The Ways of
PHILOSOPHY

The Ways of
PHILOSOPHY

Milton K. Munitz

Distinguished Professor of Philosophy

City University of New York

(Baruch College, Graduate School)

Macmillan Publishing Co., Inc.
New York

Collier Macmillan Publishers
London

Library of Congress Cataloging in Publication Data

Munitz, Milton Karl, (date)
    The ways of philosophy.

    Bibliography: p.
    Includes index.
    1. Philosophy—Introductions. I. Title.
BD21.M85   100   77-18540
ISBN 0-02-384850-2
Macmillan Publishing Co., Inc.
866 Third Avenue, New York, New York 10022

Collier Macmillan Canada, Ltd.

Printing: 7 8 9   Year: 0 1 2 3 4 5

ISBN 0-02-384850-2

Acknowledgments

Grateful acknowledgment is made to the following publishers for permission to reprint excerpts from the indicated works:

Oxford University Press: Plato's Republic, translated by F. M. Cornford.
Cambridge University Press: Descartes' Meditations, Rules for the Direction of the Mind, translated by E. S. Haldane and G. R. T. Ross.
Charles Scribner's Sons, Inc.: Martin Buber, I and Thou, translated by Walter Kaufmann
Hutchinson Publishing Group Ltd: Gilbert Ryle, The Concept of Mind
Basil Blackwell: Ludwig Wittgenstein's Philosophical Investigations and The Blue and Brown Books
Grove Press, Inc.: D. T. Suzuki, Essays in Zen Buddhism: First Series
Samuel Weiser, Inc.: D. T. Suzuki, Living by Zen

Preface ————————————————————

This book offers an introduction to philosophy for the student and general reader. Its approach seeks to fulfill the expectation and build upon the interest most persons have when they come to the study of philosophy. They expect philosophy to provide guidance in helping them to form a comprehensive view of reality and of the world in which we live. They also expect philosophy to deal with the most fundamental questions about the nature of human life: its position in the entire scheme of things, and the goals and values that should guide our conduct. The classic route to philosophy is one that recognizes the legitimacy and importance of these topics, however broad and vaguely stated they appear to be.

In trying to reach answers to these perennial and fundamental questions, philosophy as a disciplined inquiry would turn, as one of its resources, to the writings of the great philosophers. The classic route *to* philosophy would thus involve a study of the classics *in* philosophy. In this book the classics will be studied not, to be sure, as final and unquestionable sources of authority but rather as containing the proposals and insights of some of mankind's most profound and influential thinkers. Furthermore, the technical vocabulary in which many philosophers couch their answers will be introduced as an aid toward achieving precision and clarity in thought. Similarly, the various arguments used by philosophers will be examined insofar as they are relevant to dealing with certain characteristic problems of philosophy—problems that themselves arise from a concern with the basic themes already mentioned.

There is no one way of writing an introductory book in philosophy. Frequently, however, the books a person encounters on first contact with the subject may be discouraging or misleading. In my own presentation, I have tried to be on guard against certain familiar pitfalls. These include: fragmentation; narrowness; the desire to cover 'everything', however superficially; the concern to be 'up-to-date' and deal with topics of only current (and possibly transitory) interest; the cultivation of proficiency in 'analysis' for its own sake. I believe that in philosophy, above all, it is important to see the forest and not just the trees.

In writing a 'first book in philosophy', I have tried to present a clear and selective account of some of its major aspects. I have chosen those materials—whether systematic, historical, analytical, or technical—that will give the student or other reader some sense of what philosophy in its classic dimensions and in certain of its major preoccupations is all about. It is to be hoped that if this is the reader's 'first book in philosophy' it will not be the last, and that he or she will be encouraged to go on to enrich and deepen his or her knowledge of the subject in various ways.

I am much indebted to the following colleagues for their critical comments and constructive suggestions on various portions of this book: Professors William J. Earle (Long Island University), Robert A. McDermott (Baruch College), Arthur M. Wheeler (Kent State University), and William N. Whisner (University of Utah). The author alone, of course, is finally responsible for all reports of factual material and interpretive judgments.

I owe a special debt of gratitude to Mr. Kenneth J. Scott, Senior Editor at Macmillan, for his expert guidance throughout the preparation of the manuscript and for his helpful comments on its contents and mode of presentation.

Finally, I also wish to thank Ms. Shirley Lebowitz and Ms. Marcia Lind for their assistance in the preparation of the typescript.

M. K. M.

Contents ―――――――

List of Illustrations ————————

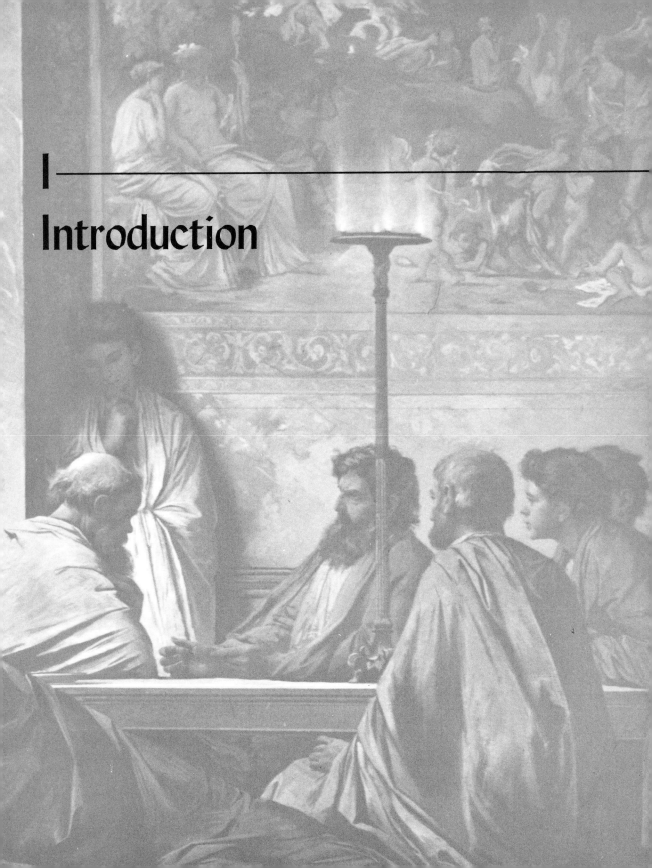

Introduction

chapter 1

On the Term

'Philosophy'

The term 'philosophy' belongs to everyday language. As ordinarily used, it is not a technical word for which we immediately require a definition if we are going to understand what someone means by it. Nevertheless, even though the term 'philosophy' is one with which we already have some familiarity, it is not a simple or noncontroversial matter to give a precise definition of the *discipline* called 'philosophy'. Now this may startle you a bit. However, there are several reasons why this is so, and I want to say a little about some of those reasons.

Of course, it is easy enough to give formulae or phrases that might sound as if they were clarifying definitions. However, when you look into some of these, you will find that they may not be as helpful as they might have seemed. For example, it is useful to recall the derivation of the term 'philosophy'. It comes from two Greek words, *philein* ('to love') and *sophia* ('wisdom'). So philosophy may be said to be the love of wisdom, and a philosopher may be thought of as one who pursues wisdom just as a lover pursues his beloved. Yet immediately upon being given this 'definition' you are likely to ask: "And what is *wisdom?* If I am pursuing wisdom, what is it that I am pursuing? For example, if I wish to say that some people are wise, what is it that I am to look for?" Suppose someone were to suggest that wisdom consists in having acquired a good deal of information, learning, and knowledge, as well as in having lived a long life and having had a lot of experience. To this you would probably want to reply: "No! Wisdom is something different from just an accumulation of experience, knowledge, and information." Of course, you will surely not want to ignore or discount the role of learning, experience, and knowledge. You cannot be a wise person, whatever it takes to be wise, you would want to say, without having some knowledge, learning, and experience. But what is it *in addition* that you must have? It should be obvious, as you begin to think about how to answer *this* question—"What are the distinctive marks of wisdom?"—that it is not any easier to answer than the question we started with: "What is philosophy?" And so, if we don't already have a clearer idea of what 'wisdom' means than we have about the term 'philosophy', we obviously have not made any real progress in clarification by defining philosophy as 'the love of wisdom'.

Furthermore, when you read what many different philosophers have to say about the nature of philosophy, you will discover that they are by no means in agreement about what it is that, as philosophers, they seek to accomplish or think they have accomplished. Thus you might turn to the commonly recognized great philosophers and ask, in effect: "What do *you* mean by 'philosophy'?" And you would find there is no single definition on which they all agree (not even that it is the pursuit of wisdom). The problem of *what* philosophy is—its goals and methods—is something on which philosophers have had major and important differences.

And yet the interesting thing is that, generally speaking, we have no difficulty—certainly when we survey the history of what is known as philosophy—in identifying the great philosophic minds: Parmenides, Socrates, Plato, Aristotle, Thomas Aquinas, Descartes, Spinoza, Leibniz, Locke, Hume, Kant, Hegel, Schopenhauer, Nietzsche, Whitehead, Dewey, Frege, Husserl, Russell, Heidegger, Wittgenstein, and others. (People's lists will differ; yet there is almost certainly going to be a reasonable amount of agreement.) Well, if these are all philosophers, did they have something in common? Did they share in something that made them all philosophers? Or is it the case that the term 'philosophy' does not designate some one common activity or interest, but instead a number of related, perhaps overlapping interests? As we begin to think about trying to answer this question, once again it will appear that there is no quick and simple answer one could give that might serve as a definition of 'philosophy' all would accept.

Instead of trying, therefore, at the outset, to mark out in some precise and rigorous way the boundaries of the discipline of philosophy, and to formulate a definition that would capture, once and for all and to everybody's satisfaction, the 'essence' of philosophy, it would be better to proceed in a more exploratory and tentative way. Let the study of philosophy, as it is carried on, yield such clarification as it can about the meaning (or meanings!) of 'philosophy' itself, along with such other clarifications of other concepts and terms as it will succeed in realizing. This device of pulling oneself up by one's own intellectual bootstraps, for philosophy, is not as viciously circular or self-defeating as it might at first glance appear. And it is surely more honest and less dogmatically confining to proceed in this way than to pretend to be able successfully to do anything else.

One thing we could say, with a fair degree of truth and accuracy, is that philosophers try to get you to accept what they have to say by thinking it through with you, by giving you arguments, by considering the pros and the cons and the reasons behind their position. They ask you to clarify *your* thoughts, or they will consider what *somebody else* proposes, and will say: "Let's examine it! Is it really so? Is it consistent? Is it clear? Does it jibe with other things we want to accept?" And in offering *their own* views they will also normally strive to *argue* their case, to offer *reasons* in support of their conclusions.

Although not all philosophers place the same degree of emphasis on reason and critical thinking, by and large—at least ever since the days of the great Greek philosophers and down to the present time—philosophy has stood for *critical analysis*. By 'critical' I don't mean something 'negative', an interest in demolishing or in tearing down. Rather I mean an interest in examining what is being considered in a logical and rational way.

Critical analysis

But critical thinking is not all there is to philosophy. For what are you going to think critically about, to reason about? What are you concerned with? What, if you will, do you want to be wise about? To have a philosophy is to have some kind of view, some kind of position. A person without a philosophy is somebody who can be swayed in any direction, or, if you ask "What do you believe?" he or she can't answer you. (It's not likely that you will find such a person.) Now it may be true that a person hasn't worked out his or her philosophy in great detail, or may be in the process of rethinking some parts of it. And, of course, there are some who devote a great deal of time and effort to formulating their philosophy. 'Professional' philosophers, certainly the great philosophers, normally devote their entire lives to this activity. Most people, then, do have 'views'—they do have a philosophy. And the task of philosophy *as a discipline* (when you do it more and more seriously) is to deepen your views, to refine, sharpen, and make them more and more solid. But when you do have a philosophic view (or a set of philosophic views), what do you have a view *about*?

Part of the answer to this is to say that to have a philosophy is to have a view about *man*. But in what respect? "A way of living," you might reply. Now what does that mean? Let me put these questions in your mind: Do not sociology, anthropology, psychology, history, economics, and politics, in some way or other, have to do with man and with 'ways of living'? Surely they do. So what is it that philosophy does, in addition to (or perhaps somewhat differently from) the way in which these other disciplines approach the topic of human beings and their 'ways of living'?

One way of answering this question is to say that philosophy is concerned with clarifying man's ideals, values, and standards of conduct. Should we say that this type of interest coincides with what some people mean by 'morals' or 'morality'? To some extent this is on the right track, although the word 'morals' itself needs to be clarified. It might be taken to suggest that we already have a fixed and clear code by which we ought to live. On the other hand, the task of philosophy is to consider critically what our code, standards, values, and goals *should be*. Philosophy *opens up* these questions for careful and explicit critical examination. And what we decide to accept, after giving this some thought, may or may not agree with what an already established code of behavior (*mores*) says these are. So to have a philosophy by which to live is to have a view of such things. It is to be able to respond to such questions as these: What is the 'meaning' of life? What are we here for? What is it all about? What is the purpose of living? How should we act? What choices should we make? What makes an action right or wrong? If I disapprove of what a person or some group does, why do I do so? Since people don't agree with one another about their modes of behavior in various situations or walks of life, what makes an action right or wrong? Am I (or are we—that is, those I agree with) in a better position to say what is right or wrong?

As we grow up, as we become reflective and self-conscious, we need to think about our own life and whether to push it in this or that direction. What should I try for? What should be my goal? Should it be to help other people? Should it be to make a lot of money? Should I devote myself to intellectual matters, to a life of scientific or scholarly research? Should I try to dominate other people and become powerful? Should I become involved in politics? Should I try to achieve a life of comfort, one filled with material possessions and with pleasures of various sorts? Should I try to become famous and be acclaimed by my fellow human beings? Should I become a religious person and do everything in this life to insure (if there is an afterlife) that I will be rewarded by an eternal life of heavenly bliss, and not be condemned to Hell? Should I try to become selfless as this is understood in, for example, Buddhism? Is life just an accident, a meaningless and utterly fruitless, absurd series of motions and actions, from cradle to grave, for the seventy or whatever number of years we are here, and then it's all over? Do you recognize these questions? Surely you have thought about these to some extent.

One of the tasks of philosophy is to formulate, to bring out into the open, and to examine critically these kinds of questions and the various possible answers to them. These are questions about *human values*. The part of philosophy that deals with these questions is known as 'ethics', 'moral philosophy', 'a philosophy of life'. When you have a view on these matters, when you've thought about and reached some answers—even if they are just tentative answers—you have something that belongs to the sphere of philosophy. You may change your mind next week! In airing your views to someone, you may say, "Such and such are my views," and that person may argue with you and say, "I think you're wrong. You should look at it this way. . . ." You may be influenced by this.

Human values

Moreover, when you do have a philosophy of human values, or purposes, or standards of conduct, it's not just something you think about, or write down, or talk about. It's something you *live by*. You act on the basis of it. It helps to determine your choices, the kinds of things you do; for example, the person you marry, whether you go to school or not, the job you accept, the kinds of foods you eat, whether you travel here, there, or not at all, and so on. Every moment of your life, in some way or other, if it is not automatic already, is filled with choices that are affected by the philosophy you have. And these choices may be made blindly or implicitly—as a result of habit, indoctrination, imitation, or blind faith. Or, on the other hand, they may be made in the light of an explicit, reflective, and critical examination; in short, on the basis of some *philosophic* analysis.

Up to now we haven't said anything about particular philosophies, but we have already formulated, in one direction, what it means to have a philosophy. It is to have a view of the purposes and goals of human life, and of what our standards for judging and guiding conduct should be, whether these affect an individual or whole groups of individuals.

Is there anything else involved in having a philosophy? Is philosophy concerned exclusively with man? Suppose I have settled, or am engaged in trying to settle, these questions about human values and standards of conduct. Is this something that can be accomplished by considering only man and excluding everything else? Is it just a view of *man* that's involved? Is it not the case that in order to have some reasonable conception of man's goals and values, one has to be able to see man himself in a broader context? But what makes up such a 'broader context'?

"Everything that exists," you might reply. That's good! There are other things in the world or in reality besides man. Let's follow that out.

What other things or kinds of things exist? Let's take individual examples. Animals, plants. Do you want to stop there? "No," you say, "there is the Earth itself." And this consists of mountains, valleys, seas, rocks, clouds, and so on. The Earth is composed of a lot of stuff. There are a lot of things happening on and in it. But of course the Earth and all that it contains do not exhaust all that exists, as the 'broader context' in which man finds himself. For example, we are sending rockets to Mars, say, or to the Moon. We know the Earth is just one planet in our solar system. And we are not quite sure of all the kinds of things we would find if we were to go exploring even on other bodies in our solar system. We know, to be sure, some of the chemicals to be found or something about the rocks on the Moon or on Mars, or about the gases on Venus and so on. Much is known, too, about the nuclear energy of the Sun, and how it generates its radiation. But the Sun itself is only one star among a vast multitude. You look up at the sky at night and what do you see? You see the Moon and perhaps some of the planets. You also see a lot of stars. You may think you see millions of stars, but as a matter of fact with your naked eyesight you can see only several thousand. But that is only a minuscule sample of an enormously larger population that exists not only in our own galaxy but in other galaxies as well. The stars that you see with your naked eyesight (including the Milky Way) belong to our galaxy. A typical galaxy is a sort of pinwheel system of billions of stars. Our Sun is one star in our own 'pinwheel' galactic system. And it's very likely there are many other planetary systems around other stars in our galaxy, containing, for all we know, millions of creatures of various sorts. At the same time, our galaxy itself is only one among an indefinitely large number of galaxies, all of which lie beyond the spatial confines of our own galactic system of stars. How vast that entire collection of galaxies is—its spatial extent—cosmologists do not know with any assurance. Nor is there any highly definite and well-established knowledge as to how long the entire system has been in existence, that is, what its overall pattern in time is. We give the name 'the Universe' to this totality or collection of all the galaxies—both those within the range of our instruments and those presumed to lie beyond their range. The Universe is made up not just of all the galaxies but rather of all the varied contents to be found in this all-inclusive domain. The Universe includes anything that can be located in it in a spatio-temporal way. It includes everything from the size of a galaxy down to such 'tiny' objects as grains of sand, mosquitoes, snowflakes, and beyond these everything that exists on an atomic and subatomic level.

Still, does that exhaust everything that exists? Is the Universe the only reality? Is all that exists contained within the confines of the Universe? Is the material Universe with all that it contains the 'ultimate reality'?

For example, your life and my life, and everything else that is brought into existence within it—are these a matter of "from dust you come and to dust you shall return"? Or is there something beyond the Universe, beyond Nature? Is there anything that is *supernatural*, lying beyond or transcending the world of space and time? What about God? That is a question many people will immediately raise. It is an obvious question. Some philosophers, in developing their view, would answer yes, others would say no, still others would say maybe (we don't know), and some, finally, would claim that the question itself is meaningless and so something for which no possible answer *could* be given. The theologies (or philosophies about God) associated with the traditional religions of the West (Judaism, Christianity, and Islam) would of course belong to the camp of the theists, those who believe in the existence of God. Their response to the question "Does God exist?" is affirmative. Yet, as we shall see, even if one is not a theist, and so does not believe in a personal God who created the world and man, there are other kinds of philosophy that would also argue that the material Universe is not the sole reality. Plato's was such a philosophy. For he too would claim that the world of things in space and time is not all that exists. There is also, Plato would say, a timeless domain of Forms (or Ideas). And then there are mystics of various sorts, who claim to be aware of a reality, or of a dimension of reality, not accessible to the senses. Indeed, such mystics would say that it is not even possible to give a literal account at all of this reality. It is something ineffable. Thus with respect to what I began by calling 'the broader context', of whose reality or existence man needs to take note, there are very many diverse views.

There are still other types of questions that belong to this general area of discussion. For example, we might ask: Is what we call 'life' fundamentally matter in motion, a matter only of complex molecular structure? And is 'consciousness' or 'mind' nothing more than a form of material behavior? Or is there something distinctive and special about the nature of mind? And do only men have minds? What about animals or plants? What, moreover, do we mean by using such concepts as 'space' and 'time'? Further, are all the events and objects in the world the products of strictly causal laws? Is there anything to be said in favor of a belief in free will?

Let us call such answers as we might give to these types of questions those that make up a 'world view' or a 'theory of reality'. Incidentally, when I use the term 'world', in the expression 'world view', I do not mean to restrict it to the Universe. By 'world', in the present context, I mean whatever one takes to be fundamentally or ultimately real. Some will say reality includes God, others will say it does not. Some will say reality is fundamentally of the nature of mind, others will say it is fundamentally

World view

of the nature of matter, and so on. To have a view about these matters is to have a world view. In philosophy the area that deals with these kinds of questions is known as *metaphysics*.

So now, notice how we have been able thus far to isolate three items or components in what we might understand by the term 'philosophy', as designating an explicit and systematic intellectual discipline or line of inquiry. We began by saying that philosophy is a matter of *critical analysis*. But about what? We went on to answer this by considering two principal lines of investigation. We considered first the question of investigating the matter of human values, goals, and standards of conduct. We called that '*ethics*'. Further, we identified something called '*metaphysics*' as an inquiry into or an account of the nature of reality. Let us put these three items together. We could say, accordingly, that *philosophy is a quest for a view of the world and of man's place in it, which is arrived at and supported in a critical and logical way*. To have 'a view of the world' is to have a metaphysics. To have 'a view of man's place in it' is to have a philosophy of life, an ethics.

The goal of the present book is to try to meet the kind of interest that most people have when they come to the study of philosophy as a discipline for the first time. They want some defensible conception or interpretation of the nature of reality and of where they fit into the entire scheme of things. Our discussions will not attempt to meet this interest by considering *all* the great variety of answers to these questions that have been worked out down the ages, or to examine each of these in depth and in all their ramifications and variations. This would clearly be beyond the scope of an introductory presentation.

The program and scope of the present book

Instead, I attempt something more modest and at the same time, therefore, perhaps more promising of success. I shall select a few (three, in fact) major and perennially attractive philosophies for detailed examination. These are the viewpoints of *Plato's philosophy, theism*, and *naturalism*. It so happens that there is a rough correlation of each of these philosophies with a historical epoch in which it came into prominence and received classic formulations and that these epochs are (roughly) successive chronologically. The philosophy of Plato, of course, defines the thought of one of the great geniuses of ancient Greek culture. The philosophy of theism received some of its most sophisticated philosophical expressions in the high Middle Ages, for example, in the thought of St. Thomas Aquinas, St. Anselm, Maimonides, and others. Finally, the philosophy of naturalism emerges in modern times under the impact of the development of science and as a result of a conscious reflection on the method and powers of science. Spinoza, in the seventeenth century, was already a major exponent and spokesman for such a point of view. In our own century, the work of John Dewey (among others) belongs to this tradition. In formulating a total philosophy, we shall also consider, at the very end of the book, the contributions made by some recent developments in philosophy.

In exploring these three major world views along with these recent developments, we shall get a glimpse of how philosophers go about their business: what their methods are, what particular problems they encounter on the way, how various critics have responded to their proposals and theses, to what extent the criticisms may be met, and how, finally, these outlooks continue to attract and engage thinking minds down to the present day.

chapter 2

The Examined Life

Socrates

Socrates devoted his life to the pursuit of philosophy. Both his life and his willingness to die for the sake of the freedom to engage in that pursuit are enshrined forever as a special part of man's intellectual history. Let us pause and examine the significance of the contribution of Socrates. Such an examination will help to amplify my earlier, prefatory remarks about the discipline of philosophy.

Socrates was brought to trial and executed in 399 B.C. at the age of seventy, which puts the year of his birth in 470 or 469 B.C. Socrates was a native Athenian and spent his life in that great city. (When his friend Crito came to visit him in prison, after Socrates had been condemned to die, and suggested that it might be possible to help Socrates escape from prison and go to another city where he would be welcomed, Socrates refused. Socrates pointed out that he had lived all his life in Athens and benefited from all that it had to offer. Even though he had been unjustly condemned, he argued, it would be unjust for him to flee now and break the law.)

Socrates took part in the Peloponnesian War and served in at least three campaigns, in which, as Plato reports, he displayed unusual courage, saved a number of lives, and exhibited great feats of endurance. His character, in general, was noted for its marked self-control and disregard for material possessions or even personal appearance. We hear about his

Socrates

going about barefoot (even on icy ground), wearing a threadbare cloak, not bathing very often, and, despite being able to consume much wine at some social affair, never getting drunk!

There were a number of occasions during his life in Athens when Socrates showed his customary independence of mind. He followed the dictates of his own conscience and what he believed to be the right, even though this meant going contrary to the judgment of the majority or coming into conflict (at great risk to his own life) with the political party in power at the time. On one occasion he stood his ground against the majority and the democratic party in power by insisting that it was illegal to permit a number of generals, who had been charged with a certain offense, to be tried collectively rather than individually. Later, when the notorious 'Thirty Tyrants' (an oligarchic, antidemocratic party) seized control, he also adamantly stood his ground, this time when it meant unjustly condemning a man arrested by the Thirty. (That party included a number of Plato's relatives. Even though Socrates was, on the whole, friendly to the members of that circle, he did not let that interfere with what he believed to be the right and just decision in this case.) The reign of terror of the oligarchic party of the Thirty Tyrants was itself later overthrown in a counterrevolution by a restored democracy. And it was this newly restored democratic party that finally brought Socrates himself to trial. This historic trial is described in Plato's *Apology*. His official accusers were Meletus (a relatively unknown young man) and Anytus (a powerful member of the democratic party, who served as the spokesman for all those who had various grounds of resentment and grievance against Socrates). At one point in the trial Socrates was given the option—after he had been found guilty of the charges of impiety and the corruption of the youth of Athens—of proposing a lighter penalty or accepting banishment, both of which, of course, Socrates refused. Instead, he argued, far from having done any harm, he had done much good, and therefore should be allowed to have free meals at public expense! He offered, however, to pay a very small fine (the amount of which would easily and willingly have been increased and paid for by Socrates' friends). But this the court found unacceptable. The vote for the death penalty received a large majority.

Instead of being immediately executed, however, Socrates was kept in prison, in order to await the return of a ship from Delos that had been sent on a religious mission. Until its return, according to law, no public executions were allowed to take place. It was during this period of waiting that Socrates was visited in prison by his many friends. Plato's account of the conversations that supposedly took place in the prison are given in his dialogues *Crito* and *Phaedo*. The latter dialogue contains the celebrated, dramatic description of the last moments in Socrates' life.

Now the hour of sunset was near, for a good deal of time had passed while he was within. When he came out, he sat down with us again after his bath, but not much was said. Soon the jailer, who was the servant of the Eleven, entered and stood by him, saying:—To you, Socrates, whom I know to be the noblest and gentlest and best of all who ever came to this place, I will not impute the angry feelings of other men, who rage and swear at me, when, in obedience to the authorities, I bid them drink the poison—indeed, I am sure that you will not be angry with me; for others, as you are aware, and not I, are to blame. And so fare you well, and try to bear lightly what must needs be—you know my errand. Then bursting into tears he turned away and went out.

Socrates looked at him and said: I return your good wishes, and will do as you bid. Then turning to us, he said, How charming the man is: since I have been in prison he has always been coming to see me, and at times he would talk to me, and was as good to me as could be, and now see how generously he sorrows on my account. We must do as he says, Crito; and therefore let the cup be brought, if the poison is prepared: if not, let the attendant prepare some.

The Death of Socrates

Yet, said Crito, the sun is still upon the hill-tops, and I know that many a one has taken the draught late, and after the announcement has been made to him, he has eaten and drunk, and enjoyed the society of his beloved; do not hurry—there is time enough.

Socrates said: Yes, Crito, and they of whom you speak are right in so acting, for they think that they will be gainers by the delay; but I am right in not following their example, for I do not think that I should gain anything by drinking the poison a little later; I should only be ridiculous in my own eyes for sparing and saving a life which is already forfeit. Please then to do as I say, and not to refuse me.

Crito made a sign to the servant, who was standing by; and he went out, and having been absent for some time, returned with the jailer carrying the cup of poison. Socrates said: You, my good friend, who are experienced in these matters, shall give me directions how I am to proceed. The man answered: You *have only to walk about until your legs are heavy, and then to lie down, and the poison will act. At the same time he handed the cup to Socrates, who in the easiest and gentlest manner, without the least fear or change of colour or feature, looking at the man with all his eyes, Echecrates, as his manner was, took the cup and said: What do you say about making a libation out of this cup to any god? May I, or not? The man answered: We only prepare, Socrates, just so much as we deem enough. I understand, he said: but I may and must ask the gods to prosper my journey from this to the other world—even so— and so be it according to my prayer. Then raising the cup to his lips, quite readily and cheerfully he drank off the poison. And hitherto most of us had been able to control our sorrow; but now when we saw him drinking, and saw too that he had finished the draught, we could no longer forbear, and in spite of myself my own tears were flowing fast; so that I covered my face and wept, not for him, but at the thought of my own calamity in having to part from such a friend. Nor was I the first; for Crito, when he found himself unable to restrain his tears, had got up, and I followed; and at that moment, Apollodorus, who had been weeping all the time, broke out in a loud and passionate cry which made cowards of us all. Socrates alone retained his calmness: What is this strange outcry? he said. I sent away the women mainly in order that they might not misbehave in this way, for I have been told that a man should die in peace. Be quiet then, and have patience. When we heard his words we were ashamed, and refrained our tears; and he walked about until, as he said, his legs began to fail, and then he lay on his back, according to the directions, and the man who gave him the poison now and then looked at his feet and legs; and after a while he pressed his foot hard, and asked him if he could feel; and he said, No; and then his leg, and so upwards and upwards, and showed us that he was cold and stiff. And he felt them himself, and said: When the poison reaches the heart, that will be the end. He was beginning to grow cold about the groin, when he uncovered his face, for he had covered himself up, and said —they were his last words—he said: Crito, I owe a cock to Asclepius; will you remember to pay the debt? The debt shall be paid, said Crito; is there, anything else? There was no answer to this question; but in a minute or two a movement was heard, and the attendants uncovered him; his eyes were set, and Crito closed his eyes and mouth.*

Such was the end, Echecrates, of our friend; concerning whom I may truly say, that of all the men of his time whom I have known, he was the wisest and justest and best.[1]

Sources

For our knowledge about Socrates and what he stood for in philosophy we are largely dependent on Plato's writings. Plato was not only a great philosopher in his own right, he was also a great literary artist, a remarkably gifted dramatist of ideas. He wrote an immortal series of *Dialogues* in many of which Socrates appears as the chief figure, the main interlocutor. There is no doubt that Socrates is very often made to serve as the spokesman for Plato himself. So it's a difficult matter to differentiate

Socrates' beliefs from Plato's when Plato puts his own words into the mouth of Socrates. One has to be especially careful in reading Plato not to take everything that Socrates is made to say as necessarily conveying Socrates' own views.

Nor can we check what Plato or anyone else attributes to Socrates by consulting Socrates' own writings—*since he left none!* Socrates' entire work as a philosopher was carried on in face-to-face conversations with people, in the *agora* (the marketplace) at Athens, in the *palaestra* (gymnasium), or at social gatherings in somebody's home. His philosophy was expressed literally through dialogue, through a talking back and forth, a process of questioning, answering, and cross-examining. He was usually surrounded by an interested and eager group of young men, listening and learning from what they heard (and happy, too, if they didn't happen to be, at the moment, the target of Socrates' irony and searching cross-examination).

There were two other contemporary writers in addition to Plato who wrote about Socrates. One was Xenophon, in a work called *Memorabilia*. However, this is a rather prosaic account—certainly as compared to Plato's—but, more importantly, it almost entirely misses the significance of Socrates as a philosopher. There is also an account given by Aristophanes in his well-known comedy *The Clouds*. Aristophanes there portrays Socrates as a rather ludicrous figure; he produces, in fact, a caricature. Aristophanes had little understanding of or sympathy with Socrates. He tends therefore not only to poke fun but also in many ways to seriously misinterpret Socrates' concerns as a philosopher. So to learn about what Socrates himself believed, we are forced, more or less, to fall back on Plato's account. (Aristotle, too, has some brief and illuminating things to say about Socrates. But Aristotle, unlike the others I have mentioned, was not a contemporary of Socrates. Aristotle was born in 384 B.C., some fifteen years after the death of Socrates in 399 B.C. Aristotle nevertheless had the advantage of studying directly with Plato for the twenty years that he belonged to Plato's Academy, and so he would have learned much about Socrates from his own teacher.)

In order to come to understand, then, what Socrates stood for, we have very few documents on which we can strongly rely. And this is true even when we turn to Plato's writings. One on which we *can* place a reasonable amount of confidence is Plato's *Apology*. For the *Apology* represents Socrates' own defense before the jury (composed of 500 men!) that considered the charges on which he was brought to trial. Plato tells us that he was himself present at the trial. Although, of course, we have no way of knowing whether Plato took notes, nevertheless there is good reason to believe that he made a serious effort not only to capture the spirit of what Socrates was saying but also pretty much to write down the substance of what he had to say. So we are going to appeal to Plato's *Apology* as our principal source for a knowledge of what Socrates stood for.

The charges brought against Socrates

The charges on which Socrates was brought to trial were two, as stated in the official indictment: first, that of 'impiety' (of refusing to believe in the gods recognized by the State) and, second, that of 'corrupting the youth'. Socrates of course feels these were trumped-up and false charges. His whole defense is intended to show up those who attack him. And he does a remarkable job of this with typical mock modesty and irony. He begins, for example, by saying, in effect: "I'm not really an eloquent public speaker or orator, so I'll have to speak in my accustomed manner, that is, in a spontaneous and unpolished way. But what I shall tell you will nevertheless be the truth." He then proceeds to make one of the most brilliant courtroom defenses ever made.

The fact is that although impiety and corrupting the youth were the nominal charges against Socrates, from what we know of the background that led up to the trial, the real reasons (as is very often the case) were primarily political. Socrates was tied in with Plato and other members of the aristocracy, the upper ruling class. He had associated with people who belonged to the oligarchic Thirty Tyrants, the party that had just recently ruled Athens during a period of violence and self-serving government. These people were now in strong disfavor with the new democratic party that came into power upon the overthrow of the oligarchic group. There were many eager to 'get' Socrates, to put him out of the way. Also, as he himself suggests (and here he is undoubtedly right in his surmise), he didn't hesitate to speak his mind and to expose the shallowness of those who claimed to have superior wisdom. By his persistence in criticism and cross-examination, especially of those who thought of themselves as being great politicians and great leaders, it is very likely he created a number of enemies who seized the opportunity to try to get rid of him.

"The Unexamined Life Is Not Worth Living"

I propose now to single out for consideration some central ideas in the *Apology*. As a text for this analysis, let us take a famous phrase in Socrates' defense, that "the unexamined life is not worth living." What does he mean by that phrase? As we examine it in its various aspects, we shall see what can be said to hold generally for any philosopher who might use this phrase, but also the special emphases that Socrates gave to it.

Critical questioning and examination of beliefs

Let us begin with the term 'unexamined' or, rather, with the positive term 'examination'. What does 'examination' in this context mean? It means, one might reply, to examine our thoughts, our actions. Socrates questions people. One way in which we could put it is to say that an unexamined life is one in which *there is no questioning*. Socrates spent his days talking with people. He didn't do this for money, the way the Sophists did.* He did it out of a concern to teach, but not in the sense of 'to indoctrinate'. He wasn't going to try to impose on other people what *his* views were. He made people *think*. Sometimes people believe they already know the answers! Socrates thought his job was not to tell them *what* they ought to believe—to give them a readymade set of doctrines—but rather to get them to think out the implications of what they were saying, to bring these implications out into the open, and to examine critically and judge their soundness. He did this for whatever topic happened to come up for discussion. For example, people might think they already know what it is to be courageous, or loyal, or just, or wise, or to enjoy a relation of friendship. But what do these terms mean? What *is* courage? wisdom? justice? friendship? loyalty? Are we really clear about these concepts? If we are questioned to state explicitly what their basic features are, can we do so without difficulty?

Socrates sometimes described himself as being a 'midwife'. Literally, a midwife, as you know, is a woman who helps another woman who is pregnant to bear a baby. Socrates was a 'midwife' of ideas. In another dialogue of Plato's, the *Theaetetus*, Socrates says:

I am so far like the midwife, that I cannot myself give birth to wisdom; and the common reproach is true, that, though I question others, I can myself bring nothing to light because there is no wisdom in me. The reason is this: heaven constrains me to serve as a midwife, but has debarred me from giving birth. So of myself I have no sort of wisdom, nor has any discovery ever been born to me as the child of my soul. Those who frequent my company at first appear, some of them, quite unintelligent; but, as we go further with our discussions, all who are favored by heaven make progress at a rate that seems surprising to others as well as to themselves, although it is clear that they have never learned anything from me; the many admirable truths they bring to birth have been discovered by themselves from within.[2]

* The Sophists were a group of itinerant teachers who, among other things, claimed to possess the kind of wisdom (which they were willing to impart to their students—for a fee) that would enable those who had acquired it to 'get ahead in life', to be successful, to have virtue, to plead one's case effectively in a courtroom or elsewhere, and so on. Plato, as we shall see later, was for various reasons hostile to what the Sophists stood for. In particular, the Sophists challenged the view that standards of right and wrong are enshrined in some absolute way in Nature, or given once and for all for all men to follow without deviation or exception. Many Sophists stressed the importance of convention as the basis of moral codes and therefore the diversity of such codes. In other words, what is regarded as right or wrong is *relative* to different societies; one cannot say there is some one absolutely correct standard that all men *should* follow.

People have ideas that are germinating or that they think are ripe and ready to come out. Socrates' task is to help bring out and develop these ideas.

Socratic dialogue

He does this by dialogue. Socrates does not say to someone whom he is trying to help in this clarification of ideas: "I have written a book in which you will find the truth about what we are talking. Read it! Study it! Memorize it!" Nor does he give a sermon or a lecture. (In general, a process of 'Socratic dialogue', as a *teaching* device, is not a 'lecturing' process. Some great teachers—perhaps you are fortunate in having had one—are known for their skill in the practice of this technique. They don't lecture *at* you, they draw *you* out. They get the student to think. They get him to say, perhaps, at the end—"I didn't really know, did I?" —or at least to see the need to question what he had all along taken for granted, or thought was correct on the spur of the moment.) So Socrates does not say: "This is what you must know if you want the truth. . . ." No! Instead he proceeds by saying, in effect: "You tell me what you think, and let's look at it." Socrates very often (and with a considerable touch of irony, to be sure) says: "I don't know the answers, but you think you know the answers. So let me learn from you. Let's see if what you have to say is correct." In summary, then, one of the philosophic tasks Socrates performs is a critical examination of people's ideas, opinions, and beliefs. This is the famous process of *Socratic dialectic*. The term *dialektikē*, in Greek, ordinarily means 'conversation'. So what Socrates does is really just to engage in a conversation, a dialogue, as his basic technique of 'midwifery'.*

In his defense, Socrates begins by trying to explain the prevalence of the various slanderous reports being circulated about himself that led to charges now being leveled against him. His slanderers say that Socrates

---

* The term 'dialectic', by the way, has another important meaning in the history of philosophy, with which this meaning of *Socratic* dialectic should not be confused. In the philosophy of Hegel, the great German philosopher of the nineteenth century, and in that of Marx (who was influenced by Hegel) you will read about the 'Hegelian' concept of *Dialectic* or the 'Dialectical Laws' (or pattern) of history. This meaning of 'dialectic' has to do with the entire process of human history, a process that Hegel read in idealistic terms, and that Marx read in materialistic terms. The dialectical process of history, as interpreted by this type of philosophy of history, involves a threefold movement from *thesis* to *antithesis* to *synthesis*. Starting with some positive, particular state of affairs (*thesis*), in culture or society, a reaction is provoked that constitutes a contradictory opposite or *antithesis* to the original thesis. Out of this opposition a new stage will emerge that serves to 'reconcile' the two and thereby accomplish a *synthesis*. This synthesis may in turn serve as the starting point that defines a new thesis, and the process may start all over again, involving a new sequence of thesis, antithesis, and synthesis, and so on! This meaning of 'dialectic' has nothing to do with the dialectic practiced by Socrates. The two meanings of the term must be kept quite distinct.

is an evildoer because he claims to be wise about all sorts of matters, for example, "about things under the earth and in heaven," and that he also teaches others to "make the worse appear the better cause." In the first place, Socrates points out, the people who make the former type of accusation (he mentions here, by way of example, the kind of caricature in Aristophanes' *Clouds*) obviously confuse him with the natural philosophers who are interested in investigating astronomical and physical phenomena. But he has no such interests, although he doesn't wish to speak disparagingly of those who do. Again, Socrates points out, he is unjustly and altogether incorrectly thought of as having the same kinds of interests as the Sophists and of teaching for money. All of these reports circulating that contain these misconceptions arise from assuming that he claims to have a special kind of wisdom that he is eager to impart to others.

He suggests that he can understand how this common picture of himself came to be accepted, and he offers an explanation for these popular misconceptions. A friend of his (Chaerophon) once went to the oracle at Delphi and asked the oracle to tell him whether there was anyone wiser than Socrates. And the oracle replied that there was no man wiser than Socrates. When he heard this, Socrates was startled and puzzled. Surely the oracle must be wrong, he thought. "I can't be the wisest of men. There must be many wiser people." So he set about trying to find out whether in fact the oracle was right, and to try to prove it wrong if he could.

And so Socrates turned to all sorts of people who were supposedly wise, who had a reputation for wisdom. For example, he went to a well-known politician and asked him his views on various subjects. And the result, Socrates reports, was the following:

When I began to talk with him, I could not help thinking that he was not really wise, although he was thought wise by many, and still wiser by himself; and thereupon I tried to explain to him that he thought himself wise, but was not really wise; and the consequence was that he hated me, and his enmity was shared by several who were present and heard me. So I left him, saying to myself, as I went away: Well, although I do not suppose that either of us knows anything really beautiful and good, I am better off than he is—for he knows nothing, and thinks that he knows; I neither know nor think that I know. In this latter particular, then, I seem to have slightly the advantage of him. Then I went to another who had still higher pretensions to wisdom, and my conclusion was exactly the same. Whereupon I made another enemy of him, and of many others besides him.[3]

Well, that was a disheartening experience. What about the poets? He turned to them next, and went through the same procedure. He talked with them, and found, once again, that when he examined them about what they themselves had written they didn't show any particular clarity, consistency, or deep understanding of their own ideas. They might write beautifully, but they didn't have any real understanding:

After the politicians, I went to the poets; tragic, dithyrambic, and all sorts. And there, I said to myself, you will be instantly detected; now you will find out that you are more ignorant than they are. Accordingly, I took them some of the most elaborate passages in their own writings, and asked what was the meaning of them—thinking that they would teach me something. Will you believe me? I am almost ashamed to confess the truth, but I must say that there is hardly a person present who would not have talked better about their poetry than they did themselves. Then I knew that not by wisdom do poets write poetry, but by a sort of genius and inspiration; they are like diviners or soothsayers who also say many fine things, but do not understand the meaning of them. The poets appeared to me to be much in the same case; and I further observed that upon the strength of their poetry they believed themselves to be the wisest of men in other things in which they were not wise. So I departed, conceiving myself to be superior to them for the same reason that I was superior to the politicians.[4]

Finally, Socrates relates, he went to the artisans—the craftsmen—those good at making various things. And indeed they did have superior 'wisdom' and knowledge about their own specialty. The trouble was that, because they had this genuine knowledge and skill in their own limited domain, they thought this also gave them an equally sound knowledge and wisdom about all sorts of other matters. And yet when they ventured into these other areas it was quite evident they lacked the wisdom they supposed themselves to have.

Well, Socrates concludes, what all this resulted in, in the first place, is that I didn't particularly endear myself to many people (especially the politicians!). In fact, I made myself a considerable number of enemies by exposing their pretensions to have a wisdom that in fact they did not have. Furthermore, Socrates points out, this experience gave me another lesson—that, in one sense, the oracle was right, after all, in saying I was the wisest of men. What I take this to mean is that, unlike others, I am genuinely wise because I am aware of my own ignorance, of my lack of wisdom. My 'wisdom' consists in my awareness and confession of *not* being wise; others haven't even reached the point of having such an awareness or of making such a confession. And so, Socrates concludes, not actually having wisdom, and not finding it among others, I go around *searching* for wisdom, and talk to various people to see if they can help me to find it.

All of this, of course, is another example of Socratic irony. His own skillful cross-examination shows him to be far from the ignorant or unwise person he says he is. On the contrary, it takes a probing mind to ask the kind of questions he does. At the same time, it is true, he doesn't want to claim for himself any final and dogmatic position. Socrates is clearly trying to help others, as well as himself, through this process of searching dialogue, to get deeper and deeper insight and clarification on various matters. So this is one aspect of the Socratic interest in 'the examined life'.

There is a second meaning of the phrase 'the examined life' that Socrates himself makes clear. The examined life is one in which there is *self-knowledge*. Socrates here stresses the same point summed up in the famous traditional saying, inscribed in the temple at Delphi: "Know thyself!" Another way in which this idea is summed up is in the statement *"Virtue is knowledge."* Finally, the same point is expressed by Socrates' assertion that his fundamental mission as a philosopher is to get people to realize that the most important thing of all is *"the care of the soul."* What do all these phrases mean? Let us first note how Socrates puts the matter.

Men of Athens, I honor and love you; but I shall obey God rather than you, and while I have life and strength I shall never cease from the practice and teaching of philosophy, exhorting any one whom I meet and saying to him after my manner: You, my friend,—a citizen of the great and mighty and wise city of Athens,—are you not ashamed of heaping up the greatest amount of money and honor and reputation, and caring so little about wisdom and truth and the greatest improvement of the soul, which you never regard or heed at all? And if the person with whom I am arguing, says: Yes, but I do care; then I do not leave him or let him go at once; but I proceed to interrogate and examine and cross-examine him, and if I think that he has no virtue in him, but only says that he has, I reproach him with undervaluing the greater, and overvaluing the less. And I shall repeat the same words to every one whom I meet, young and old, citizen and alien, but especially to the citizens, inasmuch as they are my brethren. For know that this is the command of God; and I believe that no greater good has ever happened in the state than my service to the God. For I do nothing but go about persuading you all, old and young alike, not to take thought for your persons or your properties, but first and chiefly to care about the greatest improvement of the soul. I tell you that virtue is not given by money, but that from virtue comes money and every other good of man, public as well as private. This is my teaching, and if this is the doctrine which corrupts the youth, I am a mischievous person. But if any one says that this is not my teaching, he is speaking an untruth. Wherefore, O men of Athens, I say to you, do as Anytus bids or not as Anytus bids, and either acquit me or not; but whichever you do, understand that I shall never alter my ways, not even if I have to die many times.[5]

Self-knowledge

There are a number of key ideas or terms that we now have to be clear about, especially the concepts of 'virtue' (*aretē*) and 'self-knowledge'.

The term 'virtue' in English, which translates the Greek term *aretē* as it applies to the context of thought of ancient Greece—to the thought and usage of Socrates, Plato, Aristotle, and others—does not mean what the term 'virtue' meant, for example, in Victorian times. *That* meaning has to do with the display, posture, and practice of restraint and conventionality, especially with respect to sexual conduct. In this usage (which to a large extent has already faded in our own day) a person is said to be virtuous when he or she doesn't indulge in anything contrary to the accepted mores of the society. But that's not the meaning of this concept in Greek ethics. The term 'virtue' (*aretē*) in general signifies excellence. *Aretē* means being good at something, realizing one's powers. A virtuous person is one who has well-being. To be virtuous is to be fully developed and, to use a modern term, well adjusted. A person who lives a life of virtue is one who doesn't have any shortcomings or failures, any serious weaknesses and flaws of character. The problems of morals and ethics, in a broad sense, do not have to do with correcting one's digestion, or a broken arm, and so on—although sometimes even these physical failings may result from a bad character. This would be the case, with, say, the alcoholic or the drug addict, or in general where the impairment of a person's functioning is due to his or her own choices or way of life and is not a *purely* medical (physical or physiological) problem. By and large, then, 'virtue' means 'excellence'; it means being able to function well as a person. And similarly with 'vice' as the opposite of 'virtue': vice does not mean 'breaking the laws of society', the mores, especially as these affect sexual conduct. 'Vice' means an impairment, a falling down, a weakening, a dis-ease; in short, an unsatisfactory functioning of the total individual. (We will come later to Plato's more detailed account of the various special types of virtues and vices, according to this way of thinking.)

The key to leading a life of virtue in the Socratic sense is *knowledge*. By 'knowledge' Socrates does not mean what comes from reading a lot of books, taking many courses, having a large stock of information, having a head crammed with statistics, and so on. Although some of this may be relevant, 'knowledge' in the Socratic sense is different from all of this. It means such things as making the right kinds of choices as a result of reflection; steering your way effectively and with skill through life's problems, crises, opportunities, and options; being clear about where you're heading and what means to use to achieve your ends. Such knowledge is essentially a matter of *practical wisdom*. It is the kind of wisdom to be used in the conduct of one's affairs. It is, accordingly, not a purely theoretical matter; it is not something to be achieved simply through a process of understanding. It is rather something embedded in practice, in daily living.

Practical wisdom for Socrates rests on the exercise of the most distinctive capacity that human beings possess: *reason*. Animals, too, of course, in being alive, have various needs and 'pursue ends'; but they don't have the power of reason. An animal can't *deliberate* to the extent, or in the way, that a human being can. It is this power of reason that is to be called upon by someone seeking self-knowledge. We need to distinguish this meaning of 'self-knowledge' from what is sometimes signified by the use of this phrase. For example, a psychoanalyst or a biographer may help you to know various things about yourself by bringing to light certain important events or experiences in your *past*. This kind of understanding of oneself is achieved by coming to learn (perhaps for the first time) the deep-seated *feelings* and *hidden motivations* that make you act a certain way. Such knowledge thereby helps to *explain* your present (or past) behavior. All of this no doubt is helpful. But it is not to be identified with the acquisition of self-knowledge in the Socratic sense. To have a knowledge of self in the latter sense is an ethical rather than a psychological or historical matter. It is to know what you *want* to achieve, how you *should* act, what choices you *ought* to be making *now* and as you *go on* living in the future.

The achievement of self-knowledge thus involves the practice of an *art* of living. Consider a simple analogy. Suppose I take some pieces of wood, give them to different people, and say: "Here, please make a coffeetable for me". People will do it differently. Some will have greater facility, technical ability, or creative imagination than others. Some people will botch things, others will do a so-so job, a few will turn out an excellent piece of work. Each of us, in a sense, has his own 'piece of wood' to work with. Our lives are the materials out of which we try to make the best thing we can. The 'raw materials' are 'there', in one form or another, for the entire stretch during which we are alive, however long that may be. The art of life, if it is a life that is going to be based on self-knowledge, i.e., based on the exercise of reason and on practical wisdom, is an art requiring constant attention, skill, and the making of choices as a result of careful deliberation.

Let me highlight the sort of thing Socrates means by 'self-knowledge' by putting the matter this time negatively, by drawing a contrast with other familiar approaches.

One important strand in the traditional religious ethics of Judaism and Christianity consists in having a body of rules and prescriptions for conduct. The original 'Do's' and 'Don'ts', stated in the Ten Commandments, were elaborated in great detail, with varying emphases, and in different directions, in the subsequent history of religious thought. According to this tradition, a good person is a righteous person. He or she lives in accordance with the prescribed code of behavior, i.e., the rules set down by God or enunciated by his prophets and other great religious authorities. Anyone who breaks the code is 'bad' or 'evil'. The major vice, on this view, is *sinfulness*. Remember the opening lines of Milton's *Paradise Lost?*

Of Man's first disobedience, and the fruit
Of that forbidden tree whose mortal taste
Brought death into the World, and all our woe,

With loss of Eden, . . .

According to the Old Testament, Adam did not listen to God. God told Adam not to eat of a certain tree. But Eve was beguiled by the serpent, and Eve in turn convinced Adam. They ate of the tree, in violation of God's command, and were driven out of the Garden of Eden and punished. Henceforth all men were to work by the sweat of their brow, and women to bear children in pain. God punished man for failing to obey his commandments.

This conception of sin as consisting of disobedience—as the failure to abide by preordained, authoritatively given rules—is precisely the opposite of the conception of error or 'vice' in the thought of Socrates. For Socrates, the primary vice is not sin but ignorance—failing to know where the true good lies. The determination of the good life is not to be made by some external authority. It is to be made by the individual, acting in terms of his own reason. So the person who botches things in his life is someone who is ignorant, foolish, or unwise; who doesn't have insight into what is best. Thus an adequate self-knowledge needs to be contrasted with self-ignorance, not with sinfulness in the sense of disobedience. "The care of the soul" (*psyche*), in this way of thinking, is the management of one's life by means of man's distinctive possession: reason. It is this power of reason that can (and should) guide our actions. Of course, no one ever makes a complete success of such control or management. The 'art' of life is that for which each of us, as it concerns his own conduct, is ultimately responsible. This 'art' is embodied in the management of one's own personal affairs. At the same time, it is never, even under the best of circumstances, an 'art' that takes the form of a 'perfect masterpiece'. (Even so-called masterpieces in the field of the fine arts will usually have some imperfections, perhaps slight. And, in any case, even such masterpieces will, like everything else, be subject at some time or other to neglect, deterioration, accident, or destruction.) Similarly, no one is ever completely successful in the conduct of his or her own life. However, there are obviously degrees of mastery involved in the conduct of life, as we compare different people's lives. The greater the success, the greater is the input, to a large extent, of reason. So this, in a nutshell, is another aspect of the 'examined life' that Socrates is talking about: self-knowledge and rational guidance in the conduct of one's affairs as the primary conditions for leading the good or 'virtuous' life. "Virtue *is* knowledge."

On being confronted by this Socratic emphasis on *self*-knowledge as the condition for the good life, you might ask: "What's the good of all this talk about acquiring self-knowledge, this introspective 'soul-searching', if the *society* in which we live is corrupt or badly needs change? If he is really interested in the good life, shouldn't Socrates have directed his attention to the character of the society in which he lived, and made sure that *it* was healthy?" This is not merely a challenging question, it is one that Socrates himself was aware of, and tried to answer. Here is what he says:

Some one may wonder why I go about in private giving advice and busying myself with the concerns of others, but do not venture to come forward in public and advise the state. I will tell you why. You have heard me speak at sundry times and in divers places of an oracle or sign which comes to me, and is the divinity which Meletus ridicules in the indictment. This sign, which is a kind of voice, first began when I was a child; it always forbids but never commands me to do anything which I am going to do. This is what deters me from being a politician. And rightly, as I think. For I am certain, O men of Athens, that if I had engaged in politics, I should have perished long ago, and done no good either to you or to myself. And do not be offended at my telling you the truth: for the truth is, that no man who goes to war with you or any other multitude, honestly striving against the many lawless and unrighteous deeds which are done in a state, will save his life; he who will fight for the right, if he would live even for a brief space, must have a private station and not a public one.[6]

In this passage, as well as in others, Socrates does not deny the importance of political considerations or the need for the wise management of the affairs of the state. On the contrary, Socrates is as much concerned with a well-run society as any other clear-thinking person would be. He holds the view (later developed by Plato, Aristotle, and others) that, as individuals, we cannot pursue our personal goals and live a rational life as individuals if our society is generally corrupt and unsupporting. The full consideration of the ethics of personal conduct cannot be explored in a vacuum, in isolation from the questions that concern us as members of society. The problems of politics, how the *polis* (or city-state) is managed, and particularly what its laws should be, are, for Socrates, of central importance. But speaking for himself, he believes—as does also his pupil Plato, after him—that his own role and possible contribution to the attainment of such a healthy society can best be realized in an *indirect* way. He would not himself directly take part in the day-to-day rough and tumble of politics. Instead, he would serve as a 'gadfly of the state', a searching 'midwife of ideas' for those who might aspire to become involved in politics, or in fact may already be so involved. He would, by pressing them to become clearer, wiser, and more rational in the working out of *their* ideas and plans, in the long run be of more help in achieving a well-run society than he could be by doing anything else.

Definition

I come now, finally, to a third component in the analysis of what is involved in the Socratic concept of an 'examined life'. I have stressed thus far the importance of a critical examination of beliefs and the striving for self-knowledge. However, the statement of one's beliefs or the search for knowledge of any kind (including self-knowledge) involves the use of *ideas*. In expressing our beliefs or our claims to knowledge, we use various concepts, terms, expressions, words. A typical and important form of Socratic question, in carrying out an examination, is to ask about some general concept, term, or word that is at the core of some discussion: *What does it mean?* In effect, what Socrates is asking for is a *definition*.

Plato wrote some twenty-five dialogues. In many of them Socrates is the main figure. In such dialogues, there is always one central concept

The scene in Plato's *Symposium*

under discussion (along with, perhaps, various subsidiary concepts). For example, in the famous dialogue *Symposium* the central concept is *love*. People talk about being in love. But what is love? Another dialogue, *Lysis*, has as its central theme 'friendship'. In the *Republic* the central question is: What is justice? Similarly, the *Laches* deals with 'courage'; the *Charmides* with 'temperance'; the *Euthyphro* with 'piety'; and so on.

In each such dialogue, Socrates (Plato) is concerned with the analysis of a concept that figures prominently in our view of the good life. Socrates, in each case, typically raises the question: "What is (the meaning of) . . . ?" And usually there is some eager or innocent person present who is ready to trot out his answer. In some dialogues, various proposed definitions of the concept under investigation are examined, only for it to be revealed that each of the proposals is unsatisfactory; the dialogue thus ends in a negative fashion. In other dialogues, the critical rejection of alternative definitions is followed by a constructive, positive analysis. This latter case is illustrated in the *Republic*.

In the beginning of the *Republic*, for example, Polemarchus states what he thinks justice is, then Thrasymachus offers his analysis, and so on. Socrates examines each of these definitions, shows up their weakness, and points out why they cannot at all be satisfactory. Finally, the various people present prevail upon Socrates (who at this point really speaks for Plato) to offer his own analysis. So the rest of that dialogue is a long and detailed positive or constructive analysis that proposes the correct definition of 'justice'.

Now what is Socrates looking for in a definition? Ordinarily, when you're not familiar with a word—say, 'serendipity', 'egregious', 'tetrahedron', and so on—you look it up in a dictionary to get its meaning. But a dictionary definition is not what Socrates is after. For such dictionary definitions serve simply to set out the meaning of an unfamiliar term through the use of other words with which you are already familiar and presumably already understand. There are many terms—for instance, 'friendship', 'love', 'democracy', 'courage', 'justice', 'wisdom', 'education' —whose meaning we think we already know. After all, we do use them constantly. And, as far as correct usage is concerned, this is true enough. But if you stop to ask yourself what they mean, in the sense of being able to give a carefully thought out analysis of the term, you will find that this is by no means a simple and easy matter. This is especially true for those concepts about which there is much controversy, or about which various philosophic differences may come into play. The giving of a good definition, in the Socratic sense, is one of the most difficult tasks that can be undertaken. And, when undertaken, the result may not always be successful or reflect basic agreement. Sometimes a good definition may emerge only after much thought is given to it by very many people over a long period of time. Compare the carpenter's 'definition' of a circle with the geometer's. Certainly, the carpenter's definition, which may consist basically in telling you how to draw a circle on a piece of wood with carpentry tools, may be adequate enough for his purposes. But would it satisfy the geometer? Mathematicians are still trying to define 'number', although in one sense everybody, including the mathematician, already 'knows' what a number is.

For Socrates, to give the definition of a term is to give its *essential* characteristics, those that are both *fundamental* and *common* to everything that falls within the range of that concept.[7] The test of a good definition is whether it will stand up in the face of various particular examples. If we say that A and B are friends, is what makes them friends —the features of that relationship—something that will hold wherever two people are friends? Is it common and essential for all other cases of friendship? If not, the proposed 'definition' will not serve. Nor, for Socrates, will the search for a definition be satisfied merely by giving an example or by citing a particular case. What Socrates wants is a definition that is universal, or general. It must not consist in giving some particular, isolated case. It must not confine itself to a situation in which some accidental or nonessential feature may be illustrated, a feature that need not be present in all other cases.

Some of the common failures in obtaining the kind of definitions Socrates is interested in are illustrated in various dialogues in which this kind of search goes on. Thus in the *Euthyphro* the question is posed as to what constitutes piety or holiness. And Euthyphro replies that holiness consists in doing what he is himself doing now, that is, prosecuting murderers and temple thieves. Clearly this will not do as a *general* definition of holiness or piety, as we shall now see.

Soc. And therefore, I adjure you to tell me the nature of piety and impiety, which you said that you knew so well, and of murder, and of other offences against the gods. What are they? Is not piety in every action always the same? and impiety, again—is it not always the opposite of piety, and also the same with itself, having, as impiety, one notion which includes whatever is impious?

Euth. To be sure, Socrates.

Soc. And what is piety, and what is impiety?

Euth. Piety is doing as I am doing; that is to say, prosecuting any one who is guilty of murder, sacrilege, or of any similar crime—whether he be your father or mother, or whoever he may be—that makes no difference; and not to prosecute them is impiety. And please to consider, Socrates, what a notable proof I will give you of the truth of my words, a proof which I have already given to others:—of the principle, I mean, that the impious, whoever he may be, ought not to go unpunished. For do not men regard Zeus as the best and most righteous of the gods?—and yet they admit that he bound his father (Cronos) because he wickedly devoured his sons, and that he too had punished his own father (Uranus) for a similar reason, in a nameless manner. And yet when I proceed against my father, they are angry with me. So inconsistent are they in their way of talking when the gods are concerned, and when I am concerned.

Soc. May not this be the reason, Euthyphro, why I am charged with impiety —that I cannot away with these stories about the gods? and therefore I suppose that people think me wrong. But, as you who are well informed about them approve of them, I cannot do better than assent to your superior wisdom. What else can I say, confessing as I do, that I know nothing about them? Tell me, for the love of Zeus, whether you really believe that they are true.

Euth. Yes, Socrates; and things more wonderful still, of which the world is in ignorance.

Soc. And do you really believe that the gods fought with one another, and had dire quarrels, battles, and the like, as the poets say, and as you may see represented in the works of great artists? The temples are full of them; and notably the robe of Athene, which is carried up to the Acropolis at the great Panathenaea, is embroidered with them. Are all these tales of the gods true, Euthyphro?

Euth. Yes, Socrates; and, as I was saying, I can tell you, if you would like to hear them, many other things about the gods which would quite amaze you.

Soc. I dare say; and you shall tell me them at some other time when I have leisure. But just at present I would rather hear from you a more precise answer, which you have not as yet given, my friend, to the question, What is 'piety'? When asked, you only replied, Doing as you do, charging your father with murder.

Euth. And what I said was true, Socrates.

Soc. No doubt, Euthyphro; but you would admit that there are many other pious acts?

Euth. There are.

Soc. Remember that I did not ask you to give me two or three examples of piety, but to explain the general idea which makes all pious things to be pious. Do you not recollect that there was one idea which made the impious impious, and the pious pious?

Euth. I remember.

Soc. Tell me what is the nature of this idea, and then I shall have a standard to which I may look, and by which I may measure actions, whether yours or those of any one else, and then I shall be able to say that such and such an action is pious, such another impious.

Euth. I will tell you, if you like.

Soc. I should very much like.

Euth. Piety, then, is that which is dear to the gods, and impiety is that which is not dear to them.

Soc.   Very good, Euthyphro; you have now given me the sort of answer which I wanted. But whether what you say is true or not I cannot as yet tell, although I make no doubt that you will prove the truth of your words.[8]

To sum up, then: Socrates, as a typical philosopher, is constantly asking "What is the meaning of . . . ?" or "What do you mean by . . . ?" There is the old story of the professor who came into his philosophy class one morning and began by saying: "Good morning, class!" At which point a student immediately raised his hand and asked "What do you mean by 'good'? What do you mean by 'morning'?" This is an exaggeration, of course. Nevertheless, it illustrates what goes on all the time in philosophy: putting your concepts on the table and examining them; not just taking it for granted that because the *word* is familiar you *understand* it for philosophic purposes.

(When people say "I know what I mean, but I can't express it," the reply should be "That won't do! If you know what you mean, you should be able to formulate it." It may not be a good formulation, but you should be able to give it *some* formulation. And the problem then is to examine it in a Socratic manner. There are some people, too, who, when you ask them why they believe what they do, reply "I have a feeling in my bones it is so." And to this you should respond that that's the wrong place to have your knowledge!)

So now we've got three things for which Socrates stood—three ways of articulating what he intended by 'the examined life': (1) the importance of a critical examination of one's beliefs; (2) the importance of self-knowledge; (3) the importance of clarification of key concepts through definition.

Every good philosopher who undertakes to develop a world view and a philosophy of life will normally follow Socrates, at least to this extent, as the very model of the philosophic life.

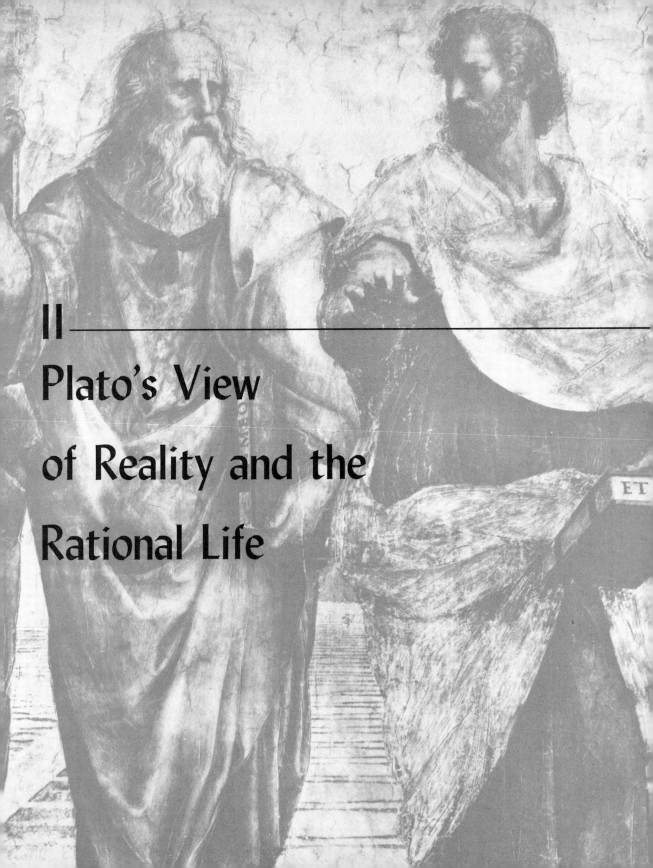

II

Plato's View
of Reality and the
Rational Life

chapter 3

Eternal Forms and

Temporal Flux

Plato (427–347 B.C.) is our first major example of a philosopher who undertook to formulate a comprehensive vision of the world and of man's place in it.

Plato's impact on the history of Western thought is immeasurable. He has lived through the centuries; his writings have been studied repeatedly and used in different ways by various philosophers. For example, some of his central metaphysical doctrines were incorporated in the philosophical outlook of those who played a major role in laying the groundwork of the theological systems of Judaism (e.g., Philo Judaeus of Alexandria [*fl.* 20 B.C.–A.D. 40] and Christianity (e.g., St. Augustine [354–430]). Others turned to him—and continue to do so—for inspiration and support in formulating their political theories and programs. Still others appeal to Plato in working out their views about the philosophy (or 'foundations') of mathematics. And so on.

Let us remember, too, that aside from those inspired to follow in his path, there are at least as many for whom Plato's major doctrines are the very embodiment of error. So he needs to be reckoned with and studied just as closely whether one comes finally to agree or to disagree with him. He cannot be ignored. Alfred North Whitehead, one of the outstanding philosophers of our own day, in a much-quoted remark, once characterized the history of Western philosophy as "a series of footnotes to Plato." This is at once a brief, forgivably exaggerated, yet true statement of the case.

Plato

Relatively few facts about Plato's life and character are known. Much of what is written derives from accounts written long after Plato's death, and contains a good deal in the way of legends and anecdotes that accumulated over the centuries. These either reflect the tendency of Plato's many admirers to attribute all sorts of marvelous qualities to him as befits their hero, or else, if they were written by hostile critics or other detractors, include many items intended to damage his reputation. Plato himself in his dialogues never writes in his own person, and refers to himself only twice. Furthermore, the rather long autobiographical account that he gives in his *Seventh Letter* has not been accepted as authentic by all competent scholars. There are very few direct or extensive references to Plato by contemporary writers, even though many of them certainly knew Plato personally or at least about him. (It seems to have been the custom of the time for a prose writer not to make direct allusions to his contemporaries.)

Plato was a member of a distinguished, wealthy, and aristocratic Athenian family. His father claimed descent from the last king of Athens.

Among Plato's own contemporaries were many relatives who were prominent in Athenian politics; they were strongly antidemocratic in both their views and their affiliations. Despite his own antidemocratic views, Plato was repelled by the excesses of the oligarchic party known as the Thirty Tyrants that seized power at one point and that included some of his own relatives. And when that party was later itself overthrown by a democratic regime, which in turn executed his own revered master Socrates, he was equally appalled by *their* excesses. Given his family background and connections, along with his own deep interest in politics, one would expect Plato to have chosen a political career for himself. However, Plato avoided the life of practical politics. He concluded after many bitter experiences and discouragements, as he tells us in his *Seventh Letter,* that "it is very difficult to manage political affairs aright [and that] all cities at the present time are without exception badly governed". Like Socrates, he preferred to spend his life at one remove from the arena of day-to-day politics and to exert, through his thought, such influence as he could on those who did directly participate in political affairs.

Plato as a young man most likely saw military service on the Athenian side in the Peloponnesian War against Sparta. As a young man he also had close contact with Socrates—an experience that had an overwhelming and lasting influence on his own life and thought. Socrates was executed when Plato was about thirty-one years old. At a later stage of his life Plato traveled to various places, including three visits, on separate occasions, to Syracuse in Sicily.

Another important fact associated with Plato's life is the founding of the Academy. Plato's own residence was named 'Academy'. It was situated a mile outside the walls of Athens. It consisted of various buildings, gardens, a gymnasium, amid a grove of trees. Here over a period of time a 'school for advanced studies' came to be founded, where various 'courses' were taught and lectures given by specialists. The subjects included mathematics, astronomy, and political theory. It is possible that Plato himself gave a number of lectures. The Academy must not be thought of on the model of a modern university, not even a medieval one. Especially in its early period it is likely that it had only very few students. Aristotle was one of the most famous of these. After Plato's death the Academy was headed by Plato's nephew Speusippus. It continued to exert an important influence on the intellectual life of the ancient world for a considerable time.

Unlike Socrates, who did not leave any writings, Plato left a considerable number when he died at age eighty in 347 B.C. These include some letters and about twenty-five dialogues. (I say 'about' because scholars are not in complete agreement about the authenticity of a number of dialogues attributed to Plato.)

Plato's Dialogues

Throughout the range of his *Dialogues,* Plato examines a great variety of themes. They include the following: the nature of reality; the structure of the physical Universe; the character of different types of government (e.g., democracy, oligarchy, tyranny) and the way a *polis* (city-state) should be run; the functions of the different classes in society; the role of women in society; the causes of war; the various methods, goals, and types of education; the structure of the human psyche, its faculties and powers; the relation of the soul to the body, including the question of whether the soul has independent existence apart from the body, prior to birth and after death; the various goods of life, and whether there is a 'supreme' good; the character of specific virtues, for example, courage, temperance, wisdom, justice, and loyalty; the nature of friendship and love; the differences between knowledge and opinion; the nature of language; the values and limitations of art and poetry; and so on. No single dialogue gives us his entire philosophy (although the *Republic* is one of the richest, and touches on a considerable number of his themes). However, the entire collection of the *Dialogues,* when taken together, gives us what we may call Plato's system of ideas.

In using the expression 'Plato system', it is important to bear in mind the following qualifications: In the first place, there is the real risk that we may be attributing doctrines to Plato that he might have denied as his own. In one of his letters, he goes so far as to discourage anyone who would attempt to sum up his philosophy:

So much I can say about writers past or future who claim that they know the things about which I am in earnest, whether by hearing them from me or others, or discovering them for themselves—that in my view they understand nothing of the matter. There is not, and can never be, a treatise of mine about it, for it cannot be put into words like other subjects of study. Only out of much converse about the subject, and a life lived together, does it suddenly, like a light kindled from a leaping flame, spring up in the soul and thenceforth maintain itself. But this much I do know, that whether written or spoken, it would be best done by me, and if it were badly written, I would be the chief sufferer.[1]

And so we have no way, in the face of this warning, that we can safely sum up his philosophy! We have to recognize that, as with other seminal thinkers who are extremely rich and suggestive in expressing their ideas, we cannot always be sure what the author believed, as contrasted with what is read *into* his writings. There is, in fact, no single set of doctrines that everyone agrees could be assigned to Plato as constituting the 'essence' of his thought. Partly this is because Plato is frequently elusive about what he is committed to. He doesn't always come out and say: "This is what I believe!" And so opportunities for interpreting what he 'really' means are opened up at every turn in his writings. This has given rise to an enormous secondary literature of 'interpretation', and there is no reason to believe it will ever stop growing.

What we may judge to be Plato's own views are at best always put into the mouth of one or another speaker in a dialogue. And Plato, like any dramatist, could always take cover, if he wished, by saying that one should not attribute to the author what he puts into the mouth of one of the characters in his 'play'. Again, even if we put this caution aside for the moment, there is the additional factor that Plato, who spent his entire life in thinking about the kinds of topics I have enumerated, underwent various shifts and alterations in his thinking. As he grew older, he had second thoughts about some of his own earlier commitments. At the very least, then, Plato's 'system' is not fixed and static. Despite some characteristic underlying continuities, his philosophy changes from his 'early' and 'middle' dialogues to his 'later' dialogues.

Having made qualifications and expressed cautions, let us now plunge ahead, anyway, and formulate what we may think of as Plato's own characteristic views!

Main Features of Plato's Philosophy

Let me begin by giving a brief and rough overview of his philosophy. As we go on, I shall fill in whatever details we need for our present purposes.

(1) A leading theme in Plato's philosophy—perhaps *the* dominant one—is the contrast between *two* 'levels', 'types', or 'domains' of reality: the material, sensible world and the domain of Forms. For this reason Plato's metaphysics or theory of reality is normally classified as being *dualistic*. Moreover, Plato not only would have us make a distinction, or recognize a contrast, between two types or domains of reality. He also would have us proceed to rank them one above the other. The 'rank' of an entity or domain of entities depends on its *degree of reality*, that is, *how much* reality it possesses. In short, Plato's metaphysical dualism insists on recognizing *two fundamental degrees of reality*, which can be assigned to the *two basic types of reality*. There are many other examples in the history of philosophy where a metaphysics claims that there are degrees of reality—that some entity or domain of entities has *priority* over or is *more fundamental* than others, and is ultimately more *real*. The reasons that different metaphysical systems give for making a distinction of degrees of reality will vary as we go from one system of thought to another. And similarly what is meant by being 'more fundamental', 'higher', or 'lower' will vary as we go from one system to another. Plato's

The 'world' of Forms and the material world

is a classic and early example of such a metaphysics. For the moment, I am concerned with giving a brief account of *his* version of a metaphysical dualism and the distinctions of degrees of reality it contains. Later, we shall see another famous example of metaphysical dualism, namely, in the system of theism with its own basic distinction between God and the World. According to that philosophy, God's being is said to have a more 'fundamental' reality, to be metaphysically 'prior', since it is the creative ground or source of the World and therefore has a *higher* degree of reality than the World does.

Plato distinguishes two types of reality: the 'world' of Forms and the ordinary world of sensible, material things. For him, the world of Forms has a higher degree of reality than the world of sensible, material things.

The world we confront in our everyday life and experience is made up of material objects, persons, and the various events and situations in the world about us—the things we can sense and observe. Each of us is part of it, this chair is part of it, this building is part of it, the trees, the animals, the clouds, the rain, the Earth, the stars, the planets—they are all part of the sensible world. All the things that we encounter in our daily life, or that the various sciences which rely on an appeal to experience inform us about, belong to what Plato would call the material world: a world spread out in space and exhibiting change. Nothing in this world is ever really fixed and permanent. Things come into existence and go out of existence. Some things last longer than others, but nothing lasts forever.

The material world: in space and time; sensed; imperfect

The everyday sensible world of material things is, first, *in time*, not eternal. Second, it is *sensed*, or open to observation. Although we can use our mind to form various opinions or beliefs about this world and what goes on in it, these beliefs will have to depend for their support on sense experience. And what we find out in this way is always subject to correction and improvement. Our beliefs are not infallible. Third, the material world, unlike the Forms, *occupies space*. Finally—and this is a point on which Plato places great emphasis—the various objects, events, and constituents of the material world are *imperfect* in various ways.

For many persons as well as according to some fully developed philosophies, the claim would be made that this material world is the *only* real world. Later on, we will study a type of philosophy, known as 'naturalism', that makes that claim, so it is not only a 'commonsensical' point of view but also one that some philosophers have sought to justify through critical analysis. But Plato disagrees with that kind of philosophy. He also disagrees with the commonsense view that it is the ordinary things of everyday experience that are the only real things. He says in effect that, yes, they are real, but actually there is another domain of which most people are totally unaware, and *that* domain—the world of Forms—is even more real, more fundamental than what common sense takes to be real.

Why should Plato have thought, even though the ordinary world of material sensible things is in time and space, is open to sensory experience, and is imperfect in various ways, that these characteristics somehow make this world *insufficiently real* and therefore there must be another type or domain of reality that is *more real?* Let me state briefly three kinds of reasons that led Plato to this conclusion.

In the first place, insofar as we recognize various things to be *imperfect* in one way or another this can only be on the basis of our having some conception of the ideal or of perfection. If I say that no circular shape I find or can make is *absolutely* circular, I must have a conception of a perfect Circle to which I can appeal as my criterion or model. Similarly, if I say that the actions of individual men and the various social or political institutions of men fall short in some degree of what is absolutely right, good, or desirable, this again implies that I have some conception of what the ideal might be.

Second, whereas in certain areas there are many persons who have conflicting or changing opinions as to the truth, there are, by contrast, other individuals who have made a thorough and careful study of the matters in question and who can be said to really *know* what the truth is; these latter individuals do not have merely another *opinion*. Whatever may be the opinions of different persons as to the formula for the volume of a sphere, the geometer *knows* what it is.

Third, whereas our senses inform us of the existence of *things* that come to be and undergo change and pass away, we also have a power of grasping with our minds the *meanings* of certain concepts that do not undergo change, meanings that do not come to be or pass away but remain fixed and invariant. For example, the concept of *equality* as having to do with length, size, or volume has a fixed and unchanging meaning even though the things that I see to be equal may not always have been equal and will not remain equal.

For Plato, these three facts—(1) our having an awareness of the ideal or of perfection, (2) the possession by some men of knowledge and not merely opinion, and (3) our grasp of certain fixed meanings—can be explained by saying there is a special domain of *entities* to which we have access. These entities are not to be found in the ordinary world of sensible and material things. They constitute these very ideal standards, objects of knowledge, and targets of fixed meanings. He calls these entities *Forms*.

Forms

(In referring to the domain or level of reality that consists of Forms, I shall spell the word 'form' with a capital 'F' in order to distinguish Plato's conception from an ordinary form.) Plato has a metaphysical *Theory of*

Forms: his notion of 'Form' is a technical and philosophical one. Sometimes, in the literature that discusses Plato's philosophy, you will also run across the use of the term 'Idea' instead of the term 'Form'. These two expressions, 'Idea' and 'Form', as used in connection with Plato's philosophy, have the same meaning. Accordingly, some writers will speak of Plato's *Theory of Ideas*. (Again, in order to distinguish Plato's use of this term from the ordinary use of the term 'idea', it is best to capitalize 'Idea'.)

What, then, are Forms (or Ideas) in Plato's sense? Let me put the matter first negatively. A Form cannot be touched, seen, heard, smelled, tasted—in short, observed or sensed in any way. It is not anything material. It is not anything that exists in space or time. "What then," you will ask, "is he talking about?" The answer is that he is talking about a special *type* of reality altogether different from what we ordinarily, and on a commonsense level, take to be 'reality'.

Characteristics of Forms:

Beyond time (eternal)

Objective and independent

Forms have the following characteristics:

(a) Forms are *beyond time*. We could also express this by saying that they are *eternal*. They don't come into or pass out of existence. They are beyond temporal flux or change. They are not the kind of things that last for only a certain time. It's not that they last forever, because they don't endure or last at all. One shouldn't even use such expressions in connection with them. They are beyond time altogether.

(b) A Form is *not an idea or a concept*. It is not a psychological event, or part of the human mind. A Form is an Idea, not an idea. The term 'idea', as standing for a psychological event, is used in such sentences as the following: "I have an idea how to make $100"; "You don't have a very clear idea of what I'm talking about"; and so on. An idea in this sense is something going on in someone's mind. It's part of a stream of thought or stream of consciousness. Plato's Forms are not ideas that are parts of human consciousness. A Form is something *objective*, not subjective. A Form is 'out there' in the world of Forms, whether we recognize it or not. To use a rough analogy: Columbus didn't invent America, he discovered it. It was there, and he came upon it. Even if Columbus hadn't discovered America, it would still be there; Europeans may not have given it a name, but it would still be there. Plato believed, similarly, that what we call a Form is objective. It is independent of human creation, or awareness, or the act of naming. For him, we can become aware of a Form, just as Columbus discovered America; but we don't create it or invent it.

Suppose someone were to ask, nevertheless: "But *where* is a Form, *where* is the domain of Forms?" To this one would have to reply that the term 'where' in the asking of this question is inappropriate, because 'where' implies or presupposes that there is some *place* or *region* where

Forms are *located*. However, such *spatial* expressions simply *do not apply* to Forms. All you can say is that *there are* Forms, and that they can be disclosed by the use of reason. However, you cannot travel to the realm of Forms by foot, plane, rocket ship, or any other means of physical transport. So Forms are objective and independent in their own 'realm' of being, although they can be disclosed to human beings through the activity of reason.

(c) Forms are *intelligible entities,* i.e., entities that can be grasped by the mind and understood, not entities that might be disclosed to our senses. The disclosure of the realm of Forms is of tremendous importance, in Plato's view, both for our understanding of the nature of reality and for the types of consequences and uses in human life that such disclosure by reason makes possible. The power to discover the world of Forms is the most distinctive capacity that a human being can possess. *Intelligible*

(d) The realm of Forms is made up of a great number of Forms, each of which is *unique* and distinct from the other Forms. Nevertheless, there are important connections of all sorts among such unique Forms, connections that hold *within* the realm of Forms. For example, Courage requires and involves Wisdom; Rectangularity and Circularity are included as cases of Plane Figure: Redness is distinct from Blueness and both are related to Color; and so on. *Unique*

(e) Each Form represents a *perfect* model or ideal type. A Form possesses to the fullest possible degree, in its own being, all the essential characteristics that belong to that Form. The essential marks of a Form can be grasped by reason and can be set out by means of a definitional formula. *Perfect*

(I shall return later to a more complete analysis of the nature of Forms.)

In our earlier discussion, we established that Plato was a dualist. Now that we have had a very brief, preliminary glimpse of what Plato means by his distinction between the two domains of reality—that of the sensible material world, on the one hand, and the realm of Forms on the other— we can also sum up what for Plato is the *relation* between these two domains. One way of stating that relationship is to say that the various objects and events in the material world, as well as human actions and institutions, are *copies* or *embodiments* (with various degrees of approximation or imperfection) of the eternal world of Forms. Thus if I have knowledge of the Form Circle—of a Form that belongs, you might say, to the 'Platonic Heaven' of Forms—then any circular shape I can find in the material world will be at best an imperfect copy of that Form. Any circular shape you could *make* (for example, that you might draw on paper, in the sand, on the blackboard, or could cut with a saw out of a *Material, sensible particulars are copies of Forms* piece of wood or metal), or again, any circular shape you could *find* in the world (say, the shape of the full moon that we can see with our eyes), will be an imperfect copy of the *Form* Circle. A five-year-old child's free-hand drawing of a circle will obviously not be as good as the circle drawn by a draftsman who has used a precision compass. But Plato's point is that even the draftsman's circle is imperfect compared to the perfect Form Circle as this is known by the geometer. So the realm of everyday things is a domain of imperfect copies of an eternal realm of Forms, copies exhibiting varying degrees of imperfection.

This has been a brief summary of the contrast between the two types or domains of reality according to Plato's metaphysics. Let it serve as an introductory statement of one major theme in Plato's general philosophy. I turn now to an account of two other themes in his general outlook.

Moral idealism and absolute standards

(2) I have been discussing up to this point a basic feature of Plato's metaphysics, his conception of the nature of reality. A second leading theme in Plato's philosophy has to do with human conduct on both an individual and a social level. There is an important connection between Plato's metaphysics and his conception of what the good life for man might be. This connection might be brought out in different ways. No doubt, Plato himself would have maintained that because there is in reality a domain of Forms distinct from the ordinary world of sensory experience and material objects, man's reason is able—through its knowl-edge of ideal Forms—to provide a guide and standard for conduct. A critic of Plato, however, who is not convinced that there is, in reality, an independent domain of Forms, might suggest instead that Plato starts out with a conception of what man's life ought to be and *projects* his conception of the ideal into the status of being, supposedly, an inde-pendent metaphysical reality. Such a critic would say that what Plato has done is similar to the case of those who say that God created man in His image, whereas, in fact, it is man who creates a concept of God in his (man's) image. In any case, whichever of these approaches one adopts—whether one follows Plato himself or his critic—there is an intimate con-nection between Plato's metaphysics and his conception of the good life for man. Neither can be understood completely without taking the other into account.

If we are going to live as human beings, Plato argues, our choices should not be left to blind impulse, tradition, convention, or brute force. They must be left, ultimately, to reason. Moreover, insofar as we are possessed of reason, Plato maintains, we have a conception of what is *ideal*—of what is *the* right and *the* good. Plato is an *absolutist*. He is convinced that just as in mathematics there is only one correct answer to a calculation, so in morals and politics there is a unique, absolute standard of what is right and good. For this reason he was strongly opposed to the views of the

Sophists. They were *relativists*. Relativism (to put it roughly) asserts: "When in Rome, do as the Romans do; when in Sparta, do as the Spartans do." Our standards of what is right or wrong are relative to the society to which we belong. Plato was opposed to any form of relativism. He believed that there is a correct standard that should be held for *all* men. It can be discovered by means of our reason. Plato, of course, recognized, as we do, that the actual behavior of persons or institutions ordinarily falls short, to varying degrees, of what the rational ideal would require, and that men's moral *opinions* do not normally coincide with what moral *knowledge*, based on reason, would assert to be right or good. It was therefore a corollary of this absolutist position, according to Plato, that the power to control social and political affairs should be vested only in those who possess genuine political wisdom and moral *knowledge*. Plato was convinced that only the wise should rule. Plato was not a democrat. He did not believe that everyone's opinion should be consulted and used as a basis for forming public policies or laws.

Those who have reason will look to the ideal. Their efforts to embody the ideal in actual behavior or social institutions will never be totally or permanently successful. Plato recognized that the world in which we live—the actual everyday world—can never be made completely perfect, rational, or ideal. However hard one may try, one always winds up with something less than perfection. Nevertheless, as a moral idealist, Plato believed that the maximum approximation to the ideal is worth struggling for. Otherwise, life would not be worth living since it might easily become barbaric or chaotic, or be only mediocre and dull.

(3) Plato believed that just as human beings have the capacity of reason, which allows them to make their life to some extent rational, so the Universe at large gives evidence of some form of rational organization. One can't point, to be sure, to the Reason or Intelligence that is operating in the world at large in the same way one can point to a *person* who possesses reason. Nevertheless, Plato is convinced there is evidence of design and order in the world on the grand scale. The order that we find in the world is not merely a matter of chance. There must be some designing Intelligence at work. Plato upheld a belief in *cosmic design*. (He was strongly opposed to the views, for example, of the atomist and materialist Democritus, who asserted in *his* metaphysics that everything that happens in the world is the result, at bottom, of the blind purposeless interaction of material atoms.) Because of this conviction, Plato's conception of the physical Universe is classified as a *teleological* one. The term 'teleological' comes from the Greek work *telos*: it means 'purpose', 'end', or 'goal'. Plato admitted that we have no way of *proving* that there is a designing Intelligence at work in the world; nor do we have any way of showing that such an Intelligence exists by directly confronting *it* by means of observa-

Cosmic design and irrationality

tional experience. Plato resorts to a myth (which he recounts in the *Timaeus*) to convey his faith in the existence of a rational Intelligence at work in the world at large. He calls this Intelligence a 'Divine Craftsman'. (It is only a 'likely story', he admits.) In saying all of this, however, Plato should not be called a 'theist' in the Christian sense. He did not claim that there is a God who created the world out of nothing. Instead, he believed that just as any craftsman uses his intelligence and imagination to work over raw materials that he finds already in existence, so, too, the 'Divine Craftsman' works over preexistent raw materials to make them as rational as possible. The result of his work—the Universe at large as we find it—is a mixture of rationality (design and order) and irrationality.

Plato argued that there is, or rather *ought to* be, a parallel between what can be accomplished in human life and what we already find on the level of the Universe at large. Man should emulate in his own life the work of the Divine Craftsman. He should introduce as much rational order into his life as possible. The 'microcosm' of human life should carry forward the rational ordering of the macrocosm, the Universe at large.

So much for a general summary of some of the leading themes in Plato's philosophy. We turn next to a more detailed examination of two of these themes: the Theory of Forms (which will occupy us for the remainder of this chapter) and the political and moral philosophy (in the next).

A Closer Look at the Theory of Forms

Why should Plato have developed the Theory of Forms? Why should he have believed, as strongly as he did, that there are such entities? This is what we have to try to understand. It is not the sort of theory that has received broad acceptance or agreement by other philosophers. Plato's most famous pupil, Aristotle, was one of the earliest and most severe critics of the theory. And even Plato himself, toward the end of his life, began to raise certain serious questions about it, although there is no evidence that he ever completely abandoned the theory. What, then, prompted Plato to develop this theory? What motivations did he have? And how did the Theory of Forms meet his intellectual needs? In what follows, I shall consider, briefly, three such motivations and show how the Theory of Forms simultaneously met all three.

Mathematical knowledge

(1) The first derives from Plato's study of mathematics, and the need, as he saw it, to explain how it is possible to have mathematical knowledge at all. Plato was greatly impressed by the certainty obtained in mathematics, as contrasted with the vagueness and uncertainty of men's beliefs in other areas. Already by Plato's time the Pythagoreans and other

Greeks had developed various parts of a theory of numbers ('arithmetic') and a theory of spatial figures ('geometry'). It is true that prior even to the work of the early Greek mathematicians, the Egyptians, Babylonians, and others had established various rules about numbers and figures. But the great glory of Greek mathematics was that it was able to set all of this out in a deductive system. Such a deductive system included accepted, self-evident starting points and conclusions whose *proofs* consisted in showing that they followed logically and necessarily from those starting points. This was the first major step in the development of mathematics as a rational discipline. Plato himself summarizes the character of the mathematical method as follows:

You know, of course, how students of subjects like geometry and arithmetic begin by postulating odd and even numbers, or the various figures and the three kinds of angle, and other such data in each subject. These data they take as known; and, having adopted them as assumptions, they do not feel called upon to give any account of them to themselves or to anyone else, but treat them as self-evident. Then, starting from these assumptions, they go on until they arrive, by a series of consistent steps, at all the conclusions they set out to investigate. . . . You also know how they make use of visible figures and discourse about them, though what they really have in mind is the originals of which these figures are images: they are not reasoning, for instance, about this particular square and diagonal which they have drawn, but about the Square and the Diagonal; and so in all cases. The diagrams they draw and the models they make are actual things, which may have their shadows or images in water; but now they serve in their turn as images, while the student is seeking to behold those realities which only thought can apprehend.[2,*]

Plato fastened upon the fact that mathematics gives us *knowledge*, not *opinion* or *belief*. The truth of a mathematical statement is something that is known with certainty; it is obtained by *reason*. Let's say I'm working in the field of arithmetic—the theory of numbers. There are very precise and definite relationships among numbers initially set out in certain self-evident, accepted starting points or axioms. Once I understand the axioms and use my reasoning powers, I can establish various other truths about numbers by showing that these other truths follow logically or rigorously from those starting points. Once you 'see' the proof (rationally follow it), you have *unshakable* knowledge about the truth of the conclusion. Anybody who might think otherwise from what you *know* to be the truth has only *opinion*. Indeed, there may be various opinions that differ among themselves. But they are all to be contrasted, as to their worth, with what is *known* to be the truth. The fact that somebody has only an opinion,

* From *The Republic of Plato* translated by F. M. Cornford and published by Oxford University Press (1941). Reprinted by permission of the publisher.

however strongly held, or uses his persuasive powers to try to get you to accept what he believes, will have no effect on you. If his opinion differs from what you know to be the case he will not be able to change your mind. Furthermore, all who use a common rational faculty, in following the mathematical proof, will come to the *same* conclusion. Once established as true, the conclusion thus established does not undergo any change. In short, a mathematically known truth is established in a rigorous, logical way, is unchanging, and is agreed to by all rational men.

Aside from these features of mathematics, there is another that impressed Plato (as he makes clear in the preceding quotation). This has to do with the contrast between what the mathematician is talking about when he establishes various things, for example, about *the* Square, *the* Diagonal, or *the* Circle, on the one hand, and the various diagrams, images, or material and sensible *examples* of what is square, diagonal, or circular, on the other. Would a geometer undertake to give a *proof* concerning various properties of a Circle by *measuring* the circular figure he has drawn on a blackboard? Of course not. Why is that? Let us take as our definition of 'circle': "a line forming a plane figure that is the locus of all points equidistant from a given point." A point has position but no length; a line has length but no thickness. And all the radii of the circle will be exactly equal in length to one another. Any circle or circular shape that someone might draw or find in the ordinary sensible, material world will fall short, in some degree or other, from the Circle with which the geometer is concerned, and about which he establishes various truths. The geometer has no objection to using, as aids to your understanding, and as teaching devices, figures drawn on the blackboard, for example. But no matter how accurate the drawing, the chalk lines drawn on the blackboard will have *some* thickness, the radii will not be *precisely* equal in length to each other, and so on. Further, the circles one draws on a blackboard were not always there, and they will be erased. And one can obviously draw *many* different circles. In short, the circular shapes one constructs (or finds) are multiple, inexact in some degree, undergo change, come into and pass out of existence. But *the* Circle about which the geometer establishes various truths cannot be, and does not need to be, drawn on the blackboard or anywhere else. It does not undergo change of any sort. It is not imperfect in any way. It is unique (there are not many Circles). And it can be approached only by means of reason, not by the senses. What we have said about *the* Circle holds for other mathematical concepts. Take Equality—another of Plato's examples.[3] A carpenter could take two sticks and try to make them equal in length. And he could get a pretty good match. He could say, pointing to two sticks: "These two sticks are 'more' equal than those two other sticks." But even the 'most' equal sticks are not *perfectly* equal. So Equality, in the mathematical sense, is again not something one finds exhibited perfectly in any sensible material. Nevertheless, we have a conception of Equality.

To sum up, then, there are these two features of mathematics that Plato tried to explain: (a) In mathematics we obtain knowledge that rests upon reason. One can give rigorous and certain demonstrations; such knowledge doesn't depend on 'counting noses' for opinions as to the truth. (b) What the mathematician makes reference to needs to be comprehended by the mind, by reason; it is not established by an appeal to the senses. In establishing mathematical truths one doesn't perform observations or experiments. (A mathematician can work with a pencil on the back of an envelope. He doesn't even need that, because all he does is work out certain relationships in his mind.) What the mathematician deals with has to be *conceived*, not *perceived*. And what is thus conceived is not material, tangible, or observable in any way.

What Plato asked himself is: How is it possible to have such mathematical knowledge? If its subject matter is not anything that one can observe with the senses, what then is it? One of the principal motivations Plato had in constructing his Theory of Forms was to be able to answer these questions. His answer, briefly, is that mathematics explores a domain of eternal, perfect, intelligible entities—the Forms.

(2) There is a second motivation Plato had for positing a domain of Forms. Plato wanted to be able to say that we have absolute and conclusive *knowledge* not only in mathematics but also with respect to what is *right and good*. Some people, when you ask them how to establish what is right or what is good, as this has to do with human conduct, would say "It's a matter of what the customs or conventions of a society say it is." Others would say "What ultimately determines whether something is considered right is simply a matter of power: Might makes right." Very briefly, these are two of the kinds of views that Plato encountered in his own day, especially as defended by the Sophists. Plato was strongly opposed to these views. Not only did he want to show their inherent weaknesses; he also wanted to be able to present an alternative approach that would not have the disastrous consequences that, in his eyes, flowed from the position of the relativist. The two views I have mentioned are presented and critically examined in Book One of the *Republic*.

Absolute moral standards

In that dialogue, the discussion starts innocently. Plato provides a perfectly natural setting in which eventually a number of participants are brought to explore some of the deepest and most far reaching of philosophic themes. Socrates comes to the house of Cephalus, an aged, wealthy, retired businessman. He's an old friend whom Socrates hasn't seen in a long time. Cephalus greets him. "Ah, welcome Socrates. Why don't I see you more often, etc., etc." Before you know it, Socrates tries to engage Cephalus in a philosophic discussion. Socrates says to him, quite 'innocently'—(and I paraphrase)—"Cephalus, here you are, an old man, wealthy and retired. What do you take to be the benefits which wealth has brought you?" Cephalus replies in a commonsensical and honest way (and again I summarize): "Well, I can face death with equanimity. It makes it possible for me not to have to cheat or deceive anyone—to tell the truth and to pay my debts." Socrates picks up that answer and begins questioning Cephalus. He asks Cephalus whether it would be the right thing to do, for example, to return a friend's weapon if, meanwhile, the person has gone mad. At once Cephalus 'smells a rat'. He realizes that he's going to get deeper and deeper into philosophical questions, so he begs off and says "I have to go perform a sacrifice." He leaves. It seems that Cephalus would much rather *do* what he thinks is proper and right than sit around and talk about it. So he turns the discussion over to his son, Polemarchus, who is much more eager, energetic, and ready to exchange wits with Socrates.

Polemarchus rushes forward with a definition of justice that once again reflects a popular conception of morality. He says, among other things, that doing justice is a matter of helping your friends and harming your enemies. It seems, at first glance, to be a perfectly acceptable statement. However, Socrates takes this 'analysis' and begins to find all sorts of flaws with it. He says (in effect): "Look! Is anybody whom you call your friend, necessarily your *real* friend? Is anybody whom you call your enemy your *real* enemy?" He thus gets Polemarchus, first of all, to distinguish real enemies from apparent enemies, real friends from apparent friends. The surface definition of doing good to your friends and not to your enemies lacks the kind of constituent that Socrates is looking for in a good definition: a precise and explicit statement of what is essential to the concept under analysis. So here is one type of weakness (vagueness and inexactness) in Polemarchus's definition. He then goes on to point out that if you are really going to harm your real enemy, then you are surely going to make him a worse man than he was before. (You might break his arm, tell malicious stories about him, burn his house down; in other words, hurt him in one way or another.) However, hurting somebody is making him worse. And Socrates asks: "How could a man who is just and good be a source of harm?" So, this is another problem for Polemarchus to think about. This kind of discussion continues. The whole point of Socrates' questioning is to show various weaknesses in popular morality: shallowness, inconsistency, vagueness, and imprecision. It is loose; it does not give us secure and carefully thought out rules and standards.

The other challenge Socrates has to face is put into the mouth of Thrasymachus.

All this time Thrasymachus had been trying more than once to break in upon our conversation; but his neighbors had restrained him, wishing to hear the argument to the end. In the pause after my last words he could keep quiet no longer; but gathering himself up like a wild beast he sprang at us as if he would tear us in pieces. Polemarchus and I were frightened out of our wits. . . .[4.][*]

After Socrates calms him down a bit, he invites him, with his customary irony, to tell the assembled company the 'real truth'. Thrasymachus proceeds to propose his own analysis, which can be summarized as follows: Justice is that which serves the interest (is to the advantage) of the stronger. What is 'right' for those who are being ruled is what is beneficial to those who rule, those who make the laws. This is the situation in all forms of government, not just in one-man dictatorships. If you want to know what is right, what is accepted, look to the ruling class and what they make others do in order to serve the interests of themselves as rulers. It may be a small group, it may be a single individual. The rulers are the ones who set the standards. And you can't ask, by way of protest: "But is it right?" No! For what is right is what they say it is!

Listen then, Thrasymachus began. What I say is that 'just' or 'right' means nothing but what is to the interest of the stronger party. Well, where is your applause? You don't mean to give it me.

I will, as soon as I understand, I said. I don't see yet what you mean by right being the interest of the stronger party. For instance, Polydamas, the athlete, is stronger than we are, and it is to his interest to eat beef for the sake of his muscles; but surely you don't mean that the same diet would be good for weaker men and therefore be right for us?

You are trying to be funny, Socrates. It's a low trick to take my words in the sense you think will be most damaging.

No, no, I protested; but you must explain.

Don't you know, then, that a state may be ruled by a despot, or a democracy, or an aristocracy?

Of course.

And that the ruling element is always the strongest?

Yes.

*From *The Republic of Plato* translated by F. M. Cornford and published by Oxford University Press (1941). Reprinted by permission of the publisher.

Well, then, in every case the laws are made by the ruling party in its own interest; a democracy makes democratic laws, a despot autocratic ones, and so on. By making these laws they define as 'right' for their subjects whatever is for their own interest, and they call anyone who breaks them a 'wrongdoer' and punish him accordingly. That is what I mean: in all states alike 'right' has the same meaning, namely what is for the interest of the party established in power, and that is the strongest. So the sound conclusion is that what is 'right' is the same everywhere: the interest of the stronger party.

Now I see what you mean, said I; whether it is true or not, I must try to make out. When you define right in terms of interest, you are yourself giving one of those answers you forbade to me; though, to be sure, you add 'to the stronger party'.

An insignificant addition, perhaps!

Its importance is not clear yet; what is clear is that we must find out whether your definition is true. I agree myself that right is in a sense a matter of interest; but when you add 'to the stronger party', I don't know about that. I must consider.

Go ahead, then.

I will. Tell me this. No doubt you also think it is right to obey the men in power?

I do.

Are they infallible in every type of state, or can they sometimes make a mistake?

Of course they can make a mistake.

In framing laws, then, they may do their work well or badly?

No doubt.

Well, that is to say, when the laws they make are to their own interest; badly, when they are not?

Yes.

But the subjects are to obey any law they lay down, and they will then be doing right?

Of course.

If so, by your account, it will be right to do what is not to the interest of the stronger party, as well as what is so.

What's that you are saying?

Just what you said, I believe; but let us look again. Haven't you admitted that the rulers, when they enjoin certain acts on their subjects, sometimes mistake their own best interests, and at the same time that it is right for the subjects to obey, whatever they may enjoin?

Yes, I suppose so.

Well, that amounts to admitting that it is right to do what is not to the interest of the rulers or the stronger party. They may unwittingly enjoin what is to their own disadvantage; and you say it is right for the others to do as they are told. In that case, their duty must be the opposite of what you said, because the weaker will have been ordered to do what is against the interest of the stronger. You with your intelligence must see how that follows.

Yes, Socrates, said Polemarchus, that is undeniable.

No doubt, Cleitophon broke in, if you are to be a witness on Socrates' side.

No witness is needed, replied Polemarchus; Thrasymachus himself admits that rulers sometimes ordain acts that are to their own disadvantage, and that it is the subjects' duty to do them.

That is because Thrasymachus said it was right to do what you are told by the men in power.

Yes, but he also said that what is to the interest of the stronger party is right; and, after making both these assertions, he admitted that the stronger sometimes command the weaker subjects to act against their interests. From all which it follows that what is in the stronger's interest is no more right than what is not.

No, said Cleitophon; he meant whatever the stronger believes to be in his own interest. That is what the subject must do, and what Thrasymachus meant to define as right.

That was not what he said, rejoined Polemarchus.

No matter, Polemarchus, said I; if Thrasymachus says so now, let us take him in that sense. Now, Thrasymachus, tell me, was that what you intended to say—that right means what the stronger thinks is to his interest, whether it really is so or not?

Most certainly not, he replied. Do you suppose I should speak of a man as 'stronger' or 'superior' at the very moment when he is making a mistake?

I did think you said as much when you admitted that rulers are not always infallible.

That is because you are a quibbler, Socrates. Would you say a man deserves to be called a physician at the moment when he makes a mistake in treating his patient and just in respect of that mistake; or a mathematician, when he does a sum wrong and just in so far as he gets a wrong result? Of course we do commonly speak of a physician or a mathematician or a scholar having made a mistake; but really none of these, I should say, is ever mistaken, in so far as he is worthy of the name we give him. So strictly speaking—and you are all for being precise—no one who practises a craft makes mistakes. A man is mistaken when his knowledge fails him; and at that moment he is no craftsman. And what is true of craftsmanship or any sort of skill is true of the ruler: he is never mistaken so long as he is acting as a ruler; though anyone might speak of a ruler making a mistake, just as he might of a physician. You must understand that I was talking in that loose way when I answered your question just now; but the precise statement is this. The ruler, in so far as he is acting as a ruler, makes no mistakes and consequently enjoins what is best for himself; and that is what the subject is to do. So, as I said at first, 'right' means doing what is to the interest of the stronger.

Very well, Thrasymachus, said I. So you think I am quibbling?

I am sure you are.

You believe my questions were maliciously designed to damage your position?

I know it. But you will gain nothing by that. You cannot outwit me by cunning, and you are not the man to crush me in the open.

Bless your soul, I answered, I should not think of trying. But, to prevent any more misunderstanding, when you speak of that ruler or stronger party whose interest the weaker ought to serve, please make it clear whether you are using the words in the ordinary way or in that strict sense you have just defined.

I mean a ruler in the strictest possible sense. Now quibble away and be as malicious as you can. I want no mercy. But you are no match for me.

Do you think me mad enough to beard a lion or try to outwit a Thrasymachus?

You did try just now, he retorted, but it wasn't a success.[5,*]

Here, once again, Socrates, as a spokesman for Plato, has to meet the challenge of Thrasymachus and those who would agree with him. Plato wants to show that it is not force that ultimately determines what is right or good but only reason. Plato was convinced that in ethics and politics,

*From *The Republic of Plato* translated by F. M. Cornford and published by Oxford University Press (1941). Reprinted by permission of the publisher.

just as in mathematics, we must make a distinction between knowledge and opinion. There is, for him, only one correct way of judging what is right or good. It is not to be determined by asking for the opinions of those who are unenlightened and ignorant. And certainly it is not to be discovered by asking those who have the greater power (the stronger army, the most money, etc.), because they too, from Plato's point of view, might be wrong. Suppose Hitler had won World War II and had imposed his way of thinking on the entire world? If you were a follower of Thrasymachus, you would say: "If Hitler had won, that would mean he was right!" And Plato would say: "Not at all! The fact that somebody comes out victorious in a *military* way does not necessarily mean that what he has done is right *morally*. His victims would still cry out from their graves that what he had done was *criminal!*" There is, Plato maintains, an absolute standard of what is right, even though human beings might not recognize it or abide by it. Yet we should appeal to it in order to appraise the actual course of events. We must appeal to it, too, as a guide to action if we would try to bring human conduct and institutions closer to the ideal. In short, Plato was a *moral idealist* who believed in absolute standards of what is right and good, standards of which we can have infallible knowledge.

Here, then, is a second motivation for Plato's Theory of Forms. The domain of Forms contains the absolute standards of what is right and good. We are not to look for such standards in daily experience, in the way in which people *actually* behave. Just as a mathematician uses his reason (not his powers of observation or sense experience) to find out about *the* Circle, so, too, in moral or political philosophy we must use reason to discover the ideal of Justice, for example, what a just society *might* be.

(3) I turn, finally, to Plato's third motivation in introducing the notion of Forms. This is connected with Plato's analysis of what underlies the fact that we make use of certain *general* concepts and expressions in language.

The meaning of general terms

To begin with, let us take a few simple sentences. Suppose I say: "Socrates is wise"; "This tabletop is rectangular"; "The Earth is spherical." We notice in each of these sentences that there is an individual object or entity that is being referred to: specifically, Socrates, this tabletop, the Earth. Such an individual object can be normally identified by sense experience. And if something once existed, but no longer does (as is the case with Socrates, who is no longer alive), we may nevertheless have ways of making reference to it by relying on reports that we take to be reliable; we fall back, for example, on available historical documents by Socrates' contemporaries. The important thing, for the moment, is that in each of the preceding quoted sentences the subjects of the sentences are particular individuals. But there is something else to be noted about the sentences we used as examples. Consider now their *predicates*, i.e., what we *asserted of* the subjects, the expressions we used to *describe* the individuals referred to. Consider, that is, the expressions 'wise', 'rectangular', 'spherical'. In the first place, we might have used those *same* predicates to describe *other* individuals. There are *many* individuals that we might have described by means of the same predicates we used to describe the individual object or person we happened to be talking about. There are other wise people besides Socrates, other surfaces that are rectangular, other objects that are spherical, and so on. Let us say, therefore, that these predicate expressions are *general*, as contrasted with the subject expressions, which are *particular* or refer to individuals.

Consider, next, that not only can I use the term 'wise' to describe Socrates and other individual persons. I also can make statements in which I say something about what it is to be wise, about wisdom itself. For example, I might utter the sentence "Wisdom is a virtue or excellence." Here the *subject* expression of this sentence is 'wisdom' and the predicate (what I say *about* wisdom) is 'is a virtue or excellence'. Now consider the use of such terms as 'wise' as a predicate in the sentence "Socrates is wise," or the expression 'wisdom' in the sentence "Wisdom is a virtue." Do *these* expressions ('wise' and 'wisdom') *themselves* refer to some individual material *object* that I can pick out and identify by means of sense experience in the way I could find Socrates in the world around me? Plato would say they are expressions that convey or name something wholly different in character from what a name like 'Socrates' refers to. Plato would say the terms 'wise' and 'wisdom' name *one* definite 'something' that is exemplified in *many* different cases or instances.

Moreover, it makes sense to inquire into the meaning, that is, the essential characteristics, of these terms. It makes sense to ask for their *definitions*, although it is ordinarily a very difficult matter to find a satisfactory definition even of many expressions with which we are perfectly familiar and use everyday: What *is* wisdom? courage? friendship? justice?

And now Plato goes one step further. He assumes that just as various proper names or other linguistic expressions we use to refer to individual objects designate something real (for example, Socrates, the Earth, this tabletop) so the terms 'wisdom', 'rectangularity', 'justice', and so on, designate or refer to something objective. The *name* 'Socrates' is part of language, but the *person* Socrates is not himself part of language; the name 'Socrates' refers to or designates the person Socrates. Similarly, Plato wishes to say, the term 'wisdom' (*sophia*) is part of language (Greek, English, or whatever), but what it refers to is not part of language. To be sure, we can't point to it in the way we can point to Socrates as an individual object. Nevertheless, just as Socrates as a person (as an individual object in the world) does not depend for his existence on his having a name, so what the term 'wisdom' refers to is also objective and does not depend for *its* existence or reality on the fact that there is some *word* in Greek, English, or some other language to refer to it. Plato wants to say there would still be Wisdom even if men did not recognize it or give it a name. Moreover, what is so named refers to something distinct and unique. Wisdom, for example, is different from Justice or Courage, just as Triangularity is different from Circularity or Rectangularity.

To explain how it is that we are able to use such terms as 'wisdom' (an abstract noun) and 'wise' (used as an adjective to describe someone) and the kinds of meaning they have (as distinguished from how it is that we give meaning to names for particular individuals in the world about us), Plato introduced the notion of Form. A Form is that to which terms such as 'wisdom' and 'wise' refer. It is something quite different in status from that to which a name for an individual object in the sensible world refers.

Yet Plato would say there is a connection between the individual objects of the sensible material world and these abstract, intelligible Forms. Plato describes the relation between these two domains as one of *participation*. Individuals 'participate' or 'share in' a common Form. However, no individual in the sensible world perfectly exemplifies the Form itself. No person is fully wise, no work of art is perfectly beautiful, no circular shape of wood or chalk is perfectly circular, no society is perfectly just (good), and so on.

Here are some passages in which Plato introduces the notion of Form in terms of the considerations I have been summarizing:

We proceed as usual and begin by assuming the existence of a single essential nature or Form for every set of things which we call by the same name.[6]

Let me remind you of the distinction we drew earlier and have often drawn on other occasions, between the multiplicity of things that we call good or beautiful or whatever it may be and, on the other hand, Goodness itself or Beauty itself and so on. Corresponding to each of these sets of many things, we postulate a single Form or real essence, as we call it. . . . Further, the many things, we say, can be seen, but are not objects of rational thought; whereas the Forms are objects of thought, but invisible.[7]

The mind, by a power of her own, contemplates the universals in all things.[8]

Must you always mean the same thing when you utter the same name, whether once or repeatedly?
The same thing, of course.
The word 'distinct' is the name of something, is it not?
Certainly.

Then when you utter it, whether once or many times, you apply it to nothing else, and you name nothing else, than that of which it is the name.
Assuredly.
Now when we say that the others are distinct from the one, and the one is distinct from the others, though we use the word 'distinct' twice, we do not for all that apply it to anything else, but we always apply it to that nature of which it is the name.[9]

Then this—I mean Justice—is a certain thing?
Certainly.
Then, too, by Wisdom the wise are wise, and by the Good all good things are good?
Of course.
And these are real things, since otherwise they would not do what they do.
To be sure, they are real things.
Then are not all beautiful things beautiful by the Beautiful?
Yes, by the Beautiful.
Which is a real thing?
Yes, for what alternative is there?[10]

Summary

Now let me summarize the foregoing points about Plato's motivations in developing his Theory of Forms. I have suggested that there are three general lines of thought that led Plato to devise his theory. One was his attempt to make sense of the accomplishments of mathematics in giving us knowledge as distinct from opinion. A second was his concern to support his conviction that there are absolute standards by which we could guide our conduct and appraise or criticize what we find in men's actual behavior and social institutions. The third was his interest in understanding what lies behind, and makes possible, the use of general terms in thought and language. These three motivations in his thought led Plato to posit the domain of Forms. *The domain of Forms simultaneously answered all three interests.* Forms are at once (1) the targets of knowledge as distinct from opinion, (2) the ideal standards or models by which we can guide our actions and provide the basis for critical appraisals of what we find in practice, and (3) the unique, eternal, and intelligible entities to which general terms and concepts refer.[11]

As we have seen, Plato's metaphysical theory of the nature of reality rests upon making a crucial distinction and contrast between two domains or levels of reality, that of Forms and that of the sensible world. Let us now examine the use Plato makes of this metaphysical theory, particularly as it affects human life. We said, at the very beginning of our discussion, that a traditional and important task of philosophy is to provide a comprehensive view of the world and of man's place in it. Plato's philosophy is a classic example of this interest of philosophy. Let us turn from Plato's metaphysics, then, to his philosophy of human life and values. Plato has much to say on this topic. One of the longest and most important sources of his views is to be found in the *Republic*. I turn next to examine some of the leading themes of that dialogue.

chapter 4

The Ideal Society

Plato's Republic

Plato's most famous dialogue, the *Republic*, deals with the nature of the good life. It does this by exploring the various answers that might be given to the question "What is justice?" However, it is important to remember that the word 'justice' (which translates the Greek word *dikaiosynē*) is to be understood as having the same broad range of meanings as belong to the terms 'good' and 'right'. Justice, as Plato treats of it, has virtually nothing to do with legal matters—for example, with decisions by a court of law. Also, it is worth bearing in mind that the title, the *Republic*, does not refer to a special type of government or political structure, a republic in the modern sense. It deals rather with matters of public concern. (In fact, that's what, in Latin, the term *'res publica'* means from which we get the word 'republic'.) The *Republic* offers a general political theory. Politics, for Plato, meant a consideration of how a city-state (a *polis*) should be run. (A city-state would normally have several thousand people in it and not be something of the dimensions of a modern *nation*-state.)

Although Plato devotes much of his attention to the character of an ideal political community, he is throughout just as much concerned with analyzing the nature of the good life for the individual. Indeed, as we shall see, there is a very close parallel between his conception of what justice (or the good life) consists in when considered on a political level and what it consists in on the level of an individual's personal life. For

Plato the separation that we make nowadays between ethics (as having to do with personal conduct) and politics (as having to do with affairs of government and state) would not have made any sense. Rather, in his approach, it would be better to hyphenate the two expressions and say that what he is concerned with is 'ethics-politics'. And this for the very good reason that one cannot explore what the good life is for the individual without also, and at the same time, taking into account what would make for an ideal society in which the individual is to lead his life. And, conversely, one cannot make any serious headway in characterizing what the good society is without having some conception of the good life for the individuals who make up the society. The two go hand in hand. And it is for this reason that when Plato comes to define what he means by 'justice' he argues that there is a common structure or pattern that characterizes justice, whether we find it in a *just society* or in the life of a *just individual*. I shall return to this point more fully later.

Justice, then, for Plato, is the supreme excellence or virtue to be aimed at in the organization of the good life for the individual or the state. Before Plato begins to build his case for this claim, and to provide an analysis of the internal structure of the just life, he formulates a challenge that some sceptic might make. Why indeed should we think of justice as an excellence at all? Why should we think of it as being a good to be striven for? Perhaps a life of injustice is, at bottom, more satisfactory! In the *Republic* Plato puts this challenge into the mouth of Glaucon (who, in real life, was Plato's brother). Here is the way he makes his case:

Glaucon's challenge:
Why be just at all?

Nothing so far said about justice and injustice has been established to my satisfaction. I want to be told what each of them really is, and what effect each has, in itself, on the soul that harbours it, when all rewards and consequences are left out of account. So here is my plan, if you approve. I shall revive Thrasymachus' theory. First, I will state what is commonly held about the nature of justice and its origin; secondly, I shall maintain that it is always practised with reluctance, not as good in itself, but as a thing one cannot do without; and thirdly, that this reluctance is reasonable, because the life of injustice is much the better life of the two—so people say. That is not what I think myself, Socrates; only I am bewildered by all that Thrasymachus and ever so many others have dinned into my ears; and I have never yet heard the case for justice stated as I wish to hear it. You, I believe, if anyone, can tell me what is to be said in praise of justice in and for itself; that is what I want. Accordingly, I shall set you an example by glorifying the life of injustice with all the energy that I hope you will show later in denouncing it and exalting justice in its stead. Will that plan suit you?

Nothing could be better, I replied. Of all subjects this is one on which a sensible man must always be glad to exchange ideas.

Good, said Glaucon. Listen then, and I will begin with my first point: the nature and origin of justice.

What people say is that to do wrong is, in itself, a desirable thing; on the other hand, it is not at all desirable to suffer wrong, and the harm to the sufferer outweighs the advantage to the doer. Consequently, when men have had a taste of both, those who have not the power to seize the advantage and escape the harm decide that they would be better off if they made a compact neither to do wrong nor to suffer it. Hence they began to make laws and covenants with one another; and whatever the law prescribed they called lawful and right. That is what right or justice is and how it came into existence; it stands half-way between the best thing of all—to do wrong with impunity—and the worst, which is to suffer wrong without the power to retaliate. So justice is accepted as a compromise, and valued, not as good in itself, but for lack of power to do wrong; no man worthy of the name, who had that power, would ever enter into such a compact with anyone; he would be mad if he did. That, Socrates, is the nature of justice according to this account, and such the circumstances in which it arose.

The next point is that men practise it against the grain, for lack of power to do wrong. How true that is, we shall best see if we imagine two men, one just, the other unjust, given full licence to do whatever they like, and then follow them to observe where each will be led by his desires. We shall catch the just man taking the same road as the unjust; he will be moved by self-interest, the end which it is natural to every creature to pursue as good, until forcibly turned aside by law and custom to respect the principle of equality.

Now, the easiest way to give them that complete liberty of action would be to imagine them possessed of the talisman found by Gyges, the ancestor of the famous Lydian. The story tells how he was a shepherd in the King's service. One day there was a great storm, and the ground where his flock was feeding was rent by an earthquake. Astonished at the sight, he went down into the chasm and saw, among other wonders of which the story tells, a brazen horse, hollow, with windows in its sides. Peering in, he saw a dead body, which seemed to be of more than human size. It was naked save for a gold ring, which he took from the finger and made his way out. When the shepherds met, as they did every month, to send an account to the King of the state of his flocks, Gyges came wearing the ring. As he was sitting with the others, he happened to turn the bezel of the ring inside his hand. At once he became invisible, and his companions, to his surprise, began to speak of him as if he had left them. Then, as he was fingering the ring, he turned the bezel outwards and became visible again. With that, he set about testing the ring to see if it really had this power, and always with the same result: according as he turned the bezel inside or out he vanished and reappeared. After this discovery he contrived to be one of the messengers sent to the court. There he seduced the Queen, and with her help murdered the King and seized the throne.

Now suppose there were two such magic rings, and one were given to the just man, the other to the unjust. No one, it is commonly believed, would have such iron strength of mind as to stand fast in doing right or keep his hands off other men's goods, when he could go to the market-place and fearlessly help himself to anything he wanted, enter houses and sleep with any woman he chose, set prisoners free and kill men at his pleasure, and in a word go about among men with the powers of a god. He would behave no better than the other; both would take the same course. Surely this would be strong proof that men do right only under compulsion; no individual thinks of it as good for him personally, since he does wrong whenever he finds he has the power. Every man believes that wrongdoing pays him personally much better, and, according to this theory, that is the truth. Granted full licence to do as he liked, people would think him a miserable fool if they found him refusing to wrong his neighbours or to touch their belongings, though in public they would keep up a pretence of praising his conduct, for fear of being wronged themselves. So much for that.

Finally, if we are really to judge between the two lives, the only way is to contrast the extremes of justice and injustice. We can best do that by imagining our two men to be perfect types, and crediting both to the full with the qualities they need for their respective ways of life. To begin with the unjust man: he must be like any consummate master of a craft, a physician or a captain, who, knowing just what his art can do, never tries to do more, and can always retrieve a false step. The unjust man, if he is to reach perfection, must be equally discreet in his criminal attempts, and he must not be found out, or we shall think him a bungler; for the highest pitch of injustice is to seem just when you are not. So we must endow our man with the full complement of injustice; we must allow him to have secured a spotless reputation for virtue while committing the blackest crimes; he must be able to retrieve any mistake, to defend himself with convincing eloquence if his misdeeds are denounced, and, when force is required, to bear down all opposition by his courage and strength and by his command of friends and money.

Now set beside this paragon the just man in his simplicity and nobleness, one who, in Aeschylus' words, "would be, not seem, the best." There must, indeed, be no such seeming; for if his character were apparent, his reputation would bring him honours and rewards, and then we should not know whether it was for their sake that he was just or for justice's sake alone. He must be stripped of everything but justice, and denied every advantage the other enjoyed. Doing no wrong, he must have the worst reputation for wrong-doing, to test whether his virtue is proof against all that comes of having a bad name; and under this lifelong imputation of wickedness, let him hold on his course of justice unwavering to the point of death. And so, when the two men have carried their justice and injustice to the last extreme, we may judge which is the happier.

My dear Glaucon, I exclaimed, how vigorously you scour these two characters clean for inspection, as if you were burnishing a couple of statues!

I am doing my best, he answered. Well, given two such characters, it is not hard, I fancy, to describe the sort of life that each of them may expect; and if the description sounds rather coarse, take it as coming from those who cry up the merits of injustice rather than from me. They will tell you that our just man will be thrown into prison, scourged and racked, will have his eyes burnt out, and, after every kind of torment, be impaled. That will teach him how much better it is to seem virtuous than to be so. In fact those lines of Aeschylus I quoted are more fitly applied to the unjust man, who, they say, is a realist and does not live for appearances: "he would be, not seem" unjust,

> *reaping the harvest sown*
> *In those deep furrows of the thoughtful heart*
> *Whence wisdom springs.*

With his reputation for virtue, he will hold offices of state, ally himself by marriage to any family he may choose, become a partner in any business, and, having no scruples about being dishonest, turn all these advantages to profit. If he is involved in a lawsuit, public or private, he will get the better of his opponents, grow rich on the proceeds, and be able to help his friends and harm his enemies. Finally, he can make sacrifices to the gods and dedicate offerings with due magnificence, and, being in a much better position than the just man to serve the gods as well as his chosen friends, he may reasonably hope to stand higher in the favour of heaven. So much the better, they say, Socrates, is the life prepared for the unjust by gods and men.[1,*]

With this challenge facing him, Socrates (speaking for Plato) undertakes in the rest of the dialogue to give his own constructive analysis of justice and to show why, indeed, the just life is to be preferred to the unjust.

Justice in the State and Individual

As I have already remarked, justice, for Plato, is a virtue whose fundamental nature or structure is to be found as much in the life of an individual person as in the way in which a whole society is organized. Since this is so, Plato proposes to undertake the analysis of justice by first seeing it 'written in large letters' on a social level. Having discerned its structure in the workings of a city-state, he will then turn to its parallels in the way a *psyche* or 'soul' might be exercised or ad-*justed*.

A moment ago, I used the expression 'the way a society is *organized*'. The use of the term 'organized', in connection with a society, is something that Plato would have found congenial. For he treats a political organiza-

---

* From *The Republic of Plato* translated by F. M. Cornford and published by Oxford University Press (1941). Reprinted by permission of the publisher.

tion very much the way in which, when one considers a person as a complex *organism*, one distinguishes his various organs. For Plato the state can be looked upon as a kind of *organism*: it, too, has various 'organs' or major parts—this time made up of the various *classes* of society—where each 'organ' has its own function and contributes in its own special way to the functioning of the 'political organism' as a whole. He would have approved of the expression 'body politic'. In short, the state is also a special kind of *individual*. Accordingly, when Plato comes to develop his political theory, he defends an *organic* analysis of the workings of a society.*

A leading concern of the *Republic* is to give a picture of an *ideal society*. You might be led to infer from this that Plato sets out to construct his own version of a Utopia, and that therefore (like many other blueprints for Utopia) it is bound to fail or have little value as a practical guide to action, because it has no connection with, or relevance to, men's actual problems. But this would not be a correct interpretation of what Plato is trying to accomplish. It is true that Plato is trying to draw a picture of an ideal society, of what the best society might be. At the same time, he is not unrealistic. He does not fail to take into account the actual forces at work in communal life or the elementary facts of human psychology as he understands them. On the contrary, his analysis is based on a full recognition of what he thinks are the actual drives, needs, and interests that people have. So although he is concerned with an ideal society, his version of the ideal (if it's going to stand any chance of being genuinely effective) will have to be built up out of, be an improvement on, and point the way to a transformation of the actual 'raw materials' that we already find at work in human nature. To this extent, then, Plato is a realist, and not a dreamy-eyed idealist. He starts out by considering what he takes to be the actual motivations of human beings and the forces at work in society. He wishes to see how these motivations and forces can be channeled and organized in a society that might become rational. In describing the ideal society, then, Plato is not describing the *Form* Justice. He is, rather, appealing to the Form Justice, as he conceives it, to describe the best possible society for people as they are *actually constituted* in the world of fact. His ideal is thus a 'mixture' (as the Universe is, too) of reason and necessity.

Plato is not writing a history of how societies *have* developed. Nor is he trying to be a prophet. He is not looking to the future and predicting how, in fact, societies *will* develop. Instead, he is attempting to give a

---

* Indeed, even in his cosmology as set out in the *Timaeus*, Plato suggests we could think of *the Universe* as itself an all-inclusive 'Living Creature'. Thus for Plato there are important parallels that might be found as we go from the level of the person, to that of the state, and even to that of the Universe.

logical analysis of the forces at work in society. At the same time, as a moral-political idealist, he is pointing to the direction in which he believes society *ought to* develop. But the ideal can be conceived only by reason. Plato has no illusions about the likelihood of the ideal ever being fully realized. He has no naive misapprehensions that someday, somewhere, his vision of the perfect society will in fact be fully realized. However, this does not in the slightest diminish the value of having a conception of an ideal society. On the contrary, it is only when people have such an ideal that they can set about to change the existing state of affairs, since they then have a criterion or plan for guiding action. The vision of the perfect society, like the mathematician's conception of the Circle, can serve as a model and guide.

Plato's version of what an ideal society might be like, as I remarked earlier, has been extremely influential. People have adapted it to suit their own needs and conceptions. And although we shall find much in Plato's account that is limited to the experience of his own historical epoch (and so does not speak to us and our problems two thousand years later), still it is remarkable how many of the sorts of things he says ring true; for many, therefore, his views have a continuing validity and relevance today. It is for this reason that Plato's work is a classic and will always remain so. Moreover, even if one violently disagrees with Plato's basic outlook on life and politics, one cannot ignore the challenge of his views.

The Growth of the Ideal Society

Formation of the first city

So let's start where Plato does. He begins by calling attention to the basic condition for the very existence and continued survival of *any* society. It is the *economic* function. This condition holds for the most primitive society as well as for the most advanced. Consider, first, the character of a fairly simple society. In such a society a good deal of the time and energy of its members are devoted to survival: to satisfying the basic needs for food, clothing, and shelter. As living creatures, we have to replenish our energy; we have to eat and drink, otherwise we die. And we have to protect ourselves against the elements. Meanwhile, new members of society are being brought into existence: men reproduce themselves. And so people have to feed, clothe, and house their children, not just themselves. It's not just a question of individual survival, but of group survival.

Does the economic function of producing the necessities of life ever disappear, no matter how developed a society becomes? The answer is no. That's why the economic function is basic: it's not just a principal preoccupation of a relatively simple society; it's a continuing concern of any society. It underlies all the other functions or activities so that if the economic base is destroyed, virtually everything else goes with it.

Plato begins by describing this function of society not only because it is basic but also because he finds illustrated in it a very important feature that he will emphasize as he goes on to consider more developed stages of society. It is the principle of *the division of labor.* "A state comes into existence because no individual is self-sufficing; we all have many needs."[2] Men are not normally Robinson Crusoes or hermits. They live in communities. Each member of the community has various needs: for food, clothing, shelter, or other material goods and services. However, by living with other persons, it is now possible to call upon the help of other members of the community; it is not necessary to do everything oneself. ". . . if the farmer is to have a good plough and spade and other tools, he will not make them himself. No more will the builder and weaver and shoemaker make all the many implements they need. So quite a number of carpenters and smiths and other craftsmen must be enlisted."[3] Thus people tend to specialize or take on particular functions or activities. Let's say I am a farmer, and am good at growing things. I will grow enough food not only for myself but also for other members of my group. At the same time, I expect that if there's another fellow who is good at making various things that I need (clothes, shoes, etc.) he will make enough not only for himself but for others as well. A system of exchange will come into use; men will be interdependent on one another. And a division of labor, of specialized functions, will characterize the life of the community. So here already on the economic level of the production and consumption of basic material goods is a twofold phenomenon of importance for the emergence and survival of any society: on the one hand, of specialization and, on the other, of interchange, coordination, and a mechanism of sharing for the benefit of all members of the society.

The division of labor

Plato turns next to consider the growth of a society beyond its fairly simple stages. He describes a society in which life is no longer confined to the satisfaction of bare necessities. Various refinements and 'luxuries' become increasingly available. At the same time, while life becomes easier and richer than life on a subsistence level, all sorts of complications begin to make their appearance. As the community grows in size and complexity, for example, there are increasingly more opportunities for acts of *injustice.* Also, the tendency to indulge in 'soft' living creates the need for physicians to cure men's illnesses. And with the increased wealth of a society or the desire of its members to acquire even more wealth, men go to war against each other.

More complex societies

The consideration of luxury may help us to discover how justice and injustice take root in society. . . . Some people, it seems, will not be satisfied to live in this simple way; they must have couches and tables and furniture of all sorts; and delicacies too, perfumes, unguents, courtesans, sweetmeats, all in plentiful variety. And besides, we must not limit ourselves now to those bare necessaries of house and clothes and shoes; we shall have to set going the arts of embroidery and painting, and collect rich materials, like gold and ivory. . . . Then we must once more enlarge our community. The healthy one will not be big enough now; it must be swollen up with a whole multitude of callings not ministering to any bare necessity: hunters and fishermen, for instance; artists in sculpture, painting, and music; poets with their attendant train of professional reciters, actors, dancers, producers; and makers of all sorts of household gear, including everything for women's adornment. And we shall want more servants: children's nurses and attendants, lady's maids, barbers, cooks and confectioners. And then swineherds—there was no need for them in our original state, but we shall want them now; and a great quantity of sheep and cattle too, if people are going to live on meat. . . . And with this manner of life physicians will be in much greater request.

The country, too, which was large enough to support the original inhabitants, will now be too small. If we are to have enough pasture and plough land, we shall have to cut off a slice of our neighbors' territory; and if they too are not content with necessaries but give themselves up to getting unlimited wealth, they will want a slice of ours. . . . So the next thing will be, Glaucon, that we shall be at war.[4],*

In this last remark, Plato gives one of the earliest statements of the view that all wars are to be explained in terms of economic motives. Elsewhere, Plato sums the matter up very simply: "All wars are made to get money."[5] When the highly developed industrial societies of our own day have gone to war with each other over colonies because these were rich sources of raw materials, they were illustrating a principle that Plato found already at work in earlier stages of human history.

Selection of guardians

Given this situation—where one group is ready to move in and take over what belongs to another group, and where those who are thus under attack need to defend themselves—a new and important complication arises. Up to now, a society engaged in primarily economic activities (a society of farmers, weavers, shoemakers, traders, hunters, carpenters, etc.) has had no need of a special group to serve as a defense. But now the state needs such a new *soldier class* whose function will be different from that of the *producer class*. For even if a society is on the whole a peaceful one and wants to mind its own business, it may find itself threatened from the outside. So it has to develop a soldier class to *protect* itself against those who want to appropriate what it has. Or else a society may be dis-

---

* From *The Republic of Plato* translated by F. M. Cornford and published by Oxford University Press (1941). Reprinted by permission of the publisher.

satisfied with what it already possesses and wants to take over what belongs to some other group; for it, again, a fighting force is necessary, this time for *aggressive* purposes. Indeed, as the society develops, it will need not only a special group of men to defend itself against attack by *external* enemies but also a group of men who will preserve law and order within, by policing the society and maintaining its *internal* security. Plato calls the class of individuals who will perform these military and policing functions the 'auxiliaries'. (At first, he simply calls them 'guardians'. However, he later subdivides the guardian group into two subgroups: those who will become *rulers* and others who remain to serve in the military-police function and are called *'auxiliaries'*.)

Just as the state in carrying on its activities of producing and consuming material goods relies on individuals with special skills and aptitudes as traders, farmers, shoemakers, weavers, and so on, so now the society needs individuals with special aptitudes for fighting and policing. The question thus arises how to select and train such individuals who will be especially good and trustworthy in performing these functions. It is at this point that Plato turns his attention, for the first time, to the role of *education* in society.

Plato's discussion of education in the *Republic* falls into two main parts, one having to do with *primary* education and the other with *higher* education. The examination of the methods and goals of primary education is introduced in the context of finding a method for selecting and training individuals who will be assigned the job of being *auxiliaries*. The nature of higher education is considered at a later stage in the dialogue, when the problem of selecting the future *rulers* of the society is taken up.

Primary education

In detailing his views on primary education, Plato adapts some features of the system of education practiced in the Athenian society of his own day. However, his intent is to make primary education a state responsibility, not as it was in his day a private or family one. Moreover, it will need to be very closely supervised and controlled in accordance with Plato's project of constructing an ideal society. Also, although such primary education would presumably be made available to the children of all classes of the society, his interest at this stage is primarily that of selecting the future guardians of the society (first the auxiliaries, and out of these, eventually, the rulers). Therefore, whereas one function of primary education would be to provide all members of the society, whatever their eventual role, with certain basic or elementary skills and information (of reading, writing, knowledge of elementary facts of history, and so on), Plato's main interest is devoted to finding those individuals who show themselves to possess the traits of character and of fitness in both mind and body that will justify their being selected to become, eventually, the guardians of the society. So although everybody gets some training in the elementary things that one should know in a minimal way, the scheme of primary education is also to serve as a selective mechanism for choosing guardians. At this stage, Plato is concerned with the course of training that will help choose those individuals who will make good soldiers. Later on, if among these selected individuals there are some still fewer individuals who show they have the promise for benefitting from a course of higher education, and becoming in time candidates for the ruling class, such individuals will be allowed to go on to such higher education.

Character training

Let's examine, now, a bit more fully, some of Plato's ideas on the nature of primary education. It is a special concern of primary education to provide *training in character*. If one catches a child or young person cheating, lying, being uncooperative, being dishonest, and so on, it is the job of those supervising the training of the young to chastise and correct him. On a playing field, the sportsman's code requires that one show certain traits and behavior. Violating the code brings condemnation. Also, a teacher will watch out during the playing of a game to see, for example, who will not run away or falter when it is necessary to attack. If a person shows himself to be cowardly or weak, it suggests that he is not the kind of individual who would, in time, make a good soldier or policeman. So there are certain virtues of character that will be stressed, praised, and so instilled. There will be certain vices—shortcomings or weaknesses—that will be pointed out and condemned.

Plato recognized that character training is achieved in various ways, not only on an athletic field or in a gymnasium. There are all kinds of subtle and not-so-subtle influences that help mold a person's character. That's why Plato gives much attention to the kinds of things a young, impressionable mind is exposed to as it undergoes the various formative processes in its development. A modern-day example would be the sorts of programs a child watches on TV. If there are no restrictions on these, and children are constantly subjected, for example, to scenes of violence and cruelty, this will be something that 'eats into' their character. Plato was very aware of this kind of influence. In his day, of course, there were other 'media' that had a broad impact on character formation. These included taking part in school plays or dramatic recitations, engaging in dances, listening to or performing music, reading the stories and myths recounted by the poets, and so on. Plato was keenly aware, in all of these activities, of the influence exerted by and on the imagination, the image-forming capacity of the young person's mind. Such image-forming capacity (let's call it 'fiction' in the sense of that which is 'made up'—it need not be false or misleading) is especially exercised in the various *arts*. The imaginative arts have a very strong influence on character formation, on the attitudes and ways of behavior that people take on. The very dances a person engages in, the music he listens to or performs, the plays he listens to or performs, the stories he listens to or reads, have an effect on the way his character develops. It is because of this fact that Plato did not hesitate to recommend a *censorship of the arts* by which children and young persons would be affected. He believed that young minds do not have the wisdom or range of experience sufficient to allow them to make their own choices as to what they should read, perform, or listen to. In his view those who *do* have such knowledge of what is right and good should make the choices for them. Thus he was in favor, for example, of expurgating passages from some of the stories told by the poets about the gods and heroes of Greek religion. These gods and heroes were the 'movie idols' of the day. Young persons reading about them in 'unexpurgated editions' were likely to take on and imitate their behavior and characteristics. But it is well known that the heroes and heroines, the gods and goddesses, frequently indulged in all sorts of immoral behavior: they lied, cheated, raped, murdered, and so on. "If *they* can do it," an impressionable youngster might easily suppose, "why shouldn't I?!"

Another side of the process of early primary education is the training of the body. Plato stresses the importance of gymnastics and sports for toughening the body. They are to go hand in hand with the training of character in order to develop a well-rounded individual: "a sound mind in a healthy body." One doesn't want underdeveloped bodies or underdeveloped minds and characters. (Someone might be a 'whiz' at arithmetic, know all the baseball statistics for the last ten years, and be a weakling or not know how to hit a ball! Or he might be a physical 'brute' with a weak character, or be 'all brawn and no brain'.)

Building strong bodies

The fully developed ideal society that Plato envisages has three classes: *producers, auxiliaries,* and *rulers.* The producer class is composed of the farmers, merchants, artisans—all those engaged in the various basic economic activities of the society without which it could not survive. The auxiliaries include the soldiers and the police force: those whose special function is to defend the society from attack by external enemies and to guard against outbreaks of lawlessness within the society. Further, it would seem that Plato intended the auxiliaries to include, in addition to the military and police, those who would enforce the policies and laws as these are determined by the rulers. In short, one may think of the auxiliaries as enlarged to include a group of 'executives'—in the sense of those who execute or carry out the rules laid down by the ruling class for the society as a whole. They would be, in some ways, comparable to those performing the various functions of a Civil Service. Finally, the rulers are those select individuals in whom the power to rule over the entire society is vested. How to select these individuals, their special qualifications and virtues, engages the bulk of Plato's attention in the *Republic.* I shall return to this theme shortly.

The three classes: producers, auxiliaries, rulers

Meanwhile, there is one point that should be mentioned in order to forestall any confusion or identification of Plato's conception of the tripartite class division of society with a rigid caste system. Plato thinks that *by and large* individuals will tend to fall into one or another of the three classes by virtue of their interests, native endowments, and abilities. However, the assignment of an individual to a particular class should not be a matter of arbitrary decision, family influence, or parentage. It should depend entirely on merit or proven ability. In short, if your father is a member of the ruling class and you show that what you're really fitted for is to be a foot soldier or to be a baker or a farmer—that's where you're going to be assigned. Conversely, if you are the son or daughter of a farmer or city person, and you show yourself to have those special traits and abilities that might qualify you to become an auxiliary or even a ruler, you will be given the opportunity to become a member of one or the other of those classes.[6] Plato's is a society of 'meritocracy', one in which a person rises as high as his abilities warrant.

Justice as health in an organically structured society

Plato turns next to an explicit analysis of where justice is to be found in the ideal society. To anticipate the main point he is going to make: *Justice is another name for the total health of an organically structured society in which each class and individual performs its specialized function in harmonious cooperation with the others.* The principle of the division of labor that we earlier noted at work on a purely economic level, even in a fairly primitive or simple society, is now broadened to encompass the workings of the *political* structure of the society as a whole in its most advanced form. In order to understand this concept of justice as a matter of organic health in society as a whole, let us take physical health in an individual person as our model. Let's suppose your doctor has given you a thorough physical examination and pronounced you in excellent health. What does this amount to? First of all, he's examined each of your organs, each with its own specialized function, and found each doing its job well (the eyes are 20–20, the heart shows no irregularities, etc.). Moreover, all these organs and functions mesh with one another: the lungs provide the oxygen that the circulatory system and the brain need, and so on. Health is a quality of organic unity and the coordinated interdependence of specialized functions. Broadly speaking, this is the model Plato has in mind in thinking of what justice amounts to in an ideal society.

Courage

Let us consider now this ideal in some greater detail. Take, first, the auxiliary class. What you look for here, as already remarked, is the carrying out of the orders of the ruling class: whom and when to fight and what laws to enforce. Given this broad function, the special virtue or excellence of this class Plato calls 'courage'. By 'courage' is meant not only bravery in battle but also in general the loyal, unflinching, and honest performance of one's duties in enforcing the laws and in challenging and overcoming those who would subvert the order and well-being of the society as a whole.

Another chief virtue is temperance. This virtue, however, is not identified *Temperance* with or confined to one special class. Rather, it signifies the readiness of both the producer and auxiliary classes to *subordinate* their own judgments on public matters to the superior wisdom of the rulers. It signifies a general quality of agreement or acquiescence that each class is ready to display with respect to the rightful possession of policy-making powers by the rulers.

The third chief virtue is wisdom. This excellence is to be sought for in *Wisdom* the policies and laws framed by the rulers. Without it, none of the other virtues would make any sense. In a very crucial way, wisdom is the kingpin, the necessary condition for the very possibility of an ideal society at all. Without wise rulers, the whole thing collapses. This is why Plato devotes as much time as he does to stating what wisdom is and how it is to be achieved.

Suppose now that these three virtues are present in the various appro- *Justice* priate classes of the society, that they are manifested in the several functions they perform. Then, Plato claims, justice—the fourth virtue—will emerge as the result of their copresence, the overall quality of health in the society as a whole. It is found in the total coordination of the specialized functions of the several classes for the benefit and well-being of the society as a whole. Justice is the quality of total harmony and health in the state. This is part of Plato's answer to the challenge of Thrasymachus, Glaucon, and Adeimantus to say what *he* thinks justice really is.

There are a few additional brief points that need to be made about the social organization I have just described.

First, it is necessary to avoid the mistake sometimes made by those who characterize Plato's society as a form of 'communism'. One may indeed genuinely raise the question (as I shall later) whether Plato's scheme isn't, after all, another type of *totalitarianism*, since it advocates the unlimited power of the state to regulate *all* the institutions or activities within the society (e.g., art, education, economic activities, the 'media'). However, this much at least can be said to differentiate Plato's society from what is ordinarily meant by a *communist* type of (totalitarian) society: that Plato's scheme allows for the accumulation of private property by what is, in fact, the largest segment of the society, the producing class. Although Plato would seek to restrain the unbounded drive toward the accumulation of wealth as a vice that tends to produce weakness and degeneracy in the society, he has no objections whatever to the possession of private property by the members of the producer class. It is only those who belong to the soldier and ruler classes who will be supported at public expense. They will not have any private property beyond the barest personal necessities. Such individuals, Plato assumes, unlike the bulk of the people who make up the economic base of the society, will not have any strong drives to accumulate large amounts of private material possessions.

Moreover, in addition to not having any private property, members of these classes will not have private families as do those in the lowest (i.e., producer) class. Instead of private family life, Plato provides for the reproduction of members of the ruling class by a publicly regulated scheme of mating and eugenic control. The offspring of such unions will not know who their actual parents are, and similarly all children born from the supervised mating festivals of a given date will be regarded as the children of all those who mated at that time.[7]

Having given his account of the life of the guardians, a life without private property and without family life, Socrates is asked by Adeimantus whether the society he has been describing would make for the *happiness* of its members, even if it is 'just'. And to this Socrates replies that the goal of achieving a just and well-ordered society

was not to make any one class specially happy, but to secure the greatest possible happiness for the community as a whole. . . . For the moment, we are constructing, as we believe, the state which will be happy as a whole, not trying to secure the well-being of a select few. . . . It is as if we were coloring a statue and someone came up and blamed us for not putting the most beautiful colors on the noblest parts of the figure; the eyes, for instance, should be painted crimson, but we made them black. We should think it a fair answer to say: Really, you must not expect us to paint eyes so handsome as not to look like eyes at all. This applies to all the parts: the question is whether, by giving each its proper color, we make the whole beautiful. So too, in the present case, you must not press us to endow our Guardians with a happiness that will make them anything rather than guardians. We could quite easily clothe our farmers in gorgeous robes, crown them with gold, and invite them to till the soil at their pleasure; or we might set our potters to lie on couches by their fire, passing round the wine and making merry, with their wheel at hand to work at whenever they felt so inclined. We could make all the rest happy in the same sort of way, and so spread this well-being through the whole community. But you must not put that idea in our heads; if we take your advice, the farmer will be no farmer, the potter no longer a potter; none of the elements that make up the community will keep its character. In many cases this does not matter so much: if a cobbler goes to the bad and pretends to be what he is not, he is not a danger to the state; but, as you must surely see, men who make only a vain show of being guardians of the laws and of the commonwealth bring the whole state to utter ruin, just as, on the other hand, its good government and well-being depend entirely on them. . . . So we must consider whether our aim in establishing Guardians is to secure the greatest possible happiness for them, or happiness is something of which we should watch the development in the whole commonwealth. . . . In that *way, as the community grows into a well-ordered whole, the several classes may be allowed such measure of happiness as their nature will compass.*[8,*]

Justice in the Life of the Individual

Plato turns from this analysis of justice on a political level to the just life for the individual. In order to describe this, he begins by giving a summary statement of the basic components in the *psychological* makeup of a human being. For just as our analysis of the functioning and virtues of the state called for a discrimination of the major classes of society, so, now, for each individual person, it is necessary to distinguish the major elements in his psyche. Having discriminated these, Plato will then establish their special virtues. At this point Plato's analysis of the makeup of the psyche closely parallels his tripartite analysis of the class structure of the state. The human psyche, too, Plato claims, has three basic elements: *appetitive, spirited,* and *rational.* These three 'faculties' of the psyche correspond to the producer, auxiliary, and ruling classes in the state. In short, there is a similarity between the stratification of a society into classes and the distinctions to be made among the different components in the psyche of an individual person.

First, consider the *appetitive* side of the human psyche. Appetites or desires, in a broad sense, may be found on *all* levels of the human psyche. However, in a more *restricted* meaning, the term 'appetite' applies especially to the animal drives of hunger, thirst, and sex. The human being shares these latter drives with the animal kingdom. (In the *Timaeus,* Plato locates these appetites, naturally enough, in the digestive and sex organs, the 'lower regions' of the human body.) These appetites drive a person toward finding what it takes to satisfy them: food, drink, and sexual release. For example, a person prowls around for food or drink, whether in a primitive or more sophisticated way (in a forest, in the family refrigerator, or in a fancy restaurant). The sex drive, too, it is needless to remind ourselves, finds satisfaction or release in one form or another. These two drives, for food and sex, are frequently the source of the most intense emotions and are capable of arousing the greatest passions.

The second level of the psyche, in Plato's analysis, is the *spirited* element. Here, it is necessary to differentiate Plato's use of the term 'spirit' from a typical religious use. In the latter, 'spirit' designates an immortal and immaterial entity, as contrasted with the material and mortal 'flesh'.

The tripartite structure of the human psyche: appetites, spirit, and reason

* From *The Republic of Plato* translated by F. M. Cornford and published by Oxford University Press. Reprinted by permission of the publisher.

To get at Plato's meaning, think, instead, of how we use the term 'spirit' when we speak of a 'spirited horse', or what we mean when we say "the team acted with a lot of spirit." Spirit, for Plato, is that side of our nature that is engaged and manifested when we act with ambition, gusto, anger, self-assertion, honor, and determination. (Again, in the *Timaeus*, Plato would locate, physiologically, the spirit in this sense in the heart and lungs.)

There is, finally, the *rational* element: man's unique capacity to deliberate, to make and evaluate judgments, and to achieve knowledge.

Every normal and fully developed person has all three powers or factors in his or her makeup. For Plato the crucial question is: What element in our psyche is dominant or uppermost? If it is the appetites, then all the emotions are bound up with one's energy as expended in obtaining food, drink, sex, and the like, and the money which is the chief means of satisfying them.[9] Although Plato criticizes this type of life, it is not on the ground that he is recommending an ascetic morality. He is not saying we ought to get rid of our appetites. On the contrary, in a normal healthy psyche one could no more get rid of them than a society could continue without its economic base. What he is saying is that the appetites need to be disciplined; a person must exercise self-control in their pursuit and satisfaction. The appetites need to be held in check by reason and not allowed to get out of hand. When this is accomplished, the virtue of *temperance*, as distinctively correlated with the appetitive side of the psyche, makes its appearance.

The spirit occupies a middle position between the appetites and reason. It can go either way. Take the social analogue for the moment. A soldier can be a mercenary in the employ of a rabid dictator, or he can act courageously under the direction of a wise ruler. Similarly, in the individual psyche, the spirited element can be under the control of the undisciplined appetites or, on the other hand, can act as an ally of a person's reason. When the spirited element acts in conjunction with reason, its excellence or virtue is what Plato calls *courage*.

Finally, the rational faculty, when fully exercised and at its optimum mode of functioning, has the special virtue of *wisdom*. A wise person knows what is best for the conduct of one's personal affairs, just as the rulers in an ideal society know what is best for the society as a whole and enact it.

Once again, justice is the supreme resultant virtue found in an individual's life when the other three virtues—of temperance, courage, and wisdom—are present. Justice is a matter of being healthy, of leading a well-ad*justed* life: of managing your sex life, your survival needs, your career, your education, your relations with other individuals, and, in general, your private affairs in such a way that you have a well-ordered life. What comes out of all of this is what Plato calls 'justice'; it is another name for *psycho-*

logical and moral health. Some people are markedly unhealthy, not just physically, but psychologically and morally; their life is in tatters, broken down, a failure. True, nobody is completely healthy any more than any actual society is an ideal society. Nevertheless, Plato's thesis is that what will make for the greatest amount of health (harmony, justice) is dependent on the way a person exercises reason and makes wise choices in the management of one's personal affairs. This is the crux of Plato's message.

The Selection of Wise Rulers

Having seen, now, the parallel that Plato draws between the structure of a just society and the life of a just individual, let us return to a closer look at the one feature in the structure of the ideal society that is absolutely essential—*the need for wise rulers*. Plato expresses this requirement by saying that in an ideal state there must be a union of wisdom and power: *philosophers must be kings and kings philosophers!*

Unless either philosophers become kings in their countries or those who are now called kings and rulers come to be sufficiently inspired with a genuine desire for wisdom; unless, that is to say, political power and philosophy meet together, while the many natures who now go their several ways in the one or the other direction are forcibly debarred from doing so, there can be no rest from troubles, my dear Glaucon, for states, nor yet, as I believe, for all mankind; nor can this commonwealth which we have imagined ever till then see the light of day and grow to its full stature.[10,*]

As we shall see, by 'philosopher' Plato is not content to mean simply one who is wise or loves wisdom. Rather, he is one who has the requisite *knowledge of what is good*. And this requirement Plato interprets in terms of how *he*, Plato, conceives of *knowledge*. First of all, knowledge is to be contrasted with mere belief or opinion. Second, knowledge is that which involves a special mode of access to, awareness, and understanding of the domain of *Forms*. Third, the kind of knowledge that is to be sought for in a truly wise man, and especially in a ruler, is the kind of knowledge that culminates in a knowledge of the *Form of the Good*. If there is going to be a well-run society, its rulers will formulate laws and policies that are rational and justifiable because drafted in the light of a knowledge of ideal Forms. Thus the philosopher-kings will rule not by whim or force; their decisions will not be arbitrary or self-serving. It is because they have an un-

---

* From *The Republic of Plato* translated by F. M. Cornford and published by Oxford University Press (1941). Reprinted by permission of the publisher.

questioned superior wisdom that Plato does not hesitate to entrust to his philosopher-rulers the absolute power to rule over the entire society, without requiring or seeking the 'consent of the governed'. The rulers are men who are wholly unselfish and motivated solely by the needs and interests of the society as a whole. They establish laws that best serve those needs and interests. It is because he makes this crucial assumption that Plato entrusts to his rulers a number of things that Plato's critics have seized upon as examples of what they find wholly questionable proposals: for example, the absolute and unquestioned right to censorship of the arts; the privelege to use various forms of propaganda or 'noble lies' to deceive the populace, in order to make possible the achievement of certain ends that are allegedly for the benefit of the people themselves; the right to practice a form of selective breeding (eugenics) for the ruling class itself that would insure, as far as possible, the production of offspring from highly selected individuals. These offspring will themselves be most likely to rise to positions of power because of their superior intellectual abilities, physical stamina, and capacities for sound character development.

In the *Republic* Plato approaches the nature of political wisdom and knowledge, and how they are to be realized, by several routes. Of these I select for closer examination (1) the celebrated Allegory of the Cave and (2) the program of higher education for all aspiring rulers of the ideal society.

The Allegory of the Cave

Next, said I, here is a parable to illustrate the degrees in which our nature may be enlightened or unenlightened. Imagine the condition of men living in a sort of cavernous chamber underground, with an entrance open to the light and a long passage all down the cave. Here they have been from childhood, chained by the leg and also by the neck, so that they cannot move and can see only what is in front of them, because the chains will not let them turn their heads. At some distance higher up is the light of a fire burning behind them; and between the prisoners and the fire is a track[1] with a parapet built along it, like the screen at a puppet-show, which hides the performers while they show their puppets over the top.

I see, said he.

Now behind this parapet imagine persons carrying along various artificial objects, including figures of men and animals in wood or stone or other materials, which project above the parapet. Naturally, some of these persons will be talking, others silent.[2]

[1] The track crosses the passage into the cave at right angles, and is *above* the parapet built along it.

[2] A modern Plato would compare his Cave to an underground cinema, where the audience watch the play of shadows thrown by the film passing before a light at their backs. The film itself is only an image of 'real' things and events in the world outside

It is a strange picture, he said, and a strange sort of prisoners.

Like ourselves, I replied; for in the first place prisoners so confined would have seen nothing of themselves or of one another, except the shadows thrown by the fire-light on the wall of the Cave facing them, would they?

Not if all their lives they had been prevented from moving their heads.

And they would have seen as little of the objects carried past.

Of course.

Now, if they could talk to one another, would they not suppose that their words referred only to those passing shadows which they saw?

Necessarily.

And suppose their prison had an echo from the wall facing them? When one of the people crossing behind them spoke, they could only suppose that the sound came from the shadow passing before their eyes.

No doubt.

In every way, then, such prisoners would recognize as reality nothing but the shadows of those artificial objects.

Inevitably.

Now consider what would happen if their release from the chains and the healing of their unwisdom should come about in this way. Suppose one of them set free and forced suddenly to stand up, turn his head, and walk with eyes lifted to the light; all these movements would be painful, and he would be too dazzled to make out the objects whose shadows he had been used to see. What do you think he would say, if someone told him that what he had formerly seen was meaningless illusion, but now, being somewhat nearer to reality and turned towards more real objects, he was getting a truer view? Suppose further that he were shown the various objects being carried by and were made to say, in reply to questions, what each of them was. Would he not be perplexed and believe the objects now shown him to be not so real as what he formerly saw?

Yes, not nearly so real.

---

the cinema. For the film Plato has to substitute the clumsier apparatus of a procession of artificial objects carried on their heads by persons who are merely part of the machinery, providing for the movement of the objects and the sounds whose echo the prisoners hear. The parapet prevents these persons' shadows from being cast on the wall of the Cave.

And if he were forced to look at the fire-light itself, would not his eyes ache, so that he would try to escape and turn back to the things which he could see distinctly, convinced that they really were clearer than these other objects now being shown to him?

Yes.

And suppose someone were to drag him away forcibly up the steep and rugged ascent and not let him go until he had hauled him out into the sunlight, would he not suffer pain and vexation at such treatment, and, when he had come out into the light, find his eyes so full of its radiance that he could not see a single one of the things that he was now told were real?

Certainly he would not see them all at once.

He would need, then, to grow accustomed before he could see things in that upper world. At first it would be easiest to make out shadows, and then the images of men and things reflected in water, and later on the things themselves. After that, it would be easier to watch the heavenly bodies and the sky itself by night, looking at the light of the moon and stars rather than the Sun and the Sun's light in the day-time.

Yes, surely.

Last of all, he would be able to look at the Sun and contemplate its nature, not as it appears when reflected in water or any alien medium, but as it is in itself in its own domain.

No doubt.

And now he would begin to draw the conclusion that it is the Sun that produces the seasons and the course of the year and controls everything in the visible world, and moreover is in a way the cause of all that he and his companions used to see.

Clearly he would come at last to that conclusion.

Then if he called to mind his fellow prisoners and what passed for wisdom in his former dwelling-place, he would surely think himself happy in the change and be sorry for them. They may have had a practice of honouring and commending one another, with prizes for the man who had the keenest eye for the passing shadows and the best memory for the order in which they followed or accompanied one another, so that he could make a good guess as to which was going to come next. Would our released prisoner be likely to covet those prizes or to envy the men exalted to honour and power in the Cave? Would he not feel like Homer's Achilles, that he would far sooner "be on earth as a hired servant in the house of a landless man" or endure anything rather than go back to his old beliefs and live in the old way?

Yes, he would prefer any fate to such a life.

Now imagine what would happen if he went down again to take his former seat in the Cave. Coming suddenly out of the sunlight, his eyes would be filled with darkness. He might be required once more to deliver his opinion on those shadows, in competition with the prisoners who had never been released, while his eyesight was still dim and unsteady; and it might take some time to become used to the darkness. They would laugh at him and say that he had gone up only to come back with his sight ruined; it was worth no one's while even to attempt the ascent. If they could lay hands on the man who was trying to set them free and lead them up, they would kill him.

Yes, they would.

Every feature in this parable, my dear Glaucon, is meant to fit our earlier analysis. The prison dwelling corresponds to the region revealed to us through the sense of sight, and the fire-light within it to the power of the Sun. The ascent to see the things in the upper world you may take as standing for the upward journey of the soul into the region of the intelligible; then you will be in possession of what I surmise, since that is what you wish to be told. Heaven knows whether it is true; but this, at any rate, is how it appears to me. In the world of knowledge, the last thing to be perceived and only with great difficulty is the essential Form of Goodness. Once it is perceived, the conclusion must follow that, for all things, this is the cause of whatever is right and good; in the visible world it gives birth to light and to the lord of light, while it is itself sovereign in the intelligible world and the parent of intelligence and truth. Without having had a vision of this Form no one can act with wisdom, either in his own life or in matters of state.

So far as I can understand, I share your belief.

Then you may also agree that it is no wonder if those who have reached this height are reluctant to manage the affairs of men. Their souls long to spend all their time in that upper world—naturally enough, if here once more our parable holds true. Nor again, is it at all strange that one who comes from the contemplation of divine things to the miseries of human life should appear awkward and ridiculous when, with eyes still dazed and not yet accustomed to the darkness, he is compelled, in a law-court or elsewhere, to dispute about the shadows of justice or the images that cast those shadows, and to wrangle over the notions of what is right in the minds of men who have never beheld Justice itself.

It is not at all strange.

No; *a sensible man will remember that the eyes may be confused in two ways —by a change from light to darkness or from darkness to light; and he will recognize that the same thing happens to the soul. When he sees it troubled and unable to discern anything clearly, instead of laughing thoughtlessly, he will ask whether, coming from a brighter existence, its unaccustomed vision is obscured by the darkness, in which case he will think its condition enviable and its life a happy one; or whether, emerging from the depths of ignorance, it is dazzled by excess of light. If so, he will rather feel sorry for it; or, if he were inclined to laugh, that would be less ridiculous than to laugh at the soul which has come down from the light.*

That is a fair statement.

If this is true, then, we must conclude that education is not what it is said to be by some, who profess to put knowledge into a soul which does not possess it, as if they could put sight into blind eyes. On the contrary, our own account signifies that the soul of every man does possess the power of learning the truth and the organ to see it with; and that, just as one might have to turn the whole body round in order that the eye should see light instead of darkness, so the entire soul must be turned away from this changing world, until its eye can bear to contemplate reality and that supreme splendour which we have called the Good. Hence there may well be an art whose aim would be to effect this very thing, the conversion of the soul, in the readiest way; not to put the power of sight into the soul's eye, which already has it, but to ensure that, instead of looking in the wrong direction, it is turned the way it ought to be.

Yes, it may well be so.

It looks, then, as though wisdom were different from those ordinary virtues, as they are called, which are not far removed from bodily qualities, in that they can be produced by habituation and exercise in a soul which has not possessed them from the first. Wisdom, it seems, is certainly the virtue of some diviner faculty, which never loses its power, though its use for good or harm depends on the direction towards which it is turned. You must have noticed in dishonest men with a reputation for sagacity the shrewd glance of a narrow intelligence piercing the objects to which it is directed. There is nothing wrong with their power of vision, but it has been forced into the service of evil, so that the keener its sight, the more harm it works.

Quite true.

And yet if the growth of a nature like this had been pruned from earliest childhood, cleared of those clinging overgrowths which come of gluttony and all luxurious pleasure and, like leaden weights charged with affinity to this mortal world, hang upon the soul, bending its vision downwards; if, freed from these, the soul were turned round towards true reality, then this same power in these very men would see the truth as keenly as the objects it is turned to now.

Yes, very likely.

Is it not also likely, or indeed certain after what has been said, that a state can never be properly governed either by the uneducated who know nothing of truth or by men who are allowed to spend all their days in the pursuit of culture? The ignorant have no single mark before their eyes at which they must aim in all the conduct of their own lives and of affairs of state; and the others will not engage in action if they can help it, dreaming that, while still alive, they have been translated to the Islands of the Blest.

Quite true.

It is for us, then, as founders of a commonwealth, to bring compulsion to bear on the noblest natures. They must be made to climb the ascent to the vision of Goodness, which we called the highest object of knowledge; and, when they have looked upon it long enough, they must not be allowed, as they now are, to remain on the heights, refusing to come down again to the prisoners or to take any part in their labours and rewards, however much or little these may be worth.

Shall we not be doing them an injustice, if we force on them a worse life than they might have?

You have forgotten again, my friend, that the law is not concerned to make any one class specially happy, but to ensure the welfare of the commonwealth as a whole. By persuasion or constraint it will unite the citizens in harmony, making them share whatever benefits each class can contribute to the common good; and its purpose in forming men of that spirit was not that each should be left to go his own way, but that they should be instrumental in binding the community into one.

True, I had forgotten.

You will see, then, Glaucon, that there will be no real injustice in compelling our philosophers to watch over and care for the other citizens. We can fairly tell them that their compeers in other states may quite reasonably refuse to collaborate: there they have sprung up, like a self-sown plant, in despite of their country's institutions; no one has fostered their growth, and they cannot be expected to show gratitude for a care they have never received. "But," we shall say, "it is not so with you. We have brought you into existence for your country's sake as well as for your own, to be like leaders and king-bees in a hive; you have been better and more thoroughly educated than those others and hence you are more capable of playing your part both as men of thought and as men of action. You must go down, then, each in his turn, to live with the rest and let your eyes grow accustomed to the darkness. You will then see a *thousand times better than those who live there always; you will recognize every image for what it is and know what it represents, because you have seen justice, beauty, and goodness in their reality; and so you and we shall find life in our commonwealth no mere dream, as it is in most existing states, where men live fighting one another about shadows and quarrelling for power, as if that were a great prize; whereas in truth government can be at its best and free from dissension only where the destined rulers are least desirous of holding office."*

Quite true.

Then will our pupils refuse to listen and to take their turns at sharing in the work of the community, though they may live together for most of their time in a purer air?

No; it is a fair demand, and they are fair-minded men. No doubt, unlike any ruler of the present day, they will think of holding power as an unavoidable necessity.

Yes, my friend; for the truth is that you can have a well-governed society only if you can discover for your future rulers a better way of life than being in office; then only will power be in the hands of men who are rich, not in gold, but in the wealth that brings happiness, a good and wise life. All goes wrong when, starved for lack of anything good in their own lives, men turn to public affairs hoping to snatch from thence the happiness they hunger for. They set about fighting for power, and this internecine conflict ruins them and their country. The life of true philosophy is the only one that looks down upon offices of state; and access to power must be confined to men who are not in love with it; otherwise rivals will start fighting. So whom else can you compel to undertake the guardianship of the commonwealth, if not those who, besides understanding best the principles of government, enjoy a nobler life than the politician's and look for rewards of a different kind?

There is indeed no other choice.[11,*]

The ascent into the world of intelligible Forms that Plato describes in the Allegory of the Cave is accomplished by those who manage to free themselves from total immersion in and preoccupation with sensory experiences of material things. In the imagery he employs, the escaped prisoners can now see real objects in the light of the Sun. The 'real objects', in Plato's two-world scheme, correspond to the Forms, and the 'Sun' corresponds to the Form of the Good. Plato's allegory is obviously intended to point up the difference between those who live in the sensible and material world of everyday experience and those who have access to the

* From *The Republic of Plato* translated by F. M. Cornford and published by Oxford University Press (1941). Reprinted by permission of the publisher.

superior reality of the domain of Forms. The true philosopher is one who, by escaping into the light, is *enlightened* by the knowledge of the Forms, and especially by the Form of the Good. Were he to return to the prisoners in the Cave and report his discovery, he would be laughed at or attacked. What he would report to have seen (understood) would make no sense to the prisoners. Indeed, once having achieved release from the Cave, those who have this pure intellectual experience would be reluctant to go back into the Cave, and especially to take on the responsibility and chores of ruling society, of governing the 'prisoners'. Plato's point, however, is that such personal predilections to remain in 'ivory towers' and to enjoy the liberation of a purely intellectual life must be denied. The welfare of the society requires that those who have theoretical wisdom and insight shoulder the responsibility of *applying* the wisdom to making practical decisions with respect to the laws and policies of the state. So philosophers must become rulers for the benefit of the society as a whole, and not primarily for their own personal benefit.

Plato undertakes to give a further analysis of the imagery of the Allegory of the Cave by giving its equivalent in terms of the program of *higher education* to which all future rulers are made to submit. As we have seen, one of the main purposes of primary education was character training, the establishment of proper habits and attitudes. The emphasis there was on *training*; a child was made to follow certain exercises, accept certain rules, acquire certain skills. It was not for the child to question *why*, or to be critical; he was simply a recipient, an absorber. On the level of higher education, however, where one is dealing with a highly select group of mature individuals whose rational capacities are of the highest order, the goal is no longer one of training, not even the acquiring of right opinions. It is rather one of acquiring *knowledge*.

The scheme of higher education

For Plato the two disciplines (or rather groups of disciplines) in which such knowledge can be acquired are *Mathematics* and *Dialectic*. In these disciplines, according to Plato, one explores the domain of Forms. They are not to be thought of as being sciences in the sense in which we have come to use the term 'science' in our own day, as applying to physics, chemistry, biology, anthropology, and so on. These are *empirical sciences*. They deal with some area of the world of nature, about which the scientist, by appealing to *observational experience*, undertakes to establish various laws or regularities. The knowledge obtained by the empirical sciences is always open to correction. The results of investigation, however well established, are only probable and never absolutely certain. They deal moreover with entities that are subject to change, development, and statistical variation. For Plato, empirical science in this sense can never give us knowledge, in *his* sense of the term. Knowledge, for Plato, must be certain and unchanging: it must deal with eternal Forms in which there is no admixture of anything sensible or 'imperfect'. For him, only in Mathematics and Dialectic can one explore the domain of Forms without having to appeal to observation of sensory experience. The knowledge obtained is pure, infallible, and perfect.

Mathematics

The program of studies in higher education begins with a thorough study of mathematics. By 'mathematics' one is not to understand, in this connection, the acquiring of certain skills or rules of thumb to be used, for example, in performing calculations with numbers—skills one presumably acquired in primary school. Mathematics, as an advanced study, among other things, will be a *theory* of numbers. Arithmetic as such a theory of numbers establishes certain theorems or truths about numbers by means of demonstration from accepted premises. Needless to say, the kinds of theorems so established need not have primarily a practical interest—let's say of the sort one will want to know in order to be able more efficiently to add up a column of figures in a grocery bill. In addition to the theory of numbers, mathematics includes a study of plane and solid geometry—once again pursued in a rational, deductive way, where the use of visible diagrams is only to serve as an aid to the imagination, not as evidence for the truths established. Finally, Plato thought of astronomy and harmonics as also being branches of mathematics. By 'astronomy' he would mean a study of the mathematical and abstract theory of solids in motion, in which the actual motions of the visible heavenly bodies in the sky are imperfect examples. The *observed* motions of the heavenly bodies serve, at best, only as a stimulus or incentive to the study of 'ideal motion' of perfectly spherical, solid bodies. Similarly, the study of harmonics is a mathematical study of the numerical basis for musical consonances. The Pythagoreans, in Plato's day, had already pointed the way to a study of this sort. What Plato has in mind is again some extension and refinement of such a purely abstract study of musical harmonies in their mathematical relationships. All of these quantitative studies will be conducted by relying on reason as the ultimate method. The future rulers will have to 'pass' all such courses in mathematics! The purpose of embarking on such studies is to have a full, secure, and clear sense of what it is to use the rational method to obtain knowledge.

Dialectic

However, this is only the beginning! Plato does not propose to stop here and put mathematicians in charge of running a society. He expects, after all, his rulers to have knowledge about what is right and wrong, about what is good and desirable, about human *values*. The study of these topics belongs to the domain of moral and political philosophy—to what he calls 'Dialectic'. Dialectic encompasses a study of the absolute standards and models for human behavior: what Plato intends when he refers to Justice, Beauty, Temperance, Courage, Wisdom, and the like. Plato makes, now, a fundamental and crucial claim. It is this: *the study of 'value' Forms by*

Dialectic will have all the rigor and rational necessity that one already finds in the domain of Mathematics. Those who have mastered a study of Dialectic will have the same basic agreement and secure infallible knowledge as the mathematician has about geometric figures and numbers. The climax and highest stage of such a study will be an incommunicable vision of the *Form of the Good.* The knowledge of that Form provides a unity, synoptic integration, and intelligibility to all other Forms, including even the mathematical ones. *Yet Plato nowhere tells us* what the internal structure, if any, of the Form of the Good is, nor does he in any way undertake to analyze or define it. He says the vision of it is ineffable, but those who have it will have an overpowering vision of the source and basis of anything. It will clarify and make sense of everything else. It yields an ultimate enlightenment, in the way the Sun serves as a source of light for everything in the visible world.

The Form of the Good

For those selected to pursue the sequence of studies in higher education, the period of primary education will have lasted until age seventeen or eighteen, followed by an intermediate period of physical and military training. The study of mathematics, as outlined earlier, will then consume a period of ten years, from age twenty to age thirty. Then from age thirty to age thirty-five there will be an intensive study of Dialectic, for all who have successfully passed the preliminary stages. Even such persons, however, are still not ready, in Plato's judgment, to assume the burdens and responsibilities of governing society. For another fifteen years (that is, from age thirty-five to age fifty) those who have hitherto been going to 'the university' and had there acquired a theoretical knowledge of Forms will be expected to go back into the 'Cave'. They will be required to study first-hand the problems and needs of the society over which, eventually, they will be allowed to rule. For these fifteen years they will occupy various minor posts of an administrative or executive sort, civil as well as military. Finally, at age fifty, those men *or* women who survive, who possess the necessary aptitude, theoretical understanding, and practical experience, will be elevated to the position of members of the ruling class. Plato, let it be remembered (contrary to the practices of his day), was a strong advocate of the equality of men and women. "Every occupation is open to both [men and women] so far as their natures are concerned."[12] The crucial point for Plato, the *only* thing that matters, is proven ability.

A Critical Evaluation of Plato's Political Philosophy

Although I have not discussed all the great variety of topics treated in the *Republic,* you will now have a sufficient glimpse of at least some of its leading themes to be in a position to understand why that dialogue has occupied the unique position it has in the history of Western philosophical and political thought. Plato's theories are not trite or colorless. They have aroused (and continue to do so into our own day) the bitterest attacks and the staunchest support and admiration. Plato has a way (as very few philosophers do) of polarizing his readers into friends or enemies. One can hardly be left neutral or indifferent.

Confronted with the kinds of views we have been examining, the recent 'enemies' of Plato have identified him as the fountainhead and arch-theoretician of *totalitarianism.** When all is said and done, it is charged, Plato's conception of an ideal society provides the framework for the practice of dictatorship. In effect, for example, one might ask: Would Plato not have approved of Hitler or twentieth-century communist states— or, at least, do not Plato's theories make it philosophically possible for a Hitler, for example, to come within the scope of Plato's scheme?

To this type of charge, the friends of Plato (and indeed Plato himself, as we see in his own account of tyranny in the *Republic*) would violently disagree on the ground that it is a serious misinterpretation of what he stood for. Plato's defenders would claim that the sort of thing one found in Nazi Germany was the *very opposite* of Plato's account of the ideal society in the *Republic*. Plato himself, when he comes to picture the *decline*, through various stages, of a society from its peak or ideal form, identifies dictatorship or tyranny as the *very worst* kind of government. It is far worse, in Plato's view, than oligarchy (rule by self-serving men of wealth) or democracy (rule by the unenlightened 'mob'). It is a fair guess therefore that Plato—had he been alive in the twentieth century to observe the practices of Nazi Germany, Stalinist Russia, or other well-known examples of totalitarian dictatorships in our own time—would have been among the first to condemn those regimes. Hitler, Goering, Goebbels, Himmler, and company were not, in Plato's eyes—we may safely assume— guided by reason and knowledge as Plato understood these. They were, on the contrary, power-hungry, prejudiced individuals of strong *opinions*. But obviously none of them had even remotely gone through the course of education and rational inquiry that Plato would have required of his philosopher-rulers. They were, instead, persons ruled by passions and virulent hatreds, using such technical and scientific know-how as they could take advantage of to serve their *immoral* and *unjust* ends.

To this 'defense' of Plato one might nevertheless make the following kind of reply: How can we be sure that if we try to enact Plato's kind of program we won't eventually be saddled with rulers who turn out to be

---

* In recent decades, three books, especially—R. H. Crossman's *Plato Today*, Warner Fite's *Platonic Legend*, and Karl Popper's *The Open Society and Its Enemies*—have spearheaded this type of attack.

dictators anyway? Isn't the big stumbling block, or, to switch metaphors, the 'Achilles heel', in his entire moral and political philosophy the assumption that one can have *infallible* knowledge of what is right and good, that there are *absolute* standards of these to which some select few individuals can appeal? How can we guarantee that there is this type of knowledge of human values to be had, and that we can entrust the rule of an entire society to some few individuals who claim to have such knowledge? According to Plato himself, the culmination of the study of Dialectic will be an ineffable vision of the Form of the Good. However, Plato nowhere tells us what the inner structure of this Form is. He claims there is an inner vision of what the Good is. What assurances do we have that when some few chosen individuals supposedly have this 'vision' they will in fact enact laws and policies that will be for the benefit of the entire society? Those who have criticized Plato's political scheme (beginning, by the way, with his own pupil Aristotle) have pointed to the inherent dangers in rule by an elite few. This is especially the case where their privileges rest on the claim that there is some esoteric or secret knowledge of absolute values they possess. One is well advised to be particularly on guard and sceptical about the very existence of such knowledge.

To continue with this critique of Plato: It may be the case that pure mathematics, which does not deal with matters of fact in the empirical world, possesses rigorous and rational proofs of its truths. And we may grant that anyone who can follow a proof in mathematics will come to accept the conclusion once he or she follows the reasoning step by step. But is the situation the same when we undertake to state 'truths' about values—about what is right, good, or desirable in the conduct of individuals or groups of persons, especially in politics? It's not at all clear and beyond question that value-judgments are open to the same kind of rational and conclusive proof as is found in pure mathematics. However, Plato thought so. Indeed, he went even further and thought that the hypotheses of Mathematics found their ultimate justification in the study of Dialectic, that is, in the insights one gets from an awareness of the Form of the Good. This is a view that no modern mathematician, or philosopher of mathematics, would accept.

To reinforce this attack on Plato's basic thesis, let us suppose, as an imaginative exercise, that we were to try to *approximate* Plato's ideal by delegating the rule of a society—let us suppose a future world-state—to the wisest men of the world. Let us suppose we were to call a world congress of philosophers from the United States, Great Britain, France, China, the Soviet Union, West Germany, Egypt, Iran, Israel, India, etc. And suppose everyone were to agree that these individuals were to draft the laws for a world-state! What do you suppose would happen? Would they be likely to show any greater measure of agreement among themselves than already is to be found in or among the various societies from which they were delegated? It would take a rather naive person to answer this in the affirmative. So Plato's dream is in a very genuine way unrealistic, not because it is unrealistic to have ideals, but because Plato has not given us inescapable and irrefutable arguments to show that there is anything to be expected in the form of absolute standards, universal agreement, and infallible knowledge in the domain of ethics and politics.

Plato claimed there is a continuity and similarity between the kinds of inquiries pursued in Mathematics and Dialectic insofar as both deal with Ideal Forms by means of reason. Many of Plato's critics would argue that there is a notable gap or discontinuity between these domains. At the very least, Plato failed to make a convincing case that there is a similarity either of method or of results in mathematics and those studies in which value-judgments play a crucial part.

Nor does this mean, of course, that *therefore* value-judgments must be left to decision by some altogether nonrational method. Rather, one would need to redefine 'reason'. As contrasted with Plato's conception of reason, many philosophers (including the American philosopher John Dewey, whose thought we shall study later) who have examined the use of reason or intelligence in the empirical sciences would propose the extension of the use of the method of experimental intelligence to human affairs. Such philosophers have a quite different conception from Plato's of what human reason is. For them, reason or intelligence, when it deals with states of affairs in the actual world, is a very fallible method whose results cannot be decked out in the form of conclusive proofs. At best, in the domain of practical human affairs, they would say all one can get are carefully thought-out plans and policies of action that have to be *tested in experience*, not judged as to their merit by consulting some supposedly eternal and fixed scheme of values. This fresh analysis of intelligence, as contrasted with Plato's, stresses the *pragmatic* role of intelligence. It does not look to pure mathematics as a model for value inquiries as Plato did; it looks instead for certain important clues to the method of the empirical sciences as a preferable model. Plato expected reason to be demonstrative, certain, and infallible, something to be exercised by an elite, whereas a pragmatist approach would stress the fragility, tentativeness, fallibility, and openness of human intelligence. Whether in empirical science, where various *hypotheses* are submitted to the test of experience, or in the domain of practical affairs, where various *plans of action* have to be evaluated by seeing how well they work out in practice, the method of reason is different from what it is in pure mathematics.

In political matters, therefore, the application of the method of experimental intelligence appeals to the considered judgment of the people affected by a particular law or policy; it is *they* who are called upon to evaluate its effectiveness, not some group of 'experts'. A democratic political philosophy would say "He who wears the shoe knows whether it pinches." However, Plato had no regard for the input of the public at large for their evaluation or consent. It should be remembered that the 'consent' of the auxiliary and producer classes consisted in their acquiescence that the philosopher-kings should rule; they were not invited to give their consent, that is, to freely and critically *evaluate* the laws to which they were required to submit. Further, unlike Plato's rulers, who look to an eternal and fixed model that does not require any *change* in their legislation, those who take empirical science as their model have a different conception of what adequacy consists in. Just as in empirical science one doesn't expect some accepted theory to necessarily remain fixed and final (it will be held on to only for as long as it 'works'), so, too, in practical affairs, where human societies are even more subject to change, there is nothing sacrosanct or eternally valid about some particular set of goals, ideals, standards, laws, or policies of action.

To sum up, then, the critics of Plato's authoritarian and totalitarian political philosophy see it as something to be challenged by those who claim to have a better insight into the nature of human reason and the superiority of a democratic political system. In a democracy, whatever its imperfections, there is an effort made to get the consent of the governed, to employ in some way the pooled judgment of all members of the society. By having periodic elections, by having delegated representatives who are required to be responsive to the demands of the electorate, one minimizes the chance for the abuse of power by a minority who would otherwise have no check over them. According to these critics, it is better in the long run to trust the pooled judgment of the many than the so-called expert judgment of the few, especially if the latter are not held accountable by anybody else but by themselves! So the upshot of the criticism made by 'enemies' of Plato's philosophy is that neither Plato nor any other absolutist has made a convincing case for his view either in theory or in practice. One remains justifiably sceptical of any such claim to absolute knowledge of absolute standards. And whatever shortcomings and abuses, in turn, a nonauthoritarian regime may itself exhibit, in the long run the people are better served by keeping control over their destinies and day-to-day modes of living in their own hands.

III

Theistic Views
of God
and the World

chapter 5

The Religious

Heritage

of the West

Plato is a major example of the flowering of philosophic genius in ancient Greece. The Platonic world view was at once a distinctive creation of Plato's own mind and a distilled restatement of many of the characteristic emphases and features of Greek 'pagan' culture. The philosophy we are about to examine, that of theism, is quite different in many ways from that of Plato, although there are certain important points of overlap.

The philosophy of theism reached one of its high points of expression in the Middle Ages. The works of the great theologians and philosophers of that period (e.g., Thomas Aquinas and Maimonides) gave doctrinal expression to a culture dominated and permeated by religion in its Judaeo-Christian form. It was a period in which some of the great cathedrals were built, and in which Dante's *Divine Comedy* was written. It is true, of course, that some aspects of the philosophy of theism had their antecedents among the Greeks. Plato's philosophy in its own way lent support to the view that there was a Supreme Intelligence at work in the design of the Universe. However, 'theism', as I shall use this term in what follows, is to be understood in connection with the dominant thought of the Judaeo-Christian outlook on the world and man. Seen against this background and that use of the term, Plato was a quasi-theist. There is an important reason for making this distinction. First of all, in developing his world view Plato did not accept the doctrine of a God who created the world *ex nihilo* (out of nothing). Second, Plato employed both reason and poetic myth or allegory as the principal methods by which he sought to support his

Contrast between Judaeo-Christian theism and Platonism; Greek religion

95

philosophy. Neither for Plato nor for the Greeks in general was there an explicit appeal to the revealed word of God as the ultimate sanction for one's outlook on the world and man. The Greeks did not have 'sacred books' in the sense in which we use that expression in connection with the Old and New Testaments or the Koran. These texts are thought by many to contain the word of God as revealed to certain chosen individuals. Although the various religious cults of the Greeks, as is the case generally, adopted certain rites and ceremonies, the beliefs used to explain and justify these practices were left to the poets and to various myths as these were handed down from generation to generation. Even though Hesiod and Homer were prime literary sources for these stories and myths, their works were not looked upon as being sacred texts containing the revealed word of God. Finally, the religion of the Greeks was typically *polytheistic*, involving the recognition or worship of many gods, whereas Judaism, Christianity, and Islam are *monotheistic* religions.

Vitality of theistic philosophy

The 'philosophy of theism', then, in the sense I shall use this expression, stands for an important and distinctive development in the history of Western thought as illustrated in Judaism, Christianity, and Islam. The religious traditions that nurtured theism have provided a world view to which countless numbers of people have subscribed over a period of many centuries, down to our own day. The philosophic foundations of the theistic world view as developed in the West were laid long before the thirteenth century. For the Christian tradition this was accomplished through the work of the Church Fathers, especially St. Augustine (354–430). Earlier, Philo Judaeus (*fl.* 20 B.C.–A.D. 40) had already made important contributions to the development of Jewish philosophy. From those beginnings, the working out, in various directions, of a theistic philosophy has continued down to the present time, with many important 'revolutions' and fresh points of departure beyond the syntheses achieved during the Middle Ages. The vast majority of individuals who read this book have probably been reared in households where, with varying degrees of emphasis, seriousness, and enforcement, the tenets of theism and its associated ethic have been propounded. Part of the growing up process, of the intellectual development of most individuals, involves coming to terms with the question of whether or not to accept this philosophy.

Major components of theism: belief in God; moral code; conception of human destiny

A crucial part of theistic metaphysics is its conception of the nature of God, and of God's relation to the world and to man. The working out of a set of doctrines about God belongs to *theology*, the special name given to a central part of theistic metaphysics. Theism also involves a philosophy of life, a conception of how man fits into the entire scheme of things. As with any philosophy of life, it takes the form of providing people with principles and guidelines according to which they should regulate their conduct. The Ten Commandments that God gave to Moses on Mount Sinai, and Jesus' Sermon on the Mount are major examples and primary sources for religious ethics. Different parts of the theistic tradition undertake their elaboration. In them one finds typical stress placed upon such concepts as love, mercy, justice, charity, obedience, hope, faith, humility, and forgiveness—all, however, within the common and broad framework of a view of reality that looks to God as their ultimate source and sanction.

In addition to providing an ethical code to guide the individual in the conduct of his or her own life, a theistic view will normally have a view of man taken collectively, of human destiny at large, and of the unfolding of human history as a whole. A classic example of this sort of thing is to be found in St. Augustine's *City of God*. An excellent summary of its basic theme is given in the following selection from George Santayana's *Reason in Religion*:

There was in the beginning, so runs the Christian story, a great celestial King, wise and good, surrounded by a court of winged musicians and messengers. He had existed from all eternity, but had always intended, when the right moment should come, to create temporal beings, imperfect copies of himself in various degrees. These, of which man was the chief, began their career in the year 4004 B.C., and they would live on an indefinite time, possibly, that chronological symmetry might not be violated, until A.D. 4004. The opening and close of this drama were marked by two magnificent tableaux. In the first, in obedience to the word of God, sun, moon, and stars, and earth with all her plants and animals, assumed their appropriate places, and nature sprang into being with all her laws. The first man was made out of clay, by a special act of God, and the first woman was fashioned from one of his ribs, extracted while he lay in a deep sleep. They were placed in an orchard where they often could see God, its owner, walking in the cool of the evening. He suffered them to range at will and eat of all the fruits he had planted save that of one tree only. But they, incited by a devil, transgressed this single prohibition, and were banished from that paradise with a curse upon their head, the man to live by the sweat of his brow and the woman to bear children in labour. These children possessed from the moment of conception the inordinate natures which their parents had acquired. They were born to sin and to find disorder and death everywhere within and without them.

At the same time God, lest the work of his hands should wholly perish, promised to redeem in his good season some of Adam's children and restore them to a natural life. This redemption was to come ultimately through a descendant of Eve, whose foot should bruise the head of the serpent. But it was to be prefigured by many partial and special redemptions. Thus, Noah was to be saved from the deluge, Lot from Sodom, Isaac from the sacrifice, Moses from Egypt, the captive Jews from Babylon, and all faithful souls from heathen forgetfulness and idolatry. For a certain tribe had been set apart from the beginning to keep alive the memory of God's judgments and promises, while the rest of mankind, abandoned to its natural depravity, sank deeper and deeper into crimes and vanities. The deluge that came to punish these evils did not avail to cure them. "The world was renewed and the earth rose again above the bosom of the waters, but in this renovation there remained eternally some trace of divine vengeance. Until the deluge all nature had been exceedingly hardy and vigorous, but by that vast flood of water which God had spread out over the earth, and by its long abiding there, all saps were diluted; the air, charged with too dense and heavy a moisture, bred ranker principles of corruption. The early constitution of the universe was weakened, and human life, from stretching as it had formerly done to near a thousand years, grew gradually briefer. Herbs and roots lost their primitive potency and stronger food had to be furnished to man by the flesh of other animals. . . . Death gained upon life and men felt themselves overtaken by a speedier chastisement. As day by day they sank deeper in their wickedness, it was but right they should daily, as it were, stick faster in their woe. The very change in nourishment made manifest their decline and degradation, since as they became feebler they became also more voracious and blood-thirsty."

Henceforth there were two spirits, two parties, or, as Saint Augustine called them, two cities in the world. The City of Satan, whatever its artifices in art, war, or philosophy, was essentially corrupt and impious. Its joy was but a comic mask and its beauty the whitening of a sepulchre. It stood condemned before God and before man's better conscience by its vanity, cruelty, and secret misery, by its ignorance of all that it truly behoved a man to know who was destined to immortality. Lost, as it seemed, within this Babylon, or visible only in its obscure and forgotten purlieus, lived on at the same time the City of God, the society of all the souls God predestined to salvation; a city which, however humble and inconspicuous it might seem on earth, counted its myriad transfigured citizens in heaven, and had its destinies, like its foundations, in eternity. To this City of God belonged, in the first place, the patriarchs and the prophets who, throughout their plaintive and ardent lives, were faithful to what echoes still remained of a primeval revelation, and waited patiently for the greater revelation to come. To the same city belonged the magi who followed a star till it halted over the stable in Bethlehem; Simeon, who divined the present salvation of Israel; John the Baptist, who bore witness to the same and made straight its path; and Peter, to whom not flesh and blood, but the spirit of the Father in heaven, revealed the Lord's divinity. For salvation had indeed come with the fulness of time, not, as the carnal Jews had imagined it, in the form of an earthly restoration, but through the incarnation of the Son of God in the Virgin Mary, his death upon a cross, his descent into hell, and his resurrection at the third day according to the Scriptures. To the same city belonged finally all those who, believing in the reality and efficacy of Christ's mission, relied on his merits and followed his commandment of unearthly love.

All history was henceforth essentially nothing but the conflict between these two cities; two moralities, one natural, the other supernatural; two philosophies, one rational, the other revealed; two beauties, one corporeal, the other spiritual; two glories, one temporal, the other eternal; two institutions, one the world, the other the Church. These, whatever their momentary alliances or compromises, were radically opposed and fundamentally alien to one another. Their conflict was to fill the ages until, when wheat and tares had long flourished together and exhausted between them the earth for whose substance they struggled, the harvest should come; the terrible day of reckoning when those who had believed the things of religion to be imaginary would behold with dismay the Lord visibly coming down through the clouds of heaven, the angels blowing their alarming trumpets, all generations of the dead rising from their graves, and judgment without appeal passed on every man, to the edification of the universal company and his own unspeakable joy or confusion. Whereupon the blessed would enter eternal bliss with God their master and the wicked everlasting torments with the devil whom they served.

The drama of history was thus to close upon a second tableau: long-robed and beatified cohorts passing above, amid various psalmodies, into an infinite luminous space, while below the damned, howling, writhing, and half transformed into loathsome beasts, should be engulfed in a fiery furnace. The two cities, always opposite in essence, should thus be finally divided in existence, each bearing its natural fruits and manifesting its true nature.[1]

Theism as a well-rounded philosophy gives human beings a set of answers to their most basic questions. It is easy to understand why it has been so pervasively adopted and influential. People know there is a God in heaven, they know why the world is the way it is, and they know in a general way where they 'belong'. To have a philosophy of this sort is what most people crave and find extremely valuable. Therefore, psychologically as well as intellectually and culturally, to have this (or any other) world view threatened or overturned marks a very serious crisis. Such a crisis has been an underlying feature of modern culture ever since the rise of science, beginning roughly with the sixteenth century. The 'warfare of science and theology' in the nineteenth century, with the emergence of Darwin's theory of evolution and its implicit challenge to the doctrine of a special act of divine creation of man, is but one example of a continuing unsettlement of the inherited traditional theistic world outlook. Our task, in what follows, is to examine the underlying commitments and claims of a theistic philosophy, to see what can be said in its support as well as to take note of certain challenges that have been brought against it.

A necessary and crucial part of the theistic world view is the belief in God. Although for some people the essence of their commitment to 'religion' is the philosophy of life or ethics it contains—with its stress on love, justice, and the like—it needs to be pointed out that if one wishes to

Central role of belief in God

detach such an ethical code as a sufficient and independent element (and perhaps, even, *attach* it to some other metaphysics, for example, a naturalistic world view) then one is no longer subscribing to a *theistic* philosophy. For a theistic philosophy the belief in God is indispensable. It provides the logical and metaphysical background, the support and ultimate sanction for the ethics associated with it. Accordingly, in what follows I shall concentrate virtually all my attention on this cornerstone of theism: its commitment to a belief in God. For if that belief is removed or brought into question, the whole integrated system of theistic philosophy is itself jeopardized and brought into question.

Another preliminary point worth making is that our interest in what follows is upon the *common core* of Judaism, Christianity, and Islam in their commitment to a belief in God. It is this commitment that unites and serves as a common basis for the major religious philosophies of the West. There are, needless to say, very many important points of doctrinal difference that separate any one major religious tradition from the others, just as there are major and important differences in the conception of God that characterize sects or traditions within each of these major religions. Our concern, however, will not be one of making a comparative study of these differences or in examining the highly technical differences that distinguish special theological doctrines from one another. Rather, we will concentrate our attention on the belief in God that runs as a common thread among the several major religious traditions. Our principal interest will be to examine the underlying belief in God: what can be said about this belief both in its favor and by way of critical comment.

The Meaning of the Term 'God'

A necessary first step in this analysis is to make clear what is to be understood by the term 'God'. There are a number of components in its standard meaning:

Uniqueness

(1) First the *oneness and uniqueness* of God. This is expressed in the familiar lines of the Jewish liturgy:

Hear O Israel: the Lord our God is One Lord; and you shall love the Lord your God with all your heart, and with all your soul, and with all your might.

'Theism', in the sense we are using this term, is to be understood as synonymous with *monotheism*—a belief in one, unique God, as contrasted with a belief in many gods, in various types of *polytheistic* religions. Monotheism is also to be distinguished from *henotheism*. A henotheistic view involves a belief in, an exclusive worship of, one tribal or national deity but does not deny that there are other gods that are legitimately worshipped by other groups. The monotheism we are concerned with doesn't acknowledge the genuine existence of any other deities than the One God, the God who is Father of all mankind, Creator of the world in which *all* men "live, move, and have their being." God is not merely supreme, one among many gods; God is alone and unique. There is only one God.

(2) God's being is distinct from that of the world. This is what is traditionally meant by saying that God *transcends* the world, or that God is a *transcendent* reality or being. Since theism subscribes to this thesis of the transcendence of God, of God's existence apart from the world, it is to be carefully distinguished from the philosophy of *pantheism*. By a pantheistic philosophy is meant one that affirms the identity of God and the world: that God is to be found in the world, that God pervades and is co-extensive with the world (or Nature) and does not have any being apart from the world. A pantheistic philosophy is thus a monistic philosophy since it upholds the view that there is only one ultimate reality, whereas theism is a *dualistic* philosophy, inasmuch as it affirms the distinctness and separation of God's existence from that of the world (Nature, the Universe).

Transcendence

(3) To say that God is transcendent is to point to the difference and separation between God and the world. However, the relation between God and the world according to theism consists in the fact that the very existence of the world *depends* on God. God is the source and ground for the existence of the world. Without God, the world would not exist at all, now or ever. If, in fact, there was an actual moment in the past when the world *began* to exist, an actual *origin* of the world (as some but not all theists believe), then without God the world would not have been brought into existence. Another way of expressing this general type of claim is to say that God is the *Creator* of the world. God brought the world into existence through his unique and supreme power of creation. Although the world and all that it contains are thus *dependent* on God for their existence, God's own being is *independent* of the world. God does not depend either on the world or on any other being (if any) for his own existence.

Creator of the world

In the theistic tradition the concept of creation is generally taken to be creation *ex nihilo*, creation out of nothing. As previously remarked, in this respect the theistic doctrine of divine creation needs to be distinguished from the Platonic myth of a Divine Craftsman who imposes a certain rational order on *preexistent* material. For theism, God not only *orders* the world in a certain selected way but also *creates* the very material on which such order is imposed. Without God's creation there would be nothing in existence aside from God, not even some preexistent material. God in creating the world creates all the creatures that it contains—the heavenly bodies, the plants and the animals, man himself. Without God's creation of the world there would be neither space nor time, nor the manifold entities we find in the world. So everything that exists, other than God, depends on God for its existence; all entities other than God are God's *creatures*.

Infinite

(4) God's power of creation is an example of God's *infinite* power. We must be careful, however, to understand the sense in which the term 'infinity' is used to describe God. It does not mean the sort of thing we have in mind when we say that a number series (for example, the positive integers) is infinite, that is, 'without end', since there is no last member to that series. Nor is God's infinity to be understood in general in any *quantitative* way. Thus if we were to conceive of space or time to be infinite, this again would be a type of infinity that is quantitative and inapplicable to God. A negative way of understanding what is meant by saying that God is infinite is to say that God is *not* finite. Although we describe God's attributes by using terminology borrowed from the way we describe traits of human beings—for example, in terms of power, goodness, and wisdom—these properties as possessed by God are wholly different from the way in which they apply to human beings. Human beings are finite and limited in their possession of these qualities. God's wisdom, power, and goodness are not finite; they are 'infinite'.

Omnipotence

To begin with, God is *omnipotent*, infinitely powerful. God's power is so great that it is the ground for the very existence of the world. In creating the world, God imposed an order and structure upon it. He 'ordained' the laws that Nature obeys—for example, the heavenly bodies 'in their courses'. According to some, since God imposed a certain order on the world, he can also suspend the operation of its laws and thereby perform *miracles*. For example, in the Old Testament, God made the Sun to stand still for Joshua. By contrast with God's omnipotence, the power of any creature *in* the world is limited or finite. Some creatures are more powerful than others, but nothing other than God is supremely or infinitely powerful.

Omniscience

God's infinity is also expressed by saying that God is infinitely wise and all-knowing. God is *omniscient*, once again in a way that makes even the wisest or most knowledgeable of men fall infinitely short of God's wisdom and knowledge.*

---

* I am reminded here of a wonderful and privileged experience I had some years ago, when I had a long private conversation at the Institute for Advanced Studies at Princeton with Albert Einstein, three weeks before his death. I had ventured to make some critical remarks about his philosophy of science in one of my books (*Space, Time, and Creation*), and he was kind enough to give me his reactions to what I had written. Among other things, one important impression I came away with from that meeting

Another dimension of God's infinity is conveyed by saying that God is *infinitely good or benevolent*. God's goodness is manifested in various ways. (Here, once more, I bring together for the sake of a simplified summary, a number of different strands in the historical development of this concept.) God is the ultimate source of all value, design, and order in the world. God is the author of rules for man's moral guidance. God establishes, in an absolute way, the difference between right and wrong. God rewards those who follow in his path and punishes those who are evil. Sometimes a person may not know why he or she suffers evil. This is the theme of the Book of Job. Job, a righteous man, is made to suffer in order to test his righteousness. And to Job's exclamations of sorrow, pain, and bewilderment, the Voice out of the Whirlwind replies

Who is this that darkeneth counsel
By words without knowledge?
Gird up now thy loins like a man;
For I will demand of thee, and declare unto me.
Where wast thou when I laid the foundations
  of the earth?

Man's finite intellect cannot probe and understand God's ways. However, the faithful will never doubt God's ultimate goodness and justice, even if God's ways are beyond man's understanding. The problem of evil is one of the most serious and difficult challenges that has been raised against the whole theistic outlook. If God is both infinitely good and infinitely powerful, how can we explain the amount of evil in the world, the suffering of innocent and righteous people? (Think of the Holocaust!) Nevertheless, the unswerving conviction of the theist is that God is infinitely good and just. A *theodicy* is the attempt made within the framework of theism to explain or accommodate oneself to the existence of evil in the world; such explanations take many forms, but we shall not stop to examine them here.*

---

was a sense of his genuine modesty and humility. Over and over again, he referred to his keen awareness of his limitations. He kept saying "I don't know, . . ." Nor, of course, was this said by way of mock modesty. And this, for me, was another example of what is (or should be!) a familiar fact of human experience: that the greater and more profound the mind, the more likely is that person to have a genuine sense of his own limitations.

* Leibniz, the great German philosopher of the seventeenth century, wrote a book, entitled *Theodicy*, in which he set out to prove that God created the best of all possible worlds. It was this attempt to justify the ways of God to man, to sanction a philosophical optimism, and to serve as an apologetic for the evils in the world as somehow necessary to the achievement of God's ultimately beneficent purposes that (Continued)

God's goodness is further conveyed by an emphasis on God's *love*. Divine love (*agape*, in the Christian sense) needs of course to be differentiated from *eros* (the kind of discriminating, desiring, and preferential love that men have, which depends on certain 'lovable' traits found in someone else). God's love is infinite, unconditional, universal, and non-preferential, a love for *all* his children. The ethic of Jesus is the highest and most sublime expression of this conception of divine love; a model that all men, in their own limited fashion, are called upon to emulate in their own behavior.

Immateriality

(5) Whereas the world is material and exists in space and time, God is *immaterial*. The various entities in the world undergo change, have various quantitative features including spatial and/or temporal extension. God, however, is not to be described in any of these ways. Since God does not belong to the world as a *part* of it, nor is God in any way identical with the material Universe, one cannot ascribe material, spatial, or temporal features to God. It is for this reason that Jews, from earliest times, had nothing but contempt for idol worshippers. An idol is made of stone, wood, or some other material. To worship an idol is to fail to acknowledge that God is 'wholly other' or different from any material object. That is why, incidentally, theists were appalled by a philosophy such as Spinoza's, since Spinoza in identifying God and Nature—in saying that they are one and the same reality—was denying the immateriality of God: he was making God an extended being, and this goes wholly against the claim of any theistic philosophy.

Instead of describing God as immaterial, theist philosophy frequently uses the terms 'Spirit' and 'Person'. God for the theist is a *personal* God. In Martin Buber's language, God is a 'Thou' not an 'It'. An 'It' is a thing, an object, not a Person. Only a 'Thou' can be the genuine focus of one's worship and love.

Man himself is a combination or mixture of flesh and spirit, of body and soul. It is only insofar as man has a spirit or soul that he represents a finite reflection of God's Infinite Spirit. Connected with this view is the belief, characteristic of theistic philosophy, in the immortality of the soul. Immortality is interpreted to consist in an afterlife for man in which his soul or spirit will have a continued independent existence of its own, separated from the body in which it was lodged or to which it was joined in its earthly career.

Voltaire ridiculed in his famous work *Candide*. There was a terrible earthquake in Lisbon on All Saints Day in 1755 in which thousands of people lost their lives. If somehow one seeks to explain this in terms of God's wrath at sinners, why were so many innocent people killed? Why indeed were churches along with the worshippers inside them destroyed in the catastrophe?

(6) Since God is immaterial and doesn't exist in space or time, God has a being that can be said to be *eternal*. However, God's eternity does not consist in the fact that God exists or endures forever, throughout an infinite time. For God does not exist in time at all, not even therefore in, or throughout, an infinite time. God has no temporal extent. God is beyond time. It is important here to make a distinction between time and eternity. Eternity does not mean everlastingness, something that never had a beginning and will never have an end. These are terms that are not properly used at all in connection with God. St. Augustine, in his *Confessions*, remarks that there are some people, who when they talk about time and the creation of the world, in the sense that it had a beginning in time, ask: "And what was God doing *before* he created the world?" The very language in which this question is expressed presupposes that *there was a time before* the world was created, and that presumably God himself existed (even though the world did not) prior to the world's beginning. To this sort of question St. Augustine replies that it is a complete mistake to suppose that there was a time *before* the world existed, since in creating the world God created time itself. And, somewhat facetiously, he says that if one persists nevertheless in asking what God was doing before the world was created, one answer that might be given is to say that he was preparing Hell for people who ask such stupid questions!

Does God Exist?

Now that we have some general sense of how the term 'God' is employed in theistic philosophy, we must turn next to consider a crucial question with which theistic philosophy has been itself much concerned. I refer to *the* single most debated and discussed question on which all critics of theist philosophy have centered their attention: the question of the *existence* of God. For, after all, what I have been discussing thus far is the matter of how the term 'God' is to be understood, the meaning to be given to this expression. Even an atheist or sceptic might have followed the account thus far without protest, if he or she believed that some reasonable degree of clarity had been achieved in setting out the *meaning* of this term and in the listing of the various descriptive properties that might be used to replace the name 'God'. In short, the *name* 'God' can be understood as a shorthand way of summing up a number of properties that are conjointly asserted to constitute the divine nature: uniqueness; transcendence; independence; power of creation; infinite goodness, power, wisdom; immateriality; Personhood; eternity.

Still, the sceptic (or anyone else, for that matter!) might ask: "*And what reason is there to believe that the name designates anything real, that there exists something to which the name can be applied?*" Clearly there is a presupposition, in the asking of this question, that there is a distinction to be made between the meaning of a term (in this case 'God') and the question of whether there exists anything to which the term might be applied. As we shall see (in the next chapter in considering the views of St. Anselm and Descartes) there is at least one type of reply to the foregoing question that challenges and *denies* this distinction as it has to do with God. St. Anselm (and others) would say that it is part of the very *meaning* of the concept of God that it requires that we think of God as *existing*. Therefore, it is argued, if one really understands what the term 'God' means, there would be no need to raise the *further* question about whether God exists, about whether the term 'God' applies to anything real. Not all philosophers, however, not even all theologians, agree with St. Anselm on this matter. In order to set the stage as neutrally as possible for the time being, therefore, I have drawn the distinction between the analysis of the *meaning* of the term 'God' and the question of establishing whether or not *there exists* an entity to which the term applies.

The issue of justifying a belief in God's existence is central because it is one on which hinges the very acceptability of a theist philosophy as a whole. If a belief in the existence of God cannot be sustained by some agreed-to method, whatever else the theist philosophy upholds can find no basis. It is for this reason that we will devote the rest of the discussion of theism to a consideration of some of the various ways in which one may undertake to deal with this question.

It is important to recognize at the outset that the problem of how to establish the soundness of a belief in God's existence is of a very special character. The problem is different from what we ordinarily take to be one of determining whether or not something exists. For God, by definition, transcends the world. He is immaterial, and cannot therefore in any literal way be observed or sensed. God cannot be seen, touched, heard, or observed, directly or indirectly. God is not an idol made of wood or stone. God cannot be found by looking through a microscope or a telescope. "Why, then," the sceptic asks, "should we believe in the existence of God?"

Consider how one goes about settling a question that arises about the existence of something when this *can be* checked by observational experience. Suppose there were a group of people who lived in a very remote part of the world and who were completely out of touch with recent developments in technology—of a sort we are familiar with and take for granted. Suppose you came in contact with these people, and in the course of living with them, learning their language, and so on, at some point described various things in your own culture. Let us assume you described to them a very remarkable kind of instrument that allowed a person to speak with another person at a very great distance, and to see that other person as you talked with him. (The telephone company calls such an instrument a 'Picturephone', and a similar device is of course television.) What would you do if one of the natives, in listening to your *description* of this remarkable instrument, expressed scepticism and said "I don't believe you. There can't be any such a thing!"? He *understood* what you were saying, all right; the *description* you gave of what you *called* a 'Picturephone' or 'Television' was clear enough, but he questioned that anything exists in fact that answers to that description. What could you do to convince such a sceptic? If it were worth your while and you wanted to go to the necessary expense, you could either install such a device in his own region or take him back to where it is already installed in another part of the world. You would *confront* him with this instrument. "Here, see for yourself!" Let's suppose he knows that his son is a thousand miles away. Yet by using this contraption he himself is able to talk with and see the image of his son as he talks with him. He would then be convinced that such an instrument does exist, because he himself had seen it in operation. Here then is a type of situation in which there is no problem of how to go about settling a sceptic's doubts *about a thing that is open to observation and whose existence can be confirmed by appealing to the senses.*

Clearly, however, this procedure of settling doubts about the existence of an observable object that is part of the world is not available in the case of questions about the existence of God. For God is not part of the world. Nor is God's nature such that he *can* be observed. God is unobservable, not because it is extremely *difficult* to observe God, but because it is a misunderstanding of what the term 'God' *means* to even suppose that if there exists in reality anything that corresponds to the name 'God', it is open at all, or 'in principle', to observation. How then is it possible to establish the soundness or acceptability of a belief in the *existence* of God?

Methods for Establishing Belief in God's Existence

The theist recognizes the importance of this question. For if we cannot use the wholly inappropriate method of observational experience, what method should we employ to establish and support the belief in God's existence? The theist examines this question of method not only to answer the sceptic but also as an integral element in defending and expounding his own philosophy. A good deal of theology and of the philosophical analysis of theological claims is devoted to this *methodological* question.

There are, broadly speaking, three types of methods on which theology relies in support of a belief in the existence of God. The first is the method of *rational argument*, the second the method of *faith*, the third the method of *religious experience*. In the method of rational argument, one starts with certain premisses whose meaning is understood and whose truth is taken as established. From these premisses one logically infers or deduces certain conclusions. However long and involved the chain of reasoning, however large the number of steps in the argument and the number of intermediate conclusions, the ultimate conclusion of the argument will be the statement "God exists." In the history of theology there have been many such arguments offered. We ourselves will examine, later, two celebrated examples of such rational arguments or proofs for the existence of God: they are known as the 'ontological argument' and the 'cosmological argument'. (The meaning of these expressions will be explained in the next two chapters.) It is characteristic, then, of the method of rational argument that instead of asking someone to accept the statement "God exists" directly, and without support or evidence of one sort or another, one is asked, instead, to begin by acknowledging certain matters as already established as true. It will then be shown that from these accepted premisses, by rigorous and sound reasoning, the statement "God exists" follows as a logical consequence. For those who fall back on this method, the premisses are taken as clearly understood and true, the reasoning from these premisses is taken to be valid or logically sound, and finally, therefore, the ultimate conclusion—the statement "God exists"—is said to be meaningful, true, and validly supported by rational argument. Those who have disputed one or another of such arguments for the existence of God will typically raise questions about, and challenge the acceptability of one or another of the various components in such arguments. They might fasten on the question of the alleged meaningfulness or truth of the premisses, the validity of the reasoning, or the meaningfulness or truth of the conclusion. We shall consider some typical examples of such criticisms later, when we come to discuss the ontological and cosmological arguments.

Another method for upholding the belief in the existence of God is the appeal to the method of *faith*. Here the term 'faith' may be used in a variety of senses. The basic and underlying claim of those who fall back on this method is that it is no use at all to try to *prove* the existence of God by rational methods: only a nonrational method such as faith is suitable and legitimate. Those who appeal to the method of faith would say that in dealing with the question of the existence of God we are not dealing with anything that can be established by reason—by a syllogism, mathematical demonstration, or any other mode of logical inference. And so a religious believer might say "I don't have to go through this process of argumentation with you. You either have such a faith in God or you don't. You're either within the 'circle of faith' or not, and it is no use to try to convince you by reason that there is a God. Speaking for myself, faith alone gives me all the assurance I need that God exists."

Sometimes a theologian or philosopher may try to establish *by rational argument* the merit of appealing to the *method of faith* as the only available and sound *method* for establishing the existence of God. Hence it is necessary to distinguish the use of the method of rational argument to establish the *statement* "God exists" from the use of *rational arguments* to establish the soundness of the *method of faith* as the only effective way of establishing the truth of the statement "God exists." Let me expand this point a bit. We need to distinguish each of the following:

(1) *Using a rational method, i.e., an argument, to establish as the conclusion of this argument the statement "God exists."*

(2) *Using the method of faith to uphold the truth of the statement "God exists." (The method of faith, so used, does not itself use any arguments.)*

(3) *Using a rational method, i.e., an argument, to support as the conclusion of such an argument the following statement: "The method of faith is the only appropriate method to use in upholding the statement 'God exists'."*

If one agrees to the soundness and truth of conclusion (3), one is then warranted in using the *method of faith* to uphold the statement "God exists." And then we have (2). In short, one could use (3) to support (2). Others might prefer to appeal to (2) directly, without benefit of a rational argument, to express their readiness to use the method of faith. We shall come later to examine and assess one example of this method of faith as this is described and upheld in William James's classic essay "The Will to Believe."

The last of these methods for warranting the belief in the existence of God is the method of *religious experience*. For those who use this method, the justification of the belief in the existence of God is a matter neither of reason nor of faith. It requires rather a very special kind of experience, an experience that some people throughout the ages have claimed to have had and that some claim, today, to have had. The use of the term 'experience' here is not intended to refer to something that involves the use of one's senses. Nor is the experience in question something that characterizes a moral, scientific, political, aesthetic, or any other type of familiar experience. Rather, the expression 'religious experience' points to something wholly distinctive. It is different in character from any of the other

Religious experience

familiar dimensions or modes of human experience. It is uniquely appropriate to, and involved in, becoming aware of God's existence. Nor can one require that this religious experience submit for *its* certification to any of the other modes of experience. It stands on its own and is its own certification.

Some of the terminology used in conveying what is covered by the phrase 'religious experience' includes additional expressions such as 'revelation', 'disclosure', 'mystical vision', 'divination', and 'encounter'. I do not mean, of course, that all of these terms are synonymous, or that those who use them would agree with one another as to the nature of religious experience. I use the term 'religious experience' to cover a number of different, yet closely related, views as to the method to be invoked in making one aware of God's existence. What all these views have in common is the agreement that such religious experience is not a matter of rational argument or of faith. I shall select for later examination, as an example of such views, those of Martin Buber.

chapter 6

The Ontological Argument

St. Anselm

Is it possible to establish the existence of God by means of a rational argument? There have been a number of attempts in the history of theology to do so. In the present chapter I shall consider a celebrated example of such an attempt known as *the ontological argument*. Ontology is the part of the discipline of philosophy that concerns itself with the central concepts of *being* and *existence*. The expression 'ontological argument' points to the fact that special attention is given in this argument to a consideration of the concepts of being and existence as these have to do with God. A classic version of the ontological argument was presented in the eleventh century by St. Anselm.

Anselm was born in 1033 at Aosta, in the Italian Alps. After being a wandering scholar for some years, at the age of twenty-seven he became a Benedictine monk of the Abbey of Bec in Normandy. He rose in ranks to become prior and eventually abbot at the Abbey. He wrote a number of famous works, including the *Monologion* and *Proslogion*, as well as others on semantics (*De Grammatico*), on truth (*De Veritate*), on free choice (*De Libertate Arbitrii*), and on why God became man (*Cur Deus Homo*). He became Archbishop of Canterbury in England in 1093 and died in 1109. He was canonized in 1494.

Variations on the ontological argument, as first formulated by St. Anselm, were presented by other philosophers in later epochs, for example,

St. Anselm

in the seventeenth century by Descartes and Leibniz. A classic attack on the argument was made by Immanuel Kant in his great work, *The Critique of Pure Reason* (1781). Far from having been laid to rest by this attack, the ontological argument continues to hold the fascination and interest of many philosophers down to the present day. Recently, a considerable literature on this argument has been produced, with some leading contemporary philosophers eager to defend it (or at least some version of it) and others equally determined to challenge it and show its inherent fallaciousness or invalidity.[1] So what we're about to study is a matter of very lively debate and philosophic vitality.

'A Priori' and 'a Posteriori'

The ontological argument for the existence of God is commonly classified as being an *a priori* argument, in contrast to other types of arguments that are classified as being *a posteriori*. (The *cosmological argu-*

ment for the existence of God, which I will discuss in the following chapter, is an example of an *a posteriori* argument.) Before proceeding to consider the details of the ontological argument, it will be necessary to stop and examine the meaning of the terms '*a priori*' and '*a posteriori*' and the importance of this classification. (By the way, these terms have a wide use in philosophy, extending far beyond the immediate topic we are considering—the existence of God—and are used in a great variety of contexts, so this is a good opportunity to become familiar with them.)

Let us consider, first, the term '*a priori*'. A point to bear in mind is that the term '*a priori*' is used to classify, from a logical point of view, either a *statement* or an *argument*. 'A priori'

A *statement* is the use of language to say something true or false: for example, "Rome is at the same latitude as New York City." There are of course various other uses of language than to make statements, for example, to utter commands ("Shut the door!") or to ask questions ("What time is it?"). One important point of difference between a statement and either a command or a question is that it does not make any sense to ask "Is it true or false?" about a command or about a question. However, of a statement asserting that something is or is not the case (e.g., "It is raining outside" or "President Kennedy was assassinated"), it *does* make sense, and is appropriate, to ask "Is it true or false?" 'Statement'

An *argument* is a sequence of statements such that from certain statements (called the 'premisses') another statement (called the 'conclusion') is said to follow logically. The basic question in considering an argument from a logical point of view is whether it is *sound* or *valid*. The terms 'validity' and 'invalidity' are best reserved for use in evaluating an argument, just as the terms 'true' and 'false' are best used in connection with statements. (In loose, popular language, 'true' and 'valid' are frequently used interchangeably, as are the terms 'false' and 'invalid'; but in the light of the basic difference between a statement and an argument, it is best to use the terms in their strict sense.) At the same time, there is an important connection between the validity of an argument and the truth or falsity of the statements that compose it. Thus, if an argument is *valid*, and in it the statements used as premises are *true*, the conclusion of such an argument will never be a statement that is *false*. 'Argument'

What, then, do we mean by describing a statement or an argument as *a priori*? The term '*a priori*' marks a logical characteristic. A *statement* is said to be *a priori* when its truth or falsity can be established without having to consult experience. '*A priori*' means *independence from experience*. It does not mean to know the truth or falsity of a statement *temporally prior* to (or *before*) we have experience. Thus the statements "A is A", "Today is either Monday, Tuesday, Wednesday, Thursday, Friday, Saturday, or Sunday", and "A vixen is a female fox" are statements whose *Examples* of a priori statements truth is known *a priori*. We don't have to appeal to some particular experience to know that each of these statements is true. The first of the foregoing examples of *a priori* statements is the Principle of Identity; the second is a tautology that exhaustively enumerates all the possibilities; the third is a definition. Similarly, some statements are known to be *false a priori*, for example, "A is both A and not-A" and "A vixen is a male animal." On the other hand, if I were to say "Today is Wednesday," the truth or falsity of this statement could not be determined *a priori*: for this I should need to appeal to *some* experience—for example, by checking a calendar along with the accepted fact of experience that yesterday was Tuesday. Similarly, the statement "A vixen is a female fox" is a matter of definition, and so is true *a priori*. On the other hand, whether the particular animal that a hunter has just shot is a vixen is not known *a priori*, but only by observation, by examining the dead creature. Statements whose truth or falsity is established by an appeal to experience— whose truth or falsity depends on an appeal to experience—are known as *a posteriori* statements.

Now consider what it means to say that certain types of *arguments* are *a priori*. Examples of such *a priori* arguments are to be found in pure mathematics. Let us take a simple and elementary argument of this sort, one from Euclidean plane geometry. You will recall the familiar theorem that the sum of the angles of a triangle is 180 degrees. In order to prove this statement, we assume the axioms of Euclidean geometry, along with the definitions of such terms as 'parallel lines', 'intersection', 'interior angles', 'alternate interior angles', and so on. Let the triangle ABC be given, with a line *DE* parallel to *BC* drawn through A.

Examples of
a posteriori statements

Example of an
a priori argument

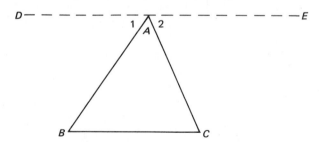

Then angle 1 = angle B, and angle 2 = angle C, since alternate interior angles of parallel lines are equal. However, the sum of the angles 1, A, and 2 is 180 degrees (a straight angle). Therefore (by substitution), the sum of the angles A, B, and C is 180 degrees (Q.E.D.). In characterizing this proof as *a priori*, what is claimed is that the validity of this proof, the derivation of the conclusion from the premises, does not depend on any appeal to observational experience, for example, to the use of protractors or rulers. It follows simply from the premises, that is, from the postulates and definitions of Euclidean geometry.*

Let us now consider, briefly, an *a posteriori* type of argument. In such an argument, the premises contain statements whose *truth* depends on experience. We start from matters of commonly accepted experience, or from reports of some particular situation that are open for observational confirmation by anybody who wants to take the trouble to do so. The pattern of an *a posteriori* argument is to start with these accepted or confirmable facts of experience and then to argue that a certain conclusion follows from these facts. Here, by contrast with an *a priori* type of argument, one does not start with certain definitions or postulates alone, but with certain facts of experience. In order for the argument as a whole to be classified as *a posteriori*, the premises will contain *some* statements (not necessarily *all*) that are themselves *a posteriori*.† Let me give an everyday example of an *a posteriori* type of argument in which the state-

*Example of an
a posteriori argument*

* There is an important phase to the discussion of this whole topic, which has to do with the development of *non-Euclidean* geometries. In such geometries (one of which is known as Riemannian, the other as Lobachevskian), the angle-sum of a triangle is different from what it is in Euclidean geometry: in the Riemannian geometry it is *greater* than 180 degrees, in the Lobachevskian geometry it is *less* than 180 degrees. These geometries were constructed by substituting different postulates for the parallel postulate of Euclid. According to Euclidean geometry only *one* parallel line to a given line can be drawn through a point outside a given line, whereas in Riemannian geometry no parallel lines can be drawn and in Lobachevskian geometry more than one nonintersecting line can be drawn through such a point. The effect of these developments in geometry was to force a reconsideration of the traditional thesis that the premises of a geometric system have to be thought of as *self-evidently true*. It came to be realized that it is sufficient for the purposes of pure geometry to take the premises as merely postulates, as assumptions. If these postulates are consistent *with each other*, this is sufficient to derive valid conclusions from them. The upshot of this whole development, however, was not to disturb—on the contrary it was to reinforce —the claim that the arguments of pure mathematics are *a priori*. This is to say that the acceptability of a conclusion in a particular system of pure mathematics does not depend on any appeal to experience, but only on satisfying the rules of logic in deriving the conclusion (theorem) from a given set of premises.

† However, in order for the argument to be classified as *a posteriori* it is not necessary that the conclusion of the argument be a statement that is itself *a posteriori*, that is, capable of direct confirmation by experience. When we come in the next chapter to discuss the cosmological argument for the existence of God, we shall see that that argument is classified as an *a posteriori* argument because its *premises* state certain commonly accepted facts of experience. And it seeks to conclude from these premises that God exists, as the only way of explaining these facts of experience. However, obviously, the conclusion of this argument, "God exists," is not itself an *a posteriori* statement, since God's existence is not at all open to direct observational experience, whereas the truth of the premises of the argument are open to observational confirmation. I reserve a fuller discussion of this cosmological type of *a posteriori* argument for later.

ments that serve as premisses and as conclusion are *a posteriori* in character. Suppose, on coming home one day, I find my house in complete disarray. The locks have been broken; the money I had in my desk drawer is missing; windows have been smashed; there are fresh muddy footprints on the carpets; my neighbors report they saw some strange individuals prowling around. All of these are facts of experience. What I infer, or conclude, from .these facts is that there must have been a burglary! (It didn't exactly take a Sherlock Holmes to figure that one out—although, mind you, it is still possible, though not very likely, on the evidence, that my conclusion is erroneous.) This then is an example of an *a posteriori* argument. It starts from certain facts of experience and reaches a conclusion that in this case is intended to *explain* the facts I started with. (By the way, not all *a posteriori* arguments need be of the sort where the conclusion of the argument explains the facts stated in the premisses. It so happens that both the cosmological argument for the existence of God and the burglary example I have just given *are* attempts to give an explanation for certain facts: in the case of the cosmological argument, as we shall see, to explain certain observed facts about the world; in my burglary example, to explain the facts about missing money, muddy footprints, etc.)

The General Pattern of the Ontological Argument

With these preliminaries in mind, let us now turn, at last, to an analysis of the ontological argument for the existence of God.

In the light of the foregoing distinctions between *a priori* and *a posteriori* arguments, it will be clear why the ontological argument for the existence of God is classified as an *a priori* argument. It does not include among its premisses any statements that report and describe matters based on an observational experience of the world. Instead, the argument hinges entirely on an analysis of the *meaning of certain concepts*. For the understanding of these concepts, it is not necessary that one appeal to certain specific observed facts of experience. All that is required is that one clearly grasp the meaning of the various concepts involved in the argument. The argument takes the general form of saying that if one does have such a clear understanding of the relevant concepts used in the premisses, then the statement "God exists," will necessarily follow as a conclusion.

The pattern of the ontological argument may be very briefly summarized as follows: A *perfect being must exist, since existence is contained in the very concept of a perfect being.* Obviously, if one is not already convinced of the existence of God, and one is merely given the foregoing summary formula, it is hardly likely, as so presented, it will carry such overwhelming power to convince, that a person would immediately, upon hearing or reading this formula, become a believer! Clearly, whatever force the argument does possess results from taking the foregoing formula apart—analyzing it minutely and carefully from every angle; then only, if at all, will it serve as a full-fledged 'argument'. So this is what we have to do now.

Incidentally, although it is customary to call the *analysis of the meaning of the concept* of a perfect being an *argument*, it is clear that such an 'argument' really consists in making *explicit* what is contained in the very definition of the *concept* of a perfect being. It is claimed by those who uphold the argument that no fresh or new item is presented in the conclusion (that God exists) that is not already contained in the premises. Those who claim that the ontological argument is valid rest their case on the fact that if one truly understands what is meant by 'a perfect being', then to deny that such a being *exists* is self-contradictory. Put the other way around, the conclusion that a perfect being exists follows necessarily from—and merely makes explicit—what is already to be understood by the term 'perfect being'. To take a simple analogy: If we take the concept 'vixen' to mean 'female fox', then to say "A vixen is female" follows necessarily from the definition, whereas to say "A vixen is a male (animal)" is self-contradictory. Analogously, if we have a clear understanding of what it is to be a perfect being, then part of the very meaning of such a concept includes existence as one of the essential marks of a perfect being. To assert that a perfect being does *not* exist is self-contradictory. This, briefly, is the strategy of the ontological argument. However, as I have already remarked, it takes a bit more discussion (quite a bit!) to try to make the claim for the existence of God as plausible or convincing as the case about the vixen being female. And, beginning with St. Anselm down to the present day, the discussion of the ontological argument has to do with the claim by the upholders of the argument that it 'works', whereas the critics deny that it does.

St. Anselm's Formulation of the Ontological Argument

Let us turn, then, to the first classic formulation of the argument as given by St. Anselm. One of the principal texts for the argument is contained in Chapter II of St. Anselm's *Proslogion*. St. Anselm begins by referring to the 'fool' mentioned in Psalms 14:1, the one who says in his heart "There is no God." What St. Anselm sets out to do is to show that even the fool has a conception of God but (because he is a fool) fails to realize that the conception of God as a perfect being requires him to say that God exists.

This very fool, when he hears of this being of which I speak—a being than which nothing greater can be conceived—understands what he hears, and what he understands is in his understanding, although he does not understand it to exist.

For, it is one thing for an object to be in the understanding, and another to understand that the object exists. When a painter first conceives of what he will afterwards perform, he has it in his understanding, but he does not yet understand it to be, because he has not yet performed it. But after he has made the painting, he both has it in his understanding, and he understands that it exists, because he has made it.

Hence, even the fool is convinced that something exists in the understanding, at least, than which nothing greater can be conceived. For, when he hears of this, he understands it. And whatever is understood, exists in the understanding. And assuredly that, than which nothing greater can be conceived, cannot exist in the understanding alone. For, suppose it exists in the understanding alone: then it can be conceived to exist in reality; which is greater.

Therefore, if that, than which nothing greater can be conceived, exists in the understanding alone, the very being, than which nothing greater can be conceived, is one, than which a greater can be conceived. But obviously this is impossible. Hence, there is no doubt that there exists a being, than which nothing greater can be conceived, and it exists both in the understanding and in reality.[2]

In order to understand St. Anselm's argument—even before one considers the various criticisms of it—we need to be clear about certain crucial expressions used in the argument; and we need, too, to take note of a certain assumption or presupposition that he falls back on in constructing his argument. First then, with respect to the crucial *terms* he employs, we need to be clear about (1) the use of the phrase 'a being than which nothing greater can be conceived' and (2) the contrast between 'something that exists in the understanding' and 'something that exists in reality'. Further, we shall need to examine (3) the *assumption* that something that exists in reality is *greater* than something that exists only in the understanding.

'A being than which nothing greater can be conceived'

(1) Consider now the expression '*a being than which nothing greater can be conceived*'. This is one of the ways in which St. Anselm describes what he means by a *perfect* being. What does the expression 'a being than which nothing greater can be conceived' itself mean? The important term in this phrase is 'greater'. Under what conditions can we say that A is *greater than B?* And, further, what does it mean to say that *nothing greater* than a particular entity can be conceived?

(i) With respect to the term *'greater'*, there are broadly speaking two ways of specifying what this means: (a) *in quantitative terms* and (b) *qualitatively in terms of degree of value, importance, or worth*. Thus, to take sense (a), I could say that A has *greater wealth* than B because A has more money than B; or A is of *greater length or volume* than B; or A extended over a *greater stretch of time* than B; or A has *greater weight* than B; and so on. On the other hand, I could say, in accordance with sense (b), that A is of *greater beauty* than B; or A showed *greater wisdom* than B; or A achieved a *greater degree of goodness, justice, happiness, saintliness*, etc. than B; and so on. One difference between sense (a) of 'greater than' (the quantitative sense) and sense (b) (the qualitative sense) is that it need not follow that if A is greater than B in some *quantitative way*, therefore it also has greater *value* of one sort or another than B. For example, it doesn't follow that if A has greater wealth than B, A must be happier than B; it doesn't follow that if painting A sold for more money than B, it was because esthetically it is a better painting than B; it doesn't follow, in short, that in general 'bigger is better'.

(ii) Further, what does it mean to say that *nothing greater than* some particular entity can be conceived? Here again we can take 'greater' in either of the senses I have just discriminated. Let us assume we can conceive of all actual or possible entities arranged in a series of *increasing quantity* of one sort or another, and also in terms of an *increasing order of value*. Thus if A lasts for a second, B for a minute, C for an hour, and so on, we can say that the succeeding members of this series endure for a greater time span than those which precede it (obviously we can also arrange objects in a series of increasing size, weight, etc.). We might also conceive of arranging entities, persons, or actions in terms, say, of increasing degrees of quality or value—for example, with respect to their esthetic depth, honesty, intellectual profundity, justice, or mercy. Once again, succeeding members of this series will have a *higher degree of value* or worth (of a given sort) than members of the series lower down in the series or preceding them. Now, in general, to say of something that *nothing greater than it can be conceived* would mean that if we were able to set up such a series, there would be some member of this series such that *every other member of the series preceded it, and none succeeded it*. Thus, if we can *conceive* what it would be to be the wealthiest person, this would mean that such a person would have greater wealth than anyone else; everyone else would have less wealth than such a person. Similarly, if we can conceive of some person or being as the wisest or most just, there would be no other individual (actual or possible) having a greater degree of these qualities; all other individuals would have lesser degrees of these qualities, and would be lower down on the scale, or be placed somewhere in the series before the individual entity that has the maximum possible or conceivable degree of the quality in question.

Now let's get back to St. Anselm. *In the passage I have quoted*, he does not specify which of these two broad senses of the expression 'greater than' he is using. Elsewhere,[3] St. Anselm makes it quite evident that when he uses the expressions 'greater than' and 'than which nothing greater than can be conceived' in connection with his use of the phrase 'perfect being' ('God'), he intends to appeal to sense (b), not to sense (a). 'Greater than' for him means having a *'higher degree of value'*, *'better than'*. 'The greatest' (= 'than which nothing greater can be conceived') means that which has *supreme value*, the highest conceivable degree of value. (It is only if he were to give *this* interpretation to 'nothing greater than . . .' that his proof for the existence of God (in the traditional Judaeo-Christian sense) would have any relevance. For God is conceived in that tradition (as we have already seen in the preceding chapter) as possessed of the highest degree of wisdom, goodness, power, love, mercy, etc.*

The distinction between
'that which exists in
the understanding'
and 'that which
exists in reality'

(2) Now let's examine the next step in Anselm's argument. This has to do with clarifying the distinction that Anselm makes between 'that which exists in the understanding' and 'that which exists in reality'. Something *exists in the understanding* when we have an idea or concept of it. We can say that a concept exists in the understanding, because we are in fact conceiving of something or other. To take Anselm's example for the moment: A painter may have an idea or concept of a painting he would like to paint, even before he has painted it. (Perhaps in this case it might be better to say he has some sort of image in his mind, rather

---

* It is worth noting, however, that if we were to take the phrases 'greater than' and 'than which nothing greater can be conceived' in sense (a), which I mentioned previously (the sense that has to do with *quantitative matters*, i.e., with *degree of inclusiveness or extent*, rather than of value), then, as it stands, the passage I have quoted from St. Anselm could be used to describe *the physical Universe as a whole*, rather than God in the traditional Judaeo-Christian sense. For the Universe, in sense (a), *is* greater than anything else included in it. It is the greatest of all physical or spatio-temporal beings, because it includes everything within it that has spatial, temporal, or material existence. Nothing can be conceived that is greater than the Universe! Indeed, when Spinoza (whom we shall study later) came to describe his *own* conception of God, in which he took God and Nature to be *identical* (one and the same reality), he was able to use the ontological argument to 'demonstrate' the existence of God or Nature. Spinoza did not think of God (or Nature) as a Person, or as having such qualities as wisdom, goodness, foresight, providential design, etc. Here we have, then, two different conceptions of 'perfection': one that St. Anselm adopted, 'perfection' in the sense of 'that which has a supreme degree of value or worth'; and Spinoza's sense, in which 'perfection' means simply 'most complete' or 'most inclusive'. On this view, God or Nature is perfect because it is the ultimate, all-inclusive, complete reality.

than, strictly, a concept.) In any case, whether or not he ever executes the painting, the image or concept exists in his mind. Again, to take some examples of our own, an economist might have an idea or concept of a wholly free market; or someone may have in his understanding the concept of an ideal society (Plato did!); or a physicist may have the concept of a particle that has neither mass nor charge. And, of course, a theologian may have a concept (in his understanding) of a God who is unique, transcendent, omnipotent, omniscient, benevolent, the Creator of the world, and the loving Father of all mankind.

On the other hand, Anselm wishes to say, some things *exist in reality*, that is, 'outside' the mind. Once the painter has painted the picture, the picture exists in reality. *Before* any such planet was ever observed, the astronomers Adams and Leverrier had the concept of a planet whose orbit lies beyond that of Uranus. When the planet Neptune was *subsequently* discovered, the real existence of the planet was thereby establishd: men were then able to say that the planet (Neptune) *exists in reality*. On the other hand, there are some concepts that do not correspond to or designate anything beyond themselves, that is, 'in reality'. For example, although one may have a concept of a unicorn, there are no unicorns in reality; they are not zoological creatures in the domain of living or extinct organisms whose existence has ever been established in the way that lions, elephants, or dinosaurs are recognized to have or have had real existence.

In short, there are, for Anselm, two ways in which something may be said to exist: (a) as a concept in the mind and (b) in reality. We can say either (1) *the concept* of X exists, or (2) X exists, or (3) both the concept of X exists and X exists. Thus whereas some things exist *only* as concepts in the understanding, there are other things of which it makes sense to say both that we have a concept of them (i.e., the *concept* of the thing exists in the understanding) and that the *entity itself exists* in *reality* (i.e., outside the mind). When this latter situation is the case, the way Anselm phrases it is to say that the entity exists both in the understanding and in reality.

(3) The next important step in the argument is contained in the use of Anselm's assumption or claim that that which exists in reality has a *greater reality* than that which exists only as a concept in the understanding. Having made the *distinction* between these two basic ways in which something may exist, he now makes the further claim that these different ways of existing—(a) as a concept in the understanding and (b) in reality—are also to be distinguished in terms of *the degrees of reality* that each possesses. He claims that if something exists 'in reality', or *both* in reality *and* as a concept in the understanding, it is greater, in the sense that it has a *higher degree* of existence, than if it exists in the under-

'Greater reality'

standing only. In short, Anselm makes the fundamental assumption that it makes sense, philosophically, to distinguish degrees of reality or existence. We have already come across the use of this type of assumption in connection with Plato's metaphysics, where Plato too draws a distinction between grades or degrees of reality, and assigns a higher degree of reality to the domain of Forms than he does to the world of sensible, material particulars. Anselm uses the same principle of distinguishing degrees of reality or existence—this time, however, to assign different degrees of reality to that which exists 'in reality' (i.e., outside the understanding) as contrasted with that which exists *in* the mind only.

A restatement and summary of Anselm's argument

Now let us follow Anselm as he puts these various items together. In the first place, even the fool, Anselm points out, has a *concept in his understanding* of a being that is greater than any other. But the fool, in denying that God exists, is involved in a contradiction. For Anselm asks us to consider that of which we have a conception when we describe it as *that than which nothing greater can be conceived*. Let me use the letter 'X' as a shorthand symbol to stand for the phrase 'that than which nothing greater can be conceived'.

The proof can be given in the following six steps:

(1) Let us assume that X *is* only *a* concept *and exists, therefore,* only *in the understanding.*

(2) However, Anselm claims, that which exists in reality is greater than that which exists only as a concept in the understanding.

(3) It follows from this that there is something greater than X *if* X *is only a concept.*

(4) And since this 'something' cannot be only *a concept, it must be something that exists in reality.*

(5) Therefore, X *(which means 'that than which nothing greater can be conceived') is not merely a concept in the understanding. It must be something that exists in reality.*

(6) Hence, if one were to deny that X *exists in reality, or affirm, instead, that* X *exists* only as a concept in the mind, *this would be self-contradictory.**

* This type of proof is known as a *reductio ad absurdum.* It consists in showing that by making a certain assumption one lands in a contradiction. Therefore, the assumption that led to this result has to be replaced. Instead, it is necessary to assume its very opposite. In our case, the assumption in question is that 'that than which nothing greater can be conceived' exists *only* as a concept in the understanding. By rejecting this assumption, one is led to its denial, to its very opposite. This is to say that X must exist in reality, and not merely as a concept.

A Critical Evaluation of St. Anselm's Argument

What, from a critical point of view, are we to make of the merit of Anselm's argument as just analyzed?

(1) One point of weakness, it can be argued, is that found in the major assumption listed in the foregoing outline of the proof in step (2), the assumption, namely, that what exists 'in reality' has a *greater reality* (or, as I have phrased it, a *greater degree of reality or existence*) than is to be found in the existence of a concept in the understanding alone. The difficulty with this is the presupposition that it makes sense to say that A *has more (greater) reality or existence than B.*

It may, of course, be granted that it makes perfectly good sense to speak of amounts or degrees of some property, whether it be a quality or a quantity. For example, we could say that A has a greater degree of skill in playing tennis than B; that A has more (greater amount of) power than B; that A shows greater regard for the welfare of his fellow man than B; that A has greater volume, or length, or durational extent than B; and so on. We may set up scales (whether rough or refined) and criteria by which we can order entities in terms of their possessing greater or lesser *amounts* of some quantity, or greater or lesser *degrees* of some quality, and so be said to stand higher or lower in some scale of values. But what does it mean to say that we can order entities, whatever they are, in terms of their 'degree of existence'? What criterion or scale do we have that measures or orders *existence as such*, and does not, in answering this question, surreptitiously equate existence with some other quality, quantity, or value? Anselm has not given us any adequate reason for making this assumption. He treats existence as if it were some quality that is comparable, in some way, to other easily recognized qualities or properties. He assumes that since we can order these other qualities in terms of 'greater' or 'lesser', 'higher' or 'lower', these discriminations also apply to existence. But why should we assume this? True, he can draw a distinction between the existence of a concept in the understanding and the existence of something 'in reality', that is, outside of the understanding. But it does not follow that because we can draw a distinction between existence in the understanding and the existence of something that is not a concept, therefore that which has nonconceptual existence has a *higher* degree of existence ('more' or 'greater' reality) than that which belongs to the concept. The *modes* of existence are different, but not necessarily of such a kind that one stands *higher* than the other.

If to have a 'greater' degree of reality belongs to something outside the mind, as contrasted with something that exists only as a concept in the mind, is it because such 'greater' degree of reality amounts to its having a higher *value* of some sort? It may be true that for most people to actually have a million dollars (in reality, i.e., in the bank) is *better, more valuable* than merely to have only an idea (or hope!) for the million dollars. But does such greater *value* of the money in the bank thereby amount to 'more or greater existence'? What if someone plans to commit arson and to burn down a hospital? He has the 'concept' in his understanding. Does it follow that if he carries out his plan (concept) and succeeds in burning down the hospital, what has happened has *greater reality*? Of course, it is far worse for the hospital to be burned down than for the person to have an idea or plan in his mind that remains unfulfilled or thwarted. But this does not mean that the idea in the mind *as an existent* is any *less* an existent (has less *reality*) than the hospital actually burned down. Why, then, is that which exists 'in reality' *greater* than that which exists 'in thought' alone? If 'greater reality' means 'more valuable', this is surely not always the case. On the other hand, if 'greater reality' means simply a *different* kind of existence, namely that which belongs to existence 'in reality' (i.e., outside the mind) as contrasted with 'existence in the understanding alone', why should such a *difference in status*, or 'location', justify one in saying that what exists 'in reality' is *greater* than that which exists 'in thought' alone?

We conclude that *existence* has no *degrees*, although many other things do—for example, various *qualities* and the *values* that attach to objects, persons, actions, institutions, and ways of life.

(2) There is a further kind of criticism frequently brought to bear on Anselm's argument. Anselm presumes that there is a difference to be made between the existence of a concept 'in the understanding' and that which exists 'in reality'. Let us grant this distinction. Indeed, the criticism developed under (1) itself accepts and uses that distinction. But let us go back to Anselm's crucial phrase 'than which nothing greater can be *conceived*' (my italics). (I previously used the letter 'X' as a shorthand symbol for this phrase.) Anselm presumes that this *phrase* can at once serve to designate *a concept 'in the understanding'* and *something that exists 'in reality'*, i.e., 'outside' the understanding. "However," a critic may ask, "what basis is there for saying that the phrase 'than which nothing greater can be *conceived*' is itself *anything more than a concept*? And what basis is there for saying that there exists anything *in reality* to which such a concept corresponds and which it may designate? Is not the claim that something exists *in reality* a matter that, in some way, must be established by going beyond the concept itself?—by taking into account or appealing to something not itself a *concept, something that we can conceive?*"

The force of this criticism can be seen most clearly by turning to another formulation of the ontological argument—given by Descartes—that displays the same characteristic weakness of the ontological argument.

Descartes' Version of the Ontological Argument

A version of the ontological argument was offered by the famous French philosopher René Descartes (1596–1650) in his work *Meditations on First Philosophy* (1641). It was this version of the argument that served as the principal target of Kant's famous attack in *The Critique of Pure Reason*. Kant's criticism is the one most often appealed to when people find fault in general with the ontological argument. Descartes writes:

. . . I clearly see that existence can no more be separated from the essence of God than can its having its three angles equal to two right angles be separated from the essence of a [rectilinear] triangle, or the idea of a mountain from the idea of a valley; and so there is not any less repugnance to our conceiving a God (that is, a Being supremely perfect) to whom existence is lacking (that is to say, to whom a certain perfection is lacking), than to conceive of a mountain which has no valley.

But although I cannot really conceive of a God without existence any more than a mountain without a valley, still from the fact that I conceive of a mountain with a valley, it does not follow that there is such a mountain in the world; similarly although I conceive of God as possessing existence, it would seem that it does not follow that there is a God which exists; for my thought does not impose any necessity upon things, and just as I may imagine a winged horse, although no horse with wings exists, so I could perhaps attribute existence to God, although no God existed.

But a sophism is concealed in this objection; for from the fact that I cannot conceive a mountain without a valley, it does not follow that there is any mountain or any valley in existence, but only that the mountain and the valley, whether they exist or do not exist, cannot in any way be separated one from the other. While from the fact that I cannot conceive God without existence, it follows that existence is inseparable from Him, and hence that He really exists; not that my thought can bring this to pass, or impose any necessity on things, but, on the contrary, because the necessity which lies in the thing itself, i.e. the necessity of the existence of God determines me to think in this way. For it is not within my power to think of God without existence (that is of a supremely perfect Being devoid of a supreme perfection) though it is in my power to imagine a horse either with wings or without wings.[4,*]

What Descartes argues is that just as it is part of the very essence of the concept of a Euclidean triangle to have an angle sum of 180 degrees, and that it would be contradictory of what we *mean* by a (Euclidean) triangle

* From *The Philosophical Works of Descartes* translated by E. S. Haldane and G. R. T. Ross. Reprinted by permission of Cambridge University Press.

to deny this property to it, so it is of the very essence of God to exist. The property of existence is one that belongs essentially to God, just as do other properties—omnipotence, transcendence, goodness, etc. It would be self-contradictory to have a concept of God as a supremely perfect being and at the same time deny existence to God. For to deny existence to God is tantamount to thinking of God as imperfect. And this, of course, is self-contradictory of the very concept of God as a supremely perfect being.

Critique of Descartes' Argument

What is one to make of the merit of this version of the ontological argument? The standard criticism runs as follows: It may be granted that men possess a concept of God. However, it does not follow that because men do have such a concept, there exists something outside the mind of which the concept can serve as a description. That something exists, other than the concept itself, cannot be established by examining or analyzing the concept alone. No amount of analysis of the meaning of a concept can ever yield the assurance or evidence that there is anything to which the concept can be applied—that there exists in fact anything beyond the concept itself and of which the concept might serve as a description. To establish such independent existence requires more than *conceptual analysis*.

'Existence' is not a predicate; existence is not a property

Another way of putting this criticism, which is essentially what Kant had in mind, is that 'existence' ('existence in reality') is not a predicate. Existence is not a *property* of something. A genuine *logical* predicate describes a property of something. For example, in the sentence "Cows produce milk" the predicate 'produce milk' describes a property of cows. But to say "Cows exist," according to Kant (and those who follow him here), does not require us to say that 'exists', as the *grammatical predicate* in the preceding sentence, is a genuine or real predicate, i.e., one that describes a *property* of cows. Take another example: Consider the sentence "Mermaids have fishlike tails." The predicate, 'have fishlike tails', describes a defining property of mermaids. It expresses (part of) the meaning of the concept 'mermaid'. Now take the sentence "Mermaids exist." Does the (grammatical) predicate 'exist' tell us anything about the *concept* 'mermaid'? Does it give us a property of mermaids? According to Kant and others, the answer is no. Even if it were true that there are mermaids in reality, somewhere on Earth or in some other part of the Universe, we should not have established the *existence* of mermaids as a *property* of mermaids. For the genuine *defining* properties of mermaids, *whether any exist in reality or not, would be exactly the same for existent mermaids as for nonexistent mermaids*. Therefore, Kant argues, 'existence' is not a descriptive property of mermaids; it does not tell us *what* a mermaid is. Existence has to do, rather, with whether or not *there is* something to which the term (concept) 'mermaid' can be applied: existence has to do with our saying *that* something is the case, not *what* a term means.

In short, no amount of the analysis of a concept into its defining characteristics will show existence (or existence in reality) among those characteristics. I can define God as infinitely benevolent, omnipotent, wise, etc. However, one cannot include 'existence' among the defining properties of God. For if one does, it is still a legitimate question whether there is anything in *reality*, i.e., 'outside the mind', or beyond the use of certain phrases and descriptions in language, to which the *concept* or term 'God' applies. The fact that one adds *the term* 'existence' to the *verbal* list of 'properties' of God—that one includes it in the *formula* defining what the *concept* of 'God' means—does not automatically guarantee that there *exists in reality* something to which that concept (or that formula) may be applied. The inclusion of the *term* 'existence' among God's 'defining properties' does not automatically insure that, independently of the verbal formula (which includes the term 'exists'), there is an *existent entity* to which that formula applies. Descartes, however, commits the error of assuming that one can make this leap from a verbal formula or concept (even if it includes the term 'existence' as part of what one means by the term 'God') to the actual existence in reality of a being that can be called 'God'.

chapter 7

The Cosmological

Argument

St. Thomas Aquinas

The cosmological argument (i.e., the argument having to do with certain properties of the world) is a classic major attempt to establish the existence of God by an appeal to reason. Various versions of the argument have been offered over the centuries by different writers. A prototype of the argument was offered by St. Thomas Aquinas. It is his formulation that I shall use as the principal text for our analysis.

Thomas Aquinas is probably the best known and most influential of all Catholic philosophers and theologians. Already in his own lifetime he was known as the 'Angelic Doctor'. His thought lies at the center of what is commonly referred to as 'Scholasticism', and expresses an important strand in the tradition of orthodox Christian philosophy and theology.

Aquinas was born in 1225 at the castle of Roccasecca near the small town of Aquino, situated between Rome and Naples. He studied at the University of Naples, where he entered the Dominican Order of monks despite the opposition of his family, who even succeeded for a while in physically detaining him and keeping him under guard. Nevertheless, upon gaining his freedom, he proceeded to Paris and Cologne to continue his studies. He lectured at the University of Paris, where he became a professor of theology in 1256. For a period of ten years, between 1259 and 1269, he lectured at various Dominican monasteries in Italy before returning to his teaching duties at the University of Paris. He was the

St. Thomas Aquinas

author of many works. These fill thirty-two large volumes and include the many-volume *Summa contra Gentiles* and the *Summa Theologica*. The latter are his best-known works and contain his most mature thought. Toward the end of his life, Aquinas underwent a strong mystical experience. It was so overpowering that he discontinued the writing of the third part of his *Summa Theologica* as well as all other writings. He told his secretary "All that I have written seems to me like so much straw compared with what I have seen and with what has been revealed to me." In failing health, he died in 1274 at the early age of forty-nine. He was canonized in 1323.

General Features of the Cosmological Argument

The use of the term 'cosmological' in connection with the cosmological argument signifies that in the course of the argument reference is made to *certain features of the world about us*. It is these commonly recognized features of the world, as found in everyday experience, that serve as the starting point and as part of the evidence on which the argument rests. It is because the argument includes reference to these empirically established facts about the world that the argument as a whole is classified as *a posteriori*. As we shall see, the premises also contain statements that are not *a posteriori*, nor is the conclusion of the argument, the statement "God exists," *a posteriori*. Nevertheless, it is because the *premisses* include some *a posteriori* statements that the entire argument is classified as *a posteriori*. In this respect it differs from the ontological argument that relies entirely on the *meaning* of certain *concepts*, in particular the *concept* of a perfect being. Furthermore, the cosmological argument seeks to *explain*, through its conclusion (the existence of God), the very facts of experience with which it starts. In contrast, the ontological argument does not seek to *explain* any facts of experience; it simply wants to show that if we start with the concept of a perfect being, then we are driven to the (same) conclusion—that God exists.

Another preliminary point: I have used the expression 'the cosmological argument' thus far. And it might be thought that there is only *one* such argument. Actually, however, not only are there many different versions of what can be classified as a cosmological argument that different authors have given, but even St. Thomas gives three separate arguments all of which are of the 'cosmological' type.*

General strategy of a cosmological argument

The general strategy of one who uses the cosmological argument is to say: "Here are certain facts of experience. I am not asking you simply to examine certain ideas or concepts. I am instead appealing to what we all find in the world around us. The only way you are going to be able to make any ultimate sense of these facts of experience is by acknowledging that there is a God who brought these facts about." Thomas Aquinas's arguments are all of this type. He starts by calling attention to such facts as these: (1) the fact of *change*; (2) the fact that the existence of various things depends on there being a *cause* for their existence; (3) the fact that the existence of certain things is such that they 'need not be', i.e. they come to be and pass away, they are 'generated' and are 'corruptible'. Aquinas shows that if we wish to account for these facts of change, of

* Actually, Thomas gives five different 'ways' of proving the existence of God. None of these includes the ontological argument, which he considered invalid. Of the five that he does offer, the first three are commonly grouped together as constituting 'the' cosmological argument. The last two are classified as *teleological*. Teleology has to do with the notion of purpose or design. In his version of the teleological argument, Thomas calls attention to what he considers certain facts of experience of the world in which order or design is manifest. Thomas argues that these facts can be explained only by a belief in a providential, infinite, benevolent, and designing Intelligence. By contrast with teleological arguments, the cosmological argument does not make reference to, or start from, anything that suggests a *purposeful* design or order.

causation, and of the perishable character of the existence of various entities, the only way of doing so, in an ultimately satisfying way, is by acknowledging that there is a supreme being, God, who brought these facts about.

Aquinas's Formulations of the Cosmological Argument

The first of Aquinas's arguments deals with the fact of *change*. It reads as follows:

The first and most obvious way is based on change. Some things in the world are certainly in process of change: this we plainly see. Now anything in process of change is being changed by something else. This is so because it is characteristic of things in process of change that they do not yet have the perfection towards which they move, though able to have it; whereas it is characteristic of something causing change to have that perfection already. For to cause change is to bring into being what was previously only able to be, and this can only be done by something that already is: thus fire, which is actually hot, causes wood, which is able to be hot, to become actually hot, and in this way causes change in the wood. Now the same thing cannot at the same time be both actually X and potentially X, though it can be actually X and potentially Y: the actually hot cannot at the same time be potentially hot, though it can be potentially cold. Consequently, a thing in process of change cannot itself cause that same change; it cannot change itself. Of necessity therefore anything in process of change is being changed by something else. Moreover, this something else, if in process of change, is itself being changed by yet another thing; and this last by another. Now we must stop somewhere, otherwise there will be no first cause of the change, and, as a result, no subsequent causes. For it is only when acted upon by the first cause that the intermediate causes will produce the change: if the hand does not move the stick, the stick will not move anything else. Hence one is bound to arrive at some first cause of change not itself being changed by anything, and this is what everybody understands by God.[1]

Argument based on the fact of change

The basic structure of this argument consists of four statements:

Outline of the argument based on the fact of change

(1) *Some things in the world are in process of change.*

(2) *A thing that is in a process of change cannot cause that change in itself; it is changed by something else.*

(3) *If that which brings about a change in something (let us call it a 'changer') is itself changed by something else, one can arrange these various changers and things changed in a series. However, an infinite series of such changers and things changed is impossible.*

(4) There must therefore be a first cause of change that initiates the series of changes but does not itself undergo a process of change. This unchanged changer is God.

The term 'change', which translates Aquinas's Latin term '*motus*', is to be understood in the broad sense that Aristotle employed. It is the one that Aquinas here adopts. According to this usage, something undergoes change when it involves one of the following: (a) a change of *quantity*, as when something grows or diminishes in size; (b) a change in *quality*, as when something changes color, or changes from cold to hot; (c) a change of *place*, as when something moves from one spatial position to another. To illustrate: an icicle grows in size; the water in the kettle boils; the billiard ball moves across the table. A widely used translation of Aquinas's text of the first cosmological argument renders the Latin term '*motus*' as 'motion'. Accordingly, the first argument is ordinarily taken as seeking to establish that there must be a First *Mover*. Inasmuch as the term '*motus*' has the broader signification of 'change', however, and since 'motion' in the sense of 'change of place' (locomotion) is only one species of change, it is somewhat misleading to confine the analysis of the first cosmological argument given by St. Thomas to this one type of change and to speak of God as a First or Prime *Mover*.

There are very many examples of change in the world about us, as found in ordinary experience. This is the basic and elementary fact from which the argument takes its point of departure. The truth of this premiss would normally be granted by most persons as beyond doubt, and we shall ourselves here so accept it. We do "plainly see" such things as leaves falling, water flowing, the sun 'rising and setting', a child growing into an adult, a person's hair turning white, and so on.

Aquinas takes as another premiss of his argument the principle that wherever there is some change of an entity from state A to state B, such change requires two conditions. First, where something undergoes a process of change, the change can be described as a transition from what is *potential* to what is *actual*. Second, wherever there is a transition from potentiality to actuality, there must be something that is already *actual* and that, by virtue of its actuality, is able to transform what was only potential into a new actuality. Let us examine each of these ideas a bit more carefully.

Suppose a ball to be at rest on a tabletop. It is not *actually* in motion. Nevertheless, it has the capacity (potentiality) to be moved. It can be pushed by someone's hand, hit with a stick, dropped, carried, etc. If none of these things happens to it, we could say it nevertheless has the potentiality for such change of place (locomotion). If someone actually pushes the ball with a stick, the potentiality of the ball to be moved is realized. It *moves;* its motion is now actual. The moving ball is in an actual process of change of position.

Things in the world have various potentialities, depending on the kind of entity they are. The ball can be moved, but it can't be made to sing "Swanee River," eat a sandwich, add a column of figures, or read Plato's *Republic.* On the other hand, a human being has very many capacities or potentialities (including the capacity to be pushed, pulled, *moved* from place to place). So the different entities in the world have different potentialities.

Having made this distinction between potentiality and actuality, Aquinas makes another point. If something (say, A) is going to have one or another of its potentialities actualized, there must be something else (say, B) already in an actual state that is instrumental in bringing about an actuality in A, in that which has the requisite potentiality. There must be an actual changer (or 'mover') that can serve as agent for transforming the change of state from that which merely exists potentially to that which becomes actual. For example, a stick in *actual* motion can bring about an actual motion in a ball at rest on a table that has the potentiality to be moved.

Aquinas points out that "the same thing cannot at the same time be both actually X and potentially X, though it can be actually X and potentially Y." If the ball is *actually at rest,* it is not *actually in motion,* although it is *potentially in motion.* In order for its potentiality for motion to be made actual, there must already be something that is *actual* that will make the ball move, for example, the actually moving hand or stick that strikes the ball and causes the ball to move. Another example: A match *could be* lit; it has the potentiality to be burned. But if it is not lit, it is not burning, not oxidizing, etc. A match cannot both be lit and be not lit at the same time in the same respect. What is "actually hot cannot at the same time be potentially hot, although it can be potentially cold." The actually lit match cannot be at the same time potentially lit, but it can at the same time be potentially a 'used-up' match.

Furthermore, that which is an actual changer or mover will have reached its own actuality through the action of still another actual changer or mover, and so on. In short, for every change there is a changer, for every motion a mover. And what is a mover or changer may itself be put into motion or undergo its own process of change through the agency of still another mover or changer.

Aquinas asks us to conceive of the possibility of arranging all these changes and changers, all these 'movers', 'motions', and 'things moved' in a series or sequence. One may use as a model here what is called a 'chain reaction'. For example, there may be an automobile accident in which one car rams into the car in front of it, because a car behind it rammed into it, and so on. Or, where a panic is created in a crowd of people trying to get out of a burning building, the person who pushes the person in front of him or falls over him is pushed from behind, whereas that pushing person is in turn pushed, and so on.

Having assumed that it is possible to set up such series of changes or motions, Aquinas next makes the crucial assumption (used as a premiss in the argument): *that such a series of changers and things changed cannot go on to infinity. It is impossible for there to be an infinite regress among the members of this series.* There must be, in other words, a First Changer, or a First Mover, and this First Changer or First Mover will not itself be *part* of the series, but only initiate it. It itself will be unchanged and unmoved, since (unlike any part of the series) it has no changer or mover that precedes *it*.

Recall Aquinas's words:

We must stop somewhere, otherwise there will be no first cause of the change, and, as a result, no subsequent causes.

Now even if we were to grant to Aquinas the possibility of arranging all changes in a single all-encompassing series (itself a very dubious assumption) the most obvious question that can be directed to the foregoing claim that "we must stop somewhere" is "*Why must* we stop somewhere?" As it stands, Aquinas simply asserts that there must be a first cause of change, since if there were no first cause there would be no subsequent causes. Now it is true enough that *if* a series does have a first cause of change, then we can account for the subsequent items in the series in terms of their connection with the first member. But Aquinas has not here given us any explicit and compelling reason to assert that a series must have a first member. Why could not the regress in the series go on to infinity? Why need a series have a first member at all? Why could there not be an infinite series composed of items of change or motion? As stated thus far, Aquinas's statement that the series must contain a first member is an example of what is known as the 'fallacy of begging the question'. In general, this fallacy consists in assuming the truth of the conclusion (the statement to be proved by the argument) as the very premiss of the argument. That is, Aquinas seeks to prove that God exists, where God is characterized (among other things) as the First, unchanging Cause of all other changes. In asserting as a premiss that a series of causes of change must have a first member, Aquinas is assuming the very thing he sets out to prove!

Now actually there is more to Aquinas's view than we have done justice to thus far. There is in the argument a tacit and unexpressed claim that, when made explicit, might lend greater weight and plausibility to the argument. Stated briefly for the moment, what Aquinas is here pre-

A series of changes must have a beginning

Fallacy of begging the question

supposing, it may be said, is that in order to give an adequate *explanation of anything* there must be a final and ultimate explanation that is both unexplained and unexplainable, and yet explains everything that follows or 'flows' from it. This is perhaps the most fundamental and crucial assumption on which all of Aquinas's arguments depend. I shall return shortly to a fuller discussion and evaluation of this assumption.

Meanwhile, let me turn to the second argument (the second 'way'). We shall find that it has a pattern similar to the first—a similar rejection of the possibility of an infinite regress, and also a tacit reliance on the same claim I have just hinted at as underlying the rejection of an infinite regress: the requirement that in any satisfactory explanation one must ultimately come to a stop in recognizing an ultimate fact that is both unexplained and unexplainable.

Argument based on causation

The second argument reads as follows:

The second way is based on the nature of causation. In the observable world causes are found to be ordered in series; we never observe, nor ever could, something causing itself, for this would mean it preceded itself, and this is not possible. Such a series of causes must however stop somewhere; for in it an earlier member causes an intermediate and the intermediate a last (whether the intermediate be one or many). Now if you eliminate a cause you also eliminate its effects, so that you cannot have a last cause, nor an intermediate one, unless you have a first. Given therefore no stop in the series of causes, and hence no first cause, there would be no intermediate causes either, and no last effect, and this would be an open mistake. One is therefore forced to suppose some first cause, to which everyone gives the name "God".[2]

It is clear that this second 'way' is of a similar pattern as the first. They differ only in that whereas the first argument concerns the causes for *changes* in the state of something (of quantity, quality, or spatial position), this argument has to do primarily with the causes of the very *existence* of something. Not only is there nothing that brings itself into existence, but once again, too, Aquinas asks us to recognize that when we do find intermediate causes for the existence of things, and arrange these in a series, such a series cannot regress to infinity. There must be a First Cause that is the ultimate cause for the existence of everything else but whose own existence is not caused by anything beyond it. And this First Cause is God.

Let us combine the main point of these two arguments. Together they turn our attention to what is involved in giving explanations in terms of causes. An appeal to causes may undertake to explain the *changes* in things or the *existence* of things. In either case, when we arrange the causes of either type into a series, the series cannot regress to infinity; there must be a first member, a First Cause.

Combining the first two arguments

God, as the First Cause, is himself unchanged. God is not a being with any *potentiality* for change, a potentiality made actual by the causal action of some already actual entity. God is not a being who undergoes a process of change from potentiality to actuality. God is wholly actual. As wholly actual, God is thus the unchanging actual, ultimate, First Cause of the changes of all other entities.

God is also the ultimate cause of the existence of all other things. He is 'the Maker of Heaven and Earth', the being who creates and maintains all things in existence. However, it makes no sense to ask for the cause of God's own existence, since God's existence is uncaused. In short, God is the uncaused First Cause of the existence of everything else.

We can combine the basic claim of these two arguments as follows: When we seek to make complete sense of the causal sequences that characterize the changes in entities and their very existence, we must ultimately come to recognize that there exists a First Cause that is the unchanging changer, the unmoved mover, the wholly uncaused causal ground for the existence of everything else.

A Critical Evaluation of the Foregoing Cosmological Arguments

What can be said, from a critical point of view, about the merit of the foregoing arguments? In order to be in a position to answer this question, it will be well to focus our attention on one central feature of Aquinas's arguments. This is contained in the premiss that there cannot be an infinite regress in the statement of causal conditions. As we have seen, in stating that there must be a first member of the series of causes, that there cannot be an infinite regress, Aquinas commits the fallacy of begging the question. However, another perhaps more plausible way of understanding what lies behind his rejection of an infinite regress can be put in another way. It is the implicit claim that to provide an adequate and full explanation for the occurrence of some process of change or the existence of some state of affairs, the process of explanation must come to an end by appealing to something that provides the full explanation for what we started with but itself is both unexplained and unexplainable.

Focusing on the nature of explanation: explanans and explanandum

Let me expand this point a bit. Every *explanation* has two parts: I shall use the expression *'explanandum'* to stand for 'that which is to be explained', and the expression *'explanans'* to stand for anything that contributes to the explanation of the *explanandum*. The *explanans* will normally be a *reason* for something, a *cause* or *condition* that accounts for something. An argument offering a explanation may have as its conclusion the *explanandum* and as its premises one or several statements that constitute the *explanans*. There may be several items in the premises of an argument, each of which is an *explanans*.

Aquinas assumes that in giving a wholly satisfactory explanation of some *explanandum*, however many contributing *explanans*-items there are, there must be some one, ultimate, and final *explanans*, either in that argument or in some other, that explains all other subordinate or 'intermediate' *explanans*-items as well.

We may represent this assumption of Aquinas by means of the following diagram:

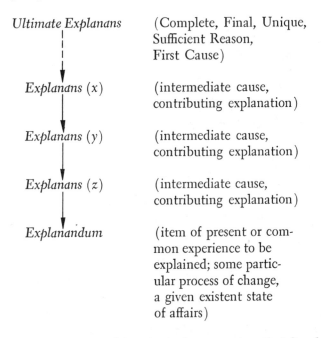

Ultimate Explanans	(Complete, Final, Unique, Sufficient Reason, First Cause)
Explanans (x)	(intermediate cause, contributing explanation)
Explanans (y)	(intermediate cause, contributing explanation)
Explanans (z)	(intermediate cause, contributing explanation)
Explanandum	(item of present or common experience to be explained; some particular process of change, a given existent state of affairs)

With respect to this principal assumption that lies behind Aquinas's cosmological argument, we must focus our attention on the requirement that *there must be a unique, final, and ultimate explanans*. What warrant is there for making this claim, for adopting this as true?

A major objection is the following: It is not the case, in giving an explanation for some particular occurrence or state of affairs (in providing an *explanans* for an *explanandum*), that the *explanans* will be considered incomplete or inadequate unless one can give, at the same time, an *ultimate* explanation for some particular *explanans*. Nor will it be the case that such an adequate explanation will be found only when we reach an ultimate explanation (or 'first cause') about which it is impossible to ask for *its* explanation. Let us consider the following cases:

Is it necessary that there be a unique, final, ultimate explanation?

(a) Suppose I am the driver of a car, and have come to rest at an intersection where the traffic light is red. My car is at rest, with no other car similarly at rest directly in front of me. A car coming at right angles across my path has a green light, and just as it crosses in front of where my car is standing, my car suddenly receives a violent impact from behind. As a result my car is pushed forward and collides with the car moving at right angles in front of me. The police ask questions; the case comes to court; the insurance companies make inquiries, since they are asked to make payments for property damage or personal injuries, etc. I am called upon to explain why I rammed into the car passing in front of me. I explain that I was at rest, waiting at a red light, but that I was pushed from behind, and this caused my car to collide with the car crossing my path. Suppose there are witnesses to corroborate my explanation, and that the evidence is not in dispute. Have I given an adequate explanation of why my car collided with the other? I think it would be correct to say that under ordinary circumstances this would be granted: I *have* given an adequate explanation. However, suppose someone were to ask me: "But why did the car behind you ram into you?" I would say: "Ask that driver!" And suppose this question were put to the driver of the car behind me. And suppose he, in turn, were to say, "I too was at rest, waiting behind the car in front of me. But suddenly my car received a terrific impact from the rear and that drove my car into the waiting car in front of me." And suppose once again this explanation is corroborated. Has this man given an adequate explanation of why *he* rammed into *my* car? I should again assume that this would be considered an explanation of *this part* of the 'chain reaction'. Now is it the case that the causal explanation I have given for *why my car was pushed* is *inadequate* until we trace it far enough back to the driver who 'started the whole sequence of events'? Not at all. At each stage the causal explanation as given is perfectly adequate. When someone asks me "But why did the car behind you push you?" he is asking a *different* and *new* question from the one I was called upon to answer, and for the event I was called upon to explain, namely why my car ran into the car that was crossing *my* path. And whether there is an adequate causal explanation for this new and fresh question does not in any way render incomplete or make inadequate the explanation I gave of why I rammed into the car crossing my path. And the same situation holds at each stage of the inquiry. Each stage of explanation (for each of the cars involved in the accident) can be as adequate or complete as the situation calls for. If, indeed, the court or the insurance company wants to know who started it all, this of course is a perfectly legitimate question because they want to know where to fix the *responsibility*. But as far as explaining in *causal* terms why my car collided with the one in front of me, I have given an adequate *causal* explanation. And there may or may not be an adequate explanation or answer to the question of *which* driver initiated the sequence of events. Suppose one does find an adequate explanation for this. And suppose it takes the form of establishing that the driver in question (the 'initiator' of the chain reaction) was drunk, that he was talking to the person sitting next to him, that he didn't keep his eye on the road, etc. In such a case we may have a sufficient and adequate causal explanation for that first impact in the chain, sufficient, that is, to fix the *legal responsibility* (or perhaps only the major share of responsibility) as far as the insurance company or court is concerned. And this may end the case. Explanations have been found sufficient for the purposes in hand, and responsibilities have been determined. Notice that it would still be possible, however, to ask about the drunk driver: "But *why* was he drunk? Why did he turn to talk to his neighbor?" and so on. And these too may be, for certain situations and purposes (for further legal or psychiatric reasons, etc.), themselves perfectly legitimate and relevant questions. And once again one may or may not get adequate explanations that would answer those additional questions, and so terminate that phase of one's inquiries. But at whatever stage one stops, it does not mean that, in so stopping, the adequacy of one's causal explanations up to that point are endangered or made suspect. Because it is still possible to go on, to ask *new* questions, and to get fresh explanations for these new questions does not mean that therefore the causal explanations given for previous or earlier questions were left hanging and rendered in any way inadequate.

Furthermore, the fact that one can go on asking new questions about new aspects of given individual events or occurrences, and getting answers to them does not require that there must be some one, final, and ultimate explanation (some one *explanans*) that is ultimate, unique, complete, and such that it explains all 'subsequent', 'subordinate', and 'intermediate' explanations (causes) while being itself both unexplained and unexplainable.

When Aquinas assumes that we can somehow arrange all individual occurrences or individual processes of change in a single sequence, and that in order to give an adequate explanation of any one of the items in this sequence we must be able to identify some one ultimate, first, cause that explains all the subsequent members of the sequence but is itself unexplained, he is simply wrong about what it takes to give adequate explanations for such individual occurrences and processes of change.

(b) Let me take another example. Suppose a child, Susie, has blue eyes, and someone were to ask "Why does Susie have blue eyes?" The reply (as given in quite elementary form) might be, "Well, both of Susie's parents have blue eyes, and as we know the Mendelian laws of inherited characteristics are such that whenever both parents have blue eyes the child will have blue eyes." In giving this explanation of the observed fact

(Susie's blue eyes) the explanation (argument) contains essentially two premisses (as *explanans*): (1) The eyes of Susie's parents are blue. (2) Whenever both parents are blue-eyed, the child will have blue eyes. The conclusion (3) (*explanandum*) therefore follows: Susie has blue eyes. In this argument, premiss (2) states a regularity or law, and premiss (1) states a particular observed fact that fulfills one of the conditions of the regularity (that the parents both have blue eyes). The conclusion (3), that Susie has blue eyes (another observed fact), is thereby explained by seeing that it follows from these two premisses. Both premisses are true and the conclusion both is true and follows validly from the premisses.

Suppose now, however, one were to ask "But why does the law about the inheritance of blue eyes when both parents are blue-eyed hold? How do you explain *it?*" It is important to see that one is now asking a new question (no longer about Susie's eyes)—this time about the *regularity* that figured in explaining the color of Susie's eyes. At the time when Mendel and other investigators established, by countless observations, regularities about the patterns of inherited characteristics, no satisfactory, confirmed explanations were forthcoming of the sort that are available nowadays. The regularities established—for example, by Mendel—are now themselves explained by appealing to the principles of the highly sophisticated scientific disciplines of genetics and molecular biology. And so the observationally confirmed regularity about the inheritance of blue eyes can itself be derived as a conclusion (as an *explanandum*) from the premisses of contemporary genetic theory that thereby serve as the *explanans* for that conclusion. However, why need it be the case that there must be a final, unique, and ultimate explanation for the facts stated by the principles of genetic theory? Would it be the case that if such an ultimate explanation were not available, all other 'intermediate' or subordinate explanations for items subsumed under them would be inadequate?

On Explaining the Existence of the World

The central question for the theist: Why is there a world at all?

To the foregoing objections it might be replied, in Aquinas's behalf, that somehow they are beside the point, they miss what Aquinas is really after. For to talk about cars in an accident, or Mendel's laws, or Susie's eyes, or even genetic theory is still to be talking about matters within the world. One can make points such as the foregoing about the nature of explanation, which are taken from examples of everyday experience or from science, but all such examples have no bearing on what Aquinas wants to say. For what he is interested in has to do with an explanation that transcends the world altogether. God, as First Cause or Unchanging

Changer, is not an item in the series of causes or changes, all of which are in the world. God is not part of the world. Therefore, to appeal to examples that have to do with processes of change or features of entities *in* the world has no bearing on God's status as the unique and ultimate explanation for *the very existence and character of the world as a whole.* In short, one may possibly grant all that has been said earlier and still maintain that the underlying force and intent of Aquinas's arguments have been missed by raising the kinds of objections I have previously mentioned.

Furthermore, it may be said, when Aquinas refers to a causal series he need not be taken as requiring that this be of such a kind that every preceding member of the series, starting with a present object or event, is to be taken as a *temporally* prior object or occurrence. My example of a car accident in which first one car hits another and then the next car hits the next, and so on, is not the model Aquinas need have in mind. (Nor, for that matter, is the other familiar example frequently employed: that in which one begins by saying that my existence is due to my parents' bringing me into the world, but their existence, in turn, is due to the fact that their parents preceded them and brought them into existence, and there must be, if we keep going in this regress, a First Cause that started this whole sequence. Once again, it needs to be said, in Aquinas's behalf, that the notion of *temporal* priority is not the crucial aspect of causality for him.) Indeed, he allows the *possibility* that it is perfectly conceivable (not at all contrary to *reason*) that there should have been an *infinite* series stretching into the past, and that the world need not have had a temporal beginning or origin in time! That the world *did* have a temporal beginning, Aquinas accepts and believes, but only on the grounds of *revelation and faith*, not as something that can be proved by rational argument.[3]

The notion of a First Cause makes sense for Aquinas quite apart from the question of whether causes *precede* effects *in time.* For the essential feature of cause on which he places his emphasis is the notion of *causal dependency.* Something is said to be the cause of something else when the latter would not exist without the operative presence of the former. (Even for causal relations between objects *in* the world, some causal conditions are simultaneous with their effects: for example, a stone resting on a cushion causes a depression in the cushion, although we shouldn't want to say that the action of the stone comes first in time and then, at a later moment in time, the depression in the cushion occurs; rather, both occur at the same time. The effect takes place as the cause is operating. The depression in the cushion depends on the stone's resting on it, along with other relevant causes or conditions that may be copresent.) In any case, the causal series in which individual objects and events in the world should be placed in order to bring out what Aquinas has in mind is one that exhibits the dependency of the *entire sequence* of events and objects in the world and of the world as a whole on a being that transcends the world altogether. For Aquinas the series as a whole, and all the individual members forming it, depends ultimately for its existence on a First Cause that is itself *independent*, and not the effect of any other creative or sustaining cause beyond itself.

The claim that the world as a whole depends for its existence on a being that is beyond the world is central not only to Aquinas's views but also to theistic metaphysics generally. We must stop, therefore, to ask what lies behind this claim. Once again we can trace the controlling assumption behind this outlook to an underlying view about the nature of explanation.

Let us begin by stressing the point that both on the level of ordinary, everyday experience and surely on the level of scientific inquiry it makes perfectly good sense to look for satisfactory explanations for the events and various phenomena in the world, even if we don't already have these explanations. The very enterprise of science rests on making the assumption that the events and phenomena *in* the world are intelligible. Science is committed to the goal of finding causal connections among events. *The interrelationship of events and objects with one another* is what underlies the search for scientific explanations. We can explain weather changes at a locality in terms of movements of air masses; eclipses of the Sun in terms of the motions of the Moon and Earth with respect to one another; the improved yield of crops in terms of the chemicals put into the soil; and so on. Where explanations are not available at all, or where prevailing explanations are not satisfactory, scientists will not give up the search. They will not throw up their hands and say the matter is simply unexplain*able*. The fact that it is hitherto unexplain*ed* is no warrant for saying it is unexplainable. Scientists take encouragement from the numerous cases in history where what is unexplained at one stage yields to a satisfactory explanation at a later stage.

A scientist's search for explanations of natural phenomena is something with which a theist has no quarrel. Yet the theist will confront all actual, future, or possible successes of science with the remark that they will still leave untouched and unsatisfied what requires an explanation. And this is the explanation for the very existence of the world itself! No matter how far scientists probe, they remain *within* Nature, *within* the cosmos, *within* the world: they trace interconnections among the various items in the world. But as scientists they never do, or can, answer the question: *Why is there a world at all, and what sustains the world as a whole in its existence?* This for the theist is the basic question. What the theist wants to know is not why some particular event occurs or some particular object exists. It may be granted that the answer to this kind of question is one that shows the connection between the object or event in question and some other object(s) or event(s). And one may continue to ask questions of a similar sort about these other particular objects and events, as one did in the first place about the original object and event. And again it may be granted that one can get explanations or answers to these questions about these new and different particular objects and events. But none of this, however far the inquiry is pushed, no matter how many satisfactory explanations of this or that event or object become available through ordinary commonsensical or scientific investigation, will ever satisfy the kind of question the theist is interested in asking. For he is primarily interested, not in the explanation of this or that particular event or object, or in any conjunction of such explanations of particular objects and events, however long this list is extended or however numerous are the items in it. He is interested in an altogether different kind of question. He wants to know about all of these objects and events taken collectively —about the world as a whole, whatever its contents and however numerous the items that make it up—what reason there is for the existence of this totality as such. Why does the world as a whole exist, rather than nothing?

Now this kind of question is a request for an explanation, too, but this time not of some particular item or individual content of the world, but of the world itself taken as an all-inclusive whole. Why does *it* exist? What reason or explanation can be given for *its* existence? This is the central question that the theist asks—and to which he is prepared to give his own answer, his own explanation. His answer is that the world as a whole is brought into existence and maintained in its existence by God. It is because God exists, and exercises his power of creation, that the world exists as his handiwork. Another way of expressing this answer is to say that the world's existence is *contingent* or dependent on God. The world would not have existed were it not for the fact that God made the world. On the other hand, in being independent of the world, God is not dependent for his own existence either on the world or on any other being. For if God were so dependent, it would mean that God's existence, too, is contingent; it could have been the case, were it not for the causal or creative action of this other 'superior' being, that God himself would not have existed. But this is nonsense. For God is not the kind of being who is in any way dependent on the creative power of some other being. And this is another way of saying that God's existence is not contingent. Another way of expressing this is to say that *God's existence is necessary*—where 'necessary' means 'noncontingent'. Therefore, if one were to ask "*Why* does God exist?" (i.e., "What explains the existence of God?"), this question shows a failure to understand the distinctive character of God's existence. Because God's existence is necessary, there is not even the possibility of ask-

The world's existence is contingent; *God's existence is* necessary

ing this question, because the question is illegitimate. It cannot meaningfully arise. When the little girl (when told by her mother that God made the world) asks "And who made God?" the reply has to be that the little girl is asking a pseudo-question.

In asking the question "Why does the world exist?" the theist is making two fundamental assumptions of his own: (1) that it makes sense to speak of the world as a whole and (2) that it makes sense to look for the reason or explanation for the existence of the world as a whole. His question *presupposes* that both these assumptions are meaningful and true. But unless one is prepared to grant the meaningfulness and truth of these presuppositions, the question itself can have no answer.

Both assumptions of the theist that lie behind asking the question "Why does the world exist?" have been challenged by many philosophers.

(1) Some philosophers (e.g., Bertrand Russell) have questioned the very meaningfulness and use of the concept of the world (or the Universe) as a whole.* According to these philosophers, it makes sense to speak of individual items (objects and events) but it makes no sense to speak of the world (or the Universe) 'over and above these'. To take a simple analogy: I could say I had breakfast this morning, but what I mean by this, it turns out, is that I had orange juice, two eggs, coffee, and toast. There was no breakfast over and above these items; it *consisted* of these items. So when I drank my orange juice, ate my eggs, ate my toast, drank my coffee, that is exactly what happened and nothing more. I did not eat breakfast in addition to or as any thing different from the items just enumerated. In a similar way, these critics would say, there are *a*'s, *b*'s, *c*'s, . . . , etc. But there is nothing more than this collection of individual entities that is to be designated as 'the world' or 'the Universe' as such.

(2) Further, it will be argued by such critics, it makes sense to look for, and, in some cases to succeed in finding, explanations for the individual items as individuals. However, it makes no sense to ask for the explanation for the world as such, as something different from the giving of explanations for individual items. When I have explained each item, taken one at a time, there is nothing left over. I cannot ask "But what about explaining the world itself?" for in giving the explanation of each item I have done all that can meaningfully be done. I can ask for and give the explanation, for example, why it rained yesterday, why the sun shines, why children resemble their parents, etc., but I cannot also ask "Why is there a world at all?" because when I have given all the explanations that can be given for the individual items, one by one, there is nothing left over about which to ask "Why does it exist as a whole?" This type of criticism was succinctly summed up in the following remark by David Hume:

* See p. 148 for Russell's comments in his debate with Father Copleston.

Did I show you the particular causes of each individual in a collection of twenty particles of matter, I should think it very unreasonable, should you afterwards ask me, what was the cause of the whole twenty. This is sufficiently explained in explaining the cause of the parts.[4]

Does the foregoing criticism of the cosmological argument itself have any merit?

(1) Let us consider, first, the claim that it makes no sense to speak of the Universe or the world as a whole. (In Chapter 14 I shall undertake a more thorough discussion of this topic.) For the moment, however, let me ask that you consider the following type of situation: Suppose you attended a concert, and that one of the compositions played by the orchestra was Beethoven's Seventh Symphony. Consider, to begin with, the use of the term 'the orchestra'. Suppose someone were to suggest there is no such thing as the orchestra as such. There are rather Messrs. So-and-So, who play first violin, also Messrs. So-and-So, who play second violin, Messrs. So-and-So, who play bassoon, . . . , etc., etc. When you have finished naming each individual, and the instrument he or she plays, our critic might suggest, you have identified all there really is to what you have called 'the orchestra'. There is no such thing as 'an orchestra' over and above, and as distinct from, each of the individuals named and the instrument each person plays. Would someone who took this view be right in his claim? It may, of course, be granted that if by denying there is an orchestra 'over and above' each of the persons enumerated it is meant that there is no *additional person* called 'the orchestra', this is altogether correct. Still, doesn't it make sense to say that the conductor is concerned, normally, with how these individuals are performing *collectively?* What the conductor along with the audience and critics is interested in is "How does the *orchestra* perform?" And by 'the orchestra' is meant the complex coordinated whole consisting of a number of individual performers who are playing in coordination with one another. Even if you were to give an account (or reproduction) of how each and every member of the orchestra played his or her own particular part of the score, you would still not have anything that would let you know how the orchestra, as a coordinated combination of all these individual performances, sounded. So there would seem to be a perfectly important sense in which we recognize the existence of the individual whole or composite called an 'the orchestra', which *is different,* as a unified whole, from merely an enumerated set of individual persons.

And, of course, the same type of analysis would apply were we to examine what we mean by saying that the orchestra played Beethoven's Seventh Symphony. True, each member of the orchestra, and each section (violas, first violins, cellos, flutes, etc.), has his or her own part. Suppose,

On the use of the concept of 'the world as a whole'

however, someone were to suggest that the symphony is nothing more than each of these parts taken one by one. Would this be correct? Is there not a sense in which the symphony, as a total composition, is something with its own characteristics that cannot be found by simply examining each player's part, one by one? Do we not have to listen to how all these parts are interrelated to each other, when taken collectively? And is not this what the *conductor's score* shows? The symphony is not another individual part, since over and above the parts there are no other *parts*. Yet there is a perfectly good sense in referring to the performance and structure of the symphony *as a whole*.

There are, of course, many examples one may give, in addition to the foregoing, where the existence of some whole has various properties that belong to it as a coordinated totality or unity of its parts. (Think of a baseball team, a painting, the human body, etc.) Admittedly there are important differences among these various examples of individual wholes. And, as we shall see later, to think of the Universe (the world) as an individual whole calls for recognizing certain important differences from any of the foregoing examples of individual wholes. Nevertheless, it may be argued, it makes perfectly good sense to think of the Universe as a distinctive individual whole. Let us provisionally understand by 'the Universe' or 'the world' the all-inclusive totality of whatever exists in space and time.

The possibility that we may be able to give a more satisfactory analysis of the concept 'the world' or 'the Universe' as a whole (which I shall attempt to give in Chapter 14) should make us pause before accepting the objection, raised earlier, to the theist's justification for using the concept of the world as a whole in his formulation of the cosmological argument. Let us provisionally accept and grant the soundness of the theist's use of the concept of 'the world as a whole'.

(2) We come now, however, to perhaps the most serious question and difficulty that can be raised with respect to the cosmological argument, even after we have allowed as legitimate the use of the concept of the world as a whole. For, as we have seen, the underlying question that drives the theist to his metaphysical position is: *Why does the world as a whole exist at all?*

The assumption that there must *be a reason for the existence of the world*

In asking the question, the theist is making the crucial assumption that *there must be a reason for the existence of the world*. This presupposition is taken as true and unquestionable. The theist assumes that just as it makes perfectly good sense to look for explanations for the characteristics of things *in* the world, so *it also makes sense to ask for the explanation for the existence of the world as a whole*. The theist wants to know *why there is a world at all, with whatever the parts it does have; not what accounts for this part, and that part, and that part, . . . , etc.* Even if one is able to explain the existence of a part of the whole by reference to other parts of the whole, and so for each part of the whole—one is still remaining *within* the whole and giving explanations 'internally'. What the theist asks is not satisfied by such internal explanations. He wants to explain the fact that *parts exist at all to collectively make a whole.* If one can successfully challenge this presupposition, and show that one does not have to accept it as the unquestioned truth the theist takes it to be, then one need not go on to dispute the answer, or any part of the answer, that the theist gives to the question. For if the question should evaporate, then there is no need to go on and consider various possible answers to the question.

What *reason* then is there to assume that there *must* be an explanation for the existence of the world as a whole? If someone were to say "It is self-evidently true," the reply to this is that it is by no means self-evident (intuitively obvious) to every one. What one wants here is an *argument*, a set of reasons to support the assumption that the world as an individual whole has a reason for its own existence. One can have *faith* that there must be such a reason. But faith is not reason, and what we are asking for at this point is an argument that would show that it is appropriate and legitimate to suppose there *must* be an explanation for the existence of the world as a whole. If one were to request a similar argument to justify the search for explanations for occurrences *in* the world, the justification could be given in various ways. For one thing, there are innumerable examples both in common experience and in science where such successful reasons and explanations for events in the world *have already been found and can be given.* However, as the philosopher Charles Peirce once put it, "Universes are not as plentiful as blackberries!" Since there is only one Universe or world, we cannot appeal to other examples of Universes in which there has been success in finding reasons or explanations for *their* existence. We cannot, therefore, be encouraged and justified to believe, on the basis of these other cases of 'explained Universes', that there must be a reason for the existence of this world of ours as well. Not at all! The situation here is completely unique. Therefore, it does no good to appeal to the principle of the explainability of the multiple entities and phenomena *in* the world. For what reason have we to generalize from what we find to hold true for the parts *of* the world to the world itself as a unique whole of such parts?

The assumption that what holds true for the parts of an individual whole *must* also apply to the whole itself is known as the *fallacy of composition.* In some cases it may be true that the properties of the parts also apply to the whole they compose. For example, if each of the parts of a watch is made of metal, then the watch as a whole is also metallic.

The fallacy of composition

However, if each member of a trio (say, Heifetz, Piatigorsky, and Rubinstein) is in his own right a first-rate performer on his own instrument, it does not follow that the trio composed of those players will be a first-rate trio. There are qualities belonging to many groups or wholes that are quite different from the qualities belonging to each of the members of the group or to parts of the whole. In summary, then, the fact that the existence of each item in the world—each occurrence, object, or phenomenon—is capable of being explained does not automatically guarantee that the existence of the world as a whole which they compose is itself also capable of being explained.

Summary: claims and counterclaims

Some of the foregoing claims and counterclaims are illustrated in the following exchange between Bertrand Russell and Father Copleston in their BBC debate in 1948.

COPLESTON: But are you going to say that we can't or we shouldn't even raise the question of the existence of the whole of this sorry scheme of things—of the whole universe?

RUSSELL: Yes, I don't think there's any meaning in it at all. I think the word "universe" is a handy word in some connections, but I don't think it stands for anything that has a meaning.

COPLESTON: If the word is meaningless, it can't be so very handy. In any case, I don't say that the universe is something different from the objects which compose it . . . what I'm doing is to look for the reason, in this case the cause of the objects—the real or imagined totality of which constitute what we call the universe. . . . Why shouldn't one raise the question of the cause of the existence of all particular objects?

RUSSELL: Because I see no reason to think there is any. The whole concept of cause is one we derive from our observation of particular things; I see no reason whatsoever to suppose that the total has any cause whatsoever.

COPLESTON: Well, to say that there isn't any cause is not the same thing as saying that we shouldn't look for a cause. The statement that there isn't any cause should come, if it comes at all, at the end of the inquiry, not the beginning. In any case, if the total has no cause, then to my way of thinking it must be its own cause, which seems to me impossible. Moreover, the statement that the world is simply there if in answer to a question, presupposes that the question has meaning.

RUSSELL: No, it doesn't need to be its own cause, what I'm saying is that the concept of cause is not applicable to the total.

COPLESTON: Then you would agree with Sartre that the universe is what he calls "gratuitous"?

RUSSELL: Well, the word "gratuitous" suggests that it might be something else; I should say that the universe is just there, and that's all.

COPLESTON: Well, I can't see how you can rule out the legitimacy of asking the question how the total, or anything at all comes to be there. Why something rather than nothing? that is the question. The fact that we gain our knowledge of causality empirically, from particular causes, does not rule out the possibility of asking what the cause of the series is. . . .

RUSSELL: I can illustrate what seems to me your fallacy. Every man who exists has a mother, and it seems to me your argument is that therefore the human race must have a mother, but obviously the human race hasn't a mother—that's a different logical sphere.

chapter 8

The Right to Believe

The irrelevance of proofs for the existence of God

The attempt to prove the existence of God by means of arguments of the sort we have been considering in the foregoing two chapters will appear to many as utterly hopeless and beside the point. A belief in God, it will be said, is not something to be established by means of 'proofs'. The having of a belief in God and the justification for the having of such a belief (if one is challenged to provide such justification) have nothing to do with demonstrative arguments. God is a Presence, not an inference. Our knowledge of him does not emerge at the tail end of an argument, as the conclusion of a chain of reasoning. If one reads, for example, the Old or New Testament, nowhere does one find 'proofs' for the existence of God. The existence of God is taken for granted. At most the prophets may inveigh against men's forgetfulness of God, or men's neglect to let a reverence for God be an active force in the conduct of their lives. But even those who show such forgetfulness by ignoring his presence are not taken to *deny* his existence.

The matter of providing proofs for God's existence largely arose with the development of the discipline of philosophical (or 'natural') theology. Such theology represents the efforts by thinkers who were not only steeped in the literature of the Bible but also greatly influenced by the heritage of Greek philosophy. Theology, as a systematic intellectual discipline (as one strand in the growth of religion in the West), was a *synthesis* of the Bible and Greek philosophy. It was from the latter influence that theology acquired its emphasis on the use of rational argument. In articulating the *system* of Jewish, Christian, or Muslim thought, the many writers belonging to these several traditions sought to enlist the use of philosophical arguments and conceptual distinctions worked out in Greek philosophy, especially in the thought of Plato and Aristotle.

Whatever the impressive character of these intellectual systems of religious doctrines, there are many who would maintain that the very essence of a religious response to the world—the *spirit* of religious commitment —is frequently absent or lost in such systems. And this is especially true when one tries to prove the existence of God by means of rational arguments. It doesn't 'work', because God is not to be found or encountered on the level of intellect and conceptual abstractions. It will be said by many, accordingly, that if we are to get back to the original roots and sources of genuine religious commitment, the appeal must be to the primary, *prerational*, *preargumentative* ways men have for 'knowing' God. The fact that the various arguments and proofs for the existence of God have been subjected to many incisive attacks (especially in modern philosophy) leaves those who have such a strong, prerational religious commitment utterly unaffected. Their position is that one should never have looked for support to rational proofs for the existence of God in the first place. To appreciate all this, we need not go back only to the original founders of the great religions of the West, or to the way in which these matters are expressed in the Bible. The primary sources of knowledge of God are *religious experience* and *religious faith*. These, it will be said, are the only sound and reliable ways of coming into the presence of God. They are available *now*, and to anyone who would open himself to the requisite experience or faith.

Sören Kierkegaard (1813–1855), the great Danish theologian (and one of the principal founders of the modern movement known as 'existentialism'), in his own passionate call for adherence to a 'genuine' Christianity, voiced a characteristic contempt for all attempts to prove the existence of God. He wrote:

And how does God's existence emerge from the proof? Does it follow straightaway, without any breach of continuity? Or have we not here an analogy to the behavior of these toys, the little Cartesian dolls? As soon as I let go of the doll it stands on its head. As soon as I let it go—I must therefore let it go. So also with the proof. As long as I keep my hold on the proof, i.e., continue to demonstrate, the existence does not come out, if for no other reason than that I am engaged in proving it; but when I let the proof go, the existence is there. But this act of letting go is surely also something; it is indeed a contribution of mine. Must not this also be taken into the account, this little moment, brief as it may be—it need not be long, for it is a leap. However brief this moment, if only an instantaneous now, this "now" must be included in the reckoning.[1]

In this and the following chapter I shall focus on two relatively recent attempts to argue for the primacy of faith and religious experience as the appropriate avenues to a 'knowledge' of God. I shall examine, first, the views of William James as presented in his classic essays "The Sentiment of Rationality" and "The Will to Believe" as an example of a call to the reliance on faith. I shall then turn, in the following chapter, to Martin Buber's celebrated account of the 'I-Thou' relation, as a forceful and influential example of what it means to stress religious experience as the 'avenue' to God.

William James

Life and character

William James (1842–1910), one of America's best-known philosophers and psychologists, was a leading figure in the development of the philosophy of pragmatism. His book *The Principles of Psychology* (1890) is universally acknowledged as a classic in its field, and an important landmark in the early development of that discipline. Among his other works are *The Varieties of Religious Experience* (1902), *Pragmatism* (1907), *A Pluralistic Universe* (1909), and *Essays in Radical Empiricism* (1912).

William James was a member of an unusually talented family circle. His brother was the famous novelist Henry James. (There is the frequently repeated remark that William wrote psychology like a novelist, whereas Henry wrote novels like a psychologist.) William James was born in New York City in 1842. His early development profited from the stimulation of a lively and spirited home environment, one that encouraged in its members the cultivation of independence of mind. William, very often in the company of his brother Henry, had the benefit of attending schools in England, France, Germany, and Switzerland. From an early age, he showed an interest in natural science and painting. (He even had serious plans, at one point, of becoming a professional painter!) He entered Harvard in 1861, with concentrations, at first, in chemistry, comparative anatomy, and physiology. In 1864 he entered Harvard Medical School, from which he received his degree in 1869. Instead of going into medical practice, however, James remained at Harvard as a member of the faculty, teaching at first anatomy and physiology, later giving courses in psychology, and eventually joining the philosophy department. (Other famous colleagues in the philosophy department who were his contemporaries included Josiah Royce and George Santayana.)

The various accounts of James's character as given by those who knew him, and also his extensive and lively correspondence, show him to have been a warm, charming, sensitive, and convivial person. Still, he suffered on a number of occasions from periods of deep depression and experienced

William James

the unsettling effects of spiritual crises. He was able, however, to emerge from these with a renewed faith in life. And his letters indicate that what helped him was the activity of philosophical thought. This thinking-through of alternatives played an important role in rescuing him from these periods of soul-sickness and in restoring his will to live. Philosophy, for James, was not solely an intellectual, dispassionate, 'academic' exercise. It lay at the very core of his being and had a deep personal meaning for him.

The Right to Believe in the Religious Hypothesis

In his essays "The Sentiment of Rationality" (1879) and "The Will to Believe" (1896) as well as in his other writings, James challenges the view of rationalists in philosophy along with those who adopt the position that all our beliefs must be guided entirely by reason and not go beyond what already available evidence allows us to affirm. James argues that especially

The legitimate role of faith

in the matter of determining our philosophical beliefs there are a variety of factors—or, to put it somewhat differently, various sides of our human nature—that not only *do* but also rightfully *should* play their role in causing us to make this or that commitment. "Pretend what we may," he says, "the whole man within us is at work when we form our philosophical opinions. Intellect, will, taste, and passion co-operate just as they do in practical affairs. . . . The absurd abstraction of an intellect verbally formulating all its evidence and carefully estimating the probability thereof by a vulgar fraction by the size of whose denominator and numerator alone it is swayed, is ideally as inept as it is actually impossible."[2]

When it is a matter of making up our minds about our most fundamental beliefs and commitments, James *argued for* the legitimate place of *faith* in justifying our choice of beliefs. The very title of James's essay "The *Will* to Believe" was, as he remarked later, a "luckless title, which should have been 'Right to Believe'."[3] In connection with religious beliefs, specifically, James is *not* simply asking us to blindly commit ourselves to a belief in God. He is not simply saying "Have faith!" or "Believe in God!" As a philosopher, he wishes to show that it is *reasonable* for men to have *faith* or to believe in God: that we have a *right* to believe in God, because that right itself can be justified as reasonable. In Chapter 5, I made a distinction between the simple use of the method of faith on the one hand and the use of *rational arguments* to support the use of the *method* of faith on the other. James's discussion clearly falls into the latter category. He proposes to give "a *defence* [my italics] of our right to adopt a believing attitude in religious matters, in spite of the fact that our merely logical intellect may not have been coerced."[4]

The *right* to believe, as James goes on to make his point, is the right to take certain matters on *faith*, even where there is insufficient evidence or reason to warrant the adoption of those beliefs.

Now, there is one element of our active nature which the Christian religion has emphatically recognized, but which philosophers as a rule have with great insincerity tried to huddle out of sight in their pretension to found systems of absolute certainty. I mean the element of faith. Faith means belief in something concerning which doubt is still theoretically possible; and as the test of belief is willingness to act, one may say that faith is the readiness to act in a cause the prosperous issue of which is not certified to us in advance. It is in fact the same moral quality which we call courage in practical affairs; and there will be a very widespread tendency in men of vigorous nature to enjoy a certain amount of uncertainty in their philosophic creed, just as risk lends a zest to worldly activity.[5]

James points out that there are many occasions in the conduct of our daily practical affairs when our faith in certain matters, even where the evidence is not all in, plays a crucial role in making certain results come about. Without the presence of faith as a kind of energizing force, the outcome of our actions and behavior might very well have been different from what it turned out to be because of the very presence of faith. It was the faith of the person that made the difference in what happened.

Suppose, for example, that I am climbing in the Alps, and have had the ill-luck to work myself into a position from which the only escape is by a terrific leap. Being without similar experience, I have no evidence of my ability to perform it successfully; but hope and confidence in myself make me sure I shall not miss my aim, and nerve my feet to execute what without those subjective emotions would perhaps have been impossible. But suppose that, on the contrary, the emotions of fear and mistrust preponderate; or suppose that . . . I feel it would be sinful to act upon an assumption unverified by previous experience,—why, then I shall hesitate so long that at last, exhausted and trembling, and launching myself in a moment of despair, I miss my foothold and roll into the abyss. In this case (and it is one of an immense class) the part of wisdom clearly is to believe what one desires; for the belief is one of the indispensable preliminary conditions of the realization of its object. There are then cases where faith creates its own verification. Believe, and you shall be right, for you shall save yourself; doubt, and you shall again be right, for you shall perish. The only difference is that to believe is greatly to your advantage.[6]

It is important not to misinterpret the point that James is making here. He is *not* saying that we can make anything at all come about merely by thinking or willing it to be so!

Can we, just by willing it, believe that Abraham Lincoln's existence is a myth, and that the portraits of him . . . . are all of someone else? Can we, by any effort of our will, or by any strength of wish that it were true, believe ourselves well and about when we are roaring with rheumatism in bed, or feel certain that the sum of the two one-dollar bills in our pocket must be a hundred dollars? We can say any of these things, but we are absolutely impotent to believe them; and of just such things is the whole fabric of the truths that we do believe in made up,—matters of fact, immediate or remote, as Hume said, and relations between ideas, which are either there or not there for us if we see them so, and which if not there cannot be put there by any action of our own.[7]

What James is arguing for is that where there is a margin of doubt about the possible outcome of a certain *action* on our behalf, then in many cases a person's strong faith and commitment to bring about a particular result will often tip the scales and be effective in getting that very result.

There are many situations in life when the adoption of a certain attitude in dealing with people will bring about a result that would not be present

The role of faith in action and interpersonal relations

otherwise. Take the matter of friendship, for example. If I take a wholly standoffish attitude toward another person, and wait to see whether that person is reliable, kind, well-meaning, and responsible, etc., and do nothing to *be* friendly myself until the other person 'proves' himself to me—the chances are that no friendship between us will ever arise. To *have* a friend one must *be* a friend. I must have faith in the other person and act in a way that shows that faith. And my very acting in this trusting way will normally bring about the result of getting the other person to respond in the same way. "How many women's hearts are vanquished by the mere sanguine insistence of some man that they *must* love him! . . . The desire for a certain kind of truth here brings about that special truth's existence. . . ."8

The importance of faith for religious belief

If we are prepared to recognize the role of faith as a valuable component in determining our practical commitments and interpersonal relationships, then, as a next crucial step, James proposes that we give the same weight to the role of faith in determining religious beliefs. For here, in one sense, the stakes are even higher than they are in the ordinary range of daily practical affairs. The choice we are faced with as to whether to accept the 'religious hypothesis' transcends in importance any other choice.

Genuine options: forced, living, and momentous

The matter of adopting the 'religious hypothesis' is what James calls a 'genuine' option. A genuine option is one that is *forced, living,* and *momentous.* Some options, he points out, are living, others dead; some forced, others avoidable; some momentous, others trivial.

1. A *living* option is one in which both hypotheses are live ones. If I say to you: "Be a theosophist or be a Mohammedan," it is probably a dead option, because for you neither hypothesis is likely to be alive. But if I say: "Be an agnostic or be a Christian," it is otherwise: trained as you are, each hypothesis makes some appeal, however small, to your belief.

2. Next, if I say to you: "Choose between going out with your umbrella or without it," I do not offer you a genuine option, for it is not forced. You can easily avoid it by not going out at all. Similarly, if I say, "Either love me or hate me," "Either call my theory true or call it false," your option is avoidable. You may remain indifferent to me, neither loving nor hating, and you may decline to offer any judgment as to my theory. But if I say, "Either accept this truth or go without it," I put on you a forced option, for there is no standing place outside of the alternative. Every dilemma based on a complete logical disjunction, with no possibility of not choosing, is an option of this forced kind.

3. Finally, if I were Dr. Nansen and proposed to you to join my North Pole expedition, your option would be momentous; for this would probably be your only similar opportunity, and your choice now would either exclude you from the North Pole sort of immortality altogether or put at least the chance of it

into your hands. He who refuses to embrace a unique opportunity loses the prize as surely as if he tried and failed. Per contra, the option is trivial when the opportunity is not unique, when the stake is insignificant, or when the decision is reversible if it later prove unwise. Such trivial options abound in the scientific life. A chemist finds an hypothesis live enough to spend a year in its verification: he believes in it to that extent. But if his experiments prove inconclusive either way, he is quit for his loss of time, no vital harm being done.[9]

By the phrase 'the religious hypothesis' James means, in part, the belief that "the best things are the more eternal things, the overlapping things, the things in the universe that throw the last stone, so to speak, and say the final word. . . . 'Perfection is eternal'."[10] This formula is of course quite vague. James doesn't stop in this passage to analyze what he means by 'the best things' or the 'overlapping things'; and the expression *'more eternal'* comes dangerously close to being sheer nonsense. Still, if we make allowances for the looseness and characteristic exuberance of James's language, it would not be a serious misinterpretation of his intent to suppose that James is here conveying the ordinary, common religious belief in the existence of God, of a being that is perfect and eternal, one whose justice, mercy, and love will insure the eventual triumph of goodness in the entire scheme of things. James's theism is a form of cosmic optimism.

'The religious hypothesis'

James's view is that the attempt to *prove* the existence of a Perfect Being is a total failure. Intellectually, there is no convincing evidence, no argument, that constrains us to adopt this belief. On the other hand, there is no disproof either. There is no counterevidence that obliges us to deny the existence of God. If we were to rely on available evidence of one sort or another, James maintains, the situation would be a stalemate, a deadlock. We can neither prove nor disprove the existence of God on rational grounds or on the basis of the facts of ordinary experience.

"Well," you might say, "if you can't prove something one way or another, the proper thing to do is to suspend judgment. Don't commit yourself." This response is especially favored by those who take a 'scientific' or 'rational' way of looking at things. "No evidence, no belief!" Indeed, the case can be made even stronger. It could be said that to commit oneself in the *absence* of evidence, or on the basis of *insufficient evidence*, is positively irrational and to be avoided at all costs. This view was forcefully stated by one of James's contemporaries, the mathematician and philosopher of science W. K. Clifford, in a famous essay entitled "The Ethics of Belief." James regarded Clifford's position as wholly erroneous, and he repeatedly attacked it. Clifford writes:

Rejection of the scientific model as not applicable to the religious hypothesis

[Belief] is desecrated when given to unproved and unquestioned statements, for the solace and private pleasure of the believer. . . . If the belief has been

accepted on insufficient evidence, the pleasure is a stolen one. Not only does it deceive ourselves by giving us a sense of power which we do not really possess, but it is sinful, because it is stolen in defiance of our duty to mankind. That duty is to guard ourselves from such beliefs as from a pestilence, which may shortly master our own body and then spread to the rest of the town. . . . It is wrong always, everywhere, and for anyone to believe anything upon insufficient evidence.[11]

The strength of this claim lies in expressing the day-to-day attitude of the working scientist. In science, the proper stance is: Wait till you get enough evidence to enable you to say whether a given hypothesis or statement is true or false. "Go out and get the evidence," the typical scientist will say, "perform the tests, make the necessary observations and experiments that will provide you with the required evidence to either confirm and uphold a given hypothesis or to disconfirm it. And if there is no evidence one way or the other, or insufficient evidence, well, then, the proper thing to do is *suspend judgment*. There is no warrant in plunging in before the matter can be settled by the evidence." And this attitude of the scientist is surely a warranted and sane one in purely intellectual or theoretical inquiries about the various phenomena and events in the world. A scientist is not forced to come to a decision. He can wait (or, better, the community of scientists can wait) indefinitely until adequate evidence becomes available. The searcher for truth can be patient and need not rush to make a decision.

It is at this point, however, that James parts company with Clifford and all those who insist that *all* our beliefs should be modeled on scientific ones. *That* attitude may be sound enough for the working scientist. However, James argues, it does not hold and should not be expected to apply to the matter of adopting a *religious belief*. Here, suspension of belief until the evidence is in is inappropriate. In this respect a religious belief is unlike a scientific judgment. We cannot afford to wait indefinitely until all the evidence, or at any rate a sufficient amount of evidence, is in before committing ourselves.

To this extent, the adoption of a religious belief is closer to and more like the adoption of a *practical* judgment of action. We have to make up our minds now, or within a definite time; we cannot postpone the decision indefinitely. Even a reasonable man who is caught in a burning building has to make up his mind what to do. He can, of course, make a quick assessment of the situation (of what exits to head for, what path to follow, etc.), but he cannot postpone a decision indefinitely. If he does (if he 'sits on the fence'), that is already reaching a decision, and he will suffer the consequences. So, in general, in matters of practical affairs, even to be guided by reasons and evidence is different from the purely theoretical context of the inquiring scientist. Action is required. A decision has to be made within a certain time; one may have a near 'deadline', or one of a more extended sort—but act one must. The same need to make up our minds and not postpone a decision indefinitely holds true for a religious belief as much as for a practical belief. It is, in James's language, *forced*.

James argues that when it comes to the adoption of a religious belief our 'will' or 'passional nature' has a right to intervene in our making a decision. It cannot be left entirely up to our intellect to decide, or to a dispassionate, neutral, evidence-gathering interest of a purely scientific mentality.

The contribution of the 'will' to believe

Our passional nature not only lawfully may, but must, decide an option between propositions, whenever it is a genuine option that cannot by its nature be decided on intellectual grounds; for to say, under such circumstances, "Do not decide, but leave the question open," is itself a passional decision,—just like deciding yes or no,—and is attended with the same risk of losing the truth.[12]

Not only is the decision about religion a matter in which our 'passional nature' has a legitimate and indeed unavoidable role to play, but to deny, on purely intellectual grounds, our right to make a decision in the absence of evidence would itself be the height of foolishness. It would be irrational. James writes:

I, therefore, for one, cannot see my way to accepting the agnostic rules for truth-seeking, or willfully agree to keep my willing nature out of the game. I cannot do so for this plain reason, that a rule of thinking which would absolutely prevent me from acknowledging certain kinds of truth if those kinds of truth were really there, would be an irrational rule.[13]

James gives basically two reasons for this position.

Pascal's wager

(1) The first reason James gives has a certain kinship with an argument presented by Blaise Pascal (1623–1662), the great French mathematician. James sums up Pascal's argument as follows:

In Pascal's Thoughts *there is a celebrated passage known in literature as Pascal's wager. In it he tries to force us into Christianity by reasoning as if our concern with truth resembled our concern with the stakes in a game of chance. Translated freely his words are these: You must either believe or not believe that God is—which will you do? Your human reason cannot say. A game is going on between you and the nature of things which at the day of judgment will bring out either heads or tails. Weigh what your gains and your losses would be if you should stake all you have on heads, or God's existence: if you win in such case, you gain eternal beatitude; if you lose, you lose nothing at all. If there were an infinity of chances, and only one for God in this wager, still you ought to stake your all on God; for though you surely risk a finite loss by this procedure, any finite loss is reasonable, even a certain one is reasonable, if there is but the possibility of infinite gain. Go then, and take holy water, and have masses said; belief will come and stupefy your scruples. . . . Why should you not? At bottom, what have you to lose?*[14]

In a similar vein, James points out that the option of casting our vote in favor of the religious hypothesis is one whose stakes are so high that it would be wholly irrational for a person to withhold making a positive decision on the grounds that he may be making a mistake, that he may be committing himself to a falsehood! James maintains that the sceptic or agnostic who denies himself the opportunity to adopt a belief in God because he does not have sufficient evidence is cutting himself off from all possible benefits of this belief.

To preach scepticism to us as a duty until 'sufficient evidence' for religion be found, is tantamount therefore to telling us, when in presence of the religious hypothesis, that to yield to our fear of its being error is wiser and better than to yield to our hope that it may be true. It is not intellect against all passions, then; it is only intellect with one passion laying down its law. And by what, forsooth, is the supreme wisdom of this passion warranted? Dupery for dupery, what proof is there that dupery through hope is so much worse than dupery through fear? I, for one, can see no proof; and I simply refuse obedience to the scientist's command to imitate his kind of option, in a case where my own stake is important enough to give me the right to choose my own form of risk. If religion be true and the evidence for it be still insufficient, I do not wish, by putting your extinguisher upon my nature . . . to forfeit my sole chance in life of getting upon the winning side,—that chance depending, of course, on my willingness to run the risk of acting as if my passional need of taking the world religiously might be prophetic and right.[15]

Pragmatic benefits of religious belief

(2) James makes a second point in support of the right to cast our vote for the religious hypothesis. It is not merely that, if there is an afterlife, a genuine belief in God would have its rewards in the afterlife. Another important reason for adopting the religious hypothesis is that a belief in God has beneficial consequences in *this* life here on Earth, and for as long as we are alive. A life based on religion and its code of ethics makes a difference: it is more rewarding than a life in which a belief in God is absent. "The second affirmation of religion is that we are better off even now if we believe her first affirmation [the belief in God's existence] to be true."[16] On the whole, James argues, the underlying 'set' or attitude toward ourselves and other persons that religion makes possible, as we go through life, is of a more desirable sort than is characteristic of those who lack

religious beliefs and commitments. James, as a pragmatist who takes into account the beneficial consequences of *having* a belief in religion, offers this fact as an argument in favor of subscribing to the religious hypothesis.

Since belief is measured by action, he who forbids us to believe religion to be true, necessarily also forbids us to act as we should if we did believe it to be true. The whole defense of religious faith hinges upon action. If the action required or inspired by the religious hypothesis is in no way different from that dictated by the naturalistic hypothesis, then religious faith is a pure superfluity, better pruned away, and controversy about its legitimacy is a piece of idle trifling, unworthy of serious minds. I myself believe, of course, that the religious hypothesis gives to the world an expression which specifically determines our reactions, and makes them in a large part unlike what they might be on a purely naturalistic scheme of belief.[17]

Insofar as the having of a positive commitment to religion affects our daily actions and the attitude we take to the world, there are *no practical differences* between the *agnostic* and the *atheist*. For whereas the agnostic *'suspends judgment'* about God's existence and the atheist *denies* that there is a God, the *practical* differences between the two disappear as far as conduct is concerned. For in suspending judgment the agnostic is not any more ready or willing to let the belief in God and God's moral guidance affect his own behavior than is the atheist. Both the atheist and the agnostic, then, are to be contrasted with the believing and 'yea-saying' theist. In this respect, both the agnostic and atheist cut themselves off from the benefits that flow from having a religious commitment at the core of one's being.

Doubt itself is a decision of the widest practical reach, if only because we may miss by doubting what goods we might be gaining by espousing the winning side. But more than that! it is often practically impossible to distinguish doubt from dogmatic negation. If I refuse to stop a murder because I am in doubt whether it be not justifiable homicide, I am virtually abetting the crime. If I refuse to bale out a boat because I am in doubt whether my efforts will keep her afloat, I am really helping to sink her. If in the mountain precipice I doubt my right to risk a leap, I actively connive at my destruction. He who commands himself not to be credulous of God, of duty, of freedom, of immortality, may again and again be indistinguishable from him who dogmatically denies them.[18]

What, however, are these practical benefits of religion that affect one's daily conduct and life 'here and now'? Why is it reasonable or advantageous, on pragmatic grounds, to believe in God and his moral code? Unfortunately, James does not say, explicitly, what are the supposed beneficial effects of having religious beliefs.[19] But he undoubtedly took for granted that these are too well known to require any elaboration on his part. Thus it is a commonly confirmed fact that persons with a strong religious faith are frequently able to maintain a remarkable serenity and strength in the face of adversity and the assorted calamities and tragedies with which everyone's life is to some degree filled. Religious faith in God's goodness enables individuals possessed of such faith to bear up in the face of life's evils in a manner that clearly differentiates them from those who, without religious faith or comparable resources, frequently 'go to pieces'. Further, insofar as one really *practices* the virtues central to a religiously sanctioned moral code such as that of Christianity—such virtues as love, compassion, humility, forbearance, charity, hope—one's own life and the lives of other persons benefited by these virtues become that much more satisfying and rewarding.

Critical Evaluation of James's Argument

James's arguments for the right to believe in the religious hypothesis, as we have seen, reduce to two principal claims: (1) We have no totally satisfactory evidence of a direct, testable sort either to support or to challenge the religious hypothesis. In the absence of such positive or negative evidence, we have a right to allow our passional nature to decide in favor of the religious hypothesis. We have a right therefore to choose that religious belief which is genuine (live, momentous, and forced). (2) The right to believe in the religious hypothesis is justified in terms of the benefits that such a belief brings to its adherents. Men's lives on earth are the better for having such a belief.

Let us consider now the soundness of the foregoing claims.

The 'right' to believe and the question of truth

(1) The right to believe, as James interprets this in the context of religion, is the right to gamble on, guess at, or opt for the *truth* of some particular worldview (or conception of God) as developed in some religion or other. I have the right, that is, to expect that, by adopting this belief, I have chosen what is *true:* that I have chosen a belief which corresponds with the nature of ultimate reality. Notice, however, that James himself acknowledges we have no way of *knowing* (on the basis of ordinary intellectual grounds of testable evidence or logical arguments) whether some particular religious hypothesis (with its metaphysical conception of God) is in fact true. In the absence of arguments or evidence all we can do, and have the right to do, he claims, is *choose* a particular religious hypothesis. But if what is basically involved is gambling, opting, or guessing, then we immediately have the right to ask what makes any one guess, option, or gamble *better* than another? If I choose (opt for, guess at, gamble on) religious hypothesis A and someone else chooses

religious hypothesis *B*, and someone else hypothesis *C*, . . . , etc., do I have any greater claim to the *truth* of *A* than the others have for the *truth* of *B*, *C*, . . . , etc.? No, I do not. Each of us has *the same right to believe* (to opt, gamble, guess). But insofar as different religious hypotheses make *different* claims about the nature of God and the character of ultimate reality, *they can't all be true, since they conflict with one another.* A Muslim's view of God is different from that of a Christian, and each of these, in turn, is different from that of a Jew.

James insists that a religious option has to be genuine, that is (among other things), *live*. Normally the question of which religious hypothesis to adopt (on the assumption that a person wished to make such a choice) is severely restricted in terms of family background, cultural inheritance, geographical region, and so on. Yet if certain options are 'dead' for particular individuals, these same 'dead' options may be very much *alive* for other individuals who come from a different family background, geographical region, or culture. And surely that other individual has as much right (on Jamesian principles) to opt for *his* live option as I have for my own. Yet why is mine any better—in the sense of assuring me of the *truth* of my option—than his? Obviously not only do I not have any such assurance, but also when all of us exercise our respective *live* options (or guesses or gambles) we can't all be choosing *the* truth; for these are incompatible with one another, and incompatible hypotheses cannot all be true. Indeed, it may be that none of them is! What this all comes down to, then, is that the right to believe is the right to guess or gamble. However, this is not to be equated with having reliable grounds for claiming that one has *knowledge* of the truth. *Believing* (in the sense of 'faith') is not knowledge of the truth. And if what is wanted is having a *true* metaphysical world view, then the right to believe, in James's sense, is not the way to obtain knowledge of the truth.

(2) The whole approach to religion in terms of 'gambling', opting for a hypothesis, or 'guessing' at the truth does violence to the very nature of religion. The language of guessing and gambling is simply inappropriate to what is involved in being devout, pious, or worshipful. A truly religious person, it will be said, does not *calculate* his or her possible losses or gains, or choose what he or she hopes will bring the greatest gain.

Moreover, even if one could reduce or eliminate this element of cold calculation, by being conditioned through repeated participation in certain rituals and ceremonies, or by being immersed constantly in certain ways of life, prayers, attendance at church, etc., this, too, at best has to do with the psychological fact that one can be programmed to 'believe' by these means. But such deliberate conditioning, however successful, in no way establishes the *truth* of one's beliefs. Obviously, the same or an equivalent type of (deliberate) programming, conditioning, or brainwash-

The irrelevance of calculation to religious commitment

*Pragmatic tests for the
truth of a statement and
of having a belief*

ing could be undertaken by altogether different religions with equally effective results. Once again, however, since the various religious philosophies are incompatible with one another, the fact of such *psychological effectiveness* tells us nothing about the *truth* of the beliefs so engendered.

(3) It is important to make a distinction between two things about which James is not always clear. One is the statement "God exists," and the other is the having of the belief in the truth of the statement "God exists." Offhand it might seem as if there is no distinction between the two. Yet this would be a mistake. The statement "God exists" is a statement that, as James himself acknowledges, is *untestable*. Its *truth* cannot be established by an appeal to any experience in support of the statement itself. Nevertheless, a person may have the belief in the truth of the statement "God exists." And the fact that a person *has* that belief and *acts* in accordance with it—that fact of having a belief in God *does* have consequences in his or her life. The merit or otherwise of having that belief *is* testable in experience. One can observe the effect that the having of the belief has on a person. Now James, as a pragmatist, was interested in stressing that it is better for us to have a belief in God than not to have it.

Let us grant that we can observe the *quality of the lives of the individuals affected by having the belief in God*. Let us grant, too, for the sake of the argument, that these are *beneficial consequences*. Does this in any way establish the *truth* or *falsity* of the statement "God exists"? There are times when James would seem to run these two matters together. But this is an outright error and philosophic fallacy. The two matters are entirely separate and distinct. The truth of the statement "God exists" must be distinguished from the belief that *it is a good thing to believe* that God exists. The truth or falsity of the statement "God exists" cannot itself be tested in experience. *Even if the having of the belief that God exists is testable* in *the quality of the life of the person* who has that belief, this has *no bearing whatsoever on the truth or the falsity of the statement "God exists."* If the statement "God exists" is untestable, that is the end of the matter. The fact that the having of a belief in God has effects on a person's life does not mean that those effects on his or her life establish the truth of the statement "God exists."

It is easy to confuse what the pragmatic test amounts to when it concerns two different types of beliefs. The first is a belief whose consequences in conduct and practice *do* determine the truth or falsity of the belief. The other is a belief in a statement where the statement cannot itself be tested in experience, yet where the having of the belief in such in untestable statement *does* have consequences in experience. Suppose, for example, I have a belief in the truth of the statement "Drinking six glasses of milk a day is good for me." This statement is testable. Indeed, if I act in accordance with my belief in the *truth* of this statement, it may turn out, as a matter of fact, that the statement is *false*. Drinking six glasses of milk a day is *not* a good thing for me. In this case, I test both the statement and the having of the belief in the (supposed) truth of the statement in the same way. I look to the consequences. And in this case the consequences of having the belief serve at the same time to test the truth or falsity of the statement.

Now consider the case where the statement in which I have a belief is itself *untestable*. And let this statement be "God exists. . . ." A person may have a belief in the truth of this statement. Let him act on the basis of having this belief. And let the consequences of having this belief be beneficial to the person as far as his life is concerned. As contrasted with the 'milk' case previously considered, there is a difference here between the statement "God exists. . . ," which is untestable in anybody's experience, and the having of a belief in the truth of this statement. The having of this belief *does* have consequences in the quality of life of a person. However, we cannot appeal to the consequences of having a belief in God on *a person's life* to determine, at the same time and by the very same facts, the truth or falsity of the statement "God exists. . . ." This is where the 'milk' case and the 'God' case are entirely different. And if James or anyone else thinks he is using the *same* type of pragmatic test in both cases, he is simply mistaken.

Summary

To sum up: Faith and the right to believe in God can be invoked only at the very most to justify certain beneficial results from having a belief in God. Faith can move mountains, and a religious faith in God *might* make our lives happier. But even if this is the case, the faith doesn't create the fact of God's existence. One cannot, by willing to believe in God, bring God into existence. And this matter of God's existence, which is at the heart of theistic metaphysics, is what we have been all along concerned with. The Jamesian pragmatic argument in behalf of a right to believe, if this is interpreted as a support for the truth of the statement "God exists," therefore has no validity whatever.

chapter 9

I-Thou

Our discussion thus far of the philosophy of theism has focused on the matter of warranting the belief in the existence of God in a way that would satisfy the requirements of philosophic criticism. We first surveyed, in connection with the ontological and cosmological arguments, two classic attempts to prove the existence of God by *inferring* his existence from certain premisses. We then turned to James's pragmatic argument and met there another attempt to justify a belief in God in terms of the *consequences* of such a belief for human life, in this world or the next. We have seen various difficulties with and objections to these different types of arguments and approaches. Indeed, according to some persons the failure of theology and philosophy to give such adequate rational justification for a belief in God means that religion is bankrupt. Religion and belief in God, they would say, belong to an 'infantile' stage in human thought. A mature, thinking individual will see through the naivetes and futilities of clinging to an outworn way of thinking. Such a person will turn to a more sober, honest, and 'realistic' way of looking at the world and man's place in it.

Martin Buber

But not everyone would agree with this conclusion. And before we move on to consider the world outlook of naturalism, we must stop to

Martin Buber

examine a recent arresting attempt to show the profound importance and appeal of a religious response to the world. Such an attempt is found in the work of Martin Buber. Indeed, he himself would probably agree with virtually all the criticisms of traditional attempts to warrant the belief in God that we have ourselves rehearsed. Yet this would not mean, for him, that religion is bankrupt; on the contrary, it would only mean that we have looked in the wrong place for the essence of religious experience and what it has to offer.

The essence of religious experience for Buber is to be found in what he describes by the use of the various terms 'dialogue', 'encounter', 'relation', and 'meeting'. *God is not an object or entity whose existence is to be inferred. God is a Presence to be addressed.* If we lack the power to address God we shall never meet him. And if we rely on thought and philosophic analyses alone, we surely shall not meet him. Indeed, in the 'court' of thought where conceptual analysis and critical evaluation of arguments are the only tools at hand or voices heard, God is not to be

Religious experience

found at all. And that 'court' has been right in turning in a verdict of 'not proven' when it comes to establishing the existence of God.

To the man who is no longer able to meet yet is able as ever to think, the only possible religious question is whether man can ascertain the existence of the gods. This question, in the absence of any experience, must be answered in the negative.[1]

It is not as if God could be inferred from anything—say, from nature as its cause, or from history as its helmsman, or perhaps from the subject as the self that thinks itself through it. It is not as if something else were "given" and this were then deduced from it.[2]

For Buber the stress must be on religious experience. And, in appealing to 'religious experience', he is not offering us another *argument* based on experience to warrant belief. He does not appeal to voices, visions, revelations of a private and esoteric sort, witnesses to miracles, and the like, all of which some would appeal to as the basis for *inferring* the existence of God and his workings as the only way of *explaining* these phenomena. Buber's appeal to religious experience is not to be taken in the sense of evidence marshalled for an argument, from which one may infer, by way of explanation, that these 'experiences' are signs of God's means of communication with men.

Buber himself does not particularly favor the use of the term 'experience' (since he takes it to mean something subjective, internal, and a matter only of 'feelings'). However, I shall continue to use it to encompass the sort of thing he is really stressing. For experience need not be thought of as merely subjective. It has to do with all sorts and modes of human interaction and relationships. For Buber, religious experience is what is of ultimate value. Neither theology nor philosophy can lead the way to God. Not even *religion* can do so, if this is understood in the sense of a set of fixed practices and a dogmatic creed. In this sense, Buber writes, "the primal danger of man is 'religion'."[3] Genuine religious experience leads to no conclusions and needs no explanation. Buber disclaims being a theologian; he has no intellectual system of beliefs about God that he is concerned to uphold by means of arguments and polemics. He reports on his own personal experiences, and in doing so, by the very authenticity and genuineness of his language, recalls the language of others for whom religious experience is a first-hand matter, not a set of doctrines learned and derived at second-hand.

Moreover the religious is not some esoteric and special domain of experience to be found on special occasions, for example, in the performance of special rites and ceremonies or the celebration of holidays. If to be religious (as this is understood in the ordinary way by most people) is to be a 'religious believer', then Buber is *not* religious in this sense. He shed orthodoxy and conventional adherence to religion early in his life. He recounts an event (at the time of World War I, when he was in his late thirties) in which this distinction between conventional religiosity and what *he* means by religious experience was brought home to him forcefully.

In my earlier years the "religious" was for me the exception. There were hours that were taken out of the course of things. . . . "Religious experience" was the experience of an otherness which did not fit into the context of life. . . . The "religious" lifted you out. Over there now lay the accustomed existence with its affairs, but here illumination and ecstasy and rapture held, without time or sequence. . . . The illegitimacy of such a division of the temporal life . . . was brought home to me by an everyday event, an event of judgment, judging with that sentence from closed lips and an unmoved glance such as the ongoing course of things loves to pronounce.

What happened was no more than that one forenoon, after a morning of "religious" enthusiasm, I had a visit from an unknown young man, without being there in spirit. I certainly did not fail to let the meeting be friendly, I did not treat him any more remissly than all his contemporaries who were in the habit of seeking me out about this time of day as an oracle that is ready to listen to reason. I conversed attentively and openly with him—only I omitted to guess the questions which he did not put. Later, not long after, I learned from one of his friends—he himself was no longer alive—the essential content of these questions; I learned that he had come to me not casually, but borne by destiny, not for a chat but for a decision. . . . What do we expect when we are in despair and yet go to a man? Surely a presence by means of which we are told that nevertheless there is meaning.

Since then I have given up the "religious" which is nothing but the exception, extraction, exaltation, ecstasy; or it has given me up. I possess nothing but the everyday out of which I am never taken . . . I know no fulness but each mortal hour's fulness of claim and responsibility. Though far from being equal to it, yet I know that in the claim I am claimed and may respond in responsibility, and know who speaks and demands a response.

I do not know much more. If that is religion then it is just everything, simply all that is lived in its possibility of dialogue. Here is space also for religion's highest forms.[4]

The 'religious', then, for Buber is coextensive with life, not a separate 'dimension' or 'part' of it.

To be religious is to be able to respond as an 'I' in a *dialogue*. We are, Buber keeps reminding us, constantly being *addressed*: by other persons, by animals, even by trees and stones, and, of course, by God. But most men have built up an 'armor' that shields them from receiving these 'signs' or 'addresses'. Most men are incapable of engaging in a dialogue, although they might be able to deal most efficiently and responsibly with the world on another level—with people and things as objects to be understood in a detached way, or to be manipulated and controlled. To be religious, in Buber's sense, is to reopen or deepen our capacities for dialogue—for meeting and encountering other persons, the world about us, and God (as God 'shows' himself in and through the world), as partners in an 'I-Thou' dialogue.*

Buber: biographical data   Martin Buber was born in 1878 in Vienna. When he was three years old his parents separated, and he went to live with his paternal grandparents in Lemberg (at that time the capital of Galicia, Austria, today called Lvov, and part of the Soviet Union). His grandfather, Solomon Buber, was a distinguished rabbinic scholar. The home of his grandfather was filled with an atmosphere of piety and learning. In it Martin received a thorough grounding in the heritage of Jewish thought, as well as a love for such classic German writers as Goethe, Heine, and Schiller. After leaving his grandparents' house at the age of fourteen, the young man discontinued all formal religious observances. He studied philosophy and art history at the University of Vienna, continued his studies at Leipzig and Zurich, and obtained his doctorate in 1904 at the University of Berlin. The works of Nietzsche, Dostoyevsky, and Kierkegaard were early influences on his thought. During this early period of his life, while settled in Germany, Buber became involved in the emerging Zionist movement. It was about this time, too, that he also started on his lifelong research into the movement of Hasidism.† Buber found in Hasidism a rich vein of

---

* Buber brings to full fruition and explicitness a point made almost tangentially by William James in his "Will to Believe." James had written:

The more perfect and more eternal aspect of the universe is presented in our religions as having personal form. The universe is no longer a mere It to us, but a Thou, if we are religious; and any relation that may be possible from person to person might be possible here.[5]

What we find in Buber's philosophy is the flowering of this idea, but divested of all 'pragmatic' arguments and supports. I am not suggesting that Buber got the inspiration for his philosophy from James. On the contrary, there were other more explicitly acknowledged forerunners of this thought. For Buber's own listing of these, see "Afterword: The History of the Dialogical Principle."[6]

† The Hasidic movement arose in Poland in the eighteenth century. The Hebrew term 'hasid' means 'pious'. The founder of the movement was Rabbi Israel Ben Eliezer (1700–1760), commonly known as the Master of the Good Name (of God)—Baal-Shem-Tov. Hasidism had one of its principal roots in the *Zohar*, a major text of medieval Jewish mysticism. In its own stress on joy, love, and fervor, Hasidism diverged radically from the hitherto dominant Rabbinic tradition and the latter's characteristic approach to religion in legalistic and intellectualistic terms.

direct, communal, intense, and joyful religious experience. It was something of that spirit that he tried to capture and incorporate in his own philosophy of dialogue and through his central thesis that "all real living is meeting." Buber summed up the message of Hasidism, as he saw it, in the following words:

The Hasidic teaching is the consummation of Judaism. And this is its message to all: You yourself must begin. Existence will remain meaningless for you if you yourself do not penetrate into it with active love and if you do not in this way discover its meaning for yourself. Everything is waiting to be hallowed by you; it is waiting to be disclosed in its meaning and to be realized in it by you. For the sake of this your beginning, God created the world. He has drawn it out of himself so that you may bring it closer to him. Meet the world with the fullness of your being and you shall meet him. That he himself accepts from your hands what you have to give to the world is his mercy. If you wish to believe, love![7]

From 1923 until 1933 Buber held the chair of Jewish philosophy and the history of religions at the University of Frankfurt-am-Main. He was forced to resign with the Nazi rise to power. In 1938 Buber left for Israel where he occupied the chair of social philosophy at the University of Jerusalem. In Israel, Buber was active on behalf of Jewish-Arab friendship and cooperation. Upon his retirement in 1951, Buber traveled to the United States where he lectured widely. He returned in 1957 for a series of lectures at the Washington School of Psychiatry. His fame was worldwide, and he was the recipient of many awards. Dag Hammarskjøld, the Secretary-General of the United Nations, and a close student of Buber's thought, nominated him for the Nobel Peace Prize. Buber died in Jerusalem in 1965 at the age of eighty-eight.

Of the many works of Buber, the most celebrated and influential is *I and Thou.** It contains the core of his thought and has been acclaimed

---

* The original title of Buber's work, in German, is *Ich und Du*. The first translation, by Ronald Gregor Smith, uses the term 'Thou' for 'Du' and the work has therefore come to be known as *I and Thou*. A later translation by Walter Kaufmann preserves the same *title* for the work as a whole, but translates 'Du' as 'You' in the text itself. However, in order to distinguish the special use of the term 'you' by Buber from its ordinary use, Kaufmann capitalizes it, and so employs the expression 'I-You' throughout. The term 'thou' is largely archaic, and has its sole remaining use in English translations of the Bible, particularly when used as a mode of address to God. Buber himself is especially concerned to show the continuity between the way in which persons address one another and the way in which they can also address and 'meet' God. In referring to the title of the work, I shall myself continue to use (as Kaufmann does) *I and Thou*. In quotations from Buber's text as translated by Kaufmann and in my discussions of these, I shall use the expression 'I-You', as he does. However, in my own reference to Buber's thought here and in other contexts in this book, I shall also use the expression 'I-Thou' as appropriate when referring to a person's relation to God.

by religious thinkers of all faiths as a religious classic of our times. Typical is the following statement by Father Donald J. Moore (a member of the Society of Jesus) in his book-length study of the thought of Buber:

I cannot speak for other religions, nor can I speak for other Christians, and I certainly cannot "baptize" Martin Buber, but I believe that in many areas his attitude and his thought are essentially one with Christianity. Or it might be better to say that we can see more clearly, because of the writings of Martin Buber, that in many areas genuine Christianity is in basic agreement with genuine Judaism. At least it must be said that we who call ourselves Christian would be much more faithful to our task and to our vocation if we could follow, each in his own way, the spirit of Buber. Perhaps Martin Buber should be called a man of universal religion, for he was indeed a man of God.[8]

Buber's ideas have had an especially strong impact on a number of contemporary Protestant theologians.* My own examination of Buber's thought will concentrate largely on the distinctions Buber works out in *I and Thou.*

The Distinction Between I-It and I-You

Buber draws a fundamental contrast between two ways in which human beings may experience the world about them. One of these is expressed by the use of the phrase 'I-It', the other by the phrase 'I-You'. The importance of this distinction is that ultimately man's relation to God can be described only in terms of the I-You relation, where God is the eternal, supreme, and unique Thou (or You). God can never be an It. However, in order to understand the nature of the relation between man and the Eternal Thou, we need first to understand the difference, in general, between I-It and I-You attitudes in man's relationships to beings other than God, for these can be of either an I-It or an I-You sort.

The two word pairs 'I-It' and 'I-You' are written in hyphenated form in order to stress the fact that the words 'I' and 'It' or 'I' and 'You' are not to be taken in isolation from one another. Thus the term 'I' has a different meaning when paired with 'It' than when paired with 'You'. The kind of 'I' I am when dealing with an 'It' is different from the kind of 'I' I am when my basic attitudes and mode of dealing with another entity are controlled and determined by an I-You relation. When, for example,

---

* For example, in the works of Emil Brunner, Herbert H. Farmer, Paul Tillich, and Karl Barth. See Maurice Friedman, *Martin Buber*, Chapter XXVII, for detailed references.

I deal with you as an *individual ego* (It), *I* am different because I take a different attitude or posture than when I respond to You as a *person.*

It is not the case . . . that the I in both relations, I-Thou and I-It, is the same. Rather where and when the beings around one are seen and treated as objects of observation, reflection, use, perhaps also of solicitude or help, there and then another I is spoken, another I manifested, another I exists than where and when one stands with the whole of one's being over against another being and steps into an essential relation with him. . . . Both together build up human existence; it is only a question of which of the two is at any particular time the architect and which is his assistant.[9]

No human being is pure person, and none is pure ego. . . . Each lives in a twofold I. But some men are so person-oriented that one may call them persons, while others are so ego-oriented that one may call them egos. Between these and those true history takes place.[10]

The first point to bear in mind in clarifying Buber's use of these word pairs is that the term 'It' (in the word pair 'I-It') is not restricted to inanimate objects or things. Anything in the world, including other human beings or animals, can be an It. Similarly, the You in the I-You relation is not restricted to other human beings or to God. Anything in the world, including even inanimate beings and animals, can, for Buber, enter into an I-You relation or meeting. In other words, anything whatsoever can be an It or a You; it all depends on which of the possibilities of a "two-fold" attitude open to us we adopt to the other entity.

Let us consider some examples of what Buber would identify as be- *I-It* longing to the domain of I-It relationships. Let us suppose I am traveling by car from New York to San Francisco. I rely on my car to get me there: my car is an It for me—a means of getting me from one place to another. When I go to a service station to get gas, the attendant who services my car is for me in that context normally just an It; he too is a means, helping me accomplish my end. Using a credit card, cashing a check at the bank, consulting a map, and asking a policeman for directions are also examples of my using Its. The same thing is true of my relationship to the motel keeper who assigns me a room for the night, the food I eat in a restaurant, and the waiter who serves me. And if I take ill and go to a hospital, the doctors and nurses, even though they are interested in my welfare, are also Its. I use them as Its to help me. And they in turn use me as an It—they treat my body's needs or they use me as a 'case' to illustrate something or other to a class of medical students making the rounds. Or a researching medical scientist may study me along with other cases to help establish some diagnostic or therapeutic generalization. If I am a journalist reporting to my newspaper or a writer gathering material for a study or a story, my experiences along the way (including the various events, people, objects, situations, places I visit, etc.) are all Its. The key words in all these interactions, by virtue of the underlying attitude I take to them, are those of *using something or someone as a means, controlling, planning, measuring, calculating, observing, reporting, manipulating, putting, finding or observing something in a certain order, place, sequence, causal connection, or means-end relationship,* and so on. In the foregoing examples, everything functions as an It. My car is an It; so are the gas station attendant, the doctor, the map I consult, the newspaper editor to whom I report, the road I travel on, etc. I am absorbed in an I-It world of relationships.

Nor is the I-It relationship in every instance to be denigrated. On the contrary. We cannot and should not try to dispense with (as if we could!) the network of I-It relationships. All of us spend much of our lives absorbed in such relationships, and must do so to some extent if we are going to survive or lead a satisfactory life. However, some people's lives are almost *completely* taken up with such I-It relationships. And Buber's point is that, however inescapable, desirable, and necessary an I-It attitude toward the world is, it is not, and should not be, all there is to human life. "Without It a human being cannot live. But whoever lives only with that is not human."[11] And he would deplore any philosophy or institutional and political scheme that attended simply to the I-It world of relationships, however accurately, efficiently, or benevolently it does so. Philosophies or social schemes that would do so leave out an important dimension of human existence. They keep us from being wholly human; they keep us from being *persons.* In an I-It world the I is an *individual ego,* not a *person.* Although the life of man can never dispense with I-It relationships, there is the ever present danger that all of life becomes absorbed in and dominated by such I-It relationships. Man then becomes dehumanized. And this, for Buber, as for many other critics and commentators, has become increasingly true of our modern world. We live in a world in which science, technology, economic activities, and power politics have come to dominate the warp and woof of our entire life and culture. Here is to be found the major disease of our time.

In our age the I-It relation, gigantically swollen, has usurped, practically uncontested, the mastery and the rule. The I of this relation, an I that possesses all, makes all, succeeds with all, this I that is unable to say Thou, unable to meet a being essentially, is the lord of the hour. This selfhood that has become omnipotent, with all the It around it, can naturally acknowledge neither God nor any genuine absolute which manifests itself to men as of nonhuman origin. It steps in between and shuts off from us the light of heaven. Such is the nature of this hour.[12]

The I-You relation into which a human being in his or her wholeness may enter takes us onto another level or dimension from that of the I-It relationship. In the course of entering into an I-You relation, the I that is engaged becomes different from the I that functions in an I-It relationship.

What, however, *is* the I-You relation? Whereas the I-It relationship, as described by Buber, is fairly straightforward, readily illustrated, and confirmed in ordinary experience, the same cannot be said about his description of the I-You relation. His account tends to verge on the poetic; it frequently is characterized by a good deal of vagueness. Moreover, some of his own illustrations are likely to arouse scepticism. Nevertheless, we can perhaps capture, with some reasonable clarity, the major features of what he intends by the I-You relation. Before we proceed to consider these, there are a number of preliminary points worth bearing in mind.

In the first place, Buber claims that the I-You relation is not restricted to relations between human beings. The I-You relation between *persons* is the most obvious, familiar, and readily confirmable kind of case. The I-You relation can also extend, however, to animals, plants, and inanimate objects; in short to all entities within the Universe whatever their nature. Any of these can be a You to my I. Finally, and at the other extreme, the I-You relation holds for man's relation to God, to the Eternal Thou (or Eternal You). Persons can use language to address one another and to enter into explicit dialogue with other human beings. However, Buber claims, we can also enter into dialogue with beings *other than* human beings. We can address and be addressed by such nonhuman beings even if it is not human language that serves as the medium of communication between us. Yet here too one can, for Buber, have an I-You relation. One can have an I-You relation, for example, with a stone, a tree, a horse. Moreover, the life of dialogue, at its most spiritually elevated level, is with God, the Eternal You (Thou).

There is another preliminary point worth making. It is not the case that the I-You relation is an 'all-or-none' affair. There are many cases in which only the barest hint or fleeting glimpse of an I-You relation may make its appearance. There are degrees of intensity with which it can be experienced. However, even at its most sustained and intense, the I-You relation cannot be maintained indefinitely or at its peak; it too lapses, or gets transformed and reduced to an I-It relationship. Nevertheless, we can distinguish among I-You relations those cases that are extremely brief, partial, and undeveloped as contrasted with those examples that are broader based and more lasting, engage the entire human being, and permeate his or her entire life.

Although 'the main portal' to the I-You relation is that which can appear between one person and another, there are examples of I-You relations holding between a person and inanimate 'things', including works of art, plants, and animals, where the work of art, the plant, or the animal ceases to be an It and becomes, however fleetingly, a You. Buber gives some examples from his own experience:

I walked on the road one dim morning, saw a piece of mica lying there, picked it up, and looked at it for a long time. The day was no longer dim: so much light was caught by the stone. And suddenly, as I looked away, I realized that while looking at it I had known nothing of 'object' and 'subject'; as I looked, the piece of mica and 'I' had become one; as I looked, I had tasted unity. I looked at it again, but unity did not return.[13]

I contemplate a tree.

I can accept it as a picture: a rigid pillar in a flood of light, or splashes of green traversed by the gentleness of the blue silver ground.

I can feel it as movement: the flowing veins around the sturdy, striving core, the sucking of the roots, the breathing of the leaves, the infinite commerce with earth and air—and the growing itself in its darkness.

I can assign it to a species and observe it as an instance, with an eye to its construction and its way of life.

I can overcome its uniqueness and form so rigorously that I recognize it only as an expression of the law—those laws according to which a constant opposition of forces is continually adjusted, or those laws according to which the elements mix and separate.

I can dissolve it into a number, into a pure relation between numbers, and eternalize it.

Throughout all of this the tree remains my object and has its place and its time span, its kind and condition.

But it can also happen, if will and grace are joined, that as I contemplate the tree I am drawn into a relation, and the tree ceases to be an It. The power of exclusiveness has seized me.

This does not require me to forego any of the modes of contemplation. There is nothing that I must not see in order to see, and there is no knowledge that I must forget. Rather is everything, picture and movement, species and instance, law and number included and inseparably fused.

Whatever belongs to the tree is included: its form and its mechanics, its colors and its chemistry, its conversation with the elements and its conversation with the stars—all this in its entirety.

The tree is no impression, no play of my imagination, no aspect of a mood; it confronts me bodily and has to deal with me as I must deal with it—only differently.

One should not try to dilute the meaning of the relation: relation is reciprocity.

Does the tree then have consciousness, similar to our own? I have no experience of that. But thinking that you have brought this off in your own case, must you again divide the indivisible? What I encounter is neither the soul of a tree nor a dryad, but the tree itself.[14]

When I was eleven years of age, spending the summer on my grandparents' estate, I used, as often as I could do it unobserved, to steal into the stable and gently stroke the neck of my darling, a broad dapple-grey horse. It was not a casual delight but a great, certainly friendly, but also deeply stirring happening. If I am to explain it now, beginning from the still very fresh memory of my hand, I must say that what I experienced in touch with the animal was the Other, the immense otherness of the Other, which, however, did not remain strange like the otherness of the ox and the ram, but rather let me draw near and touch it. When I stroked the mighty mane, sometimes marvelously smooth-combed, at other times just as astonishingly wild, and felt the life beneath my hand, it was as though the element of vitality itself bordered on my skin, something that was not I, was certainly not akin to me, palpably the other, not just another, really the Other itself; and yet it let me approach, confided itself to me, placed itself elementally in the relation of Thou and Thou with me. The horse, even when I had not begun by pouring oats for him into the manger, very gently raised his massive head, ears flicking, then snorted quietly, as a conspirator gives a signal meant to be recognizable only by his fellow-conspirator; and I was approved. But once—I do not know what came over the child, at any rate it was childlike enough—it struck me about the stroking, what fun it gave me, and suddenly I became conscious of my hand. The game went on as before, but something had changed, it was no longer the same thing. And the next day, after giving him a rich feed, when I stroked my friend's head he did not raise his head. A few years later, when I thought back to the incident, I no longer supposed that the animal had noticed my defection. But at the time I considered myself judged.[15]

It is between persons where the I-You relation can most clearly be seen. The I-You relation is not a 'mystical' union of two beings, nor is it necessarily or especially an intellectual matter. "The life of dialogue is no privilege of intellectual activity like dialectic. It does not begin in the upper story of humanity. It begins no higher than where humanity begins. There are no gifted and ungifted here, only those who give themselves and those who withhold themselves."[16] Nor, as I have remarked already, is it necessary that the relation be enduring or deep. Yet it is unmistakable when it occurs. Nor, for that matter, is the explicit use of *speech* or vocalization necessary in order for the I-You 'dialogue' between persons to take place. There are moments when such a relation may manifest itself in silence, and yet where a 'dialogue' is present.

Imagine two men sitting beside one another in any kind of solitude of the world. They do not speak with one another, they do not look at one another, not once have they turned to one another. They are not in one another's confidence, the one knows nothing of the other's career, early that morning they got to know one another in the course of their travels. In this moment neither is thinking of the other; we do not need to know what their thoughts are. The one is sitting on the common seat obviously after his usual manner, calm, hospitably disposed to everything that may come. His being seems to say it is too little to be ready, one must also be really there. The other, whose attitude does not betray him, is a man who holds himself in reserve, withholds himself. But if we know about him we know that a childhood's spell is laid on him, that his withholding of himself is something other than an attitude, behind all attitude is entrenched the impenetrable inability to communicate himself. And now—let us imagine that this is one of the hours which succeed in bursting asunder the seven iron bands about our heart—imperceptibly the spell is lifted. But even now the man does not speak a word, does not stir a finger. Yet he does something. The lifting of the spell has happened to him— no matter from where—without his doing. But this is what he does now: he releases in himself a reserve over which only he himself has power. Unreservedly communication streams from him, and the silence bears it to his neighbour. Indeed it was intended for him, and he receives it unreservedly as he receives all genuine destiny that meets him. He will be able to tell no one, not even himself, what he has experienced. What does he now "know" of the other? No more knowing is needed. For where unreserve has ruled, even wordlessly, between men, the word of dialogue has happened sacramentally.[17]

An I-You relation between persons may spring up, unexpectedly at any moment and in any place. "Real dialogue is continually hidden in all kinds of odd corners and, occasionally in an unseemly way, breaks surface surprisingly and inopportunely . . . as in the tone of a railway guard's voice, in the glance of an old newspaper vendor, in the smile of the chimney sweeper."[18] Such a meeting may spring up between teacher and students, or between musical performer and audience, and "no factory and no office is so abandoned by creation that a creative glance could not fly up from one working-place to another, from desk to desk, a sober and brotherly glance which guarantees the reality of creation which is happening."[19]

An I-You relation between persons is not something planned and calculated. I do not use the other person as a means to accomplishing some end of my own. The You whom I meet comes not from a seeking on my part, but by an unforeseen 'act of grace'. And when I have this relation I am not self-conscious, holding back, acting in a reserved and formal way. I am not thinking of the effect I am having on You. Nor am I acting in the light of certain rules, concepts, prescriptions. All of these—means-end use, anticipated consequences, memories of the past, rules, concepts, self-consciousness—*intervene* between I and You. In order for the I-You meeting to come about, there must be a *directness* and *presentness* in our relation where all such *intermediaries* are absent. "The relation to the You is unmediated."[20] Directness is a matter of *immediacy*. Nothing stands between us. The musical performer who is not playing for effect or in a studied and calculating way; the lecturer who is not following a prepared outline but who 'gives of himself' in an unselfconscious way; the lover who opens himself or herself to a beloved not for the sake of self-gratification or because of the feelings enjoyed; the friend who gives his whole person without reserve—all these exhibit the sort of thing Buber means by 'directness'.

The I-You relation is also marked, for Buber, by *mutuality* or reciprocity. "My You acts on me as I act on it. Our students teach us, our works form us."[21] (It must be remembered that Buber argues for the possibility of an I-You relation holding not only between persons, but also between persons and animals, plants, and inanimate objects. It must be said, however, by way of criticism, that such confirmation by examples can plausibly be found where the You's are other human beings, and to some extent even where the You's are animals such as horses or dogs. However, Buber has failed to make it clear in what sense we can say that a tree or a stone *responds* to us and that the mutuality of the I-You relation holds for *all* types of entities.)

Finally, even the most deeply established I-You relation cannot be sustained indefinitely among persons. The You reverts to an It, and my relation accordingly changes. "[It] is the sublime melancholy of our lot that every You must become an It in our world. However exclusively present it may have been in the direct relationship—as soon as the relationship has run its course or is permeated by *means*, the You becomes an object among objects, possibly the noblest one and yet one of them, assigned its measure and boundary."[22] Two friends or two lovers, as Buber remarks, experience over and over again how the I-You relation gets transformed and reduced to an I-He or an I-She relationship. The person to whom one once wrote a love letter or with whom the silent communication of a glance was sufficient to insure 'meeting' may become the object (subject) of reminiscences or of biography—or even, for that matter, the subject for 'psychological' analysis or scientific study! In short the You has become an It. Although the possibility is always present for renewal of an I-You relation, it cannot be anything but delicate, fragile, and subject to dissolution.

The Eternal Thou

The crown and summit of the life of dialogue has to do with the I-You relation between man and the Eternal Thou. The I-Thou relation to God is in many ways similar to other I-You relations. "With regard to the relation between the human way to God and that to the fellow man, I was and am simply concerned that both relationships are essentially similar, because both signify the direct turning to a Thou and both find their fulfilment in actual reciprocity."[23] The meeting with the Eternal Thou, however, is not an end point in the life of dialogue where all other meetings between man and other men, or between man and other objects or creatures, or between man and works of art, are left behind. These other meetings are not *replaced* by the meeting with the Eternal Thou. On the contrary. It is only through these other 'meetings' that one comes to be able to address God. The Eternal Thou is to be found only in and through these other meetings. God is not a transcendent being apart from the world, or apart from man's status and experience in the world. All other 'meetings', 'dialogues', all other I-You relations are themselves illumined, enriched, and take on a special 'hallowing' when 'encompassed' by the meeting with the Eternal Thou. The meeting with the Eternal Thou, when it does come as the fruition of all other meetings, has an overpowering effect. Its impact is unmistakable; it colors the rest of a person's life.

At times it is like feeling a breath and at times like a wrestling match; no matter: something happens. The man who steps out of the essential act of pure relation has something More in his being, something new has grown there of which he did not know before and for whose origin he lacks any suitable words. . . . Nothing, nothing can henceforth be meaningless. The question about the meaning of life has vanished. . . . You do not know how to point to or define the meaning, you lack any formula or image for it, and yet it is more certain for you than the sensations of your senses.[24]

At this point an obvious question arises. Let us assume one is not (like Buber himself, or the biblical man of faith, or anyone else immersed in a particular religious language and tradition) ready to take for granted the *existence of the Eternal Thou.* Such a 'nonbeliever' would ask: "What am I to understand by the phrase 'the Eternal Thou'? What reason is there to believe that there is some being or 'person' I can so address? I already know about stones, and trees, and works of art, and people—and I can see perhaps what is meant by someone like Buber who thinks of an I-You relation between myself and *these*. But I don't myself have an antecedent assurance, based on training and cultural endowment, that there is an Eternal Thou. Since the Eternal Thou is not a stone, a tree, a work of art, or a human being, how do I know that when I address the Eternal Thou that there is anything to answer to this mode of address? What stands 'out there', if anything, to *receive* my address, to *meet* me, to *respond* to me in dialogue?"

Our first task is to see how Buber himself would reply to these perfectly normal and legitimate questions. (He was quite familiar with them.) Whether or not his replies will ultimately satisfy the questioner or sceptic is another matter, and I shall defer until later a critical evaluation of Buber's views. Meanwhile, let us first attend to stating Buber's own position. And here, in setting this out, I shall divide my exposition of his views into two main phases. In one phase, in reply to the foregoing kinds of questions, his answers take essentially a *negative form*. He tells us over and over again what the Eternal Thou *is not*: what mistakes and mis-interpretations we should avoid in coming to understand the use of this expression. In the other phase, there is what may be considered his more positive and constructive analysis, that in which he proceeds to tell us something more or less definite about what he means by the expression 'the Eternal Thou'. One of the things we shall ourselves later want to consider, from a critical point of view, is how well these two phases of his discussion (the negative and the positive) cohere with one another.

The first and most important point to bear in mind is that the Eternal Thou is not an It, not an object. Other beings with which we might establish an I-You relation (a stone, tree, human being) at the very least are Its, even if they do not become You's for me. But the Eternal Thou is not, and can never be, an It. To treat God as another—even very special —'object' is to make the most fundamental mistake of all. It is a mistake that even theologians and most philosophers make. They regard God as a special entity of some sort: different, to be sure, from other types of entities, but nevertheless one with his own properties and attributes. They list these properties and set them in their interrelationships with one another. These philosophical theologians construct a *system* of doctrines about the nature of God's being and God's relation to the world and to man. Buber rejects all such theological or philosophic attempts to *describe* God or his properties, to say various things *about* God, in short to give us *knowledge* about God. He denies that we can have any knowledge *about* God. For to think that we can is to treat God as if God were another kind of object. And this is already to have made God into an It.

By its very nature the eternal You cannot become an It; because by its very nature it cannot be placed within measure and limit, not even within the measure of the immeasurable and the limit of the unlimited; because by its very nature it cannot be grasped as a sum of qualities, not even as an infinite sum of qualities that have been raised to transcendence; because it is not to be found either in or outside the world; because it cannot be experienced; because it cannot be thought; because we transgress against it, against that which has being, if we say "I believe that he is"—even "he" is still a metaphor, while "you" is not.[25]

Buber rejects any use of spatial or other terms of description in addressing the Eternal Thou. Such terms, even if used symbolically, have the tendency to mislead, and to make us think of God as an It. Take the matter of asking (and attempting to answer) the question about whether God is *in* the world or *beyond* it. The very language is borrowed from spatial descriptions of ordinary objects in relation to one another. The wine is *in* the bottle; the open fields lie *beyond* the outskirts of the town. These terms we understand. Suppose one were to ask, concerning the relation between God and the world: Is God *in* the world or *beyond* it? What do the terms 'in' and 'beyond' now mean in relating God and the world, if they are not to be taken in their literal meanings as used in connection with the wine in the bottle or the fields and the town? Even if we attempt to give a symbolic interpretation to these terms, are we not already on the road to objectifying and thingifying God? Buber thinks so, and says at one point:

"World here, God there"—that is It-talk; and "God in the world"—that, too, is It-talk. . . .[26]

For Buber, as for Pascal before him, the distinction must be made between, on the one hand, the God of the philosophers and of the theologians—those who tend to 'logicize' God and place him neatly within some system of ideas—and, on the other, the 'living' God of Abraham, Isaac, and Jacob. The latter is the Eternal You addressed, not expressed. The former is a being or It encased in a system of ideas and doctrines, about whom arguments arise and evidence is sought and disputed about his existence or properties. Buber rejects all attempts to fix his own approach to the Eternal You by means of a theology. He tells us: "I am absolutely not capable or even disposed to teach this or that about God."[27]

Buber condemns all approaches to God as a knowable Being or Entity as illustrating what he calls 'gnosis', which is, in general, the view that one can have knowledge (even if only of a limited sort) about God. In a special sense of the term 'agnostic', Buber is an agnostic. He denies that we can have any knowledge about God. Ordinarily the term 'agnostic' stands for one who doesn't know *whether* God exists. An agnostic, in the ordinary use of this term, suspends judgment. Buber is *not* an agnostic in this sense. Buber has no genuine doubts about the existence of God and sees no reason to suspend judgment about his existence. On the other hand, the question of the existence or nonexistence of God is not for Buber a real question. It cannot be settled by argument or evidence. He does not wish to enter the arena of argument about the existence of God, because this already mistakes how God is to be thought of. It thinks of the term 'God' as a *name* for a special kind of object, It, or entity. And in thinking of 'God' as a name to be ascribed to some entity, one has missed the whole point. Buber prefers to use the expression 'Eternal Thou' because by means of this locution he is addressing God, not naming him. And in addressing him the very question of his existence does not even arise.

Moreover, there is connected with the gnostic approach to God another dangerous consequence that deflects men from a true meeting with God. If God is a being about whom one can have knowledge, then God will also be thought of as a being who has various powers of a very special sort, for example, that enable God to respond to prayers (make the rain come, heal the sick, insure victory in battle with one's enemies, etc.). And this way lies the path of *magic*. Magic rests on a belief in supernatural and special powers possessed by a being that can control things and make things happen. For Buber this is superstition. It is a corrupted view of the nature of God. One should not pray to God to perform special favors or to accomplish special acts. This is to treat God as a very powerful object or It. However, the Eternal Thou is not an object, It, or Power at all. The only legitimate and meaningful use of prayer is of a different sort altogether.

We call prayer in the pregnant sense of the term that speech of man to God which, whatever else is asked, ultimately asks for the manifestation of the divine Presence, for this Presence's becoming dialogically perceivable.[28]

Positive features

I have been expounding up to this point what I have referred to as the 'negative' side of Buber's account of God or the Eternal Thou. However, even though, as we have just seen, Buber disclaims for himself the capacity of giving any description of God or his attributes, he himself does not stop at this point. In *addressing* the Eternal Thou, as well as in various accounts that Buber himself gives of what it means to address the Eternal Thou, he does not and cannot avoid altogether the use of certain selected *ways* of addressing God. In the very language he uses for such address he thereby betrays, through the use of chosen phrases, *some implicit claims about* the nature and character of the Eternal Thou. And Buber is himself forced to admit as much. In doing this, he sets out what I have called his constructive or positive views about the Eternal Thou.

Although Buber frequently makes use of certain traditional terminology associated with more orthodox doctrines about God—terms such as 'eternity', 'Creator', and 'Love'—the one expression that perhaps is most crucial for him and to which he gives special attention is the term 'Person'. For, after all, the very use of the expression 'Thou' or 'You', in addressing the Eternal Thou (or You), presupposes that God is, in some sense or other, a Person. Buber is quite clear about the fact that he is opposed to any philosophy that rejects the use of the term 'Person' in relation to ultimate reality. It is on this ground that Buber criticizes the philosophy of Spinoza. For Spinoza (as we shall ourselves see more fully in Chapter 11) rejects the notion of a *personal* God. Buber, on the other hand, maintains that "it is permitted and necessary to say that God is *also* a person."[29]

But if God is (also) a person, what are we to understand by this? Buber's reply consists in showing to what extent we must distinguish the personhood of God from other more familiar examples of persons. When we describe a human being as a person, we are able to identify him as one among other human persons: a human person is a member of a wider class, of a plurality of persons. But God, Buber claims, is not a person in this relativized sense, not a member of a plurality. God is utterly unique; God is an *absolute person*. "It is as the absolute person that God enters into the direct relationship to us."[30]

If this characterization of God as an absolute person seems less than satisfying, Buber would argue that this is because all terminology borrowed from the ordinary domain of discourse as used in connection with familiar entities is ultimately inappropriate and 'paradoxical' when applied to God. All terms used to 'describe' God escape the critical condemnation of ordinary *logical* analysis because *all* concepts ultimately fail in their application to God. Thus if one were to reply that whenever we use the term 'person' in its ordinary and familiar sense it applies to someone who is limited, whereas we are now being asked to extend the use of this expression to a Thou who is unlimited and absolute, Buber would say that this complaint has no merit. For in dealing with God we are dealing with what is "superlogical"; with respect to all discourse about the Eternal Thou "the law of contradiction does not hold valid."[31]

There is another distinction between the ordinary use of the term 'person' as holding in the I-You relation between human beings and the use of the term 'Person' when this is used for the Eternal Thou: When we are able to establish an I-You relation with another human being, the I-You relation is with an entity that is *also* an object, an It. Indeed, the two attitudes (the I-You and the I-It) are often intermingled in our responses to human beings. Only on very rare occasions do we ever reach or sustain for any length of time an I-You relation. And where the I-You relation evaporates there is always the I-It relationship that remains. The person whom I 'meet' and with whom I have a dialogue is *also* an individual entity whom I can observe and describe. Indeed, there cannot be an I-You relation with ordinary entities unless it were also possible to have an I-It relationship with them. The I-You relation is 'superimposed' on an object with which I can have an I-It relationship.

But all this does not apply to the I-You relation with the Eternal Thou. For God is not *also* an object. God is not in space or time. God cannot be described or observed. God cannot be manipulated or controlled. The only way of meeting God is in terms of a *pure* I-You relation. The I-You relation to God is not superimposed on an I-It relationship, for God can never form part of an I-It relationship. Once my relationship to the Eternal Thou evaporates, there is no It to which I can point. I as an It am still here, but not God, because God never is an It. For this reason, Buber rejects the request of a sceptic who wants at least to identify God in a way that would establish his existence as an objective entity, *apart* from the I-You relation. For the sceptic, as a neutral and dispassionate 'observer', by that very posture forecloses the only way open to 'know' God, that is, by addressing and meeting him in the I-Thou relation.

Some Critical Comments

Does Buber's philosophy provide a convincing support for the outlook of theism?

(1) There is no doubt that the distinction, *in general*, between man's "twofold attitude" of I-It and I-Thou calls attention to something of importance and has much to recommend it. The I-It attitude, in particular, clearly collects innumerable examples, and aptly characterizes them. Buber's terminology not only describes the character of our everyday relationship to inanimate objects but also holds true for the way we normally treat plants and animals or indeed human beings themselves. Nor need this fact be deplored. For, as we have already seen, even when we treat another human being as an It, this may not always be because we are *using* that individual for our own selfish purposes. The I-It relationship may also describe those interactions in which that relationship holds for the *benefit* of the other individual, as is the case where the surgeon operates on a patient or the airplane pilot carries his passengers safely from one place to another.

It is not the I-It category that poses any serious conceptual difficulties or fails to have interesting and successful applicability. Difficulties arise rather, first, with respect to the sharp distinction that Buber typically makes between the I-It and the I-You categories, and, second, with the way in which he seeks to clarify and apply the category of the I-You relation. It must be said in his favor, of course, that to make clear the basic *contrast* between these attitudes or postures, he presents them very often as if they were mutually exclusive and exhaustive, as if they somehow neatly divided all human relationships into one or another of these two types. At the same time, it must be granted, Buber himself recognizes there are many 'mixed' or 'impure' cases in which the two are intermingled. Does the mother who takes care of her infant child, in diapering, cuddling, or feeding it, treat her child as an It or as a You? It would be a futile exercise in classification to attempt to assign the responses of the mother as one rather than the other. And Buber himself, I think, would agree to this.

But what about the I-You relation? Here once again it may be granted that Buber has isolated and called attention to a valuable and all too rare dimension of human existence. There are undoubtedly genuine cases in which *persons* function toward other *persons* without *self*-consciousness, without motivations of selfish use or scientific objectivity. Since, however, Buber insists on incorporating the element of *mutuality* or *reciprocity* in the I-You relation, it is very doubtful that he has made out a plausible case for saying that we can have *mutual* and *reciprocal* I-You relations to inanimate objects or to plants. And whether a *reciprocal* I-You relation can be had with *all* forms of animal life is equally debatable. (One might argue for the borderline case of an I-You relation with one's own dog, but can you say the same for your goldfish?) To say that the other partner in the I-You relation "responds" requires that we accept the following highly questionable position: We must be prepared to attribute 'minds' of some sort to *all* entities in the world. This is a position known as 'panpsychism'. If one were to adopt this position (i.e., to attribute minds to stones, trees, goldfish, etc.) one would be stretching the term 'mind' to such a degree as to put in question whether the term has not lost all its usefulness.

(2) The major difficulty in Buber's philosophy has to do with his account of the Eternal Thou. Buber repeatedly insists that he has no doctrine to teach, that he is not engaged in theology, that he does not wish to say (or express) anything *about* God, that anyone who claims to have knowledge about God is to be distrusted because he has already converted God into an It and thereby completely fails to meet God. God can only be addressed, not expressed. And so on.

There are two principal types of questions that need to be raised in connection with these claims. The first has to do with the matter of *consistency*. Can Buber use language in the way he does—in addressing the Eternal Thou as well as in making the various assertions he does about the I-You relation to the Eternal Thou—without going back on his own claim that he has no knowledge to teach about God? The second question has to do with the *meaning* of the expression 'Eternal Thou', even when this expression is used as a mode of address in man's meeting with God.

(a) Buber fails to abide by his disclaimer that he has any doctrine to impart *about* God. Indeed, he cannot avoid failing so long as he continues to use his own favorite expressions in addressing God; knowledge-claims about God are already implicit in the very use of these modes of address. Moreover, Buber's writing, far from shunning the opportunity to give his own views about God as the Eternal Thou, are filled with many doctrinal assertions. It is true that Buber makes no attempt to *systematize* the various things he says about God, nor does he give arguments in the manner of St. Anselm, St. Thomas Aquinas, Maimonides, or other theologians. Nevertheless, systematic or not, there are a number of characteristic *statements* that he repeatedly makes about God and that, as such, convey his beliefs about God's nature.

To begin with, the very expression 'Eternal Thou', used as a mode of address to God, already commits Buber to the statement that God is a *Person*. He says as much: "God is *also* a Person." "God loves as a personality and He wishes to be loved like a personality."[32] Recall our earlier discussion (p. 184) in which Buber maintains that although the term 'person' in connection with God needs to be taken in a stretched or metaphorical way, one can nevertheless also say that God is an *absolute* Person (unlike the relativized, plural examples of human persons) and that God, as a Person, can never be an It.

Further, the Eternal Thou (as the very mode of address indicates) is *eternal*. Buber also characteristically and repeatedly speaks about the *divine power and glory*. "The great images of God fashioned by mankind are born not of imagination but of real encounters with real divine power and glory."[33] God needs man as much as man needs God, and God "*wishes to be accepted and loved* in his deepest concealment."[34] God *addresses* mankind: "Everything, being and becoming, nature and history, is essentially a divine pronouncement, an infinite context of signs meant to be perceived and understood by perceiving and understanding creatures."[35] God as our Meeter is also our Maker. God is the *Creator of the world* and all that it contains. The *purpose* of God in his Creation is that the world may be hallowed: "Everything is waiting to be hallowed by you; it is waiting to be disclosed in its meaning and to be realized in it by you. For the sake of this your beginning, God created the world."[36] "Among the teachings of faith in transcendence, that one does not appear to me unworthy that sees God as having created man for communication with God."[37]

Examples of Buber's statements about God's properties and intentions can be multiplied. But there is no need to continue to do so. For it is obvious from the preceding quotations that Buber does not abstain from making various substantive claims *about* God. And insofar as he does make such explicit claims, or leave them implicit in the very modes of address to the Eternal Thou, Buber is inconsistent in denying that he *knows* various things about God. And if he abstains from trying to justify or support these knowledge-claims by means of arguments, this still does not mean that he does not make these knowledge-claims or have these convictions. It is still perfectly in order, therefore, for someone to require evidence, reasons, and support for these statements, even if Buber shies away from the issue. He cannot at once make knowledge-claims and avoid the philosophic obligation to support those claims.

(b) In addition to the question of Buber's own inconsistency, there is the perhaps more fundamental question that has to do with the *meaning* of the phrase 'the Eternal Thou'. It is obviously the case that it has *some* meaning. The quotations I have given, along with many other similar passages from his writings, show in a general way what sort of being Buber conceives the Eternal Thou to be. In raising the question of meaning, I do not intend to deny this fact. Rather, I wish to ask whether Buber as a philosopher has given a sufficiently clear and detailed *analysis* of the meaning of this phrase (over and above the use of the standard expressions taken from the Bible or from Hasidic literature) that would suit the needs of a philosophic interest in a clear, carefully articulated, and coherent world view. Of course, one may always regard Buber's language as an extended sermon, exhortation, poem, or species of rhetorical and edifying discourse. But Buber himself claims that he is interested in doing something more. He tells us that he has a primary interest in philosophy.

I am not merely bound to philosophical language, I am bound to the philosophical method, indeed to a dialectic that has become unavoidable with the beginning of philosophical thinking.[38]

Philosophy, for Buber, is a matter of making clear that which has been given to him by 'the experience of faith'.

So, from the vantage point of philosophic criticism, are Buber's efforts successful at conveying in philosophic terms his own first-hand experience of faith? Is his use of the expression 'the Eternal Thou' sufficiently clear to satisfy the requirements of philosophy? Buber makes statements of the following sort as to how we are to understand the relation of God and the world.

God is not an object beside objects and hence cannot be reached by renunciation of objects. God, indeed, is not the cosmos, but far less is he Being minus cosmos. He is not to be found by subtraction and not to be loved by re-duction.[39]

I hold the concept of a "supernature" to be a false and misleading one. Above nature is no supernature, which must, in order to be so named, offer, so to speak, a structural analogy to nature, represent a "kingdom" above that of nature. Above nature is only God. He is above nature, and bears it and perme-ates it, as He is above the spirit and bears it and permeates it. Both are grounded in Him, and He is as little bound to them as to all the other realities, unknown and unknowable to us, that are grounded in Him. He pours out His grace right through all chains of causation, but that is He alone and no super-nature.[40]

Let us assume we understand clearly enough the statement that God is not an *object*, also that God is not the *cosmos*. Both are negative state-ments, telling us what God is *not*. As for the statement that God is not 'Being minus the cosmos', it is less than clear how this is to be understood. If 'Being' is here taken as a designation of an entity different from the cosmos yet somehow distinct from it, then Buber has not made sufficiently clear what kind of entity the term 'Being' does designate, or how we might go about certifying the reality of such an entity. On the other hand, Buber apparently also wishes to deny that God is a Being distinct from the cosmos. He wishes to deny the reality of God as somehow 'minus' the cosmos. But if God is not a Being *minus* the cosmos, and is not a Being *identical* with the cosmos, how are we to conceive of God's relation to the cosmos? The philosophic answer to this crucial question is not given by Buber. No claim to adequacy in building a world view can be made in behalf of a philosophy that leaves such a central question un-answered or insufficiently explained.

The same criticism would also obviously apply to the other passage quoted, where Buber challenges the view that God can be characterized by the use of the term 'supernature'. Once again, we may accept Buber's denial that God's 'kingdom' is to be thought of on the structural analogy with anything to be found in nature or man's experience. So far, so good. But when Buber nevertheless goes on to assert that "above nature is only God" and fails to give any analysis of his own use of the expression *'above'* —leaving it again as only (presumably) metaphoric—he fails to meet the needs of philosophy. We are left completely in the dark as to how to interpret this statement.

Another crucial difficulty with the use of the expression 'Eternal Thou' is that it is addressed to an absolute Person, different from all other persons. The Eternal Thou as an absolute Person is not located, as any finite and limited person is, in a body. When we call out to the Eternal Thou, how do we know there is anything that could answer to this call?

Buber replies that this is a matter of 'risk' or faith, and not of knowledge. Philosophy, however, requires reasons for the reliance on the *method* of faith, and Buber refuses to give us any *arguments* for this.

One final point. Buber maintains that all 'finite' I-You relations find their fulfillment and consummation in the meeting of an I with the Eternal Thou.

Extended, the lines of relationships intersect in the eternal You.

Every single You is a glimpse of that. Through every single You the basic word addresses the eternal You. The mediatorship of the You of all beings accounts for the fullness of our relationships to them—and for the lack of fulfillment. The innate You is actualized each time without ever being perfected. It attains perfection solely in the immediate relationship to the You that in accordance with its nature cannot become an It.[41]

Let us grant the merit and validity of Buber's stress on the character of such I-You relations with 'finite' you's that each of us, after his or her own experience, can confirm in that experience. What justification is there for saying that all such finite I-You relations are somehow incomplete until they 'intersect' and find perfect fulfillment in a meeting with the Eternal You? Buber himself stresses "the melancholy fate of man" to have all his I-You relations evaporate and replaced by I-It relationships. *Perhaps this is all that can be expected or found in human experience.* The notion of 'intersection' or of a final consummation and perfection to be found only in an I-You relation with an Eternal Thou remains insufficiently substantiated. It could be argued that the relation to an Eternal Thou can be removed from one's world view without impairing or reducing to a state of incompleteness the multiple I-You relations a person might manage to find and enjoy during his or her life in this world.

IV

Naturalistic Views
of the Universe
and Man

chapter 10

Science and the

Modern World

The term 'naturalism' is sometimes used in philosophy to designate a type of world view that is to be contrasted with the supernaturalistic world view of theism. As contrasted with the theistic claim that God is the ultimate reality, distinct from Nature and the ground of the existence of Nature (the Universe), a naturalistic metaphysics will regard Nature (the Universe) as itself the ultimate reality. Further, those who favor a naturalistic outlook in philosophy in general will be strongly influenced by the role that science has come to play in our lives. They will look to science both as a source of detailed factual truths about the world in which we live and as representing a *method* of acquiring truth that is to be preferred to other methods.

    What I have just said by way of giving a rough description of the term 'naturalism' must be taken as no more than helping to fix the use of a convenient label for grouping a number of viewpoints in the history of thought that have a certain family resemblance to one another. But it is important not to equate convenience with precision. As with other *'ism'* terms, it would be virtually impossible to give a definition of 'naturalism' that would be sufficiently clear and precise to allow us to neatly demarcate examples of naturalistic views that fall within the area so defined from those outside its definitional boundaries. Moreover, a given thinker who might welcome the use of the term 'naturalism' to describe his own views might wish to deny that same label to someone else who uses the very same term to describe his own outlook. We must begin then by acknowl-

'Naturalism'

edging that the term 'naturalism' encompasses a wide range of examples, having important differences from one another. In short, we should not expect this or any other classificatory label of a philosophic viewpoint to be anything more than a moderately useful device for grouping various views that have significant areas of overlap and affinity with one another.

There is another general preliminary comment that needs to be made before we proceed to discuss the philosophy of naturalism. In our survey of major world views, we have thus far considered the philosophy of Plato and the world view of theism. There is a certain very rough chronological sequence in the way in which these philosophies came to fruition and formulation. The first is a prominent example of the flowering of Greek intellectual genius in the fifth and fourth centuries B.C. The second is the legacy of an outlook developed at the height of the Middle Ages in the thirteenth century. The third, naturalism, became ever more dominant from the seventeenth century down to the present day. Our present concern with these philosophies, however, is not primarily historical. Not only does each major type of philosophy have adherents during other periods than the one in which it happens to come to dominance, or in which it receives a classic statement and formulation, it would also be a mistake to assume, without actual examination of the arguments in behalf of each philosophy, that what comes later is therefore necessarily better. I have selected each of these major points of view because they continue to be live and interesting options for philosophy at any time. For example, there are many persons in our own day, as in earlier epochs, for whom some aspect of Platonism gives the true philosophy, whereas for others the outlook of theism represents the truth; such persons would prefer their own viewpoint to that of naturalism.

Finally, although the major representatives of a naturalistic outlook whom I shall consider are drawn from writers in the history of thought since the seventeenth century, it should not be overlooked that there were important examples of naturalistic philosophy in earlier epochs, for example, in the thought of Democritus and Aristotle in ancient Greece, and, once we go beyond our own Western heritage, in the long-established traditions of Indian and Chinese thought.

A major, influential, and ground-breaking example of naturalistic philosophy in modern thought is to be found in the philosophy of Spinoza. I shall turn to an examination of his philosophy in the following chapter. As a preparation for this analysis, it will be helpful to consider two stages in the broad development of the background of Spinoza's thought. One has to do with the importance of the revolutionary accomplishments of science at the beginning of the modern period, the second has to do with the redirection given to philosophy by Spinoza's contemporary, Descartes.

The seventeenth century was a remarkable period. In terms of intellectual brilliance and creative accomplishments, it can be compared with other great and relatively brief periods marked by an outburst of genius—for example, fifth and fourth centuries B.C. in ancient Greece, the thirteenth century in medieval Europe, and the Italian Renaissance of the fourteenth and fifteenth centuries. In this connection, it is sufficient to recall some of the great names of seventeenth-century thought: Francis Bacon, Kepler, Galileo, Harvey, Pascal, Descartes, Spinoza, Leibniz, Newton, Huygens, Boyle, Locke. If you were to ask yourself what were the distinctive accomplishments of that century, there would be little doubt that the major thing you would note, in contradistinction to earlier epochs, is the remarkable flowering of *science*.

The seventeenth century and science

We ourselves, living in the twentieth century, take science so much for granted that it is hard for us to realize that science has not always been a dominant force in human history and culture. It certainly was not a dominant force in the Middle Ages, and it had only a brief flurry of creative development, primarily in mathematics and astronomy, in ancient Greece. The pursuit of science, as we know it, was reasonably well under way in sixteenth-century Europe, and it has continued to flourish and grow ever since with an accelerated pace. Wherever we turn we see its fruits. Perhaps its most obvious form of impact is to be seen in technology. Aside from the purely intellectual gratification that an *understanding* of Nature's laws brings, *applied* science consists in the use of that understanding to control and manipulate Nature to serve man's practical needs. Men build machines, harness sources of energy, develop the arts of medicine, agriculture, engineering, and so on. The understanding and control of Nature's forces that science makes possible exist in a form and to a degree surpassing anything to be found in earlier epochs or cultures, where reliance was placed on other *methods* of comprehending the world.

Let us briefly recall some of the early accomplishments of the development of science in the modern world. One of the first of these important steps was achieved in the science of astronomy. The common cosmological picture used by medieval man (as indeed by men generally, in ancient times) was a geocentric one: the Earth is taken to be at rest at the center of the Universe. The planets, the Sun, the Moon, and 'the sphere of the fixed stars', each in its own period of revolution, are observed to revolve around the fixed Earth. This picture was built up out of ideas derived both from the Bible and from Greek science and philosophy (especially Aristotle and Ptolemy), as well as, of course, from the familiar facts of ordinary experience. According to the component derivative from the biblical account of creation incorporated in the prevalent medieval world picture, not only is the Earth the center of the Universe but also man

Copernican revolution

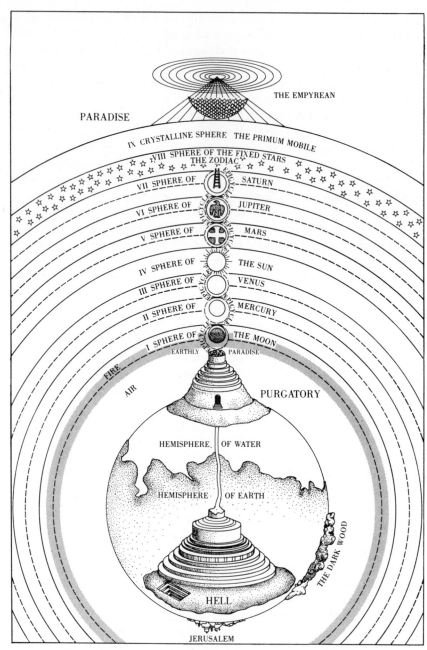

THE EMPYREAN

PARADISE

IX CRYSTALLINE SPHERE   THE PRIMUM MOBILE

VIII SPHERE OF THE FIXED STARS
THE ZODIAC

VII SPHERE OF   SATURN

VI SPHERE OF   JUPITER

V SPHERE OF   MARS

IV SPHERE OF   THE SUN

III SPHERE OF   VENUS

II SPHERE OF   MERCURY

I SPHERE OF   THE MOON

EARTHLY   PARADISE

FIRE

AIR   PURGATORY

HEMISPHERE   OF WATER

HEMISPHERE   OF EARTH

THE DARK WOOD

HELL

JERUSALEM

Dante's scheme of the Universe: A typical medieval view

himself is the pinnacle of God's creatures on Earth. God created the world in order that man may work out his salvation both in this world and in the life to come.

A vivid summary of the world picture of a medieval man is given by Anatole France in his book *The Garden of Epicurus*:

We have some trouble in picturing the state of mind of a man of olden times who firmly believed that the earth was the center of the world and that all the stars turned round it. He felt under his feet the souls of the damned writhing in flames, and perhaps he had seen with his own eyes and smelled with his own nostrils the sulphurous fumes of Hell escaping from some fissures in the rocks. Lifting his head he contemplated the twelve spheres, that of the elements, containing the air and fire, then the spheres of the Moon, of Mercury, of Venus, which Dante visited on Good Friday of the year 1300, then those of the Sun, of Mars, of Jupiter, and of Saturn, then the incorruptible firmament from which the stars were hung like lamps. Beyond, his mind's eye discerned the Ninth Heaven to which saints were rapt, the Primum Mobile or Crystalline, and finally the Empyrean, abode of the blessed, toward which, he firmly hoped, after his death two angels robed in white would bear away, as it were a little child, his soul washed in baptism and perfumed with the oil of the last sacraments. In those days God had no other children than men, and all his creation was ordered in a fashion at once childlike and poetic, like an immense cathedral. Thus imagined, the universe was so simple that it was represented in its entirety with its true shape and motions in certain great painted clocks run by machinery.[1]

Try to imagine what a shock it was to men's thought to have this familiar picture of the world challenged and eventually shattered. You will then begin to sense the intellectual upheaval brought about at the dawn of modern science with the revolutionary changes introduced by the science of astronomy in the work of the Polish astronomer Nicolaus Copernicus (1473–1543). This upheaval did not end with the gradual acceptance of Copernican astronomy. The eventual undermining of the medieval picture of the world came about over a period of time with the successive achievements of physics, chemistry, biology, and psychology, as these emerged into well-established disciplines whose results challenged outworn beliefs.

Copernicus himself was primarily an astronomer. However, his scientific discoveries produced intellectual shock waves that have come to be justifiably referred to as the 'Copernican revolution'. His major work, *On the Revolutions of the Heavenly Spheres* (1543), demonstrated that a more successful explanation of the planetary motions can be given by a heliocentric scheme than by a geocentric scheme. Copernicus showed, in other words, the superiority of an astronomical theory that takes the Sun as the center of the planetary system, where the Earth is one of the planets revolving around the Sun, over a theory that regards the entire system of the Sun, the Moon, the planets and the sphere of the fixed stars as revolving around a fixed central Earth. The major intellectual impact of this theory—apart from its technical merits—was to displace the Earth from having the privileged position in the Universe. With such a displacement of its privileged position, men naturally began to question other things. They even began to feel the first stirrings of doubt as to whether man himself occupies a privileged position in the entire scheme of things as the orthodox world view assured.

Copernicus's own principal interests, however, were not in these broader issues so much as they were in trying to give an acceptable theory of planetary motions. Indeed, in devoting his attention to this essentially technical problem, Copernicus was in many ways quite conservative. For example, he continued to use the technique of assigning epicycles in accounting for planetary motions. This technique of representation rested on the requirement that the paths of heavenly bodies be circular in shape or compounded of such circular shapes. The requirement was based on a dogma, inherited from Greek thought, according to which it was thought that only the circle exhibited the 'perfect' shape appropriate to the motions of heavenly bodies. Copernicus continued to adhere to this ancient dogma in his own constructions. This presupposition was not finally overthrown until Kepler showed how a far better fit for the observational data could be given by taking the planets to move in elliptical orbits. Another example of Copernicus's conservatism (for all the revolutionary significance of his heliocentric theory) was his adherence to the notion that there is a privileged position occupied by a single body at the *center* of the Universe, and that the sphere of the fixed stars revolves around this center. For Copernicus, the Sun was this center not only of the planetary system but also of the entire Universe. This view was itself, of course, later abandoned when it came to be realized that the Sun is but one among a myriad of stars, that it does not itself occupy any special privileged position among such stars (surely not as the center of the entire Universe), and that there is moreover no single 'sphere of fixed stars'.

Galileo (1564–1642), a great Italian astronomer and one of the founders of modern physics, lent his influential support to Copernicus's views in his famous work *Dialogue Concerning the Two Chief World Systems: Ptolemaic and Copernican* (1632). In arguing for the superiority of the Copernican system, Galileo incurred the hostility not only of the entrenched academicians for whom the word of Aristotle was the final authority but also of the Church itself, whose stake in defending a geocentric conception of the world was bound up with preserving its own elaborately worked out orthodoxy. For example, the professors at the

Frontispiece of Galileo's *Dialogue Concerning the Two Chief World Systems: Ptolemaic and Copernican*

University of Florence even refused to look through the telescope that Galileo had constructed and used to observe, for the first time, four satellites of Jupiter; they were convinced, on the basis of their texts, that there could be no such entities. And the Inquisition* insisted "that the doctrine that the sun was the center of the world and immovable was false and absurd, formally heretical and contrary to Scripture, whereas the doctrine that the earth was not the center of the world but moved, and has further a daily motion, was philosophically false and absurd, and theologically at least erroneous."[2] Galileo was called before the Inquisition and forced "to

---

* The Medieval Inquisition was established by Pope Gregory IX in 1233. Its function was to investigate charges of heresy. Those found guilty were given various degrees of punishment, ranging from burning at the stake down to penance, fines, confiscation of property, and imprisonment. In 1542 Pope Paul III assigned the Inquisition to the Congregation of the Holy Office.

abjure, curse, and detest the aforesaid errors." Galileo's *Dialogue* (along with the works of Copernicus and Kepler) was placed on the Index,* from which it was not removed until 1835.

Descartes

The Copernican revolution clearly illustrates two features to be found in any major upheaval in scientific thought. In the first place it exhibits the power a radically novel scientific theory has to reorient the ways in which scientists will henceforth think about a particular domain of natural phenomena and thereby determine the lines of research they will pursue. The Copernican theory in astronomy set new tasks for astronomical observers, for example, Tycho Brahe (1546–1601), the Danish astronomer who undertook extensive observational studies of the positions of the planets. It also encouraged the theoretical researches of Kepler (1571–1630) in finding a more adequate planetary theory; and it initiated a series of investigations that eventually led to the major achievement of Isaac Newton (1642–1727) in systematizing and unifying the laws of the entire field of terrestrial and celestial physics. A second result of the Copernican revolution (as of any major scientific revolution) consisted in the wider repercussions of a philosophic sort it brought about. The Copernican revolution forced a basic rethinking of man's conception of the world and his place in it. The Copernican theory of course was only the first of many scientific 'revolutions' to follow that had similar broad impacts. Other examples are the biological theory of evolution developed in the nineteenth century, relativity theory and quantum mechanics in the early part of the present century, and the results now beginning to emerge from the science of molecular biology in genetic research.

By the seventeenth century the flowering of science was well under way. The remarkable strides of science and its effective challenge to older ways of thinking became a matter of increasing interest, especially to philosophers. Their distinctive concern, as philosophers, was to step back, as it were, from the particular discoveries of science and to reflect upon the total phenomenon of science as a human institution and activity. Although individual philosophers themselves sometimes made important discoveries in science, their major task as philosophers consisted in undertaking to analyze and evaluate the role of science as a method of inquiry, what its practice signifies for our entire outlook on the world, and how we are to conceive the relations of science to other dimensions

---

* The Index is a list of publications Catholics are forbidden to read as endangering their faith.

of human experience, for example, to religion, politics, and ethics. The seventeenth century is especially noteworthy not merely for its many important advances *in* science but also for the number of important contributions to the philosophy *of* science and to the formulation of altered philosophic conceptions of the Universe and of man that the developments of science helped bring about. All the major philosophers of that period—Descartes, Spinoza, Leibniz, and Locke—were much preoccupied with these latter themes and wrote extensively on them.

In this connection, the work of René Descartes has special significance. Descartes is one of the founders of modern philosophy. Many of the problems and preoccupations of philosophers in the entire period from the seventeenth to the twentieth century show the unmistakable impact of his thought.

Descartes' major and overriding interest was to provide a rational foundation for knowledge. Reason, he argued, is essentially deductive; that is, it starts from self-evident premises and reaches, through a series of necessary steps, a demonstratively established conclusion. The model for such a method is to be found in mathematics. Descartes makes the claim that man's quest for knowledge in *any* domain, whether in science or metaphysics, can be made to yield to the same method of strict rational investigation. In particular, the entire world of natural phenomena, on a

The Cartesian revolution

René Descartes

material and spatial level, is a vast mathematically intelligible mechanism whose essential, detailed structure will yield eventually to patient rational investigation by the science of mathematical physics.

In the course of arguing for the broad thesis that only those beliefs that are supportable by reason can lay claim to give us knowledge of the truth, Descartes stresses the need to consider the source and warrant for all the varied beliefs that men acquire and maintain. In giving attention to this matter, he brought into special prominence the field of philosophy known as *epistemology*. The general concern of epistemology (or theory of knowledge) is to investigate the nature and limits of the mind's powers to attain truth. Although not all philosophers who followed Descartes in taking up the investigation of these questions agreed with Descartes' own answers, the central importance of this whole topic became, as a result of the impetus of his thought, an important theme in all of modern philosophy.

Finally, Descartes has much to say on the relation of the mind and body in the human being. Recognizing (indeed insisting on) the important differences between the mind and body, he also tries to make their *relation* clear and intelligible. His efforts in grappling with this 'mind-body' problem once again set the stage for a lively and important theme whose discussion continues to engage a good deal of attention in modern philosophy.

The foregoing are some of the topics in philosophy proper that Descartes opened up for discussion in a fresh and challenging way. Descartes' answers to these questions, as well as the very nature of the questions he posed, justify the use of the expression 'Cartesian revolution' to describe the impact of his thought. Taken together, the Copernican and Cartesian revolutions usher in the period of modern thought. Each in its own way accomplished a major incursion into the outlook of medieval man and set the stage for important developments to come.

I have thus far stressed the way in which Descartes is to be regarded as a founder of modern thought for whom the fact of science (its already achieved results, its future promise, and its method) is the central preoccupation of his thought. This picture, however, is somewhat overdrawn in the interest in bringing out the lasting importance of Descartes in the emerging pattern of modern thought. The more balanced fact is that Descartes' thought was in many ways only a transition between the dominant medieval world view and the modern one. For Descartes was sufficiently immersed in medieval thought not to allow him to abandon all of its central teachings in his own revolutionary proposals. As we have already seen in our earlier discussions of the ontological argument for the existence of God, Descartes' version of that argument is a classic and influential statement. Moreover, Descartes undertakes in his metaphysics to show not only how a belief in God can be established by pure reason but also how, once established, God's relation to the world and to man guarantees that the world itself is open to man's rational, *scientific* exploration and understanding. Some aspects of traditional theology, therefore, are integral parts of Descartes' total metaphysics.

Further, as we shall see, Descartes continued to adhere to the notion of an immaterial soul-substance distinct from the body. This item in his philosophy was also an inheritance from a broadly religious outlook on the world, one that he saw no reason to discard. It was nevertheless one that he desperately sought to reconcile with, and adjust to, his mechanistic conception of the world. So Descartes, in these respects, was not a complete and thoroughgoing naturalist. The components of a retained theism were still sufficiently strong in his total outlook to warrant our calling him a transitional figure to modern thought, as well as, in other respects, a founder of modern thought. By and large, Descartes was an innovative thinker when he functioned as a scientist and a philosopher of science; his use of theological and religious concepts (although no doubt sincere on his part) is largely derivative and a recasting of inherited dogmas.

René Descartes was born in 1596 in the village of La Haye in Touraine, France. From age eleven to age nineteen he studied at the Jesuit college at La Flèche, where he was given a thorough and typically scholastic education in classical literature ('letters'), history, rhetoric, philosophy, theology, and mathematics. In his autobiographical work *Discourse on Method* (written in 1637, when Descartes was forty years old) he describes his experiences at La Flèche. Although he recalls with admiration the excellent quality of his teachers, he speaks in largely contemptuous terms of the entire course of instruction, except for what he learned in mathematics. He begins by telling us "I have been nourished on letters since my childhood, and since I was given to believe that by their means a clear and certain knowledge could be obtained of all that is useful in life, I had an extreme desire to acquire instruction. But so soon as I had achieved the entire course of study at the close of which one is usually received into the ranks of the learned, I entirely changed my opinion." In short, although he entered upon his studies with considerable eagerness and optimism, at the end he emerged (except for his respect and admiration for the certainty of mathematics) disillusioned with what his studies gave him. He recognizes the value of a study of the classical literature of the ancients, in that it may be compared to the values of travel to other countries: "It is good to know something of the customs of different peoples in order to judge more sanely of our own, and not to think that everything of a fashion not ours is absurd and contrary to reason, as do those who have seen nothing." But too much time spent in such studies of the past may leave one ignorant of the present. "When one employs too much

Descartes' life and works

time in travelling, one becomes a stranger in one's own country, and when one is too curious about things which were practised in past centuries, one is usually very ignorant about those which are practised in our own time." Furthermore, the study of literature (or even history), with its reliance on imaginatively constructed (or reconstructed) stories, can be misleading because removed from reality. "Fables make one imagine events possible which in reality are not so, and even the most accurate of histories . . . at least omit in them all the circumstances which are basest and least notable; and from this fact it follows that what is retained is not portrayed as it really is. . . ." He was at first impressed by the arts of eloquence and rhetoric, and was 'enamoured' by poetry, but realized that as languages of 'agreeable fancies' they were not primarily devoted to establishing the truth in a serious and systematic way. As for theology, its dogmas were offered as ultimately based on revelation and faith. Although "Philosophy . . . has been cultivated for many centuries by the best minds that have ever lived . . . nevertheless no single thing is to be found in it which is not subject of dispute, and in consequence which is not dubious. . . ." Even such disciplines as physics, medicine, and law, as taught, were derived from the shaky foundations of traditional philosophy, for example, from Aristotelian principles, and so were not themselves sources of sound knowledge. Only in mathematics did Descartes find a type of study that gave him delight and in which he could have confidence "because of the certainty of its demonstrations and the evidence of its reasoning."

At the age of eighteen, Descartes left behind him his formal studies of the world of books to embark on a study of the 'book of the world'. He writes:

I employed the rest of my youth in travel, in seeing courts and armies, in intercourse with men of diverse temperaments and conditions, in collecting varied experiences, in proving myself in the various predicaments in which I was placed by fortune, and under all circumstances bringing my mind to bear on the things which came before it, so that I might derive some profit from my experience. For it seemed to me that I might meet with much more truth in the reasonings that each man makes on the matters that specially concern him, and issue of which would very soon punish him if he made a wrong judgment, than in the case of those made by a man of letters in his study touching speculations which lead to no result, and which bring about no other consequences to himself excepting that he will be all the more vain the more they are removed from common sense. . . .[3],*

The broadening of his experience, through travel, brought him in contact with ways of life and manners that had

* From *The Philosophical Works of Descartes* translated by E. S. Haldane and G. R. T. Ross. Reprinted by permission of Cambridge University Press.

almost as much diversity as I had formerly seen in the opinions of philosophers. So much was this the case that the greatest profit which I derived from their study was that, in seeing many things which, although they seem to us very extravagant and ridiculous, were yet commonly received and approved by other great nations, I learned to believe nothing too certainly of which I had only been convinced by example and custom. Thus little by little I was delivered from many errors which might have obscured our natural vision and rendered us less capable of listening to Reason.[4,][*]

As a way of 'seeing the world', Descartes went to Holland in 1618 and served as un unpaid volunteer in the army of Prince Maurice of Nassau. The following year he transferred to the army of the Duke of Bavaria, and so came to Germany. It is doubtful that Descartes was ever involved in any active fighting. He was able, accordingly, during long stretches of his soldierly inactivity and peace to devote a good deal of time to meditating on those problems and projects of a scientific and intellectual sort that occupied the center of his attention. The focus of all of these was the idea of accomplishing a unification of all branches of knowledge that are susceptible of rational, deductive treatment. It was to show how these several departments of learning could all be brought within the scope of a single, all-encompassing set of principles and where the details of these separate sciences could all be rationally deduced from these common principles.

It was at this period that Descartes recounts a momentous experience in his life, a series of three dreams he had on November 10, 1619. The dreams Descartes had that night gave him such an intense awareness of this project of rationally unifying all the sciences that he regarded his vision of this goal during his dreams as a prophetic endorsement of his own life's vocation. 'The Angel of Truth' who visited Descartes during his dreams filled him with such conviction as to the merit and importance of this ideal that he did indeed spend the rest of his life in carrying out this mission in his various researches and writings.

After leaving the army, Descartes traveled for a number of years in Germany, Holland, and Italy. For a brief period, from 1625 to 1627, he lived in Paris, enjoying the leisured life of a gentleman, with some mingling in society, gambling, and brief love affairs. Although he is reported to have had a duel resulting from one such affair, and although later Descartes fathered an illegitimate daughter (to whom he was much attached, and whose early death at the age of five grieved him deeply), he was by temperament apparently not a person capable of deep romantic emotions. His relations with women were largely 'platonic'. His principal

---

[*] From *The Philosophical Works of Descartes* translated by E. S. Haldane and G. R. T. Ross. Reprinted by permission of Cambridge University Press.

passions in life were primarily intellectual. During this period Descartes began a work in Latin whose English title is *Rules for the Direction of the Mind* (not published until 1701). From 1628 to 1649 Descartes lived in Holland. Here he found the necessary solitude, quiet, and freedom from distraction that he desperately craved and that enabled him to carry out his writing. (A large part of his writing, incidentally, was in the form of correspondence with eminent thinkers of the day.) In addition to his writings in philosophy, mathematics, and physics, Descartes carried on experiments in optics and physiology. He ground his own lenses; he studied anatomy by buying and dissecting the carcasses of animals obtained from local butchers. While living in Holland, Descartes finished a scientific work entitled *Le Monde* (1634). However, when he had heard that Galileo had been condemned by the Inquisition for advocating the Copernican system, Descartes, who was anxious to avoid any confrontation with the Church, halted the publication of his own work. The year 1637 saw the publication of four works: the *Geometry* (which contains his famous discovery of the method of analytic geometry), the *Dioptric*, the *Meteors*, and the largely autobiographical *Discourse on Method*. These works were written in French and were intended for a wide, nonacademic audience.

His *Meditations on First Philosophy* (1641) is a major philosophical work. In it Descartes offers the metaphysical foundations for scientific thought. This work includes a detailed account of Descartes' conception of deductive method; his views on God, the world, and man; his views on matter and mind. Descartes had shown the manuscript, before publication, to a number of the leading philosophers and scholars, among them Thomas Hobbes and Pierre Gassendi. Their 'Objections', along with Descartes' 'Replies', form a valuable and important part of the work. Other works of Descartes were *The Principles of Philosophy* (1644) (which he dedicated to a royal friend and disciple, Princess Elizabeth, daughter of the Elector Frederick) and *The Passions of the Soul* (1649). Queen Christina of Sweden, eager to learn more of Descartes' views, had prevailed upon him to come to Stockholm. He arrived there in September 1649. The Queen insisted on having her lessons as early as 5 A.M. Descartes all his life had been a late riser, spending the entire forenoon in bed reading and writing; the radical change of schedule, plus the extreme rigors of a winter in Sweden, worked extreme hardship on his health and morale. He caught pneumonia and died on February 11, 1650.

Descartes' central vision

Descartes' central vision was the conviction that the physical universe is a single, unified, mathematically intelligible mechanism. It was this vision that totally preoccupied him and to whose elaboration and defense all his other interests and energies were subordinated and in whose behalf they were enlisted. His own scientific and mathematical works as well as his writings in philosophy (in metaphysics, theology, epistemology, and ethics) were all centered either on amplifying this central vision, in providing foundations and arguments in its support, or, finally, in finding ways of accommodating those features of our experience that do not seem to be easily brought within the scope of this vision. An example of this last problem has to do with the fact that the human being has a mind that is altogether different from a body, and so apparently not subject to explanation by the science of mechanics.

A summary of Descartes' thought can thus be given under the following three headings:

(1) *The innovative core and central vision of Descartes' philosophy is the claim that the physical universe is a mathematically intelligible mechanism.*

(2) *The metaphysics, epistemology, and philosophy of science that Descartes works out are in support of this central vision.*

(3) *The mind-body problem arises from the attempt to find a place for man's possession of consciousness in a mechanical universe.*

In what follows, I turn to a brief analysis of each of these aspects of Descartes' philosophy.

The Physical Universe As a Mathematically Intelligible Mechanism

Descartes looked to a single all-encompassing science of mathematical physics to make the physical universe as a whole intelligible.

'Mathematics' means exactly the same thing as 'scientific study'. . . . As I considered the matter carefully it gradually came to light that all those matters only were referred to Mathematics in which order and measurement are investigated, and that it makes no difference whether it be in numbers, figures, stars, sounds or any other object that the question of measurement arises. I saw consequently that there must be some general science to explain that element as a whole which gives rise to problems about order and measurement, restricted as these are to no special subject matter. This, I perceived, was called 'Universal Mathematics'. . . .[5,*]

In turning to mathematics as the paradigm discipline that gives us certain and rational knowledge, Descartes is following in the tradition of

* From *The Philosophical Works of Descartes* translated by E. S. Haldane and G. R. T. Ross. Reprinted by permission of Cambridge University Press.

Plato. However, there is an important difference between Plato and Descartes. For Plato, mathematics yields rational knowledge of an independent domain of Forms in which there is no admixture of anything material, changeful, or sensible. For Descartes, however, it is mathematical *physics*, and not just 'pure' mathematics, that can give us rational demonstrative knowledge. We can have mathematical knowledge of the material, sensible world—the world of bodies in motion. The concept of the *physical universe* as a mathematically intelligible mechanism is what distinguishes Descartes' rationalism from Plato's vision of human reason exploring a timeless and independent domain of Forms.

Descartes himself was a creative mathematician. His discovery of the fundamental principles and techniques of analytic (coordinate) geometry marks an important milestone in the history of mathematics and science. Hitherto geometry on the one hand and the theory of numbers (arithmetic and algebra) on the other were independent disciplines. Descartes showed how to unify these disciplines: how to write algebraic equations for geometric curves and other spatial figures. The rich and powerful language of numbers could now be used to express the basic facts about spatial structures and geometric relationships.

Descartes' approach to physics was dominated by the conviction that analytic geometry is the ideal mathematical language for describing physical phenomena. Descartes assumed that the entire domain of physical phenomena could ultimately be brought within the scope of the science of mechanics, that part of physics dealing with the motion of bodies. Descartes' own investigations in optics, astronomy, and the physics of musical sounds, as well as his vision of all future programs for research in physics, were concerned to show how one can formulate the laws of motion of material bodies in the language of geometry. His greatest successes in this direction were to be found, as it turned out, *not* indeed with respect to the *motions* of bodies but rather in areas such as optics, where his geometrical approach led to successful formulation of the sine law for the refraction of light. For purposes of explaining and describing the phenomena of motion of bodies (especially *accelerated* motions), the 'static' language of analytic geometry proved insufficient. Later in the century the development of the differential and integral calculus, in the hands of Newton and Leibniz, provided the necessary mathematical tools for this purpose. The Cartesian dream of the 'geometrization of physics' gave way in the seventeenth century to Newtonian mechanics. Newton's approach to mechanics turned out to be far more successful than Descartes' in dealing with facts of motion.*

* Interestingly, it wasn't until the twentieth century that the project of a fundamental *geometrical* approach to physics was revived and given strong impetus with the emer-

Descartes' views about the physics of matter and motion included a number of distinctive theses: (1) all of physical nature is a plenum; there is no void or empty space anywhere in the Universe; (2) there are no atoms, that is, indivisible particles of matter; (3) all motions of bodies can be explained in terms of whirlpools of material particles (vortices) that vary in size and velocity; and (4) (the most fundamental claim of all) the essential attribute of all matter is *extension*. Extension as the essential property of matter can be described wholly in the language of geometry:

We have only to attend to our idea of some body, e.g. a stone, and remove from it whatever we know is not entailed by the very nature of body. We first reject hardness; for if the stone is melted, or divided into a very fine powder, it will lose this quality without ceasing to be a body. Again, we reject color; we have often seen stones so transparent as to be colorless. We reject heaviness; fire is extremely light, but none the less conceived as a body. Finally, we reject coldness and heat and all other such qualities; either they are not what we are considering in thinking of the stone, or at least their changing does not mean that the stone is regarded as having lost the nature of a body. We may now observe that absolutely no element of our idea remains, except extension in length, breadth, and depth.[7]

Descartes' vision of the physical universe as a single, mathematically unified, intelligible mechanism, all of whose detailed motions and phenomena could be brought within the scope of a single set of principles, was a bold and grand hypothesis. The verification of this hypothesis was certainly not carried out by Descartes, who recognized the enormous difficulty in implementing such a program. Indeed, it was not even Descartes' specific recommendations on what physical principles might serve this purpose that proved convincing to other scientists. Descartes' proposals were put aside in favor of the far more successful principles of Newtonian mechanics. Newton, in his great work *The Mathematical Principles of Natural Philosophy* (1687), carried out with enormous and impressive success the Cartesian proposal, if not all the details, of a mechanization of physics. Newton showed how his fundamental three laws of motion and universal law of gravitation made it possible to deduce, and thereby explain, the entire range of physical phenomena observed over the centuries. These phenomena included the familiar laws of statics (e.g., Archimedes' law of the lever) and the laws of terrestrial mechanics (e.g., Galileo's law of falling bodies, the laws of the pendulum), as well as the laws of planetary motion formulated in Keplerian astronomy.

gence of Einstein's theory of relativity. The recent interpretation of relativistic physics in John Wheeler's *Geometrodynamics* is very close in spirit to Descartes' original dream.[6]

Newton showed that the concepts of mass and force (including gravitational force) were needed to explain the acceleration of bodies. Newton's language of the calculus was the precise mathematical tool needed for the formulation of laws of motion of bodies. The Newtonian synthesis accomplished in its own way what Descartes had only dreamed of: a universe made intelligible to a science of mathematical physics. Newton's framework for the science of mechanics served until the beginning of the twentieth century, when it was challenged by newer developments in quantum physics and relativity theory.

Still, even if the implementation of Descartes' vision did not take on exactly the form he expected, the fact is that many since Descartes' day have been inspired by the type of goal to which he so intensely subscribed. Spinoza was one such early philosophic supporter of the general view that all of Nature possesses a single unified intelligible structure. Others inspired by the Cartesian ideal in our own day may no longer expect to find the fundamental principles underlying all natural phenomena expressed in Cartesian or Newtonian concepts, or perhaps even in some refined and transformed science of physics in particular. Still, the guiding ideal of a single *unified*, all-inclusive system of science that will make *all* natural phenomena intelligible is likely to remain a metaphysical commitment to which many scientists and philosophers adhere.

How valid is this commitment? Are we obliged to accept the claim that Nature does have a structure that would be revealed and articulated by a unique and final system of concepts and principles? One reply is that certainly there is no *proof* that there *must be* such a unique and final description of Nature's structure. The conviction that there is such a system of final Truth to be captured and set down once and for all must remain a matter of *faith*. Nor can one appeal to the history of science for evidence that there must be such a unique intelligible structure. For the progress that the history of science exhibits can be made intelligible without presupposing that all stages in the progress of science converge on a unique 'solution'. It is possible, for example, to say that one scientific theory is *better* than another without having to assume that there must be some one, final, *best* theory.

Metaphysical Foundations: Rationalism

For Descartes, the Universe is a vast and complex mechanism whose laws are nevertheless discoverable by reason. Galileo once remarked that the Book of Nature is written in mathematical language and he who understands that language can understand Nature. This remark also sums up the core of Descartes' conviction. Yet this was not enough for Descartes. He wanted to extend the vision of intelligibility and of a rational structure at the heart of reality beyond the purely physical world. He wanted to extend the case for rationality by claiming that reason has the power to discover the truth concerning the whole range of man's intellectual interests. Reason could determine the truth not only in mathematical physics but also wherever men raise serious questions about the nature of God, and about the relation of God to the world and to man. Descartes was convinced that on these matters, too, men could attain rational knowledge, answers that would have all the clarity and demonstrable certainty available in mathematics. However, Descartes realized that on these broader issues men have the widest differences of judgment. His problem was: How can we be sure that we are going to get *the* correct view? We know how to obtain the demonstrably correct view in mathematics. Yet how can we be sure to get equally certain truths concerning general philosophical questions? Descartes was convinced that this could be done. His philosophy was going to show the way.

Descartes' contributions to epistemology, philosophy of science, and metaphysics were made in order to provide an underpinning for his central thesis that the physical universe is a mathematically intelligible mechanism. In carrying through this broad philosophical project (as distinct from working out the details in the physics itself), Descartes stressed the importance of *reason*. He was convinced not only that mathematics and mathematical physics are cardinal examples of where the method of reason is successful, but also that in philosophy itself (as distinct from science) the same broad reliance on reason is to be championed. Descartes' *rationalism* is the *philosophic* apologetic, framework, and support for a reliance on reason as the only reliable method of attaining truth in any area. Part of his work as a philosopher, therefore, when writing on epistemology and philosophy of science, is to analyze the *method and criteria of reason*. The other major part of his work as a philosopher—when working out his own metaphysical views about God, the physical universe, man, and the nature of consciousness—is to *employ* the method of reason in support of the various metaphysical conclusions he reaches. We turn, now, to examine both these aspects of his philosophic rationalism.

Descartes' approach to philosophy: the importance of reason

The Nature of Reason

Descartes makes it quite clear that his model for the analysis of the *method* of reason is to be found in geometry.

Those long chains of simple and easy reasonings which the geometers use to arrive at their most difficult conclusions made me believe that all things which are the objects of human knowledge are similarly interdependent, and that if one will only abstain from assuming something to be true which is not, and always follow the necessary order in deducing one thing from another, there is nothing so remote that one cannot reach it, nothing so hidden that one cannot uncover it.[8]

General rules for the direction of the mind

With the deductive method of rational proof as employed in geometry as his model, Descartes tells us how he adopted for himself four general rules of method (for the 'direction of the mind') that he resolved to employ in all contexts where he was concerned to know the truth.

The first of these was to accept nothing as true which I did not clearly recognize to be so: that is to say, carefully to avoid precipitancy and prejudice in judgments, and to accept in them nothing more than what was presented to my mind so clearly and distinctly that I could have no occasion to doubt it.

The second was to divide up each of the difficulties which I examined into as many parts as possible, and as seemed requisite in order that it might be resolved in the best manner possible.

The third was to carry on my reflections in due order, commencing with objects that were the most simple and easy to understand, in order to rise little by little, or by degrees, to knowledge of the most complex, assuming an order, even if a fictitious one, among those which do not follow a natural sequence relatively to one another.

The last was in all cases to make enumerations so complete and reviews so general that I should be certain of having omitted nothing.[9]

The marks of reason: clear and distinct ideas, certainty

For Descartes, reliance on the method of reason involves a deliberate and conscious rejection of rival ways of justifying one's beliefs and the claim to know the truth. One who adheres to the method of reason will reject any appeal to what others think, i.e., to *authority* or *custom*. The method of reason will allow only what can be certified by *any* man possessed of the 'clear light' of reason. He will accept as true only those judgments that are composed of *clear and distinct ideas*. Such judgments are incapable of being doubted. This last feature is important. For, according to Descartes, what is characteristic of reason, as distinguished from other methods of acquiring and justifying beliefs, is that reason gives us truths that do not allow of rationally possible alternatives, i.e., that something should be true for you but not for me. Consider the matter before us as thoroughly as we can, we cannot rationally conceive of its being otherwise. Reason gives us *indubitable* truths. Another way of saying this is that *rational knowledge gives us certainty*. What one knows on the basis of reason is not a matter of conjecture, or of probability. Descartes is here restating a point made long before him by Plato, who also argued that knowledge, as distinguished from belief, offers certainty. And, like Plato before him, Descartes finds such indubitable, certain, nonconjectural knowledge preeminently available in mathematics. Descartes wishes to urge (and here he departs from Plato) that we should use the very same method of reason to reach demonstrable conclusions not only in mathematics but in metaphysics as well. Descartes, in his metaphysics, does not claim to give simply a 'likely story'. He claims to establish indubitable truths about God, the Universe, and man's soul. These truths are as unshakable and certain as anything the geometer can establish about the properties of triangles. He takes it as a rule that one should "reject all . . . probable knowledge and make it a rule to trust only what is completely known and incapable of being doubted."[10]

How are we to obtain such certainty? Descartes is not content simply to answer "By the use of reason!" He analyzes the nature of reason. He finds that reason consists essentially in two 'operations of the mind': *intuition* and *deduction*.

By intuition I understand not the unstable testimony of the senses, nor the deceptive judgment of the imagination with its useless constructions; but a conception of a pure and attentive mind so easy and so distinct that no doubt at all remains about that which we are understanding. Or, what amounts to the same thing, intuition is the undoubting conception of a pure and attentive mind, which comes from the light of reason alone and is more certain even than deduction because it is simpler. . . . Thus everyone can see by intuition that he exists, that he thinks, that a triangle is bounded by only three lines, a sphere by a single surface and other similar facts that are far more numerous than most people think because they scorn turning their minds toward such easy matters.[11]

Intuition assures us of the truth of statements composed of ideas that are at once simple, clear, and distinct. It is employed in our acceptance of the truths of definitions (which set out the essential properties of a concept) and of axioms (first principles or premises) whose truth is so self-evident and self-guaranteeing that they do not require any more basic statements from which they need to be derived.

However, intuition is not all there is to reason: there is also *deduction*.

One might wonder why we have added another mode of knowledge besides intuition, one that proceeds by deduction, *by which we understand all that is necessarily concluded from certain other facts already known. This procedure was necessary, for many things are known with certainty that nevertheless are not evident in themselves, simply because they are deduced from true and known principles by the continuous and uninterrupted movement of a mind that clearly intuits each step. Thus we know that the last link of a long chain is connected with the first, even though we do not see at a single glance all the intermediate links on which the connection depends; it is enough that we examine them successively and remember that from first to last each was attached to the next. Therefore we here distinguish intellectual intuition from certain deduction by the fact that some movement or succession is conceived in the latter but not in the former. Besides, evidence is not necessarily present for deduction, as it is for intuition, but deduction acquires its certainty in some way from memory. From this we may conclude that those propositions that follow immediately from first principles are known, according to our point of view, sometimes by intuition, sometimes by deduction; but that the first principles themselves are known only by intuition, whereas the remote conclusions are known only by deduction.*[12]

By 'deduction', then, Descartes means that act of the mind by which one derives, through a series of necessary logical steps, one statement from another. If I accept *p* then I must accept *q*, and if I accept *q* then I must accept *r*. . . . The outcome of a chain of deductive steps is the conclusion ('theorem' in mathematics). In a deductive argument each step is necessary and is logically entailed by previous statements whose truth has been established either by previous deductions or on the basis of intuition.

Intuition and deduction "are thus the two most certain paths to knowledge. No others should be admitted by the mind, and all the rest are to be rejected as suspect and liable to error."[13]

Some critical comments

Descartes' conception of knowledge as based on the use of the method of reason (as he understands that method) is open to a number of critical objections.

One important line of criticism calls attention to the fact that the model Descartes appeals to—geometry—can no longer be looked to as itself giving the kind of truth Descartes assumed it does. The development of *non-Euclidean* geometries, since Descartes' day, undermined the very reliance on supposedly intuitive or self-evident axiomatic truths. It has been shown how a consistent, non-Euclidean geometry can be built up that starts with premises altogether different from those of Euclid's geometry. The development of such alternative yet internally consistent systems of geometry casts doubt on the assumption that the premises of a mathematical system need be self-evident. On the contrary, it would now be generally recognized in the philosophy of mathematics that the only requisite in setting up a mathematical system is not that the premisses be uniquely self-evident truths but simply that they be *consistent* with one another. Similarly, the definitions of the mathematical system are not to be thought of as stating unquestionable, intuitively obvious *truths*. Definitions, rather, are simply conventional stipulations or formulae that state how a certain term is to be used. The definitions and postulates of a mathematical system, then, are not to be thought of as giving intuitively self-evident truths about world. The sole task of a 'pure' mathematical system is to derive the logical consequences of a given set of premises. The matter of the factual truth of a mathematical system is replaced by a concern with the internal consistency of the deductions. Equally valid and consistent deductions can be made from many possible alternative sets of postulates.

If a unique system of factual truth is not to be found even in geometry, the very model used for all rational truth and knowledge, it becomes highly questionable whether one should expect to find such rational knowledge, resting on a unique set of self-evident premises, in *any* sphere of intellectual inquiry, particularly in metaphysics.

A second, related type of criticism of Descartes' rationalistic conception of knowledge would question the claim that the concept 'knowledge' must be so defined that only what is *certain* can be called 'knowledge'. By rejecting anything that has any element of conjecture, probability, tentativeness, or corrigibility in it, Descartes, as has already been pointed out, is adhering to a conception of knowledge traceable to Plato's sharp distinction between knowledge and opinion. In opposition to this Platonic view, which looks to pure mathematics as the model for 'rational knowledge', let us consider what would happen if we looked, instead, to empirical science as our model. In empirical science, knowledge of the world is obtained through a process of testing hypotheses by observation and experiment. In empirical science it is not the case that only what is absolutely certain (i.e., not subject to possible improvement, replacement, or correction) is considered to belong to *scientific knowledge*. On the contrary, the body of scientific knowledge is marked by its always being open to correction, change, and improvement. Indeed, there is nothing in empirical science that is absolutely indubitable or certain. Science gives results that are at best highly probable and well confirmed. Descartes' model of mathematics as the area in which the use of reason is best exemplified would thus be replaced. By making this shift in models, the following major result is achieved: instead of a sharp and unbridgeable distinction between knowledge and opinion, there would be only *differences in degree* of evidential support and probability among different opinions or beliefs. And what would be taken as belonging to 'knowledge' or the 'truth' would belong to that part of the spectrum of human beliefs that consists of the most probable and highly confirmed beliefs.

The Method of Universal Doubt

Descartes' principal interest as a philosopher was not only to analyze and champion the *method* of reason (as he understood it) but also to show how that method could be *applied* in constructing a single unified rational system of thought in which all our beliefs could find their logical place and rational support. He worked at this project in all his major philosophic writings, especially in the *Meditations on First Philosophy* and *The Principles of Philosophy*. "All philosophy," he tells us, "is like a tree. The roots are metaphysics, the trunk is physics, and the branches are all the other sciences which can be reduced to three principal ones: medicine, mechanics, and morals."[14]

Metaphysical foundations

To carry out this ambitious project, and to show which beliefs are to be included in such a rational system, Descartes finds it necessary to undertake a wholesale examination of the various beliefs men have hitherto accepted as true. Of this vast collection, Descartes proposes to retain only those that meet the test of reason. All the others, however sanctioned by authority, custom, and tradition, will be rejected. He will admit into his reconstructed system only those beliefs that satisfy reason. And this means they either are self-evident (intuitively true) or else capable of strict deduction from intuitively accepted premises. The main task in establishing this reconstructed system of beliefs is to get the foundations right and secure. The foundations in the Tree of Knowledge belong to *metaphysics*. In such a total system of rationally established knowledge there will be not only fundamental metaphysical truths but also the truths of mathematical physics and all other beliefs resting on these metaphysical foundations.

Methodological scepticism

How, then, is one to obtain these correct metaphysical foundations? In answering this crucial question, Descartes makes a revolutionary proposal and comes up with a technique with which his philosophy is forever linked, and by which it will always be remembered: Descartes proposes to use the most thoroughgoing *doubt* or scepticism as a way of challenging and getting rid of any belief that cannot withstand it. Only those beliefs will be retained that are indubitable. He will get rid of what can be doubted and discard that about which the slightest doubt can be felt. Descartes' scepticism is accordingly a *methodological scepticism*. It is used as a method to ultimately reach that which cannot be doubted. Descartes does not emerge with scepticism as the *result*. He does not maintain that the human mind cannot ever attain truth, that it cannot ever get secure knowledge. On the contrary, Descartes' view of the world is the least sceptical of philosophers' views. He is strongly convinced that the human mind, through reason, can obtain certain knowledge. His use of scepticism is a technique to 'wipe the slate clean' of all that can be doubted in order to readmit only what cannot be doubted. His methodological scepticism is a tool used in the service of a secure and confident rationalism.

He begins by trying to find a premise that will be intuitively self-evident. He will then undertake a process of reconstruction from that starting point. He will see what other beliefs logically follow from this premise.

As deduced consequences, they will be allowed to stand because they too will resist all sceptical efforts to dislodge them. Let us now follow Descartes as he puts this strategy into practice.

The first point Descartes makes is that in attacking the soundness of various beliefs to which he, as well as others, would normally subscribe, he is not denying that their provisional retention may be justified on practical grounds. However, he is interested in questioning even these beliefs in the interest of achieving a system of knowledge that will meet the rigorous requirements of reason. He says:

I had noticed for a long time that in practice it is sometimes necessary to follow opinions which we know to be very uncertain just as though they were indubitable . . . but inasmuch as I desire to devote myself wholly to the search for truth, I thought that I should take a course precisely contrary and reject as absolutely false anything of which I could have the least doubt in order to see whether anything would be left over after this procedure which could be called wholly certain.[15]

With this as his general goal, Descartes enters upon the path of wholesale methodological scepticism, a 'bomb blast' technique of leveling everything to the ground! He summarizes the first targets on which his scepticism is directed as follows:

Thus, as our senses deceive us sometimes I was ready to suppose that nothing was at all the way our senses represented them to be. As there are men who make mistakes in reasoning, even on the simplest topics in geometry, I judged that I was as liable to error as any other and rejected as false all the reasoning which I had previously accepted as valid demonstration. Finally, as the same precepts which we have when awake may come to us as when asleep without their being true, I decided to suppose that nothing that had entered my mind was more real than the illusions of my dreams.[16]

Notice Descartes' technique. He is not going to take up one belief at a time and ask whether it can be doubted. He doesn't ask: "Is this really a table in front of me?" "Is the Earth spherical in shape?" "Is this really my hand?" "Is $4 (427 + 351) = 3112$?" and so on. He is not going to try to enumerate all his beliefs and examine them one by one. This would clearly be an impracticable and virtually interminable task. Instead, he considers the general sources on which we normally base the most solid of our beliefs. And these, he finds, fall generally into two classes: those that come to us through our senses (of sight, hearing, touch, etc.) and those that we obtain as a result of a process of reasoning or calculation.

Now for Descartes these ordinary ways of warranting our beliefs, although for the most part reliable enough, sometimes mislead us; they

Unreliability of the senses and reason

misinform and lead us astray. Timeworn examples are that we see the railroad tracks converge, and we see the stick in the water as bent. And then, of course, there are the cases of mirages and hallucinations: the parched man in the desert who sees the oasis, the 'lost weekend' drunk who sees pink elephants, and so on. Even our 'reason' sometimes leads us into making errors: we add a column of figures and reach the wrong answer, we accept a conclusion of an argument as valid when it is in fact invalid. Finally, we all have had dreams or nightmares that seemed as 'real' as anything in our waking life. When reminded of these experiences in which we have been misled, we claim to be able, nevertheless, to correct our senses, to rectify the errors in our faulty reasoning, to realize upon awakening that we have been dreaming.

However, Descartes asks: What assurance do we have that what we appeal to in order to correct our mistakes—further sense experience, more circumspect and careful reasoning, waking life—is itself to be trusted as giving us the truth? May it not be that these experiences too are infected with error? Is it not possible, as a matter of principle, *to doubt these too?* If, for example, our senses sometimes mislead us, why may it not be the case that they *always* mislead us, and that they do so even in those cases in which we place the greatest confidence? After all, if it is a matter of *subjective certainty*, am I not just as subjectively certain that this is a desk in front of me as when I am in the grip of an illusion or hallucination? So why should I trust my so-called normal sense experiences? Perhaps they too, despite my subjective certainty in what they inform me about, are misleading. In short, Descartes argues, it is theoretically possible to doubt even our most robust, 'wide awake', and sober sense experience.

And the same goes for our normal trust in reason, or the fact that we can normally distinguish dream experiences from waking ones. Perhaps even our so-called waking experiences are themselves just another form of dream experience, and what we take to be real is not there at all! If you thought the stick was really bent, and were just as convinced of that, well, then, how do you *know* (how can you be absolutely certain) that this is a chair in front of you, and that you are not dreaming all of this? "Well," you may reply, "if I were to think *that*, I would really be mad!" Descartes would agree that, from a practical point of view, it would be madness to doubt all these things. This doesn't bother him in the least. He is interested in finding, if he can, an absolutely solid and indubitable foundation for the whole system of rational beliefs, whatever the relative confidence we place in our ordinary everyday judgments. Descartes asserts that since our senses and our reason sometimes mislead us and are fallible, we cannot trust them ever to give the indubitability or infallibility for which we are searching. If I'm going to be a thoroughgoing sceptic and doubt anything about which there is the least possibility of doubt (even though I would not in normal circumstances, and for practical reasons, entertain such doubts), well, then, let it be doubted and discarded! It is not suitable as a firm and indubitable foundation for a system of rational beliefs. If what we are seeking is an intellectually secure body of judgments about the world, then Descartes requires that we be as sceptical as possible in order to find, if we can, the bedrock beliefs about which we could not be sceptical even if we tried.

To all of this scepticism about the senses and reason, and our alleged uncertainty about how to distinguish dream experiences from waking life, someone might say that there is no reason to be so distrustful of our God-given faculties, for if we believe in a benevolent God he surely would not have given men such weak and unreliable ways of dealing with the world. Is not a belief in God a sufficient bulwark against all this corrosive scepticism? To this suggestion, Descartes replies that we can, as a legitimate step in scepticism, even doubt the existence of such a benevolent and non-deceiving God.

How do I know that He has not brought it to pass that there is no earth, no heaven, no extended body, no magnitude, no place, and that nevertheless [I possess the perceptions of all these things and that] they seem to me to exist just exactly as I now see them?[17]

To bolster this proposal, Descartes asks us to imagine that there is an evil demon who constantly deceives us!

Hypothesis of an evil demon

I will suppose, then, not there is a supremely good God, the source of truth; but that there is an evil spirit, who is supremely powerful and intelligent, and does his utmost to deceive me. I will suppose that sky, air, earth, colors, shapes, sounds and all external objects are mere delusive dreams, by means of which he lays snares for my credulity. I will consider myself as having no hands, no eyes, no flesh, no blood, no senses, but just having a false belief that I have all these things.[18]

We seem to have a total wreck on our hands! All our beliefs have been examined and found wanting! I am not certain there is a world 'out there'. I have no knowledge that God exists. I even question that I have a body! Everything I have hitherto normally accepted on the basis of my senses and reason is to be rejected as unreal or false.

It is at this point, where scepticism seems to have done its worst and *no* belief seems to be left standing, that Descartes steps in and points to a halting place to this total destruction. He offers us the one loophole, the one indestructible judgment that survives all this wreckage. This solution

"Cogito ergo sum"

offers to serve as a secure rock and foundation on which a new rationally secure structure of knowledge could be rebuilt.

But I soon noticed that while I thus wish to think everything false, it was necessarily true that I, who thought so, was something. Since this truth "I think, therefore I am" [Je pense, donc je suis; cogito, ergo sum] *was so firm and assured that all the most extravagant suppositions of the sceptics were unable to shake it, I judged that I could accept it without hesitation as the first principle of philosophy I was seeking.*[19]

The statement "I think, therefore I exist" (sometimes referred to as the '*cogito*', for short) is an axiom, a self-evident truth that withstands the most thoroughgoing doubt. For doubting, as one form of consciousness, one form of 'thinking', is itself involved in the process of carrying through the act of doubting everything else. I cannot doubt that I am doubting, for in the very attempt to cast doubt on the fact that I am doubting, I am already exhibiting the existence of the act of doubt. Doubt anything you wish, but you can't doubt that there is something going on, the doubting itself. To deny *that*, or to doubt the genuine existence of the act of doubting, is self-defeating and inconsistent. In the very act of doubt, I show that I exist at least as a doubter. This much is certain and indubitable. *It* cannot itself be doubted. It is therefore intuitively certain. Since I have a clear and distinct idea of this *truth*, I must recognize that it is beyond all possible doubt. It can serve therefore as a 'first principle' of philosophy, a firm foundation on which to erect a system of knowledge.

With this self-evident axiom "I think, therefore I exist" as his first principle, Descartes proceeds to construct a system of rational knowledge. He will admit into this new structure only those judgments that meet the requirements of reason, that is, of being, like the *cogito*, either intuitively obvious and self-confirming or deductively derivable from such axiomatic premises.

Doubting requires a thinking substance

What then, Descartes asks, follows necessarily from this first principle? He is assured thus far only of the fact that he exists insofar as he is engaged in a process of doubting or thinking. "Thought is an attribute that belongs to me; it alone cannot be separated from me. I am, I exist, that is certain. But how often? Just when I think."[20] What is required, if I am going to make sense of the fact that I exist insofar as I am thinking? Descartes' answer is that the only way of making sense of this is to say that *he is a thing which thinks.*

I am, however, a real thing and really exist; but what thing? I have answered: a thing which thinks. . . . What is a thing which thinks? It is a thing which doubts, understands, (conceives), affirms, denies, wills, refuses, which also imagines and feels.[21]

This of course is a crucial step. It shows that in answering the question of how to make sense of the fact or activity of thinking (doubting) Descartes is convinced that the *only* way of doing so is to attribute that activity to a *thing* or *substance* that can perform this activity. He believes that a necessary consequence of the fact that there is an activity of thinking is the assertion that there must be a thinking substance (*res cogitans*) to perform this activity. Up to this point he has brought into question the existence of his own body as well as all other bodies, since the belief in their existence depends on the credibility of the senses. Thus he cannot yet allow that any bodily substances exist. However, at least his own thinking substance, his own mind, must be acknowledged to have a *bona fide* reality.

I knew that I was a substance the whole essence or nature of which is to think, and for its existence there is no need of any place, nor does it depend on any material thing; so that this 'me', that is to say, the soul by which I am what I am, is entirely distinct from body, and is even more easy to know than is the latter; and even if body were not, the soul would not cease to be what it is.[22]

Having established to his own satisfaction the indubitable truth that he exists as a thinking substance, distinct from the body, Descartes proceeds to draw the consequences of this fact. His next major step is prove the existence of other entities, in particular the existence of an 'external' physical world. He must find a way of getting beyond the contents of his own consciousness and establishing the existence of entities outside his consciousness. Descartes does this in several steps. The first is to establish the existence of God. He thus undertakes to deduce from the fact that he exists as a thinking substance that God must exist. For in examining the fact and character of his own existence, Descartes recognizes that as a thinking and doubting substance he is less than perfect.

God exists

Reflecting on the fact that I doubted, and that consequently my existence was not quite perfect (for I saw clearly that it was a greater perfection to know than to doubt), I resolved to inquire whence I had learned to think of anything more perfect than I myself was; and I recognized very clearly that this conception must proceed from some nature which was really more perfect.[23]

Insofar as he recognizes himself to be an imperfect being, and yet also having the idea of a Perfect Being, Descartes argues that as an imperfect being he cannot be the cause of his own existence. Furthermore, in having the conception of a Perfect Being, he sees clearly and distinctly that it is of the very essence of such a Perfect Being to exist. The first of these arguments is a version of the cosmological argument for the existence of God. The second is a version of the ontological argument. By the use of these arguments, Descartes is able to assure himself on rational grounds of the existence of a Being beyond the existence of his own thinking substance.

Reestablishing a confidence in reason

According to Descartes, a belief in God, rationally secured, carries with it the conviction that God is an infinitely benevolent and perfect Being. Since God is benevolent, he would not be a deceiver nor would he endow man with a mind that has a capacity for forming clear and distinct ideas in using his reason and yet be trapped into falsehoods by a 'malicious demon' or through any other distracting source of error. Men can have complete confidence, therefore, in their God-given faculty of reason. They can be assured of the truth of those judgments that are composed of clear and distinct ideas. Error, according to Descartes, is a failure of man's free will. It arises from a readiness to give one's assent to judgments composed of confused ideas and to those that rest in an unquestioning and uncritical way on the senses alone.

That which I have just taken as a rule, that is to say, that all the things that we very clearly and very distinctly conceive of are true, is certain only because God is or exists, and that He is a Perfect Being, and that all that is in us issues from Him. From this it follows that our ideas or notions, which to the extent of their being clear or distinct are ideas of real things issuing from God, cannot but to that extent be true.[24]

With God as the guarantor of the reliability of human reason, Descartes now has the way clear to reestablish the use of reason as the final source of truth. As it concerns the physical universe, this truth is given to us by the science of mathematical physics. It discloses the essential properties of bodies, and this, for Descartes, as we have seen, consists in their geometrical properties. Here, then, Descartes reenters once more the world of bodies in motion, and with it the opportunity for understanding its structure by means of a geometricized science of mechanics. With this step, he has provided the sought-for metaphysical foundation to support his vision that the truth about the physical world is to be found in the science of mathematical physics.

Summary of the argument

To summarize the major steps in Descartes' argument: (1) methodological scepticism serves to wipe the slate clean of all dubitable beliefs; (2) the *cogito* is the first firm axiom of a reconstituted system of rational knowledge; (3) the mind is a thinking substance; (4) God exists; (5) God as a benevolent being gives us complete confidence in the use of the method of reason (of clear and distinct ideas, of intuition and deduction) to establish the truth, in particular in mathematical physics. Such, in bare outline, is the system of Descartes' metaphysical rationalism, as a support for his controlling vision of the intelligibility of the physical universe.

Critique of Cartesian Rationalism

Descartes' rationalistic philosophy has been subjected to a variety of criticisms, both by his contemporaries and by later thinkers. The following are some standard criticisms:

(1) To begin with, as we have seen, the method of universal doubt that Descartes employs is undertaken in behalf of a search for absolutely indubitable premisses. I have previously mentioned one type of criticism that sees as misguided this whole enterprise of modeling metaphysics on a supposedly unique system of absolute mathematical truth. It may be questioned whether in any domain of factual truth one can achieve a unique, deductive system of truths resting upon a foundation of indubitable premisses. If metaphysics is thought of as concerned to give us factual truths about the nature of reality, then it is a misdirection of effort to try to find indubitable premisses for such metaphysical knowledge. Any statement (or set of statements) that undertakes to give a true account of some state of affairs is open to two sorts of criticism.

(a) For one thing, the evidence of observational experience must be appealed to, at some point, in support of any claim to factual truth. However, whatever depends on observational experience for its support is always open to correction or modification by ongoing experience. Hence there is always an element of tentativeness, i.e., *some* degree of *un*certainty that must accompany any factual statement, since our observational experience is never complete and exhaustive.

(b) Another hindrance to any claim of already being in possession of (or even to search for) indubitable factual truths is this: Any statement about an actual state of affairs requires the use of some manmade concepts for its interpretation (description or explanation). However, there are many different possible ways of 'looking at things,' many different conceptual frameworks that might be used for this purpose. Although some conceptual schemes may be *preferred*, for various reasons, to others, there is no convincing reason to believe that there is only *one* among these various possible conceptual schemes that already captures (or might capture) once and for all, and in some unique, final, and complete way, the whole truth.

(2) A second criticism of the method of universal doubt is that it is artificial. Descartes proposes that we doubt everything about which there is the least possibility of doubt. But doubt, as Charles Peirce pointed out, is not something that can be manufactured or aroused unless we genuinely feel it. And we normally have no reason to question *everything* all at once. Doubts arise at particular junctures of experience, with respect to particular beliefs. We may question the truth of some previously accepted belief because we come to recognize certain facts to be in conflict with

the belief, or because some fresh turn of events calls that belief into question. When this happens, we would normally set about removing the challenged belief and replacing it with one in which we have greater confidence. *Genuine* doubt, in other words, is always focused on some *particular* belief. What Descartes proposes is a *wholesale* doubt of everything at once. And this is both artificial and uncalled for. We have no reason to question everything at once. When we pretend to question something for which we have no good reasons to be distrustful, we are doing violence to the normal use of human intelligence.

The foregoing charge of artificiality brought against Descartes' use of scepticism is not incompatible with acknowledging that, for him, scepticism is a tool, a methodological device of ridding the mind of whatever is open to doubt. For even as a tool or method, scepticism need not be wholesale (calling everything into doubt simultaneously) in order to be effective. One could employ the method of scepticism *piecemeal* and avoid the charge of artificiality. For in fact it is often both useful and important to question some belief about which there is some genuine doubt, in order to see whether it can withstand such criticism.

Another way of making substantially the same criticism as the foregoing is to call attention to a logical fallacy in Descartes' justification for calling into question all our customary beliefs. As we have seen, he divides the principal sources of all beliefs into two main categories, those derived from the use of the senses and those based on the appeal to reason. And he says that each of these faculties *sometimes* misleads us. However, since sense and reason sometimes mislead us, he argues, we are justified (for purposes of the carrying through of universal doubt) in distrusting them in *all* cases. But this is a logical fallacy. It does not follow that because *any one* of my beliefs might be in error (can be called into question) therefore *all of them together* can be called into question. (The same fallacy would be committed by some one who argued that because *any one* person may turn out to be unreliable and dishonest, therefore *everyone* is to be distrusted and *all* people are unreliable.)

(3) A third major criticism of Descartes' argument has to do with his claim that the only way of making sense of the activity of doubting (of the *cogito*) is to affirm that there must be a *thinking substance*, an immaterial entity that performs the various activities of thinking, willing, imagining, doubting, etc. Descartes here takes over, in an uncritical way, the notion of a soul substance widely prevalent in medieval thought. He unhesitatingly accepts the interpretation of mental phenomena as requiring the concept of mind as a substance, without critically examining other possibilities. What appeals to him as indubitable and as a deliverance of the natural light of reason—that we possess a soul or mind substance—is far from being a matter on which everyone would agree. In

short, under the heading of 'indubitability' or being 'a clear and distinct idea', Descartes is allowing an inherited dogma that he imbibed as student at La Flèche to be introduced into his system of thought as a deliverance of the 'natural light of reason'. And this is but another example of how, under the guise of 'reason', a philosopher may dupe himself into believing he has achieved the absolute truth.

(4) Finally, critics have pointed to the weak step in Descartes' system in his attempt to prove the existence of God by means of certain variations on the cosmological and ontological arguments. I have myself examined his version of the ontological proof in an earlier chapter and pointed out its shortcomings. His version of the cosmological argument is no stronger than other classic statements of that type of argument. As a link, therefore, in his deductive program for securing a metaphysical foundation for his vision of the physical universe as a mathematically intelligible mechanism, it does not really succeed. It is the least original part of Descartes' whole approach, and has whatever difficulties belong in general to a theistic philosophy.

The Mind-Body Problem

In working out his theory of reality, Descartes stressed the importance of geometricized physics in giving us an understanding of the physical world. For his more general metaphysical views, Descartes also used a number of distinctions worked out in classical and medieval thought. Central to this inherited, traditional conceptual framework were the concepts of substance and attribute. Descartes, in common with the tradition of medieval thought, distinguished corporeal and spiritual (incorporeal) substances. God is an infinite immaterial mind, an incorporeal spiritual Substance who creates the world and exists independently of the world he creates. The world is composed basically of two types of entities. There are the various bodily or material substances that make up the physical universe. They are the subject matter for investigation by the science of physics. Man, however, *alone* among the creatures to be found in the created universe, is a composite being, having both a body and a mind. A human individual is an entity that consists of two interrelated substances, one corporeal and the other spiritual or mental. All other entities in the Universe, aside from human beings, are only material. Descartes believed that even so-called living entities other than man are essentially bodies, purely physical entities. He thought that since animals lack a mind or spiritual substance of the sort that man alone possesses, they are only machines—*automata*. In principle, all that is to be found out about the behavior of animals, as of any other material entities, will yield its secrets to the principles of mathematical physics. For all entities in the world, other than man, are fundamentally or essentially nothing but bodies in motion.

Psychophysical dualism

In describing man's nature, Descartes defended a position sometimes classified as *'psychophysical dualism'*. Since a human being is a combination of two substances, a body and a mind, each has its own essential properties or attributes. Those that belong to the body are to be understood by physics. But physics cannot hope to make clear the nature of mind. For the concepts with which physics works are not applicable to the mind and its properties. The mind does not occupy space and has no extension; it does not move as a body can. The various modes of consciousness (thinking, feeling, perceiving, doubting, imagining, willing) cannot be described and explained through the language of physics and geometry.

In upholding this view, Descartes maintains two theses: (1) the body and the mind are *distinct* and *separate* from each other; (2) although distinct and separate, the body and mind *interact with* each other. On the first point he is quite explicit.

All that we clearly perceive can be made by God in the manner in which we perceive it. But we clearly perceive mind, that is, thinking substance, without body, that is to say, without extended substance; and conversely, body without mind (as everyone will readily grant). Hence at least by the divine power the mind can exist without the body, and the body without the mind. Now substances that can exist one independently of the other are really distinct. Thus the mind and the body are substances that can exist independently of one another (as I have just proved). Therefore the mind and the body are really distinct.[25]

Despite the fact that the mind and body are distinct substances, they form a single, integrated, although composite, human being. They are obviously interrelated in some way.

Nature . . . teaches me by these sensations of pain, hunger, thirst, etc., that I am not only lodged in my body as a pilot in a vessel, but that I am very closely united to it, and so to speak so intermingled with it that I seem to compose with it one whole. For if that were not the case, when my body is hurt, I, who am merely a thinking thing, should not feel pain, for I should perceive this wound by the understanding only, just as the sailor perceives by sight when something is damaged in his vessel; and when my body has need of drink or food, I should clearly understand the fact without being warned of it by confused feelings of hunger and thirst. For all of these sensations of hunger, thirst, pain, etc., are in truth none other than certain confused modes of thought produced by the union and apparent intermingling of mind and body.[26]

This interrelation of body and mind occurs not only when the changes in the body are experienced and noticed by the mind, as when light rays impinge on the eye (a part of the body) and I *see a* color (mental event), but conversely when the mind is able to bring about various changes in the body, as when I *choose* to get up from a sitting position and walk. These facts of interrelation of body and mind call for explanation. How can the mind bring about changes in the body, or the body bring about changes in the mind, if these are distinct substances, one material, the other immaterial? This is a crucial difficulty for Descartes' philosophy.

Pineal gland

Descartes' solution to this problem is presented in his late work *The Passions of the Soul* (1649). He there argues that "although the soul is joined to the whole body, there is yet in that a certain part in which it exercises its function more particularly than in all the others." That part, Descartes thought, is the pineal gland, situated near the top of the brain. Descartes chose this as the point at which mind and body interact because, unlike other parts of the body that have their double or counterparts, it is a unique entity. Also, as Descartes falsely believed, the pineal gland did not occur in animals, which had no soul or mind and so had no need for a point of junction between mind and body. It is to the pineal gland that the 'animal spirits' (fluids that course through the 'nerve-tubes') transmit messages, for example, from the mind's free choices; they thereby convey its 'instructions' to the appropriate muscles of the body. Conversely, it is through the pineal gland that the incoming bodily messages are transmitted to the mind and then take on the form of sensations and ideas in the mind.

Thus, for example, if we see some animal approach us, the light reflected from its body depicts two images of it, one in each of our eyes, and these two images form two others, by means of the optic nerves, in the interior surface of the brain which faces its cavities; then from there, by means of the animal spirits with which its cavities are filled, these images so radiate towards the little gland which is surrounded by these spirits, that the movement which forms each point of one of the images tends towards the same point of the gland towards which tends the movement which forms the point of the other image, which represents the same part of this animal. By this means the two images which are in the brain form but one upon the gland, which, acting immediately upon the soul, causes it to see the form of this animal.[27]

The weakness of this solution

It is obvious that this 'solution' to the body-mind problem will not work. For one thing, if the mind is by definition an immaterial substance, how can it make *contact*, literally, with anything material—through the agency of the material pineal gland, or by changing the direction of the 'animal spirits' (fluids) *in* the body? And, conversely, if the body is material and all its changes are at bottom mechanical motions, how can such bodily changes and motions affect something wholly immaterial and produce ideas or images in the mind? The solution is incoherent and inconsistent with the very concepts and principles used in formulating the problem. Indeed, not only the followers of Descartes (let alone his critics) but even Descartes himself recognized the weakness of his position. He writes:

That the mind, which is incorporeal, is capable of moving the body, neither general reasoning nor comparisons drawn from other things can teach us; yet none the less we cannot doubt it, since certain and evident experiences make it manifest to us every day of our lives.[28]

Descartes' theory of the precise mechanism or causal route by which the mind and the body interact is thus clearly unsatisfactory. Nevertheless, the 'mind-body' problem in philosophy is still often *stated* in such a way that the crucial distinction made in Descartes' formulation of the problem—that the mind and body are both substances and that they somehow 'interact'—is still retained in many accounts. Gilbert Ryle identifies this Cartesian way of formulating the problem as the model of the 'ghost in the machine' and as the 'official doctrine' held by most people. He describes it as follows:

There is a doctrine about the nature and place of minds which is so prevalent among theorists and even among laymen that it deserves to be described as the official theory. Most philosophers, psychologists and religious teachers subscribe, with minor reservations, to its main articles and, although they admit certain theoretical difficulties in it, they tend to assume that these can be overcome without serious modifications being made to the architecture of the theory. . . .

The official doctrine, which hails chiefly from Descartes, is something like this. With the doubtful exceptions of idiots and infants in arms every human being has both a body and a mind. Some would prefer to say that every human being is both a body and a mind. His body and his mind are ordinarily harnessed together, but after the death of the body his mind may continue to exist and function.

Human bodies are in space and are subject to the mechanical laws which govern all other bodies in space. Bodily processes and states can be inspected by external observers. So a man's bodily life is as much a public affair as are the lives of animals and reptiles and even as the careers of trees, crystals and planets.

But minds are not in space, nor are their operations subject to mechanical laws. The workings of one mind are not witnessable by other observers; its career is private. Only I can take direct cognisance of the states and processes of my own mind. A person therefore lives through two collateral histories, one consisting of what happens in and to his body, the other consisting of what happens in and to his mind. The first is public, the second private. The events in the first history are events in the physical world, those in the second are events in the mental world. . . .

It is customary to express this bifurcation of his two lives and of his two worlds by saying that the things and events which belong to the physical world, including his own body, are external, while the workings of his own mind are internal. This antithesis of outer and inner is of course meant to be construed as a metaphor, since minds, not being in space, could not be described as being spatially inside anything else, or as having things going on spatially inside themselves. But relapses from this good intention are common and theorists are found speculating how stimuli, the physical sources of which are yards or miles outside a person's skin, can generate mental responses inside his skull, or how decisions framed inside his cranium can set going movements of his extremities.

Even when 'inner' and 'outer' are construed as metaphors, the problem how a person's mind and body influence one another is notoriously charged with theoretical difficulties. What the mind wills, the legs, arms and the tongue execute; what affects the ear and the eye has something to do with what the mind perceives; grimaces and smiles betray the mind's moods and bodily castigations lead, it is hoped, to moral improvement. But the actual transactions between the episodes of the private history and those of the public history remain mysterious, since by definition they can belong to neither series. They could not be reported among the happenings described in a person's autobiography of his inner life, but nor could they be reported among those described in some one else's biography of that person's overt career. They can be inspected neither by introspection nor by laboratory experiment. They are theoretical shuttlecocks which are forever being bandied from the physiologist back to the psychologist and from the psychologist back to the physiologist. . . .

What sort of knowledge can be secured of the workings of a mind? On the one side, according to the official theory, a person has direct knowledge of the best imaginable kind of the workings of his own mind. . . . A person is . . . generally supposed to be able to exercise from time to time a special kind of perception, namely inner perception, or introspection. He can take a (non-optical) 'look' at what is passing in his mind. Not only can he view and scrutinize a flower through his sense of sight and listen to and discriminate the notes of a bell through his sense of hearing; he can also reflectively or introspectively watch, without any bodily organ of sense, the current episodes of his inner life. This self-observation is also commonly supposed to be immune from illusion, confusion or doubt. A mind's reports of its own affairs have a certainty superior to the best that is possessed by its reports of matters in the physical world. Sense-perceptions can, but consciousness and introspection cannot, be mistaken or confused.

On the other side, one person has no direct access of any sort to the events of the inner life of another. He cannot do better than make problematic inferences from the observed behaviour of the other person's body to the states of mind which, by analogy from his own conduct, he supposes to be signalised by that behaviour. Direct access to the workings of a mind is the privilege of that mind itself; in default of such privileged access, the workings of one mind are inevitably occult to everyone else. For the supposed arguments from bodily movements similar to their own to mental workings similar to their own would lack any possibility of observational corroboration. Not unnaturally, therefore, an adherent of the official theory finds it difficult to resist this consequence of his premises, that he has no good reason to believe that there do exist minds other than his own. Even if he prefers to believe that to other human bodies there are harnessed minds not unlike his own, he cannot claim to be able to discover their individual characteristics, or the particular things that they undergo and do. Absolute solitude is on this showing the ineluctable destiny of the soul. Only our bodies can meet.[29]

In his book *The Concept of Mind* (1949), from which the foregoing description of "Descartes's Myth" has been taken, Ryle sets out to challenge its central thesis. It would take us too far afield, on the present occasion, to follow Ryle's arguments and proposals in any detail. There are many philosophers who are troubled not only by the way that Descartes formulated the matter but also by Ryle's own intended replacement for a Cartesian point of view. The problem of finding an acceptable way of dealing with the facts of consciousness and mental life continues as a lively topic not only among psychologists but among philosophers as well.[30]

chapter 11

Nature and Man's Well-Being

Spinoza is a major spokesman for a naturalistic world view. Indeed, in modern philosophy his thought is the earliest clear and important example of such a point of view. So a contrast between Descartes and Spinoza is helpful at this point. For all of Descartes' fresh orientation toward a world view that put science at its core, his philosophy was still sufficiently tied to the medieval outlook of theism to disqualify the use of the term 'naturalism' to appropriately describe it. Not so with Spinoza. Spinoza, although himself steeped in medieval thought, is more than just a 'transitional' figure. He consciously and deliberately set out to challenge and overturn some of the basic premises of traditional theism. He did not appeal to a traditional belief in God, as did Descartes, to support a conception of the world as a scientifically intelligible whole. Thus whereas Descartes remained an orthodox Catholic until the end of his life and a sincere believer in God, Spinoza was excommunicated by the Orthodox Jewish community of Amsterdam. His 'atheistic' and 'materialistic' views were strongly incompatible with the central metaphysical beliefs of Orthodox Judaism, as well as with those of any other variety of traditional theism.

Spinoza

Baruch (Benedict) Spinoza was born in Amsterdam, November 24, 1632. His parents were members of the Jewish community, most of whom were refugees who had settled in that city beginning in 1593, after having

Life and works

Baruch Spinoza

escaped the Inquisition in Spain and Portugal. The young Republic of the Netherlands had recently declared its independence from Spain, and in doing so had made possible a greater degree of religious toleration and freedom of thought, which gave it, therefore, a unique status among the countries of Europe.

Spinoza's grandfather and father were influential members of the Jewish community of Amsterdam. Baruch's father, Michael Espinoza, was a prosperous businessman and also held important posts in the Synagogue. Baruch, as a child and young man (from the age of five until he was eighteen), received a typical thorough education in the religious school attached to the Synagogue. The course of study included at different stages, a close study of the Bible, the Talmud, and medieval Jewish thinkers including Ibn Ezra and Moses Maimonides. Spinoza as a young man had begun to make a serious study of various secular writers. His command of languages included Spanish, Portuguese, Dutch, Italian, French, Latin, and, of course, Hebrew. He was thus able to acquire an increasingly wide familiarity with, and knowledge of, the great classical writers of the past.

One of Spinoza's teachers was Rabbi Manasseh ben Israel, the author of several books that contained numerous references to such figures as

Euripedes, Virgil, Plato, Aristotle, Duns Scotus, and Albertus Magnus. It is quite likely that Spinoza was first introduced by this cultured man to the wider domain of non-Jewish philosophy, the science of the day, and the literature written in Latin.

At about this time Spinoza also began a more systematic study of Latin and the sciences with an unorthodox ex-Jesuit named Francis Van den Ende, who opened a school in Amsterdam in 1652. It was through Van den Ende's influence that Spinoza came to learn more thoroughly of various unorthodox movements in political thought, as well as of the philosophy of Descartes. Spinoza made a thorough study of the writings of Descartes (whose death had occurred in 1650). Spinoza's book *The Principles of Descartes' Philosophy* (1663) (the only one published under his name during his lifetime) was devoted to an exposition of Descartes' philosophy.

Spinoza's father died in 1654, when the young man was twenty-two years old. Spinoza went to live at the house of his teacher, Van den Ende, where he assisted in the instruction of pupils. Although the seeds of his growing separation from the practices and orthodox beliefs of Judaism had already been sown, Spinoza became increasingly estranged from the Jewish community. The rupture finally occurred when the elders of that community found it necessary to take the serious step of excommunicating the young man. The official ban was voted and pronounced in July 1656, and Spinoza was henceforth totally excluded from the Jewish community. The document that decreed his excommunication declared "it has been

Spinoza's Grave

resolved . . . that the said Espinoza should be anathematised and cut off from the people of Israel. . . ." (It is interesting to note that, hundreds of years later, the newly established government of Israel, in partial rectification of a historic act of narrow dogmatism, erected at Spinoza's gravesite in the churchyard at the Hague a tombstone on which there is the single Hebrew word conveying the sentiment 'your people are with you'.)

Having been banished from Amsterdam, Spinoza at first settled in a small village nearby. He supported himself by being a lens grinder. His skill at making lenses for eyeglasses, microscopes, and telescopes was apparently of a high enough order to bring his work to the attention of the famous Dutch physicist Christiaan Huygens (1629–1695) and the celebrated German philosopher and mathematician Gottfried Leibniz (1646–1716). Nevertheless, the inhalation of the fine glass dust aggravated his developing tuberculosis, from which he eventually died. Spinoza was a man of frugal and simple habits. His principal energies and concern were with the pursuit of philosophic studies. It was these to which he devoted himself with all the intensity of a man driven by the highest spiritual ideals.

An early unfinished work from this period, *Treatise on the Improvement of the Understanding*, contains, in its opening pages, memorable autobiographical remarks that recount Spinoza's search for a path of life for himself, on which he finally settled and to whose realization he committed the rest of his life. Although Spinoza had dissociated himself from all orthodox religious beliefs and practices, he nevertheless was, by temperament and commitment, a man who never left the 'religious' orientation to life. He was a deeply spiritual person even though, from the point of view of the ordinary religious believer, a nonbeliever. The nineteenth-century writer Novalis once described Spinoza as a "God-intoxicated man." And that description is in some ways an apt one, although not of course if the concept of 'God' is understood in the traditional way. For in Spinoza's view the constant awareness and love of God (as he interprets what this is to mean) *is* the supreme good of life. In this sense, Spinoza is at one with the whole religious tradition in affirming that the highest good of life is "union of the mind of man with God." Spinoza's major work, the *Ethics*, is devoted to the clarification of what this means. It marks the culmination of a long and intricate philosophic analysis. I shall return later to examine some of the details of the general metaphysical world view, the psychology, and the ethics that support his conclusion. In the opening sections of *Improvement of the Understanding* Spinoza indicates how he came to single out the love of God as the highest good of man. He begins by telling us how, when he stopped to reflect about what most people (as evidenced by their life-styles and behavior) choose as the major goods of life, he found these were largely unsatisfactory.

After experience has taught me that all the usual surroundings of social life are vain and futile; seeing that none of the objects of my fears contained in themselves anything either good or bad, except in so far as the mind is affected by them, I finally resolved to inquire whether there might be some real good having power to communicate itself, which would affect the mind singly, to the exclusion of all else: whether, in fact, there might be anything of which the discovery and attainment would enable me to enjoy continuous, supreme, and unending happiness.[1]

Spinoza claims that the usual things to which people devote their energies and with which they are involved are, to a large extent, vain and futile. In any case what people take to be good or bad is in fact relative to their own dispositions—to their own attitudes and interests. What Spinoza is looking for is a good that is not vain and futile, and one, moreover, that would be not merely relative to a person's fluctuating mental attitudes and individual, variable interests. He is looking for a good that is genuine and objective, a good that, as he puts it, would be "continuous, supreme, and unending."

"Well," you might ask, "what's wrong with the things men normally pursue? What makes them 'vain and futile'?" Spinoza replies:

For the ordinary surroundings of life which are esteemed by men (as their actions testify) to be the highest good, may be classed under the three heads— Riches, Fame, and the Pleasures of Sense: with these three the mind is so absorbed that it has little power to reflect on any different good. By sensual pleasure the mind is enthralled to the extent of quiescence, as if the supreme good were actually attained, so that it is quite incapable of thinking of any other object; when such pleasure has been gratified it is followed by extreme melancholy, whereby the mind, though not enthralled, is disturbed and dulled.[2]

Spinoza, following an ancient classification that goes back to Aristotle, identifies these most prevalent conceptions of the goods of life as the pursuit of sensual gratification, the striving for fame (or honor) and the possession of material goods and wealth.

Spinoza's criticism of choosing sensual gratification (of which food and sex are the most obvious examples) as one's major preoccupation is not made on the ground that he wishes to advocate, instead, some ascetic morality that would recommend repression of normal desires. On the contrary, Spinoza recognizes that pleasures (along with material goods) are a necessary and valuable part of the complete life for a human being. What he is criticizing is the kind of life in which the pursuit of pleasure becomes so all-absorbing that it not merely blocks out other important things but even in its own terms does not yield any genuine, total, or lasting satisfaction. There is something ultimately frustrating about making the pursuit of pleasure one's supreme good. It is not merely the obvious unsatisfactoriness of a life marked by an *overindulgence* in sensual gratifications that Spinoza condemns. Even where one's life is bound up primarily with the attainment of ordinary pleasures, there is something ultimately unrewarding about a total preoccupation with these. They are evanescent, temporary, 'perishable'. You've 'had it', and then its over! Nothing permanent or lasting remains. And sometimes, too, indulgence leads to feelings of 'melancholy' or 'sadness' and to one's 'repenting' (acknowledging the mistaken judgment in its pursuit). The pleasure once had was, after all, not genuinely satisfying! Now this might not be true, to be sure, of all such experiences. But Spinoza claims that because of the evanescent character of pleasures, and the fact that they frequently turn out in their aftereffects to be less rewarding than expected, a life primarily devoted to sensual gratifications is an unsatisfactory one.

Spinoza next turns to the other two popular types of goals that many people pursue.

The pursuit of honors and riches is likewise very absorbing, especially if such objects be sought simply for their own sake, inasmuch as they are then supposed to constitute the highest good. In the case of fame the mind is still more absorbed, for fame is conceived as always good for its own sake, and as the ultimate end to which all actions are directed. Further, the attainment of riches and fame is not followed as in the case of sensual pleasures by repentance, but, the more we acquire, the greater is our delight, and, consequently, the more we are incited to increase both the one and the other; on the other hand, if our hopes happen to be frustrated we are plunged into the deepest sadness. Fame has the further drawback that it compels its votaries to order their lives according to the opinions of their fellow men, shunning what they usually shun, and seeking what they usually seek. . . . All the objects pursued by the multitude, not only bring no remedy that tends to preserve our being, but even act as hindrances, causing the death not seldom of those who possess them, and always of those who are possessed by them. There are many examples of men who have suffered persecution even to death for the sake of their riches, and of men who in pursuit of wealth have exposed themselves to so many dangers, that they have paid away their life as a penalty for their folly. Examples are no less numerous for men, who have endured the utmost wretchedness for the sake of gaining or preserving their reputation.[3]

The pursuit of fame or wealth is just as unsatisfactory as a candidate for being the 'supreme good' of life as is sensual gratification. This good, too, is evanescent and 'perishable'. In pursing fame, a person may be in the limelight one day and forgotten the next. And instead of concentrating on the intrinsic worth of what he might accomplish, such a person depends too readily on what *others* will think or approve. People are fickle, and fashions change. As for the accumulation of material goods and wealth, once again Spinoza does not deny that in any decent life one will require this satisfaction to some degree; what that degree is will differ from person to person. However, for many people the pursuit of wealth and material possessions never comes to an end. The more they have, the more they want. As a result, since their desires are limitless, such persons are basically never satisfied with what they already have.

Spinoza diagnoses the root cause for the ultimate unsatisfactoriness of these ordinary conceptions of what should be our final and supreme good of life:

All these evils seem to have arisen from the fact that happiness or unhappiness is made wholly to depend on the quality of the object which we love. When a thing is not loved, no quarrels will arise concerning it—no sadness will be felt if it perishes—no envy if it is possessed by another—no fear, no hatred, in short no disturbances of the mind. All these arise from the love of what is perishable, such as the objects already mentioned. But love toward a thing eternal and infinite feeds the mind wholly with joy, and is itself unmingled with any sadness, wherefore it is greatly to be desired and sought for with all our strength.[4]

Spinoza sums up the common shortcomings of riches, fame, and pleasure as unsuitable final goods of life: our emotions are bound up with the things we love and pursue. The character of what we love will bring us happiness or unhappiness, joy or various disturbances or anxieties of the mind (envy, jealousy, anger, fear, hatred, remorse, etc.). In the first place, the kinds of 'objects' that make up the pursuit of riches, fame, and pleasure are perishable. Our joy in these is at best short-lived, not enduring or 'permanent'. And, of course, when they are not had in the amount most men crave, this will itself bring dissatisfaction. The second drawback is that normally the pursuit of the aforementioned goods involves our being in competition with our fellow men who are pursuing the same 'objects'. You will want the same profitable business deal or promotion your competitor wants. You may not be the only one in love with the same wonderful girl. If you are an artist or a performer, you will want your novel, concert, or painting to be given acclaim and rewards in preference to those of your rivals. And so on. The competition for these limited goods brings with it well-known anxieties.

Spinoza is looking for a good that will not be of such a nature that the more I have of it the less you can have, and also of such a nature that it will be a source of continuing satisfaction and not evanescent. Love of it will bring tranquility, stability, and freedom from anxiety. Spinoza gives at this point a brief characterization of that supreme good:

It is the knowledge of the union existing between the mind and the whole of nature. This, then, is the end for which I strive, to attain to such a character myself, and to endeavor that many should attain to it with me. In other words, it is part of my happiness to lend a helping hand, that many others may understand even as I do, so that their understanding and desire may entirely agree with my own. In order to bring this about, it is necessary to understand as much of nature as will enable us to attain to the aforesaid character, and also to form a social order such as is most conducive to the attainment of this character by the greatest number with the least difficulty and danger. We must seek the assistance of Moral Philosophy and the Theory of Education; further, as health is no insignificant means for attaining our end, we must also include the whole science of Medicine, and, as many difficult things are by contrivance rendered easy, and we can in this way gain much time and convenience, the science of Mechanics must in no way be despised. But, before all things, a means must be devised for improving the understanding and purifying it, as far as may be at the outset, so that it may apprehend things without error, and in the best possible way.[5]

This brief statement of how Spinoza envisages the ultimate good of life summarizes the underlying motivation for all his writings and activities during the rest of his short life. His major book, the *Ethics*, works out the details of the requisite metaphysics, psychology, ethics, and theory of knowledge. Other writings, such as the *Theological-Political Treatise*, fill out in certain directions other details. The foundation of the entire scheme, the supreme good—what Spinoza here describes as "the union of the mind with the whole of nature"—is what he also describes as "the intellectual love of God." I shall return later to what these phrases mean and what lies behind them.

During the period when these central thoughts were taking shape in Spinoza's mind, he lived at various places where he could find the necessary quiet to do his writing and thinking. He lived for some years (1660–1663) in the small village of Rijnsburg (near Leyden), where he acquired a number of friends among the circle of Collegiant and Mennonite Christians. Their nondogmatic views, tolerance, simplicity, and kindness gave him the warmth of fellowship with kindred spirits as well as an increasing number of admirers. During this period, the first formulations of his own philosophy began to take shape in such early works as *Metaphysical Thoughts* (which was appended to Spinoza's version and exposition of Descartes' philosophy, *The Principles of Descartes' Philosophy*), his more substantial *Short Treatise on God, Man and His Well-Being* (completed in 1660), and the (uncompleted) *Treatise on the Improvement of the Understanding* (1661).

Spinoza left Rijnsburg and took up residence in Voorburg, near the Hague, where he remained for a period of seven years (1663–1670). It was here that he began working on the *Ethics*. His reputation by now had begun to grow, and he was sought out (in person or by correspondence) by a number of eminent men. These included the famous physicist Christiaan Huygens, Henry Oldenburg (one of the first secretaries of the Royal Society in London), and Jan de Witt, the Grand Pensionary of Holland (virtual head of the United Provinces of the Netherlands), who was the leader of the antimonarchist, republican political party. In 1670 Spinoza's *Theological-Political Treatise* was published anonymously, and is among the earliest and most important contributions to the discipline of 'higher criticism', i.e., the analysis of the text of the Bible from a scientific point of view. The principal motive Spinoza had for writing this book was to expose the narrow "prejudices of the Theologians" whose support was being given to strengthen the antidemocratic forces and a general repression of freedom of thought.

Spinoza spent the remaining years of his life (1670–1677) in the Hague. It was here that he brought to completion the *Ethics* (not published until after his death) as well as a number of other works: a *Hebrew Grammar*, a Dutch translation of the Bible (which he was dissatisfied with and destroyed), a *Political Treatise*, and essays *On the Rainbow* and *On the Calculation of Chances*. In 1672, when the French invaded Holland, Jan de Witt and his brother were brutally murdered by their political enemies, on the supposed grounds that they were appeasers. The assassins were led by a faction loyal to the Prince of Orange, William III, later to become King of England. When Spinoza heard of this act of violence to his friend and supporter, he burst into tears, overcome with grief and anger. He was so enraged that he wanted to post at the scene of the crime a placard he wrote denouncing this act of "the very lowest of barbarians." He was luckily restrained, however, by his landlord, who locked the door and thereby undoubtedly kept Spinoza from sharing the same fate as the de Witt brothers.

Spinoza's thought, meanwhile, was being widely discussed—sometimes with great fervor by religious dogmatists who were eager to extirpate the influence of this 'atheist', but also sometimes with admiring interest by those who recognized in his philosophy the qualities of greatness and originality. The German philosopher Gottfried Leibniz, who had read some of Spinoza's works, sought him out and had many conversations with him. In 1673 Spinoza was invited to become a professor of philosophy at the University of Heidelberg. After thinking about the offer for some weeks, however, Spinoza finally decided to decline the opportunity because he feared he would have to surrender his independence and freedom of thought that he treasured so much.

Spinoza's health was gradually deteriorating. Years of hard work and a weakening constitution took their toll. (It is reported that there were times when Spinoza was so involved in his writing that he would not leave his rooms for days at a time or his house for as long as three months!)

He died February 21, 1677, and was buried in a hired grave in a church-yard at the Hague. The sale of his few meager possessions (mostly books) brought just enough to pay for the cost of his funeral and burial. Spinoza combined a profound elevation of spirit and a moral integrity and purity of character that very few persons attain.

General Orientation of Spinoza's Thought

The title of Spinoza's major work, the *Ethics*, indicates that his principal interest is to formulate the nature of the good life for man. However, one can't get a clear grasp of what this good is without an understanding of the world in which man is situated, the reality that provides the background for its pursuit. Spinoza therefore devotes much of his attention to developing his world view or metaphysics. In order to get an initial glimpse of the distinctive and revolutionary character of what he has to say on this latter theme, we do well to bear in mind two major clues: (1) Spinoza's rebellion against the metaphysics of traditional theism and (2) his stress on the emerging role of science as the tool for making Nature intelligible.

Traditional theism rests on three central doctrines: (1) God's being is distinct from (transcends) that of the world. The existence of the world and all that it contains is the outcome of an act of Divine Creation. God both is immaterial and possesses infinite power, freedom, goodness, and wisdom. (2) Despite the attribution of various properties to God, his being is so utterly different and unique ('wholly other') that God's nature is ultimately beyond the grasp of man's finite intelligence. One can know *that* God exists, but not in any clear and definite way *what* God is. God is not accessible to (transcends) human understanding. (3) On certain special occasions and through the agency of certain select individual persons, God discloses certain truths to mankind. Such disclosures take the form of revelations, direct communications by God to his chosen prophets. These persons, in turn, bring the 'message' of these revelations to others who then undertake to interpret, act on, and teach men to heed and obey the revealed word of God. Man's reason can be enlisted in support of the truths established by revelation, but cannot be regarded as competent to judge or criticize that which is given through revelation.

Rejection of theism

These three doctrines (God's distinctness from the world, God's ultimate inaccessibility to human understanding, and the independent and unquestionable source of truth in revelation) are fundamental items in traditional theism. They are common to Judaism, Christianity, and Islam. *One way of summing up Spinoza's philosophy from a negative point of view, is to say that he rejected each of the foregoing doctrines of theism.*

He rejected, first of all, the view that God is distinct and different from the world. There is only one ultimate reality, which he continues to call 'God'; but for him God is identical with Nature. Another term that Spinoza uses to refer to this one ultimate reality is 'Substance'. So 'God, 'Nature', and 'Substance' are different names for one and the same reality. Furthermore, Spinoza denies that God (Nature) is unintelligible. On the contrary, Spinoza defends the claim that, in principle, Nature is open to exploration and understanding by man's reason. Science, in particular, makes increasingly intelligible the structure and interconnection of the various parts of Nature. The continued progress of science will fill out the details of Nature's (God's) intelligibility. Metaphysics has a grasp, in a general intuitive way, of God's (Nature's) attributes. Both metaphysics (in recognizing the general, essential structure of Nature) and science (in working out the specific causal connections among the multitudinous parts of Nature) are together founded on the conviction that reality is open to man's understanding. God (Nature), far from being 'wholly other' and transcending the powers of human intellect, is accessible to man's reason. Finally, Spinoza rejects the traditional appeal to revelation as a final and unquestionable source of truth. For him, whatever truth we discover about the world and whatever goals and standards are to be set for human conduct are matters for human reason to decide. It is reason, not revelation that is the source of metaphysical and scientific truth, as well as the source of moral guidance. There is no divine being, a supreme and unquestioned authority and arbiter, from whom man passively receives his basic knowledge and guidance. It is man himself who has to discover the truth with his own unaided powers. Through the researches of the various sciences, man, bit by bit, establishes the truth about the world in which he lives. Through a growing understanding of our own human nature (through psychology and moral philosophy), we can become increasingly clear about the powers of the human psyche and the ways of maximizing the goods of life.

Spinoza's championing of the competence of reason, and of the method of science to make Nature intelligible, is one obvious point at which his philosophy is strongly influenced by Descartes' thought and shares with the latter the general scientific optimism of the age. Spinoza's account of the different 'grades' of human knowledge is the basis, on the one hand, for his rejecting any reliance on nonrational ways of supporting our beliefs and, on the other hand, of his identifying, constructively, the positive and reliable ways in which rational beliefs can be secured.

Three grades of human knowledge

In the *Ethics*, Spinoza accordingly distinguishes "three grades of human knowledge." The first consists of 'inadequate' ideas, whereas the second and third represent, each in its own way, types of what he calls 'adequate' ideas. The first grade of knowledge is that in which men rely in an uncritical way on the senses, memory, imagination, hearsay, and tradition as sources of beliefs. This type of knowledge is made up of "confused or inadequate ideas." As "knowledge from vague experience" and as mere opinion, it falls short of giving true and certain knowledge. When men believed that the Sun actually rises and sets and moves around a fixed Earth, because that is what they saw with their eyes, this was an example of a belief belonging to the first grade of knowledge. Similarly, when a person repeats and uses some formula of arithmetic learned in school, without ever having had it proved or knowing how to give the proof, again this is a belief taken as true on the basis of hearsay or authority. Spinoza does not claim that everything obtained from the senses or on the basis of authority and hearsay is unreliable. But if we have no way of critically evaluating such beliefs by reason, or establishing their truth on the basis of a scientific and rational proof, then we are unable to discriminate what is genuinely true from what is not. So the first grade of knowledge is, in general, unreliable.

It is only when, through reason, men reach the second and third grades of knowledge that they obtain the certainty of having the truth. For example, the science of astronomy gives a more correct picture of the relationships between the Sun and planets than do the uncritically accepted deliverances of eyesight. In general, the various sciences, in undertaking to give rational justification and proofs for their conclusions, exhibit the use of "adequate ideas." Insofar as they are able to determine the cause-effect connections among the parts and events of Nature, the various sciences are able gradually to find patches of lawfulness and mathematical order in Nature. Not all sciences have made equal progress in this way. Nor is there a single, already achieved, complete system of knowledge that uncovers the entire complex network of interconnections among all parts of Nature. Yet the progress of science as a whole may be measured by the extent to which it links up hitherto disconnected areas of knowledge with one another, and probes more and more deeply into the more complex and hidden recesses of Nature's mechanism.

It is not altogether clear what Spinoza means by the third grade of knowledge, which he calls *scientia intuitiva* (intuitive science or knowledge). Since this is the highest grade of knowledge and is composed entirely of adequate ideas, we may suppose that it has to do with man's awareness, on a metaphysical level, of the virtual unity and completeness of knowledge. We have an intuitive vision, by way of projection, of what a completed science of Nature as a single all-inclusive individual whole would contain. It would show all of Nature to be a unified and intelligible whole in which everything occupies a logical and causal place in interconnections with everything else. We cannot now, of course, or perhaps ever, hope to fill in all the details of this vision. Yet Spinoza here shared with Descartes the conviction that man's reason and science can make steady progress in disclosing that intelligible structure, because Nature itself *is* an orderly and thoroughly intelligible whole. This intuitive reason links up with what Spinoza calls "the intellectual love of God." It marks the culmination of man's spiritual quest for true blessedness.

Spinoza's Ethics: *Method and Subject Matter*

Thus far we have had a brief glimpse of the broad direction and orientation of Spinoza's thought, especially in contrast to the traditional theistic type of philosophy. I turn next to a fuller statement of some of the positive details of Spinoza's system. For this purpose it is necessary to consider what he has to say in his most mature and comprehensive work, the *Ethics*. The full title in Latin is *Ethica Ordine Geometrico Demonstrata* (*Ethics Demonstrated in a Geometrical Manner*). It is one of the most tightly written, technical, and difficult of all the major classics in the history of philosophy. Much of it is obscure, and frequently the lack of clarity or intelligibility can be laid to a failure on Spinoza's part to express his thought with sufficient explicitness and amplification. As a result, many parts of the work, along with certain fundamental aspects of Spinoza's system, have been the topics for widely different interpretations by various commentators. Despite these hazards and obstacles to a clear understanding of what he has to say, the work is of sufficient richness, originality, and general profundity of thought to repay the closest study.

Let us pause, for a moment, to consider the phrase "Demonstrated in a Geometric Manner" in the title of Spinoza's work. Spinoza, as a close student of Descartes' philosophy, shared with him the general ideal of applying to the broader domain of philosophy the same standards and methods of deductive rational thinking already to be found in mathematics. The general pattern of exposition of Spinoza's work is, therefore, cast in a 'geometric' or deductive format. Although Spinoza discusses such topics as the nature of God, knowledge, the human mind, emotions, freedom, and blessedness, he wishes to present his case in such a way that no rational person will be left in doubt as to the truth of what he has to say. As in geometry, the model of a deductive system, he starts with certain Axioms and Definitions, offered as self-evident truths. From these he derives, in a strictly demonstrative way, various Propositions (i.e., theorems and their corollaries). The work is divided into five Parts. Each Part has its own set of Axioms, Definitions, and Propositions. In addition, there are various Appendices and other sections in which Spinoza breaks away from a strictly formal and compact mode of presentation to expound his thoughts more informally.

Deductive format

Spinoza's use of the strict geometric or deductive method as a model for giving us factual truth about the world has the same virtues and limitations as other attempts at this method described in earlier parts of this book. His Axioms are by no means always unquestionably self-evident. Nor can we look to his Definitions to state intuitively obvious truths. Moreover, it is undoubtedly the case that the proofs of the Propositions (Theorems) lack the degree of rigor and precision one would look for in an actual mathematical demonstration. But to stress and merely criticize these shortcomings, legitimate enough from one point of view, without regard to Spinoza's speculative system, is to miss his main accomplishment. What he has to say—the genuine outline of his thought—needs to be extracted from the various statements he makes, whether they be Axioms, Definitions, Propositions, or Appendices. These, taken together, should be considered as so many different formulations of his basic theses or principles. Whatever merit his system of thought possesses belongs to the total vision offered by these fundamental principles.

Organization of the Ethics

One further preliminary word about the organization of the *Ethics*. The First Part is entitled "Of God" and lays the groundwork of the main metaphysical scheme. It introduces and deals with such central technical concepts as the nature of Substance, Mode, and Attribute. The Second Part is entitled "Of the Nature and Origin of the Mind." Here is to be found Spinoza's account of the relation of body and mind, and the various types of ideas and knowledge to be found in the human mind. The Third Part is entitled "Of the Origin and Nature of the Affects." It treats of the emotions—the kinds of things that stir us up and move us—the kinds of changes in the human psyche that make us other than purely intellectual, thinking beings. In the Fourth Part, entitled "Of Human Bondage or of the Strength of the Affects," Spinoza examines the passions. These are the emotions that we should dominate, but ordinarily fail to do so; instead, they come to dominate us. When in the grip of the passions, men are not free. The ultimate concern of Spinoza's psychology and ethics is to point the path to a therapy or release from bondage. The Fifth Part, "Of the Power of the Intellect or of Human Liberty," contains the clues to the various techniques and routes by which man may become free and achieve the supreme good of life, a life of blessedness and of peace of mind. Spinoza begins the *Ethics* with a discussion of God, and in this last part comes back to the intellectual love of God—man's ability to see things "under the aspect of eternity." It is primarily through this means that man can achieve the supreme good of life—the sort of thing that in the *Treatise on the Improvement of the Understanding* Spinoza refers to as "the union of the mind with all of Nature."

This sketch of the contents of the *Ethics* makes clear that Spinoza's ultimate interest is properly ethical, i.e., an analysis of what makes life worth living, what are the goods of life, and what constitutes the distinctive resources man has for achieving a life of well-being in Nature. Everything else in the book—the metaphysical discussion of the nature of God, the psychology, the theory of knowledge, the theory of emotions, and so on— are all by way of preparation and necessary background for delineating the life of freedom from bondage and the serenity and blessedness that comes with an intellectual love of God.

We turn now to a closer look at some of the details of this broad system of ideas.

Substance (Nature or God), Attribute, and Mode

The three central concepts in Spinoza's theory of reality are those of Substance, Attribute, and Mode. The first of these concepts, that of Substance, Spinoza defines as follows:

By substance, I understand that which is in itself and is conceived through itself; in other words, that, the conception of which does not need the conception of another thing from which it must be formed.[6]

Spinoza's conception of Substance

Two Axioms need to be considered along with this Definition of Substance:

I. Everything which is, is either in itself or in another. II. That which cannot be conceived through another must be conceived through itself.[7]

These three statements (the Definition and two Axioms), when clarified, contain the core of Spinoza's metaphysics. To see the significance of the formulation that Spinoza gives to the term 'substance', we need to understand both the standard, inherited philosophic uses of this term and the revolutionary new content that Spinoza gives it.

The concept of 'substance' has been a familiar and central one in philosophy ever since the days of Aristotle. It was used over and over again by various philosophers in subsequent epochs (as it has been, indeed, down to the present day) to serve the needs of expressing their own distinctive viewpoints. Spinoza was neither the first nor was he to be the last to take over this well-worn concept and use it to convey a central thesis in his own metaphysics. To see the radical changes in the way he uses this concept in his own system, we do well to take note of some of its earlier standard meanings and uses. So let us consider three prominent examples of these standard uses, each of which, as we shall see, Spinoza rejects in favor of his own account.

(1) The first important technical meaning of the concept of substance is to be found in Aristotle, who assigns it a central place in his own metaphysics. Aristotle thought of substance as something that is exemplified by ordinary objects: by persons, plants, animals, and the various inanimate things encountered in daily experience. There are manmade and natural substances. An individual tree is a substance; so is a particular rock, dog, or person. Men and some animals make things. Men build houses, make tools, furniture, machines; beavers build dams, birds make nests. These constructed substances (artifacts) result from reshaping and transforming the raw materials found in Nature so that they may serve particular purposes and needs (the chair to sit on, the nest to protect the fledgling, etc.). In the Aristotelian use of this concept, there are *many substances.* For example, Nature is constituted of many different natural *kinds* of substances (stars, rocks, ants, human beings, butterflies, etc.). Belonging to each kind are numerous *individual* substances (this rock, you or I, this oak tree, etc.).

Each individual substance has certain properties (qualities, powers, traits, characteristics, features). For example, this rock is hard, has a rough surface, weighs two pounds, is gray, is lying on the ground next to this tree, and so on. Other individual substances have their own properties. That table is made of wood, is highly polished, is colored brown, is forty inches high, etc. This man is twenty years old, speaks English, is good at mathematics, is married to that young woman, etc. In short, the various things in the world are qualitied, propertied, and related to one another in multitudinous ways.

The individual substances may be grouped in terms of various properties they have in common. Individuals may resemble one another, have various properties in common. Both you, the stone, and the coffee-table, if dropped from a height, will fall. A human being and an animal can digest food and hear sounds. The leaves on the tree and your coat may both be green. On the other hand, various individual substances belonging to distinct natural kinds or classes will have certain properties restricted to the members of that particular class. All men are rational animals: they have the power or capacity of reason. This is a distinctive capacity to plan, deliberate, inquire, and understand, which only men possess and which sets them off from other animals as well as from other entities in the world.

Another aspect of the Aristotelian conception of substance has to do with the distinction between an individual substance and what can be asserted of an individual substance by means of the various predicates we use to describe the individual substance. I can say "Socrates is snubnosed," "Socrates is wise," "This tabletop is brown." I can use general terms ('brown', 'wise', 'snubnosed', etc.) and predicate these properties of individual objects. Aristotle would express this by saying that properties are *in* something else. However, an individual substance is not, in the same way, *in* anything else. For an individual substance (e.g., Socrates) is not itself a property. Rather, individual properties are *in it*. Wisdom is in Socrates as a property of Socrates, but Socrates is not 'in' anything else. Properties, qualities, relations, powers, require for their existence that they be *in* (or attached to) individual substances. The brownness of this table cannot *be*, unless there is an individual table in which this brownness can exist, in which it inheres, to which it belongs. In this sense, properties are *dependent* on substances for their existence. However, substances are independent.

Would the table exist if it were not brown? Would Socrates exist if he were not the teacher of Plato? Aristotle would say: "Yes!" The tabletop need not be brown to be a tabletop: it could be colored white. Socrates might not have met Plato. On the other hand, if a table did not have a surface at all, it would not be a table. If Socrates had not been possessed of reason, he would not have been a person or human being at all. Some properties are thus *essential* to certain entities, if they are going to be that kind of entity. On the other hand, other characteristics are *accidental* (or nonessential). They might have been absent altogether, or, if present, undergo change, lapse, or vary from one individual to another in the same class. For example, a person may learn to speak Turkish who never knew this language before. However, not all human beings speak Turkish. Speaking Turkish is not essential to being a human being, nor is the color brown essential to being a tabletop. However, having the capacity of reason is essential to being a human being; having a relatively flat surface is essential to serving as a table.

Spinoza's conception of substance in many important respects is in basic disagreement with Aristotle's. Perhaps the most important point of difference is that whereas for Aristotle there are *many* substances, for Spinoza there is only *one*. Substance, in Spinoza's view, is unique. It would therefore probably be best, in differentiating his use of this term, to capitalize it. What Aristotle calls 'substances' Spinoza will describe by the use of the term '*mode*'. According to Spinoza, there are many modes, all of which belong to one, unique Substance.

Spinoza's modes and Aristotelian substances

We have now to see what led Spinoza to this conclusion. Interestingly, we may find the clue to Spinoza's reasoning by following through with the distinction in Aristotle between substance as independent and 'in itself', as contrasted with that which depends for its existence on substance and inheres in it. The brownness of the table, we said, could not exist unless there were a table to belong to, or of which it is a part or aspect. Substances are that *in* which various properties inhere, to which they belong. On the other hand, substances do not belong, as properties do, to other things. In this sense they are independent and exist 'in themselves'. Spinoza, we may suppose (in reconstructing the process of his reasoning), came to believe that even so-called substances are not genuinely independent and self-sufficient. They, too, depend for their existence on other things. Although to be sure this table, or Socrates, or this tree is not as such merely a property, nevertheless each of them is part of some wider and more inclusive whole, or system, or network of things. If the brown surface could not exist by itself—it has to be the surface of some object—it is likewise true, Spinoza would say, that the table itself depends for its existence on other things. It is linked in all sorts of ways with other things. Take these away and the table could not exist or be independent or self-sufficient, either. For one thing, the table is 'in' something else in a purely spatial sense (in this room, which is in turn in this building, etc.). But the table is 'in' something else not only spatially but also in the sense in which it is *in a network of causal interconnections* with other things. The table is supported by the floor, requires a certain range of temperature within which it can retain its solidity, was made by a carpenter, is used now by human beings as a table, and so on. A particular human being, likewise, is what he or she is by virtue of the innumerable lines of interconnection with other things that sustain the person in existence and give the person the characteristics he or she has. Take all of these away and the human being no longer exists as an individual. A person's very existence, along with one's qualities and relations, show one to be as *dependent* on other things as the brown surface of the table is dependent on the table. If this is true of so-called substances—that they are 'in' other things, and are conceived (understood) through other things—then as far as the matter of 'independence' and 'dependence' is concerned, there is no fundamental difference between so-called substances and properties. Both are 'in' something else, conceived through something else, and hence 'dependent'.

Substance, for Spinoza, is unique and all-inclusive

Yet, Spinoza would continue, as we follow through this network of interdependencies, we realize that whereas there are wider and wider wholes and networks into which any part, fragment, item, or individual entity can be placed, there must also be an absolute, all-inclusive whole or all-encompassing network of which everything else is a part or fragment. This absolute whole itself is not part of some still more fundamental whole. By definition, an absolute whole is not a partial or dependent relative whole. It is that of which everything else is a part or an aspect. However, it itself does not belong to, or inhere in, anything else. Only *it* is truly and genuinely *in* itself, and is therefore to be *conceived* through itself. If, indeed, the term 'substance' is to be used to stand for that which is 'in itself' and is 'conceived through itself', then there can be only *one* Substance. It will be an absolutely all-inclusive whole that is not linked with anything else in causal terms. It is not an *effect*, i.e., *dependent* on anything else. And this is what makes it absolutely unique. It is, by contrast with everything else found within it, independent and self-sufficient. This utterly unique whole is what Spinoza means by '*Substance*'. He also uses the terms 'God' and 'Nature' to designate the same unique all-inclusive and ultimate reality.

Everything within Nature—all the parts or fragments or aspects of this Substance—Spinoza calls '*Modes*'. You and I, this table, the thunderstorm yesterday, the Sun, this mosquito—these are so many modifications or modes of this one Substance. We and all these other entities belong to Nature, much as the various waves of the ocean are but partial fragments of the ocean and could not exist or be conceived apart from the ocean of which they are modifications, states, or modes. Ultimately, therefore, to conceive (to understand or explain) the existence and character of any particular fragment or modification of Substance or Nature, I have got to see it in its place within the whole. Although no one ever succeeds, at any given time, in having a complete understanding of any fragment, nevertheless one can understand it more and more the wider and more subtle the lines of interconnection one can trace from it to other parts of Nature.

(2) The second traditional view of substance that Spinoza rejects is associated with the philosophy of theism. In that philosophy, as we have seen, there is a fundamental distinction between the Uncreated, Eternal, Infinite, Immaterial, and wholly Transcendent Divine Substance, on the one hand, and the created, material, spatial and temporal, dependent substances belonging to 'the world', on the other. In this sense traditional theism adopts a *dualistic* metaphysics. Spinoza rejects traditional theistic metaphysics because for him there is only one ultimate reality, which he too will call 'God'. However, unlike in theism, God will be identified with Nature. God is not immaterial, transcendent, the creative source of Nature. God and Nature are identically the same reality. Spinoza's metaphysics is thus monistic, not dualistic.

Although Spinoza uses the term 'God' synonymously with 'Nature' (and 'Substance'), he does not think of God in all of the ways in which traditional theism does. Thus, as we shall see, for Spinoza God is not a Designing, Providential Intelligence. God is not the Moral Governor of the World. Nature (or God), for Spinoza, is amoral. Nature operates according to strictly causal laws, and has no moral purposes or ultimate goals that control it in behalf of mankind or any other constituent of its all-inclusive content and order. Hence Spinoza is *not* a pantheist, as many people mistakenly suppose, if the term 'pantheism' means that

The concept of substance in theism

God is conceived as a force that permeates all of Nature, a force or power that somehow governs all events to insure the eventual triumph of some benevolent design.

The concept of substance in Descartes

(3) For Spinoza, since there is only one Substance, there cannot be two distinct *types* of substance. The third conception of substance Spinoza rejects is that illustrated in Descartes' conception of man as a composite being consisting of two distinct substances, a body and a mind. According to this view, there is in the human being an immaterial, thinking substance or mind distinct from yet able to interact with the extended, material, unthinking bodily substance. Spinoza not only rejects the distinction between God and the world, he also rejects the distinction between the mind and the body. The latter distinction is to be found not only in Descartes' philosophy but also in the whole religious tradition that makes a crucial distinction between an immortal soul and a mortal, material body. In order to see why Spinoza rejects this traditional body-mind dualism, we must turn to his account of the distinction between the *Attributes* of Extension and Thought.

Extension and Thought

Spinoza's conception of Attribute

We have thus far considered the distinction Spinoza makes between Substance and its modes. A third basic concept in Spinoza's metaphysics is that of Attribute. Here again Spinoza takes over a standard term used in traditional philosophy and theology and gives it a fresh and distinctive application in his system of thought. He writes:

By attribute, I understand that which the intellect perceives of substance, as if constituting its essence.[8]

And he adds to this the following definition of God:

By God, I understand Being absolutely infinite, that is to say, substance consisting of infinite attributes, each one of which expresses eternal and infinite essence.[9]

To get at Spinoza's meaning of the term 'Attribute', let us first hint at it by using some simple analogies. Suppose there are a variety of objects and persons on the stage of a theater where the stage is absolutely dark. I shine a bright green light onto the stage. Everything is now visible, but appears as colored green. Next, I change the color of the stage light to red. Once again everything is lit up in the same color, this time red. The two colors in which everything appears—red and green—are, for purposes of *rough analogy*, comparable to the ways in which the Attributes of Substance 'light up' Substance and all the modes contained in Substance.

Take another analogy: Suppose a man were to commit suicide by jumping off a cliff. One could examine that event solely from the perspective of the physicist and treat this event as a case of a falling body. The laws and concepts used in describing and explaining the event (the accelerated rate of fall, the time taken, etc.) apply to *any* falling object, whether it be a stone, the limb of a tree, or a man's body. On the other hand, a psychologist or biographer would use an entirely different perspective on the event. Why did the man commit suicide? Did he have an unhappy family life? Was he despairing over the loss of his job? Did he think he was suffering from a fatal disease? To understand the motivations and psychological causes of the event is clearly to use a different set of concepts for describing and explaining the event than the physicist did. These are two possible but yet essentially different ways of looking at the same event.

Consider, finally, the following example. Suppose, as a printer and typesetter, I were to look at a book and examine the printed marks on the page simply as physical objects, paying attention solely to the size of the print, the color, the width of the margins, and the shape of the letters, and were to disregard anything having to do with the *meaning* of the words, the *style* of the author, the *truth* of what he is saying. On the other hand, as a reader or book reviewer, I would surely concentrate on the latter features. Once again I have two alternate, equally legitimate, yet completely different ways of looking at the same material.

Spinoza claims that Nature (Substance, God) and all the modes that belong to it may be perceived or approached in terms of one or another Attribute of Substance. Each will 'light up' or disclose Substance or any given mode (or modes) within it. And *everything* in Nature will belong to or exhibit one or another Attribute. It isn't the case that some modes fall under one Attribute and other modes under a different one. Rather, everything in Nature falls under one Attribute, and all the *same* modes —everything all over again—also fall under a quite different Attribute.

For Spinoza there are only two Attributes of Substance known to man. These are Extension and Thought. Under the Attribute of Extension everything in Nature has a physical, material, or bodily dimension. Every part of Nature occupies space, endures through time, and interacts with other bodies. At the same time, everything in Nature can be viewed under the Attribute of Thought. This can be understood in two ways: (1) Everything possesses some level or kind of mind. (2) Everything can be seen as part of a logical structure, where the 'idea' that characterizes it links up with other ideas (other entities) in a logically intelligible system of ideas.

A key passage in which Spinoza formulates this aspect of his metaphysics is the following:

The order and connection of ideas is the same as the order and connection of things.[10]

In amplification of this, Spinoza says:

Substance ·thinking and substance extended are one and the same substance, which is now comprehended under this attribute and now under that. Thus, also, a mode of extension and the idea of that mode are one and the same thing expressed in two different ways. . . . Whether we think of nature under the attribute of extension, or under the attribute of thought, or under any other attribute whatever, we shall discover one and the same order, or one and the same connection of causes; that is to say, in every case the same sequence of things. . . . When things are considered as modes of thought we must explain the order of the whole of nature or the connection of causes by the attribute of thought alone, and when things are considered as modes of extension, the order of the whole of nature must be explained through the attribute of extension alone, and so with other attributes.[11]

In interpreting this passage, there is one idea of which we can be reasonably sure. Spinoza would reject the view that there are special and distinct kinds of entities or substances we call 'bodies' and 'minds'. Instead, he would claim, everything should be viewed as having a mental (or thought) aspect and a physical (or bodily) aspect. These are different ways in which the parts of Nature reveal themselves, and in which Nature as a whole appears.

When viewed in terms of the Attribute of Extension, Nature is a system of interacting bodies in space and time, having mechanical properties. It is the field of study for an enlarged science of mathematical physics. Human beings, along with everything else in Nature, are parts of this system. They 'have' bodies only in the sense that (seen under the Attribute of Extension) they function and interact in a *bodily way*. Of course, we need not deny that the mechanical or bodily aspect of some things (modes) is more complex than that of others. Our own bodily mechanism, as human beings, is more complex than that of an oyster or a stone.

We may also understand Spinoza to be saying that when we regard the various modes of Nature in terms of the Attribute of Thought, there is a corresponding complexity in the degree of their responses as 'minds'. For all things can be considered as being in some degree 'animated'. On this interpretation of what Spinoza means by 'thought', he is here defending a form of *panpsychism*. This is the view that everything in Nature has some degree or type of 'mental' activity. The degree of 'mental' activity or responsiveness of a mode is correlated with the degree or type of complexity that it has when viewed in terms of the Attribute of Extension—as a bodily mechanism.

If everything can be said to have a 'mind', it does not mean, we may interpret Spinoza to be saying, that everything interacts as a 'mind' with other things in the same way or on the same level. For example, only man has a mind capable of reason and logical thought, of producing adequate ideas that enable him to understand the world about him. Man *thinks,* and is conscious. But not everything in Nature (not all modes) is similarly endowed.

When man thinks, some of his ideas are adequate, others inadequate. (Recall the distinctions Spinoza draws among three grades of knowledge.) When we use our power of thinking to form adequate ideas in the sciences, for example, we can trace the causal connections among interacting bodies. The world of bodies becomes intelligible as a vast and complex mechanical system. The system of *ideas* of this *mechanical system* is, however, also a *logical system of ideas.* Certain ideas, expressed as conclusions, follow in a required *logical* way from other ideas, expressed as the premises of the system. By this means we have entered onto another dimension of the world. It is no longer only a mechanical system of bodies causally interacting with one another. That same system of extensional bodies is also a logically interconnected system. The ideas we have of them 'in' our mind (when we think adequately) correspond to the actual *logical* structure that these events exhibit. The world is a logical and rationally intelligible structure. This is what Spinoza means when he asserts that "The order and connection of ideas is the same as the order and connection of things." This famous statement sums up the core of Spinoza's rationalism. The pattern of bodily events in the world has the same kind of logical connectedness as we would find in a mathematical system. The very same relation in which one bodily or extensional event *causally* follows from another, by virtue of a causal necessity, is at the same time also a *logical* connection. If the idea of one event (the cause) is stated in our premises, then the idea of another event (the effect) is deducible as a *logical necessity* from the first idea. For Spinoza, causal necessity and logical necessity are ultimately two different ways (under the Attributes of Extension and Thought) of expressing the same rational structure of things. To say that the order and connection of ideas is the same as the order and connection of things is to say that Nature, when viewed in terms of the Attribute of Thought, is a logical system. To the extent that men have adequate ideas, as thinking minds, they are no longer merely being pushed and pulled as bodies. Their minds (thought, ideas) are now 'in' a logical system. They *understand* the world. Spinoza is con-

"The order and connection of ideas is the same as the order and connection of things"

vinced that there is a complete logical order *to be* discovered. That Order of Nature exists even if men don't know it in all its details, at any given time.

Thus whereas our bodies are limited and confined in space and time, our thinking powers, even though themselves also finite and limited, can range widely and deeply. Our power to think lifts us out of our bodily, spatiotemporal limitations. We can scan vast distances and times, and uncover the logical interconnections of things. The world becomes intelligible. It is this power of the human intellect to understand the world that, according to Spinoza, offers the only genuine blessedness and 'salvation' possible to man. Our bodies are finite and mortal, as are, of course, our thinking powers. But in using our thinking powers to understand the 'eternal' logical order of things we can become in that measure 'immortal' too.

Causal Determinism

There is one further theme that requires examination in rounding out this summary of Spinoza's conception of the world. This has to do with his view that the world is a completely deterministic causal order. Here again Spinoza is rebelling against traditional theism, according to which there is an all-powerful Being who imposed a certain order on the world at Creation, and who can also suspend, at any time, the operation of that order. God, in other words, can interfere with the established lawful pattern of events and perform miracles. God has an infinite freedom and power to do whatever he wills. He does whatever he does in order to achieve certain ends or goals (which may or may not be known to man). God, being both benevolent and omnipotent, has a providential interest in the world and in man. He orders things so that his chosen teleological order will eventually be carried out. If someone violates God's commandments he will be punished. In short, in the traditional world view, the world is a designed system. It is a system in which God operates by free choice and in which man, too, as a finite image of God's infinite properties, has the power of free will. Man, too, insofar as he exercises free will, can make things happen without being causally predetermined to act in a certain way. According to theism, man can act to achieve his own purposes (which, of course, will not always be benevolent or morally approvable).

Spinoza's rejection of cosmic design, free will, miracles

Spinoza rejects all such ideas. He rejects the notion of cosmic design and of a teleological order controlling the events in the world. He also rejects the notion of free will, whether supposedly possessed by God or by man. According to Spinoza, whatever happens does so because of the presence and operation of causes that are necessarily followed by certain effects. The world is a causally determined order, not a designed one. It makes no sense, for Spinoza, to ask *why* events happen, if this means to look for some purpose (traditionally called a *'final* cause') that has been set by some Designing Intelligence. Science, in giving us an understanding and explanation of events, tells us *how* things happen, in exemplifying certain strict and inviolable sequences of cause and effect. Furthermore, there is no free will in Nature or in man that can suspend the laws of Nature. The laws of Nature are not the sort of thing that *can* be suspended. Given certain causes, certain effects *must* follow in the same way in which, given the axioms and definitions of a mathematical system, the theorems must follow. The causal order of Nature is a necessary order, just as a mathematical system exhibits a logical necessity linking premises and conclusions.

Spinoza heaps his scorn on those who would look at Nature as a theater of events that can be understood in terms of divine or human choice. A famous passage in which Spinoza ridicules this approach is the following:

It is commonly supposed that all things in nature, like men, work to some end; and indeed it is thought to be certain that God Himself directs all things to some sure end, for it is said that God has made all things for man, and man that he may worship God. . . .

Do but see, I pray, to what all this has led. Amidst so much in nature that is beneficial, not a few things must have been observed which are injurious, such as storms, earthquakes, diseases, and it was affirmed that these things happened either because the gods were angry because of wrongs which had been inflicted on them by man, or because of sins committed in the method of worshipping them; and although experience daily contradicted this, and showed by an infinity of examples that both the beneficial and the injurious were indiscriminately bestowed on the pious and the impious, the inveterate prejudices on this point have not therefore been abandoned.

For it was much easier for a man to place these things aside with others of the use of which he was ignorant, and thus retain his present and inborn state of ignorance, than to destroy the whole superstructure and think out a new one. Hence it was looked upon as indisputable that the judgments of the gods far surpass our comprehension; and this opinion alone would have been sufficient to keep the human race in darkness to all eternity, if mathematics, which does not deal with ends, had not placed before us another rule of truth. . . . Nature has set no end before herself and . . . all final causes are nothing but human fictions. . . .[12]

Spinoza then points out that those committed to the view that everything has a purpose will never cease to look for such purposes:

For, by way of example, if a stone has fallen from some roof on somebody's head and killed him, they will demonstrate in this manner that the stone has fallen in order to kill the man. For if it did not fall for that purpose by the will of God, how could so many circumstances concur through chance (and a number often simultaneously do concur)? You will answer, perhaps, that the event happened because the wind blew and the man was passing that way. But they will urge, why did the wind blow at that time, and why did the man pass that way precisely at the same moment? If you again reply that the wind rose then because the sea on the preceding day began to be stormy, the weather hitherto having been calm, and that the man had been invited by a friend, they will urge again—because there is no end of questioning—But why was the sea agitated? Why was the man invited at that time? And so they will not cease from asking the causes of causes, until at last you fly to the will of God, the refuge for ignorance.[13]

In Spinoza's example, the man's walking along a certain path can be understood in terms of a sequence of causes. The stone's being dislodged, again, can be understood in terms of a particular causal sequence (the rainstorm, the loosening of the soil, the blowing of the wind, etc.), in terms of known laws of geology, meteorology, and so on. The rainstorm would have happened whether or not the man was on his way to visit his friend. And the man went to visit his friend because he received an invitation and followed a certain path. What happened was the combined, resultant effect of these independent causal lines, in which every event is causally explainable. The occurrence was not, therefore, prearranged or designed. Those taking a theistic view will argue that there must have been a deliberate, intended arrangement of these events so that God may carry out his design. For Spinoza such a belief is a form of superstition. You don't really *know*, and yet you *suppose* that it's all a matter of deliberate design. It is much more sound and rational, however, to recognize that what happened can be accounted for as the result of the intersection of a number of causal lines, each of which is determined in its own way.

Spinoza argues that, however difficult it is to do, one must stand back and understand *any* event in the world in an objective way. We must understand all the events in the world, including what happens to human beings, as parts of a causally determined network or pattern. Spinoza believes that, to the extent we can understand Nature in this way, we can achieve a certain peace of mind and are freed from anxiety, fear, hatred, and other 'passions'. Spinoza writes:

All things, I say, are in God, and everything which takes place takes place by the laws alone of the infinite nature of God, and follows . . . from the necessity of His essence.[14]

From the supreme power of God, or from His infinite nature . . . all things have necessarily flowed, or continually follow by the same necessity, in the same way as it follows from the nature of a triangle, from eternity to eternity, that its three angles are equal to two right angles.[15]

Notice that Spinoza still uses the old religious terminology according to which everything happens because of God. But whereas on the older view the reasons why God acts are to be understood in terms of his chosen purposes, for Spinoza 'God' is another name for Nature or Substance. In Nature (God), there is no will or design operating, only a strict, morally neutral causal order. Spinoza uses the traditional terminology and 'pours new wine into the old bottle'.

These four concepts—(1) Substance (Nature or God), (2) Mode, (3) Attribute, and (4) Causality—are the four pillars on which Spinoza's entire metaphysical system rests. They provide the background and framework for his treatment of human psychology and for his examination of the ethics of the good life for man. We turn to these topics next, by way of conclusion.

Of Human Bondage and Freedom

Individual persons are finite modes of Substance. Man is not a special creation of a transcendent Deity. Man, along with everything else, is a part of Nature and the product of causal laws. In this sense we can say that, along with pebbles, thunderstorms, roses, stars, apes, etc., man is part of God. For God *is* Nature.

What sets off man as a part of Nature from other parts (at least those we know of), according to Spinoza, is that "man thinks"; he is a rational animal. And this fact is of central importance in Spinoza's philosophy, as it is in the entire tradition of humanistic, rational ethics, ever since the days of the Greeks. The *good* life for man is a life of reason. Human reason makes possible a life of *virtue*—of excellence. And it is through the exercise of reason that man can become *free*. He can cease to be merely a body or an animal, moved by causes and forces over which he has no control and which he does not understand. Also, insofar as a man is capable of forming adequate ideas, he can be freed from the vices and passions that beset his life. He can cease to be guided by inadequate ideas and can enjoy a life of what Spinoza calls 'active emotions'.

A life of reason does not mean leading a purely 'intellectual' life. For example, Spinoza remarks:

It is the part of a wise man, I say, to refresh and invigorate himself with moderate and pleasant eating and drinking, with sweet scents and the beauty of green plants, with ornament, with music, with sports, with the theatre, and with all things of this kind which one man can enjoy without hurting another. For the human body is composed of a great number of parts of diverse nature, which constantly need new and varied nourishment, in order that the whole of the body may be equally fit for everything which can follow from its nature, and consequently that the mind may be equally fit to understand many things at once.[16]

A rational life for a complete human being is one in which both our animal and social needs and our intellectual and spiritual interests are incorporated and satisfied.

Man's freedom does not consist in escaping from the network of causes and effects through the exercise of 'free will'. It consists, rather, in having adequate ideas as the determinants of conduct, on both personal and social levels of behavior. Spinoza argues that the belief in free will is a superstition. It derives from a failure to acknowledge the strictly determined pattern that holds for all the parts of Nature.

Thus the infant believes that it is by free will that it seeks the breast; the angry boy believes that by free will he wishes vengeance; the timid man thinks it is with free will he seeks flight; the drunkard believes that by a free command of his mind he speaks the things which when sober he wishes he had left unsaid. Thus the madman, the chatterer, the boy, and others of the same kind, all believe that they speak by a free command of the mind, whilst, in truth, they have no power to restrain the impulse which they have, to speak, so that experience itself, no less than reason, clearly teaches that men believe themselves to be free simply because they are conscious of their own actions, knowing nothing of the causes by which they are determined: it teaches, too, that the decrees of the mind are nothing but the appetites themselves, which differ, therefore, according to the different temper of the body. . . . These decrees of the mind, therefore, arise in the mind by the same necessity as the ideas of things actually existing. Consequently, those who believe that they speak, or are silent, or do anything else from a free decree of the mind, dream with their eyes open.[17]

Active and passive emotions

Spinoza's account of the human psyche, i.e., the life of a human being involving its bodily and mental aspects, stresses the role of the emotions or 'affects'. We are 'affected', stirred up, undergo *e-motions*, through various causes and factors. The emotions, on both a bodily and a mental level, either help or hinder us, increase or diminish our power of acting. The emotions that stir us can be either 'active' or 'passive'. In Spinoza's terminology, there are times when we can be said to *act* (or, have active emotions), and this occurs when our emotions are guided by adequate ideas. At other times (again, in his special terminology), we *suffer* because we undergo various passions, i.e., passive emotions; and this occurs when we are in the grip of inadequate ideas. We are governed in the latter case by images or by opinions that have no rational basis in fact. Under these conditions we develop various passions of fear, hatred, envy, and the like. When dominated by these passions, we more often than not hurt other people as well as ourselves. A passion is a form of vice. It marks the lowering of the vitality or well-being of the individual. If the human being, as he goes through life, is thought of as a complex and ever-changing scale of performance or level of vitality, then active emotions mark the raising of the level of performance, passions and suffering the lowering of the scale of performance. A lowering of vitality and well-being is an impairment of functioning. The modern term for certain types of malfunctioning is 'neurosis'. For Spinoza, when a person suffers from neuroses (in his terminology, is 'in bondage'), this is primarily due to cognitive deficiencies, i.e., from his having wrong-headed ideas. The individual doesn't understand the true linkage of facts and is held in bondage to his inadequate ideas. He suffers the tortures of the damned because he lets images and opinions determine his behavior. Anticipating some of the leading insights of modern psychotherapy, Spinoza recognizes that an essential condition of winning release from neuroses, anxieties, and tensions comes from *understanding* ourselves. What forces have acted, or are acting, on you to bring about your present condition? A person cannot genuinely win freedom unless he has this understanding.

Spinoza uses the term 'passive emotions' or 'passions' because *they* control *us*. We are the passive objects, the slaves, of their domination. The only way to achieve release from bondage is through the substitution of active emotions. We gain control over our behavior and act freely when two conditions are satisfied. First, we must understand our own and other people's behavior, or other relevant occurrences in Nature. However, Spinoza insists, understanding alone will not free one from bondage to passions. The second necessary condition is to replace one emotion by another. The 'bad' (passive) emotion has to be replaced by a 'good' (active) emotion. It takes one emotion to 'drive out' another. "An emotion can only be controlled or destroyed by another emotion contrary thereto, and with more power."[18] Mere understanding—reading a lot of books, listening to someone who makes things clear to you, and your saying "Yes, I understand"—these alone will not free you from your passions. Your understanding has to be supplemented, or rather implemented, by an altered set of emotions and feeling-attitudes. Spinoza, in Parts Three and Four of the *Ethics*, gives a lengthy and detailed analysis (too complex to be examined here) of the various active and passive emotions and of how to go about substituting one for the other.

Virtue and vice

'Virtue', in Spinoza's ethics, is another name for strength and power of acting.* It comes with the presence of rational understanding and active emotions. It is the condition of the free and happy life. In this sense, virtue is its own reward. 'Vice', contrariwise, is another name for lack of strength, for a lowering and hampering of the exercise of one's powers, for being a slave to one's passions—the mark of the unhappy man. For Spinoza, the essence of morality is not fulfillment of some externally imposed set of rules, commandments, or moral 'laws'. To be moral is not primarily a matter of performing one's *duty*, of doing what is *right*, or of doing what *ought* to be done. The controlling notions of moral philosophy have to do with those that make for the enhancement of life (the maximization of its virtues), and the minimalization of its vices, in the preceding uses of these terms.

The intellectual love of God; blessedness

I have summarized thus far, in general terms, Spinoza's account of the differences between active and passive emotions, virtue and vice, freedom and bondage. However, there is another side to human life not covered by these concepts. For these concepts center primarily on the guidance and control of the psyche's activities insofar as men are endowed with certain biologically based drives, and are possessed of various needs and interests as members of social groups, interacting with their fellow men. The other dimension of human life with which Spinoza is very much concerned, but which is not covered by the foregoing analysis, is a side we may call 'spiritual' or (in a guarded use of this term) 'religious'. Spinoza himself (for all his atheism) was a deeply religious person. He therefore sought within the framework of his naturalistic philosophy to give ample scope to what, in the older tradition, was called the desire for 'salvation' or 'blessedness'. If and when realized, the state of blessedness would lift a person out of an exclusive preoccupation with animal needs or social concerns and involvements. Suppose a person were able to somehow solve all his or her personal problems, and suppose, too, people had solved all their social problems of living together. Needless to say, Spinoza does not claim that this is ever likely to occur. Nevertheless, let us suppose a suitable combination of inherited circumstances, rational understanding, and successful direction of human affairs allowed men to secure for themselves a sufficient degree of leisure, comfort, technological control, social well-being, and personal freedom from anxieties and neuroses. This would still not define all that a human being as such can achieve. A person's life would still be incomplete without the kind of elevation of spirit Spinoza calls 'the intellectual love of God'.

Such love arises from the exercise of the human power of reason to give

* Recall Plato's conception of *aretē* (virtue), to which Spinoza's view has a close resemblance.

one adequate ideas on the third grade of knowledge (intuitive science). One has a genuine intuitive and philosophic grasp of the fact that Nature (God) as a whole is a thoroughly intelligible structure. One who has such an understanding experiences a deep satisfaction, pleasure, or joy in this awareness. This pleasure or joy is called 'love' by Spinoza. Nor does one who has such a love of God ask or expect that God will love him in return. For this would not make any sense. To have an intellectual love of God is to see everything 'under the aspect of eternity'. It is to see everything as flowing from the nature of God. This 'flowing' happens not as the outcome of divine *decree* and as a matter of will on the part of a supremely powerful Ruler. Instead, whatever belongs to Nature is seen as having logical necessity. In the face of this acknowledged rational necessity, a person is able to experience the joy and love that understanding brings. It is not fear that makes him submit to God's will, or have faith in God's goodness, mercy, and justice. It is the calm resignation and serene accommodation to a pervasive logical necessity in Nature that could not be otherwise than it is. The achievement of this state of mind is what Spinoza means by 'blessedness'.

Perhaps there are very few people in the world who are able to practice the kind of awareness or love Spinoza is talking about. (Einstein once said that his religion was that of Spinoza). In any case, for Spinoza the scaling of this height is what is at once the most difficult yet, of all rewards of human existence, the most 'permanent' and satisfying. The concluding passage of the *Ethics* contains Spinoza's famous description of this supreme good:

I have finished everything I wished to explain concerning the power of the mind over the affects and concerning its liberty. From what has been said we see what is the strength of the wise man, and how much he surpasses the ignorant who is driven forward by lust alone. For the ignorant man is not only agitated by external causes in many ways, and never enjoys true peace of soul, but lives also ignorant, as it were, both of God and of things, and as soon as he ceases to suffer ceases also to be. On the other hand, the wise man, in so far as he is considered as such, is scarcely ever moved in his mind, but, being conscious by a certain eternal necessity of himself, of God, and of things, never ceases to be, and always enjoys true peace of soul. If the way which, as I have shown, leads hither seem very difficult, it can nevertheless be found. It must indeed be difficult since it is so seldom discovered; for if salvation lay ready to hand and could be discovered without great labor, how could it be possible that it should be neglected almost by everybody? But all noble things are as difficult as they are rare.[19]

The foregoing summary of some of the main features of Spinoza's philosophy has ignored much that in a more technical and thorough analysis would call for discussion. Much in Spinoza's thought is obscure.

Concluding comments

A good deal represents his own unsatisfactory attempt to take over and use some of the basic concepts and principles of medieval thought and adjust these to the needs of the naturalistic and science-oriented philosophy he was concerned to espouse. There is much, too, in his thought that has been the subject of controversial and divergent interpretations by various Spinoza scholars. Finally, there are weaknesses in his philosophy that are not unique to him alone, but are indigenous to any rationalistic scheme of thought. We have previously noted some of these in connection with our discussion of Descartes' philosophy. The most searching criticisms of Spinoza (apart from those made by the whole theistic tradition, which would reject, *in toto*, the basic presuppositions and orientation of his thought) are those made by fellow naturalists who work within the same broad tradition to which he contributed so much. Some of these latter criticisms emerge from a more scrupulous and altered conception of the power of human reason, and of the scientific method that is one of its most sophisticated exemplifications. We shall see one example of this methodological type of criticism by a fellow naturalist when we turn, in the next chapter, to a study of Dewey's account of the nature of *experimental intelligence*. And towards the end of this book (in the concluding section of Chapter 14), the present author, in setting out some of his own views, will offer some suggestions for the formulation of a naturalistic philosophy that, while building on some of Spinoza's insights, will also point in other directions.

chapter 12

Pragmatic Humanism

To move from the thought of Spinoza to that of John Dewey is to move from the thought of a seventeenth-century European rationalist to that of a twentieth-century American pragmatist. Spinoza was nurtured in medieval thought but held captive by the Cartesian vision of an orderly, mathematically intelligible world. Living in the Netherlands, Spinoza was surrounded by a society grappling with the problems and conflicts brought about by the rapidly developing commercial revolution. Dewey, of pioneer New England stock, was sensitive to the newer scientific developments of the nineteenth and early twentieth centuries (especially in biology and psychology), and was preoccupied with the social and cultural problems of a rapidly changing industrial society. For him, man's reason is not a searchlight that can disclose an orderly, rational universe. At best, human intelligence is an important but relatively little-used instrument for introducing, in an experimental and tentative way, patches of order into our lives and into our experience, but with no assurance that such order as we can establish is either final, permanent, or complete. Meanwhile, the problems of society have become more complex. Technology has transformed our lives. And conflicts of all sorts among groups of men have become more extensive and in some cases highly dangerous.

In many ways, the contrast between two thinkers could not be greater. The differences in their thought symbolize and express the radical changes brought about in Western culture in the relatively short span of some two hundred and fifty years. Each places his confidence in human reason, but the conception of what this amounts to is given a wholly different analysis by Dewey and by Spinoza. Yet each in his own way remains a naturalist, even though, once again, what 'Nature' signifies has undergone basic changes. Spinoza has a strong sense of the cosmic dimensions of Nature, and sees it largely in mechanistic and mathematical terms. Dewey, on the other hand, is more preoccupied with the foreground of human nature and with the domain of man's practical problems. He focuses on the opportunities man has for *transforming* his physical and social environment and for redirecting and controlling human affairs to better serve human needs.

Having said all this, we must still remember that Spinoza and Dewey, for all their differences, are both working within the same broadly defined tradition of naturalistic and humanistic thought. Each in his own way stresses that man is a product of Nature, that Nature is the ultimate reality, and that man must look to his own resource of intelligence to secure such well-being or happiness as he can.

John Dewey

Dewey's life and influence

John Dewey, one of America's leading philosophers, was born in Burlington, Vermont, in 1859, and died in 1952. His long life, in spanning the last half of the nineteenth century and the first half of the twentieth, reflected many important intellectual and cultural developments of that uniquely eventful period. As a prolific writer (of forty books and over seven hundred articles) and as an active participant in many political and cultural movements, Dewey was greatly influential in his thought. One of his avenues of influence is to be found in the reworking and articulation of the pragmatist philosophy that he inherited from Charles Peirce and William James. Another was Dewey's important contributions to the theory of education, which resulted in changes in the practice of education in this country as well as others.* Dewey's work in philosophical psychology, his analysis of art and aesthetic experience, his theory of political democracy, and his treatment of the nature of humanistic ethics have also had deep significance and impact.

Dewey placed great stress on the concept of *growth* as the key to

* An example of the influence of Dewey's ideas in the field of education outside the United States resulted from his extended visit to China in 1919–1920. When the Chinese Communists came to power years later, one Communist educator wrote "If we want to criticize the old theories of education, we must begin with Dewey. The educational ideas of Dewey have dominated and controlled Chinese education for thirty years, and his social philosophy and his general philosophy have also influenced a part of the Chinese people."[1]

John Dewey

understanding various aspects of human experience. His own intellectual development underwent many changes, and whatever continuity there is in his thought is to be found in his adherence to and clarification of the use of the *method* of experimental intelligence and the application of that method to diverse contexts and problems.*

Dewey's childhood and youth were spent in New England. The ruggedness, simplicity, and faith in the democratic process that permeated the life of the community left their imprint on his character and ways of thought. Dewey attended the University of Vermont, and upon graduation taught, briefly, in the high school of Oil City, Pennsylvania. He later enrolled in the newly established graduate program at The Johns Hopkins University. Although Dewey, as a graduate student, took a course in logic with Charles S. Peirce, the great American logician and founder of prag-

---

* A few months before his ninetieth birthday, he remarked "Only in the last two years have I come to see the real drift and hang of the various positions I have taken." I was present at his ninetieth birthday celebration (1949), a testimonial dinner in his honor at the Hotel Commodore in New York. There were many laudatory speeches by eminent persons—labor leaders, statesmen, educators, and others. Dewey came late in the evening (after most of the speeches) and rose to make his own comments. It was, by all odds, the most impressive address of the evening. Two characteristic notes were struck in his remarks: the importance of courage and a guarded hopefulness in facing the world, and the need to look to the future and not dwell on the past.

matism, he did not fully appreciate at the time the importance of what Peirce had to offer. It wasn't until years later that Dewey himself came to recognize the great significance of Peirce's work in logic and the philosophy of science. He then acknowledged his indebtedness to Peirce. Upon the completion of his doctorate in 1884, Dewey joined the faculty of the University of Michigan. During these early years, his growing interest in psychology and education showed itself through the publication of a number of books in these fields. In 1894 Dewey was appointed chairman of the department of philosophy, psychology, and education at the University of Chicago. He founded a laboratory elementary school (popularly known as the Dewey School), where his fresh ideas in the field of educational philosophy were implemented and tested. An association with the famous social settlement, Hull House, founded by Jane Addams offered another avenue to Dewey for exploring at first hand some of the problems of individuals aggravated by the rapid changes in American urban society. Dewey came to Columbia University in 1904, where he remained for the rest of his life. His eminence as a philosopher and educator was increasingly recognized throughout the world, and he was invited to lecture in various countries, including Japan, China, Turkey, Mexico, and the USSR. Dewey retired from teaching in 1930 but continued an active life of writing and participation in various public affairs.

Naturalistic humanism

Dewey's thought unmistakably belongs to the tradition of naturalism. Insofar as Dewey looked to science for his illustrations and guidance, it was to the biological and social sciences rather than to the physical and astronomical ones (or to mathematics). His own interests were primarily with the problems of people living in society. For the most part his thought centered in those aspects of human experience that were the topics of interest for politics, economics, law, educational, and aesthetic theory. It is in this sense that Dewey is a humanist. Yet Dewey's approach as a naturalistic humanist was grounded in his own distinctive version of pragmatism—what came to be called 'instrumentalism'. For Dewey's major stress was on the importance of using intelligence as the principal *instrument* in guiding the growth and enrichment of human experience. It stressed the importance of looking to the consequences of our various choices to determine their actual worth.

Philosophical Implications of Biological Evolution

The novel idea of an origin of species

The year 1859 in which Dewey was born saw the publication of Darwin's *Origin of Species*. This work had an impact comparable in many ways to the revolutionary effects of the works of Copernicus and Newton in earlier epochs. Like these, Darwin's work altered the course of scientific research for a long time to come in a particular scientific discipline. The consequences of the new scientific theory also had wider repercussions in man's total philosophy—in his conception of the world and of man's situation in it. Dewey himself, years later, in an essay entitled "The Influence of Darwin on Philosophy" (1910) discussed some of the significance of Darwin's work. Dewey sums up the broader implications of Darwin's theory as follows:

That the publication of the "Origin of Species" marked an epoch in the development of the natural sciences is well known to the layman. That the combination of the very words origin and species embodied an intellectual revolt and introduced a new intellectual temper is easily overlooked by the expert. The conceptions that had reigned in the philosophy of nature and knowledge for two thousand years, the conceptions that had become the familiar furniture of the mind, rested on the assumption of the superiority of the fixed and final; they rested upon treating change and origin as signs of defect and unreality. In laying hands upon the sacred ark of absolute permanency, in treating the forms that had been regarded as types of fixity and perfection as originating and passing away, the "Origin of Species" introduced a mode of thinking that in the end was bound to transform the logic of knowledge, and hence the treatment of morals, politics, and religion.[2]

By now the concept of an origin of species is so familiar that it is hard for us to remember how shocking and revolutionary an idea it was when first proposed. Aristotle, who first systematized the science of biology in ancient times, made central use of the concept of a species, but he did not think of a species as having an origin, change, or extinction. In Aristotle's approach (which remained the underlying conceptual orthodoxy in biology down to Darwin's day), the notions of origin, growth, and death applied to individuals *within* a species but not to species themselves. An individual person is born, matures, declines, and dies. However, the species to which an individual belongs (the class or collection of such individuals) is unchanging as a class or species. This notion persisted well into the seventeenth century and no hint of the natural origin or change of species is met in, for example, the writings of Spinoza or any other major thinker of the period. With Darwin, evolution (the coming into existence of species, their gradual change in characteristics, and in some cases their extinction) became a well-established fact about Nature. For example, biologists can trace the evolution of the species horse and can also reconstruct the ultimate disappearance of the class dinosaurs. The idea of *change* is no longer restricted to the careers of individuals; it applies to that of classes of individuals as well. Instead of change taking the form of repetitive patterns or sequences of changes, illustrated in the life of numerous individuals within a species, the theory of evolution introduces the idea of novelty itself in the notion of change. New species come into existence that never existed before. The general possibility of fresh developments, of an 'open future', becomes a commonplace that displaces the sense of Nature as a fixed domain in which basic patterns are established once and for all, and which hold without change for all time—past, present, and future.

Man a product
of Nature

The biological theory of evolution served to strengthen the naturalistic view of man as a product of Nature. Man as a species is a twig on a branch of the tree of life that evolved over the course of long periods of time, and through the operation of causal laws. The existence of human beings as a species is not to be understood as the outcome of an act of special creation on the part of a transcendent Deity. Man was brought into existence along with cockroaches, whales, dinosaurs, oysters, and a host of other creatures, all through the operation of natural causes. Nature doesn't care for one more than another. The world was not made to serve man more than it was made to serve any other creature. Rather, man was made by Nature as a result of its own creative energies, at the same time that Nature's creative capacities were exhibited in an unplanned, undesigned way in many other cases as well. The fact of organic adaptation in the structure and functioning of living things has natural, not supernatural, causes and sources. It is not necessary to invoke the notion of a Designing Mind in order to account for the facts of life. The Darwinian principle of natural selection made the older notions irrelevant and obsolete:

If all organic adaptations are due simply to constant variation and the elimination of those variations which are harmful in the struggle for existence that is brought about by excessive reproduction, there is no call for a prior intelligent causal force to plan and preordain them.[3]

This result of the Darwinian theory brought with it the well-known debates and 'warfare' between science and theology in the late nineteenth century and early part of the twentieth century. Many people, for whom the notion of a divine creation of man was still an item of orthodox belief, found the biological revolution hard to accept. Heated debates filled the journals and popular press as the aftermath of the Darwinian revolution. People took sides, as somebody once picturesquely summed it up (although inaccurately), on whether man "was a risen ape or a fallen angel." The Scopes case in Tennessee (dramatized in the well-known play and movie *Inherit the Wind*) showed the intense feeling aroused when a high school teacher who taught the theory of evolution in his classes was brought to trial for doing so. Needless to say, this sort of thing is no longer a cause for agitation, since the scientific fact of biological evolution and the genetic mechanisms that make it possible are increasingly understood and well confirmed. Dewey himself did not place great emphasis on the science-religion controversy sparked by the Darwinian theory, because for him the superiority of science as a source of factual truth was not a matter for doubt.*

An understanding of human life in the setting of biological evolution enables Dewey to give an analysis of the nature of human intelligence that distinguishes his approach from those of earlier naturalists. Man's chief resource in his struggle for survival and the basis for his superiority to other forms of life is his possession of intelligence. 'Mind' is not a name for some ghostly and spiritual substance. It designates, rather, the variety of special *activities* and *functions* that belong to an individual person as a complex *organism*. Man 'has' a mind insofar as he can engage in the various activities of 'mentalizing' or minding. Man can think (understand, plan, anticipate, evaluate) and, on the basis of all this, act. He can act intelligently. Intelligence functions as a *practical instrument*. It is man's chief means for coping with his natural environment. It enables him, within limits, to control and direct its occurrences. It is his primary resource for achieving dominion over other forms of life. In its biological setting, man's use of intelligence as a practical instrument takes on a different coloration from what it does if one stresses the use of reason as an opportunity for contemplation and understanding for their own sake. Dewey repeatedly attacks what he calls the 'spectator theory of mind.' For example, both Aristotle and Spinoza, two other leading naturalists at different periods before him, placed greatest stress on the use of reason for *understanding* the world, and thereby in making possible the highest value of human life. The word 'theater' has the same general root as the word 'theory'; it has reference to the act of beholding, viewing, enjoying, or witnessing a spectacle. To understand the pattern of the course of events in the great theater of the world as a whole—this for Aristotle or Spinoza affords man the supreme satisfaction of which a human life is capable. Not so for Dewey. Although he doesn't deny the satisfactions of purely 'theoretical' vision and intellectual understanding, for him these values must in turn be linked with their consequences in further experience as conditions for, and links to, a more adequate *practical* control over our environment and over the course of our own lives. Intelligence,

The role of intelligence when viewed in a biological context

* In his book *A Common Faith*, Dewey proposes a reinterpretation of religion that shows how it can be compatible with his own dominant naturalistic world outlook. His reinterpretation of religion would take religion—or rather the religious attitude—as something that should be concerned essentially with *giving expression to certain ideals* to which human beings can aspire. For Dewey, then, 'God' is not the name, as it is in traditional religion, for a special entity apart from Nature. It signifies, instead, the sum of those values that men hold dearest, and that might serve to inspire and guide man's own deepest commitments and loyalties.

for Dewey, is primarily an instrument for *transforming* the environment, for *making things happen*. Intelligence becomes a means for adjustment, manipulation, interaction, and control, not just for contemplation.

Intelligence and Experience

Intelligence and problematic situations

The concept of intelligence as a practical instrument or method for solving problems, and as the most effective resource for contributing to the enrichment and growth of human experience in its various personal and cultural dimensions, is the keystone of Dewey's philosophy. The function of intelligence, according to Dewey, is to help solve *particular* problems by formulating plans and hypotheses and testing them through their consequences in practice. Dewey stresses the fact that human life, in large part, is a matter of encountering various problematic situations. These are always specific and particular problems. The method of intelligence is the method for solving such problems. What distinguishes the method of intelligence from other methods is the fact that the soundness and acceptability of any proposed solution must be tested by the quality of consequences for further experience. All this sounds obvious, commonplace, and simple. However, the detailed application of this idea, indeed even the very willingness to use this method in the various domains of experience, has revolutionary significance.

Dewey's emphasis on the importance of using the *method* of intelligence gives his philosophy a certain cast that distinguishes it from other philosophies. Dewey doesn't offer a fixed system of principles, goals, or truths. Many who read Dewey are put off because they expect to find a set of doctrines or principles—of particular factual truths or a specific set of recommendations for conduct. In his numerous writings and in his own personal participation in various social, educational, and political movements during his lifetime, Dewey did take a stand and advocate particular courses of action. For example, he played an active role in founding the Teacher's Union and also the American Association for University Professors. He did express, in various articles and speeches, his own views about the participation of the United States in World Wars I and II. He made known his stand on the flagrant miscarriage of justice in the Sacco and Vanzetti case* and in the Bertrand Russell case.† He came out

---

* The shooting and killing of a paymaster and a guard at a shoe factory in Massachusetts in 1920 led to the indictment and eventual conviction of two anarchists, Sacco and Vanzetti. Many persons, at the time, thought that their conviction was unwarranted and was influenced by the fact that they were radicals. See Felix Frankfurter, *The Case of Sacco and Vanzetti* (1927), and G. L. Joughin and Edmund M. Morgan, *The Legacy of Sacco and Vanzetti* (1948).

strongly against the terror of the Stalinist regime and other forms of dictatorship and helped found the Committee for Cultural Freedom. At the end of World War I, he participated in the movement to gain suffrage for women. (There is an anecdote in this connection that during a parade down Fifth Avenue, made up for the most part of women suffragettes, Dewey joined the parade and did not notice that the placard he carried read "Men can vote! Why can't I?") These various activities represent Dewey's use of the method of intelligence, according to his own best judgment at the time. But these examples are *not* the fixed core of Dewey's philosophy. If anything is 'fixed', it is not this or that substantive judgment of his, this or that advocacy or condemnation of a particular course of action. Instead, the essential 'message' of Dewey's philosophy is the importance of using the *method* of intelligence. In one sense, then, there is no *content* to his philosophy. He gives a method, and to many people the constant harping on a method seems very thin and open-ended. But that's the whole point. The method has to be applied over and over again to particular situations, where the content and needs are determined by the particular situation. He refuses to anticipate all the varied kinds of situations in which people might find themselves or to anticipate and advocate certain solutions.

The common idea of a pragmatic philosophy is that the validity and soundness of any proposal—whether it be a plan of action, a reform in a code or laws for behavior, a hypothesis in science, a way of interpreting a work of art, and so on—are to be judged in terms of its consequences. Does our ongoing experience lend it support or not?—*this* is the crucial question. Dewey's appeal to experience needs to be contrasted with two traditional views concerning the nature of experience. One such concept (which goes back to Aristotle) is that experience is an accumulated deposit or fund of *past* experience, the fruit of tradition and custom. To appeal to the 'voice of experience' in this sense is to sanction a way of thinking or of doing things on the ground that it has worked in the past, which constitutes adequate reason for not tampering with it now. Dewey's analysis of experience is quite different. He does not, to be sure, want to

The pragmatic appeal to experience contrasted with traditional conceptions

† The Bertrand Russell case concerns the appointment of the celebrated philosopher Bertrand Russell to a chair of philosophy at The City College of New York in 1940. Because of Russell's unconventional views on sex and marriage, and various incidents in his own life, this appointment was attacked from several quarters. A bishop of the Protestant Episcopal Church, William T. Manning, wrote a letter to the press denouncing the appointment. Other attacks followed, and eventually the matter came to trial before Judge John E. McGeehan, who voided the appointment. After various legal maneuvers and countermoves, the appointment was finally withheld. The case aroused an enormous amount of discussion in the press and throughout the academic world. For a full account, see John Dewey and Horace M. Kallen (editors), *The Bertrand Russell Case* (1941). See also Ronald W. Clark, *The Life of Bertrand Russell* (1975).

say that because something has worked in the past, *therefore* it is no longer valid. This in itself would be the *un*intelligent attitude to take. It represents a wholesale judgment, instead of an examination, one by one, of each case of what we do inherit from the past and a consideration of the possible merit of continuing to follow and adopt what has worked in the past. It *may* be that the same way of thinking or acting will continue to work well now and in the future.

Another type of appeal to experience to which Dewey is opposed is that in which 'experience' signifies what an individual undergoes in the immediate present, primarily in the form of sensations and perceptions. Experience, in this approach, is personal rather than social, present rather than past. Once again, Dewey does not wish to minimize the importance of what experience in this sense can give us by way of valuable information. But for him the appeal neither to the past nor to the immediate present is sufficient. The way to judge whether an idea is sound—in science, morality, educational practice, politics, law, or any other domain —is to let *future, ongoing experience* decide its worth. *"Will it work?"* This is the essential demand of a pragmatist philosophy. Does it meet our needs in the long run; does it solve the problem? If the answer is yes, then hold onto it as long as it continues to work! As soon as it shows it no longer meets the needs, as soon as it falters and breaks down, the time has come to consider whether or how to modify or replace it. If a new and better way is found, it will itself have to be tested by the appeal to consequences, by its ongoing effectiveness.

To anyone living in the twentieth century the achievements of science are a commonplace. For Dewey it is obvious that the reason for the success of science lies in the use of its method. What we call 'scientific method' is the clearest example—the example *par excellence*—of the use of the method of experimental intelligence. Each of the sciences (physics, chemistry, biology, psychology, and so on) uses the scientific method in determining the truth—the laws, facts, ways of explaining the phenomena —in its own special domain. Each science uses the method of experimental intelligence to determine the truth about molecules, rocks, stars, plants, human beings or whatever be the particular subject matter under investigation. Men have confidence in the results achieved by science— both the understanding it gives and the control (through its various applications) it makes possible—because its results are confirmable; they are repeatedly tested in experience. So much is a commonplace. Dewey doesn't stop here. On the contrary, this is where he starts.

The main problem of modern culture: healing the breach between science and values

What about areas such as politics, morals, or, in general, so-called nonscientific dimensions of human experience? Here it is obvious not only that the method of intelligence is not widely appealed to or used, but also that many persons would claim the method of experimental intelligence is incompetent to deal with these questions. For Dewey this 'dualism', this contrast between the domain of facts and values—between what can be established as a *matter of fact* by scientific investigation and what *ought to be*, what is good or right—is the most glaring fact of the world in which we live. It is the source of the most serious flaw in men's thinking, and hence in the persistence of the various turbulences and chaotic patches characteristic of human culture. For Dewey *the* main problem of modern culture is to heal this breach, to overcome this dualism. It is Dewey's main thesis that until, first of all, men recognize the need to apply the method of experimental intelligence to all domains of human affairs, and then patiently, step-by-step, apply and reapply that method to the settlement of their various problems, the chaos and the turbulence will persist.

As my study and thinking progressed, I became more and more troubled by the intellectual scandal that seemed to me involved in the current (and traditional) dualism in logical standpoint and method between something called "science" on the one hand and something called "morals" on the other. I have long felt that the construction of a logic, that is, a method of effective inquiry, which would apply without abrupt breach of continuity to the fields designated by both of these words, is at once our needed theoretical solvent and the supply of our greatest practical want. This belief has had much more to do with the development of what I termed, for lack of a better word, "instrumentalism", than have most of the reasons that have been assigned.[4]

Dewey makes essentially the same point in his Gifford Lectures, *The Quest for Certainty:*

The problem of restoring integration and cooperation between man's beliefs about the world in which he lives and his beliefs about the values and purposes that should direct his conduct is the deepest problem of modern life. It is the problem of any philosophy that is not isolated from that life. . . . Its central problem is the relation that exists between the beliefs about the nature of things due to natural science to beliefs about values—using that word to designate whatever is taken to have rightful authority in the direction of conduct. A philosophy which should take up this problem is struck first of all by the fact that beliefs about values are pretty much in the position in which beliefs about nature were before the scientific revolution.[5]

When it comes to settling disagreements and conflicts of value (of what they want, of what they think is right or good) men are still living for the most part in a world in which nonrational methods are resorted to: violence, tradition, impulse, imitation, indoctrination and so on. And the result is all about us. Men are at each other's throats; social disorders of various degrees of intensity and seriousness prevail; men lead personal lives of frustration and despair. Dewey's claim is that men will not begin to even deal with these problems until they forsake the reliance on these nonrational techniques and turn to the method of experimental intelligence. The use of this method will not guarantee that all our problems will be solved either completely or permanently. To believe this is itself to be unintelligent. It is to fail in describing the human situation in a precarious and changing world. Dewey's point is nevertheless that our best chances for improving the human condition, for making headway in dealing satisfactorily with human problems in which conflicts of value appear, is to use the method of intelligence to deal with these conflicts. To explore Dewey's thesis in greater detail, we need then to study two central points: first, we have to get some sense of what he understands by the method of experimental intelligence; second, we have to see what, for him, its extension to the areas of value decision would involve.

The Method of Experimental Intelligence

Dewey devoted much attention to the analysis of the method of experimental intelligence. In one of the last and most important of his books, *Logic: The Theory of Inquiry* (1938), he gives a highly compressed formula or definition that sums up his conception of 'inquiry' (another name for the *method of experimental intelligence*):

Inquiry is the controlled or directed transformation of an indeterminate situation into one that is so determinate in its constituent distinctions and relations as to convert the elements of the original situation into a unified whole.[6]

Let us take this apart. I do so by making a number of distinctions that Dewey calls attention to in the work cited, as well as in many of his other writings over a period of many years. Much of what I am about to summarize is not exclusive to Dewey, indeed, is rather commonplace, and would be found in any elementary treatment of the pattern of scientific inquiry. That it is commonplace owes not a little to the influence of men like Peirce and Dewey in giving us an understanding of these matters.

Controlled inquiry

Dewey describes inquiry as a *controlled* or *directed transformation* of one type of situation into another. The kind of thinking or inquiry he is concerned to analyze has a specific purpose or goal: that of deliberately *changing* a situation. Controlled thinking is to be contrasted with the type of 'thinking' illustrated in daydreaming or in the random association of ideas. There are times when a person may be sitting quietly, perhaps reminiscing, or letting one idea succeed another. He is not motivated or driven by some particular need or goal. It wouldn't make any special difference to the character of the thought if ideas turned in one direction rather than another. By contrast, the kind of thinking Dewey is concerned to analyze is controlled by the need to achieve a particular goal. It arises from the need to reach a particular end. It does make a difference in which direction a person's thoughts turn. One *judges* or *evaluates* ideas in terms of whether they contribute to the achievement of the goal in question.

The controlled thinking Dewey examines has to do with *problem solving*. What Dewey calls a 'problematic situation' is otherwise described as an 'indeterminate situation'. The purpose of inquiry is to transform the indeterminate situation (the problematic situation) into a determinate situation (into one where the problem has been solved). The purpose of inquiry (the method of experimental intelligence) is to lead from the indeterminate, problematic situation to the solved, determinate situation. *Problem solving*

Take a simple, everyday example. Let us suppose you are going somewhere in your car. Things are going along smoothly. You are a pretty good driver, and all of your responses are by now fairly automatic. You stop at red lights, you slow down when some one passes into your lane, you make the appropriate turns, and so on. For the most part, you are not thinking about these things. You may be listening to the radio, or conversing with your friends. Now suppose, as you are thus driving along smoothly, the engine begins to sputter and almost immediately stops right in the midst of traffic. You're caught up short. There has been an interruption, a break in an otherwise continuous and smoothly running activity. At this point you have got to do something. You still have the objective of getting to your destination, people are honking their horns, and so on. This is a simple example of what Dewey calls a '*problematic situation*'. In general, a problematic situation is a breakdown in the continuity or relatively smooth functioning of our lives at some point or other. Illustrations abound. On a personal level, an individual may be thrown out of a job, may become ill, may have to find a new place to live. On a social level, widespread unemployment, acts of terrorism and violence, inflation, the threat of war, and deterioration or disruption of various social services are other familiar examples. In science, inquiry is controlled by the need to find answers to all sorts of problems, whether they be persistent and deep-seated ones or transitory and relatively superficial ones.

Let us go back to our simple car example. In the situation I have described, the solution to the problem is in principle already available to someone who has the requisite knowledge and skill. A car, as something man made, has a mechanism whose working is already understood with varying degrees of expertness by many persons such as professional or amateur mechanics. You may try to deal with the situation yourself. Or you may call upon professional help. What, briefly, does one do? You think of the possible reasons why the car stopped running, check out the ones that seem most likely, in order to see whether this or that proposed solution does in fact work. If your experience, understanding, and skill are rich enough to include the 'right answer', you will be able to make the car run again. You will be on your way. The break in continuity of your activity will have been removed, and a 'determinate situation' of smooth functioning will have replaced the 'indeterminate situation'. The problem has been solved. Many of life's relatively simple and routine problems can be solved *if* the techniques for their solution are already known to those possessed of the requisite professional training or of rich enough imagination and skills. The intelligent thing to do, if one does not have the requisite knowledge oneself, is, wherever possible, to seek such help: one seeks out the plumber, doctor, engineer, counselor, or other expert.

But what does one do when the problem is both relatively *novel* and *complex*, and where the type of solution is not of a standard sort, already known to somebody? Here the challenge arises for the method of *creative* intelligence. Dewey's analysis of what the use of this method entails identifies the several stages in its operation. The method of intelligence does not guarantee that a solution *will* be found. Nevertheless, Dewey insists, if a satisfactory solution is to be found at all, it will be the persistent use of this method that will in the long run be most effective and successful.

Identifying the problem *Identifying the problem* is the first important phase of any controlled inquiry. The first point to bear in mind is that no situation is *wholly* indeterminate or problematic. Some things are *not* in question; certain facts are accepted and recognized for what they are. If everything were in doubt or problematic, it would be impossible to deal with the situation at all. Even for someone caught in a burning building there are certain recognizable facts that are not in doubt or problematic, and that define the fixed and unquestioned contours, the 'givens' of the situation.

The first step then is to search out the constituents of a given situation which, as constituents, are settled. When an alarm of fire is sounded in a crowded assembly hall, there is much that is indeterminate as regards the activities that may produce a favorable issue. One may get out safely or one may be trampled and burned. The fire is characterized, however, by some settled traits. It is, for example, located somewhere. Then the aisles and exits are at fixed places. Since they are settled or determinate in existence, the first step in institution of a problem is to settle them in observation. There are other factors which, while they are not as temporally and spatially fixed, are yet observable constituents; for example, the behavior and movements of other members of the audience. All of these observed conditions taken together constitute "the facts of the case." They constitute the terms of the problem, because they are conditions that must be reckoned with or taken account of in any relevant solution that is proposed.[7]

In the example just considered, there is no problem about *what* the problem is: it is obviously to get outside the burning building safely. There are many cases, however, where the first stage of inquiry, that of identifying what precisely the problem is, is not as obvious or clear-cut. The clear statement of what the problem is may not be evident at once or by any superficial contact with the situation.

It is a familiar and significant saying that a problem well put is half-solved. To find out what the problem and problems are which a problematic situation presents to be inquired into, is to be well along in inquiry. To mistake the problem involved is to cause subsequent inquiry to be irrelevant or to go astray. Without a problem, there is blind groping in the dark. The way in which the problem is conceived decides what specific suggestions are entertained and which are dismissed; what data are selected and which rejected; it is the criterion for relevancy and irrelevancy of hypotheses and conceptual structures. On the other hand, to set up a problem that does not grow out of an actual situation is to start on a course of dead work, nonetheless dead because the work is "busy work".[8]

Problems, we have said, can be of all sorts and dimensions of complexity. They may be personal or social, practical or intellectual, scientific or outside the sphere of science. Let me consider, by way of further example, a famous problematic situation in science: that which arose with the outcome of the famous Michelson-Morley experiment in physics. At the time Michelson and Morley performed their experiment, most physicists believed there was a unique substance called 'Ether', filling the entire space of the Universe and serving as the medium through which all electromagnetic radiation (including light) was propagated. Physicists accepted Newton's system of mechanics as the way to describe and explain the motions of bodies. They also accepted Maxwell's system of electromagnetic principles for purposes of describing and explaining the phenomena of radiation. These twin pillars of classical physics had stood the test of repeated application. They were therefore sets of principles or theories in which physicists had virtually complete confidence. Michelson and Morley set out to determine the motion of the Earth through the Ether. They set up an optical apparatus that involved the use of split light beams whose measurement and characteristics would enable them to determine the motion of the Earth with respect to the Ether. The calculations performed were made on the basis of the accepted Newtonian and Maxwellian theories. These calculations led to the making of certain predictions about what should be observed. The apparatus was of course carefully checked, and the experiment was repeated several times. The outcome of the experiment, however, was contrary to the predicted result! This is the celebrated case of the 'negative outcome of the Michelson-Morley experiment'. The result created a sensation in the world of physics. It posed a serious problem: *How to explain the negative outcome of the experiment?* The problem arose because of a break or discontinuity in the accustomed way of thinking. The adequacy of the accepted theories was clearly being challenged. Results were found that were in conflict with the predictions of classical physics. Although there were many attempts to solve the problem, some by ingeniously trying to salvage the classical physics and 'explain away' the discrepancy, it was the more radical proposal of Einstein's theory of relativity that most satisfactorily explained the result of the experiment and that therefore finally came to be accepted.

Hypotheses as proposed solutions

Given a reasonably clear and well-recognized problem, what next? What is immediately called for in order to make any progress toward the solution of the problem is to undertake the formulation of various proposed solutions to the problem. These are known as *hypotheses*. A hypothesis is a tentatively entertained plan of action, policy, explanation— or whatever else is called for by the situation—as the way of resolving the initial difficulty. A hypothesis is a *possible* answer to the problem. To go back for a moment to our simple car breakdown example. Given the problem, a hypothesis that might flash through your mind is "Maybe the spark plugs are wet." That's a hypothesis. Others might also suggest themselves, even to an amateur mechanic. Where the correct type of answer is already available and known to some expert, clearly it is a matter of enumerating the possible hypotheses. These will be of a finite number: the sorts of things to look for that might be listed in a 'troubleshooting' manual. However, where a situation is novel and complex, and where therefore a standard solution is not already known, where does one get likely hypotheses? What is called for is an act of creative thinking.

Is there any way of guaranteeing that in the face of a novel and complex problem someone will come up with a fruitful hypothesis? The answer is no. It is true that if a fruitful hypothesis is to be found at all, it will most likely be found by one who already has a good deal of familiarity with the general area under investigation. The more knowledge one has of a given area of investigation, the more fruitful and rich are likely to be the number of hypotheses proposed. Given a highly technical problem in physics, for example, it is far more likely that the trained physicist will come up with a fruitful hypothesis than the layman. But there is no guarantee that even the trained physicist will do so. What cannot be automatically produced or controlled is the factor of creativity. One can't automatically produce or train an Einstein any more than one can train or produce a Shakespeare, Mozart, or Michelangelo. Einstein not only was steeped in theories and results of physics and mathematics; his fusing some of these ideas and bringing them together in the form of his proposal of the theory of relativity was an act of creative imagination. Einstein tells us that at one point "It came to me!" Creative insight 'comes' to certain minds and not to others. To this extent, the method of experimental intelligence, in being dependent on acts of creative imagination, is not a routine and automatic procedure. It may take the labor and creative proposals brought forth over a considerable period of time and by a whole community of investigators to solve a problem.

An important stage in inquiry, even before submitting any hypothesis to the test of actual experience, is to examine the implications of the hypothesis, to explore its conceptual ramifications, to ask what *would* be the case *if* it were true. This *exploration in thought of the possible consequences* of a particular hypothesis is a preliminary phase that serves two functions. First, it checks, even in advance of the testing of a hypothesis, whether it is sufficiently in agreement with already well-established facts or the needs of the situation to merit serious attention. And sometimes it may be possible to eliminate certain hypotheses that fail to meet this requirement of *consistency* with uncontested facts or requirements. If, in the simple car example, a hypothesis that crossed your mind is "Perhaps I've run out of gas," you may judge it not even worth checking because you know that just a few miles back you filled the tank with gas. Similarly, if a hypothesis is in flagrant contradiction with well-established theories and accumulated results in science, the community of scientists will be reluctant to give it any further attention. Whenever possible, one doesn't get rid of beliefs that have stood the test of time. Now this consideration will not always be a convincing one, and the elimination of a possible hypothesis on these grounds may turn out to have been unwise or too hasty. Maybe you *had* filled the tank, but in fact, without your realizing it, the tank developed a leak and you lost all the gas! Even though Einstein challenged the basic, long-established principles of Newtonian mechanics, it turned out that his theory was, after all, a better one than Newton's. Suppose, however, that the preliminary examination of a fresh hypothesis suggests it is to be taken seriously. A second function that the preliminary *conceptual* analysis of the implications of a hypothesis performs is to provide various *predictions* of what would be found in actual experience if the hypothesis is true or will work.

Examining the implications of a hypothesis

What distinguishes the *empirical* sciences from disciplines such as pure mathematics is the need to submit a hypothesis to the *test of observational experience*. The appeal to experience is for the purpose of confirming or disconfirming the predictions of a hypothesis. Most people, when they

Actual testing by experience

think of science, immediately think of performing experiments. Experiments and observation in general are, of course, highly important, but they must be seen as undertaken in the light of a hypothesis that they serve to test, to either confirm or disconfirm it. It is the *hypothesis* that leads to the performance of experiment or the making of observations. The appeal to experience must be seen as part of a course of inquiry, as a step in the testing of a hypothesis.

The pragmatic criterion for finding solutions

It will be experience—the way the proposed hypothesis (plan of action, proposed explanation, diagnosis of the difficulty) works itself out and is tested—that determines whether the hypothesis is sound or not, whether it solves the initial problem. This is where the *pragmatic* criterion, the appeal to consequences, comes to the fore. Where a hypothesis does not stand the test of ongoing experience it will be rejected, whatever may be claimed for it on the grounds that it is intuitively obvious, esthetically appealing, consistent with previous experience, or sanctioned by the authority or eminence of its author. And if one goes through the various proposed hypotheses, one at a time, and each is rejected for the same pragmatic reason that it doesn't work, the problem continues, or else is handled in some arbitrary and nonrational way! On the other hand, if among the set of proposed hypotheses, one hypothesis emerges that does satisfactorily meet the pragmatic test, then one can, to that extent, speak of a *solution*. A solution is had when a well-confirmed hypothesis (as judged by the needs of the situation) is found. If it is, after all, wet spark plugs, then I can simply dry them or replace them, and if I find that my car is able to move again, that is the end of the matter. Smooth functioning, continuity, has been restored. Since Einstein's theory not only meets the need of explaining the negative outcome of the Michelson-Morley experiment but also makes various other predictions all of which are confirmed, at the same time that it explains many other isolated facts not adequately accounted for by Newtonian mechanics, and, moreover, explains and predicts successfully everything Newtonian mechanics does successfully, one can then say that relativity theory offers a superior solution to the initial problem than is offered by any other proposed hypothesis.

The two limits of every unit of thinking are a perplexed, troubled, or confused situation at the beginning and a cleared-up, unified, resolved situation at the close. The first of these situations may be called pre-reflective. It sets the problem to be solved; out of it grows the question that reflection has to answer. In the final situation the doubt has been dispelled; the situation is post-reflective; there results a direct experience of mastery, satisfaction, enjoyment. Here then, are the limits within which reflection falls.[9]

The key to understanding Dewey's philosophy is his emphasis on the role of intelligence in making possible an enriched and growing experience. We have now had a glimpse of some of the ideas included in Dewey's analysis of the method of experimental intelligence. One way of examining his philosophy is to see how his central thesis about the nature of intelligence is applied in the various domains of human experience with which he is concerned: scientific knowledge, politics, moral philosophy, educational theory, and so on. And, as an added way of coming to the heart of his views, it helps considerably to see his views in opposition to and contrast with—and they were so deliberately and consciously—Plato's philosophy and the various forms of rationalism derived from Plato. For Dewey's concept of intelligence is at fundamental odds, almost at every point, with Plato's concept of reason. From a loose and general point of view, both may be said to stress the unique capacity of man's possession of 'reason'. However, their analysis of what this means is wholly different. Consequently, it would be misleading to group them under a common banner.

Distinctive features of Dewey's approach to the concepts of knowledge and intelligence

Contrast with Plato

We turn, first, to a brief summary of Dewey's views on the nature of *scientific knowledge*. The clearest and most extensive application of the method of experimental intelligence is to be found in the domain of science. When the achievement of scientific knowledge is understood as the result of the application of the method of experimental intelligence to the solution of particular problems, various things come to light that are ignored in other approaches.

The character of scientific knowledge

What is known, if it is the outcome of a process of inquiry as the solution to a problem, is a *product* of such inquiry. What is known is something that emerges at the tail end of a process of search; it is something *made* or constructed as the result of such a process, and cannot be understood apart from this context. Knowledge is not, as it was for Plato, a disclosure of some realm of Being (of eternal Forms) or even, as it was for Descartes or Spinoza, the rational apprehension of some unique intelligible structure in Nature. There is no antecedent pattern already in existence that is there to be known, to be disclosed or revealed to man's reason as by a great searchlight. What man comes to know he creates or produces—under various constraints to be sure—since it is not completely a free and uncontrolled creation. But it is man (individual scientists) who fashions and produces, in his various linguistic formulations, what is known. Without man's activity in *making* or *constructing* knowledge-products, there would be no knowledge. Man, as inquirer, can formulate many different statements of laws or regularities in natural phenomena, theories to explain such laws, descriptions of 'matters of fact'. Various formulations compete with one another, and some are better than others.

The outcome of a successful inquiry yields a statement (belief, judgment, linguistic formulation) that is *warrantedly assertible*. It emerges as a result of successful test and competition with *available* rival hypotheses. At a given time, it is the one best supported by the evidence, the one most adequate to meet the various needs and requirements of the situation. It is confirmed, confirmable, and coherent. The choice of such a statement embodies the claim that one now knows, i.e., can deal with, the initial data or given items of information in an adequate way. But to say that one has an item of knowledge, in this sense of having a statement that is warrantedly assertible, is a relative matter, not absolute. Dewey does not sanction the sharp division found in the Platonic and rationalistic tradition between infallible, certain, demonstrative knowledge on the one hand and variable, fallible opinion or belief on the other. For Dewey and the whole pragmatic tradition, there is only one category, not two: *All* items that belong to the domain of scientific *knowledge* are variable, open to correction, and tentatively retained for as long as they work. All knowledge *is* opinion. But opinions vary in their weight of support and merit, in their *degree of warranted assertibility*. There is nothing certain and final about *any* claim to knowledge. This thesis is what Peirce calls the *doctrine of fallibilism*. Dewey subscribes to it. It means there is nothing established once and for all, or as eternally true, through the use of 'reason'. There are only so many different conclusions (termini of inquiry) that are retained because the evidence *so far* supports them. However, there is nothing sacrosanct or infallible about any conclusion. No statement of any so-called law, no theory, no description is so conclusive and certain (beyond any possible doubt) that it might not be supplanted by some better one. All knowledge-products of empirical science are open to correction, amendment, replacement, and improvement.

Finally, all knowledge that is the outcome of a process of inquiry belongs to a *continuum of inquiry*. Any particular solution to a particular problem marks the termination of a unit or instance of the application of the method of experimental intelligence. But inquiry in science is an ongoing affair with no single final or supreme end. What may be the solution to one problem may, in turn, open up fresh problems for research, and if these in turn are solved, still others, and so on. The method of experimental intelligence needs to be applied and reapplied, over and over again, however broad or deep, narrow, or relatively superficial the problems may be. The domain of scientific inquiry, in short, is open ended. There is no eternally fixed, already complete system of knowledge and truth *to be* discovered or revealed. Knowledge getting is a temporal and historical affair. The *process* of acquiring (producing) knowledge-items that may occupy the life of a single investigator, or a whole community of investigators during some epoch, or even mankind as a whole throughout its entire history takes place in time. And the fruits of inquiry at any particular stage of inquiry—the successful outcome of inquiry at that stage—are the *products* of that inquiry; they cannot be divorced or understood apart from their historical and cultural context.

Intelligence and Human Values

The extension and application of the method of experimental intelligence to those areas of human experience encompassed by the terms 'politics', 'morals', 'practical interests', 'value considerations'—in short, everything that concerns us as individuals in our personal affairs or as members of various social groups—constitute the principal theme of Dewey's philosophy. This is where the impact of his originality and the reorientation of his thought are most clearly to be seen. In the domain of practical human values, characteristic problems do not arise simply from the desire to *understand*, that is, to provide a satisfactory *explanation* or *description* of some phenomenon. Problems in the areas mentioned, as contrasted with the predominantly intellectual interests of science, are primarily of *how to act, what to do*, what choices and direction to give our conduct, whether personal or social. In interacting with our physical environment or our fellow men, we are called upon either to *change* something or to *conduct* ourselves and *act* overtly in a particular way so that the practical problems that face us might be solved.

Dewey uses a number of technical expressions to convey the main lines of his analysis. Let us examine some of these.

One set of terms involves the distinction between a *descriptive* and a *practical proposition* (or judgment). *Practical judgments*

Propositions exist relating to agenda—to things to do or be done, judgments of a situation demanding action. There are, for example, propositions of the form: M. N. should do thus and so; it is better, wiser, more prudent, right, advisable, opportune, expedient, etc., to act thus and so. And this is the type of judgment I denote practical. . . .

A right or wrong descriptive judgment (a judgment confined to the given, whether temporal, spatial or subsistent) does not affect its subject matter. . . . But a practical proposition affects the subject matter for better or worse. . . .[10]

In a *descriptive* judgment one is concerned to give a true account of some state of affairs. For example, one may report on the surface features of the Moon, or give the statistics of unemployment among unskilled workers for the last ten years. (We may also understand Dewey to include, in this context, statements that offer *explanations* of certain state of affairs, as a type of descriptive judgment. For example: The river over-flowed its banks because of the very heavy rains.) When you make a descriptive judgment you may not be primarily trying to *do* anything about the situation you are describing. Insofar as you are making a purely descriptive judgment, you are simply giving an account of some subject matter. And your descriptive judgment is either true or false; either it correctly reports what is the case with sufficient accuracy for the purposes at hand, or it mistakes the facts and is therefore false.

A practical judgment, by way of contrast, makes a proposal to change a situation, control or prevent the occurrence of an event, correct an abuse, reform a state of affairs, or make things better by satisfying an interest or need. In a practical judgment one is not simply standing back and re-porting on what is *found* to be the case; one is instead judging what needs to be *done*. A practical judgment calls for action on the part of an agent or agents. Dewey's interest in making this distinction between a descriptive and a practical judgment is to argue that *the same broad pattern of in-quiry and problem solving we have been calling 'the method of experi-mental intelligence' can be and ought to be applied in determining the worth, soundness, or acceptability of a practical judgment as is involved in judging the truth or falsity of descriptive judgments.*

Practical problems of course are of varying degrees of complexity. What to do about the breakdown of my car in traffic is an example at one end of the spectrum, and what to do about the various tensions and disloca-tions of society—war, crime, starvation, disease, unemployment, etc.—are examples of practical problems at the other end. Dewey does not argue, in any simple-minded fashion, that at any given time men can solve all their problems with equal success or ease, even with the use of the method of intelligence. However, his thesis is that unless men turn to the use of the method of experimental intelligence, they will never solve their serious problems, for the use of this method is their only hope.

Value judgments

Dewey refines the concept of a practical judgment by introducing the expression '*value judgment*'. A value judgment is a type of practical judg-ment. To make a value judgment, for Dewey, is to make a practical judgment. And in saying this, Dewey sets himself at once in opposition to the major traditional conceptions of 'values' and 'value judgments'.

A judgment of value is simply a case of a practical judgment, a judgment about the doing of something. This conflicts with the assumption that it is a judg-ment about a particular kind of existence independent of action, concerning which the main problem is whether it is subjective or objective. It conflicts with every tendency to make the determination of the right or wrong course of action (whether in morals, technology, or scientific inquiry) dependent upon an independent determination of some ghostly things called value-objects— whether their ghostly character is attributed to their existing in some transcen-

dental eternal realm or in some realm called states of mind. It asserts that value-objects mean simply objects as judged to possess a certain force within a situation temporally developing toward a determinate result. To find a thing good is . . . to attribute or impute nothing to it. It is just to do something to it. But to consider whether it is good and how good it is, is to ask how it, as if acted upon, will operate in promoting a course of action.[11]

Examples of 'traditional conceptions of values', whose approach Dewey rejects, are found in Plato's philosophy and those associated with some forms of conventional religion. According to these traditional views, to make a correct value judgment one must check any proposal of what should be done, or any evaluation of whether something is good or right, against a predetermined code, standard, Form, rule, ideal, law, or commandment—against some scheme or table of 'eternal values'. These 'eternal values' are what Dewey refers to as 'ghostly value objects'. We are asked to consult *them* (as already given to us in some finished and clear way by some 'voice of authority' whether it be Reason, God's revelation, conscience, or the deliverances of an innate 'moral sense') to determine whether or not our value judgments are correct. It is they that put the stamp either of approval or of disapproval on how we should act. Nor does it make any difference, for Dewey, whether one thinks of such value codes as being 'out there' in some objective way (in God's will, the Platonic world of Forms, or Nature's 'law') or as to be found in some subjective, inner state of mind (for example, in the supposedly clear dictates of conscience or of moral intuitions). In either case such alleged value objects are fictitious and spurious. He says, in effect, "A plague on both your houses!"

According to Dewey, judgments of value are not to be decided upon in any of the foregoing ways. They are to be decided by looking to their consequences, not to their alleged sources. This involves considering their anticipated results or, if acted upon, their *actual* results in the context of some particular situation. It involves seeing to what extent the value judgment meets the needs and solves the problems being faced. To see the sort of thing Dewey has in mind, let us consider some typical simple examples.

Suppose someone were to ask "Is rain a good thing or a bad thing?" Dewey would say that the question cannot be answered as it stands without considering a possible answer in some concrete situation. It is not a matter of making an immediate response, as if somehow rain carried with it one or another value quality. What is called for, instead, is a process of *evaluation* that would take into account various considerations and factors. From the immediate personal point of view of one who is 'caught in the rain', one might say "I don't like the rain. It's bad. I'm getting wet. It's uncomfortable." Suppose, however, a farmer has a problem of getting sufficient water for his crops. If you met the farmer out in the field, and asked him, as it rains, "Is the rain good or bad?" he might very well admit that he doesn't like being drenched any more than you do. But he subordinates his immediate reaction to his more controlling interest as a farmer, and says "The rain is good." His evaluation of the rain is made in terms of a means-end relationship. He judges the rain to be *good for* his crops. In short, something is neither good nor bad in itself nor by possessing some inherent value quality. It needs to be seen in the context of a more inclusive situation, where it functions either to inhibit or to promote the accomplishment of some end, to be good or bad for something else with which it is bound up.

A judgment of value needs to be taken not as an *immediate* judgment but as a judgment that notes the *mediation* (the relationships) between, say, rain and crops, and judges the value in the light of the relevant consequences or effects of the rain. Passing a value judgment is done in the light of these relationships and consequences, and where the consequences taken into account are not simply those foreseen but those that actually happen. In the case of the rain, where there is little to be done about its occurrence or nonoccurrence (except for the installation of an irrigation system), whether in fact the rain is good, even for the crops, *remains to be seen*. There may be too much rain or too little; the rain may be accompanied by damaging high winds, and so on. The initial judgment "This rain is good for the crops" will itself have to be tested in the light of the *actual* consequences, the ongoing course of experience. And the same goes for any value judgment that proposes a course of action and places a value (asserts that such and such will be good, right, meet the needs, solve the problem). Its soundness or correctness has to be tested in experience, just as a scientific hypothesis, in order to be judged true or false, must meet the tests of observation as well as other relevant considerations.

Consider another simple example: the matter of judging the value of food. Sometimes what is called 'agreeable food' may not in fact be

food for me; it brings on indigestion. It functions no longer as an immediate *good; as something to be accepted. If I continue eating, it will be after I have deliberated. I have considered it as a means to two conflicting possible consequences, the present enjoyment of eating and the later state of health. One or other is possible, not both—though of course I may "solve" the problem by persuading myself that in this instance they are congruent. The value-object now means thing judged to be a means of procuring this or that end. As prizing, esteeming, holding dear denote ways of acting, so valuing denotes a passing judgment upon such acts with reference to their connection with other acts, or with respect to the continuum of behavior in which they fall.*[12]

In making a value judgment as to whether the food I am eating is good, the answer is not to be found by making reference to my immediate feelings or how the food tastes. The food may be *satisfying now*, but is it *satisfactory*? "To declare something satis*factory* is to assert that it meets specifiable conditions. It is, in effect, a judgment that the thing 'will do'. It involves a prediction; it contemplates a future in which the thing will continue to serve."[13] Dewey, of course, does not discount the importance of *immediate* valuations. His concern is to argue that any intelligent evaluative judgment must take into account the consequences beyond the immediate present in making an appraisal.

The simple examples offered above—of judging the goodness or badness of rain, or of eating certain foods—might seem almost trivial and irrelevant to the general question of deciding matters of *moral values*. But Dewey's whole philosophy protests against this kind of separation. Morality is not something apart and distinct from all the innumerable situations encountered in daily life. The *same* principles illustrated in handling these simple cases are precisely the ones that would also apply on the level of more complex, 'serious', and far-reaching situations. *There is no separate domain of morals or moral values.* Morality has to do with all the various kinds of situations in which individuals and groups of individuals (societies) find themselves. There are no situations or acts that might not have moral significance or involve the making of a moral decision. Moral values are to be found throughout all dimensions of personal or social behavior.

No separate domain of moral values

Every act has potential *moral significance, because it is, through its consequences, part of a larger whole of behavior. A person starts to open a window because he feels the need of air—no act could be more "natural", more morally indifferent in appearance. But he remembers that his associate is an invalid and sensitive to drafts. He now sees his act in two different lights, possessed of two different values, and he has to make a choice. The potential moral import of a seemingly insignificant act has come home to him. Or, wishing to take exercise, there are two routes open to him. Ordinarily it would be a mere matter of personal taste which he would choose. But he recalls that the more pleasing of the two is longer, and that if he went that way he might be unable to keep an appointment of importance. He now has to place his act in a larger context of continuity and determine which ulterior consequence he prizes most: personal pleasure or meeting the needs of another. Thus while there is no single act which* must *under all circumstances have conscious moral quality, there is no act, since it is a part of conduct, which may not have definitive moral significance. There is no hard and fast line between the morally indifferent and the morally significant.*[14]

Moral values are coextensive with the whole range of human experience, not isolated and distinguished from those that are economic, political, medical, legal, educational, sexual, dietary, scientific, esthetic, and so on. Moral values are embedded in and permeate the very texture of all human experience.

Moral judgments

The crucial questions concern how, when they do arise, moral judgments are to be decided. Value judgments, for Dewey, as we have seen, are a species of practical judgments; similarly, *moral* judgments are in turn a species of value judgments, hence ultimately a subclass of practical judgments. *His approach to the way in which moral-value judgments are to be decided, the decision of whether something is morally good or right, is ultimately continuous with and guided by the same general emphasis on the need to apply the broad method of experimental intelligence in deciding these moral judgments as would be involved in deciding the worth of any other type of judgment.*

A moral situation is one in which judgment and choice are required antecedently to overt action. The practical meaning of the situation—that is to say the action needed to satisfy it—is not self-evident. It has to be searched for. There are conflicting desires and alternative apparent goods. What is needed is to find the right course of action, the right good. Hence inquiry is exacted: observation of the detailed makeup of the situation; analysis into its diverse factors; clarification of what is obscure; discounting of the more insistent and vivid traits; tracing the consequences of the various modes of action that suggest themselves; regarding the decision reached as hypothetical and tentative until the anticipated or supposed consequences which led to its adoption have been squared with actual consequences. This inquiry is intelligence. Our moral failures go back to some weakness of disposition, some absence of sympathy, some one-sided bias that makes us perform the judgment of the concrete case carelessly or perversely. Wide sympathy, keen sensitiveness, persistence in the face of the disagreeable, balance of interests enabling us to undertake the work of analysis and decision intelligently are the distinctively moral traits—the virtues or moral excellences.[15]

Dewey insists that moral decisions must not be made in the abstract, by appealing to some fixed rule, principle, or scale of values. A situation calling for a moral decision is a particular situation; the perplexity or problem consists in determining what to decide to do in order to resolve *this* particular perplexity or conflict. General rules are to be treated not as fixed and inviolable principles that come readymade and under which the present situation is to be subsumed as an instance and thereby settled. On the contrary, rules, principles, and standards are at best instruments, aids, or guides to be used for whatever help they might afford; they are not to be treated as themselves unquestioned or unquestionable. *Their satisfactoriness is to be judged in terms of how well they guide us in dealing with this or similar particular situations.* It is always the particular situation that, for Dewey, is the focus of deliberation and needs to be approached with whatever resources one can call upon to help resolve it. What Dewey stresses is the need to "transfer the burden of the moral life from following rules or pursuing fixed ends over to the detection of the ills that need remedy in a special case and the formation of plans and methods for dealing with them."[16]

One result of adopting this approach is to abandon the view, so prevalent in traditional moral philosophies, that there is a unique scale of values that should guide all our choices, and that in this scale of values there is some one *supreme good* in life to which everything should be subordinated. For Dewey there is no such fixed scale of values, nor is there a *unique supreme value*.

No unique supreme value

In the first place, there are many different values. And which of the many goods competing for realization is to be chosen cannot be decided on in a general way or independently of an examination of the needs of a particular individual or a group of individuals in some concrete situation. To make an intelligent moral judgment about what is good or right is not to make some wholesale or abstract judgment. It is to make a judgment about what is right or good for the problematic situation under consideration. To see this point, consider for the moment, by way of analogy, what holds in situations that are not primarily moral. A scientist doesn't simply set out 'to understand the world'. When he goes to the laboratory or to his study to carry on his research, he is preoccupied at any given time with trying to solve some particular problem, to answer some particular question. Consider, similarly, what could be meant by saying that men seek to realize various types of value in their lives.

We cannot seek or attain health, wealth, learning, justice or kindness in general. Action is always specific, concrete, individualized, unique. And consequently judgments as to acts to be performed must be similarly specific. To say that a man seeks health or justice is only to say that he seeks to live healthily or justly. These things, like truth, are adverbial. They are modifiers of action in special cases. How to live healthily or justly is a matter which differs with every person. It varies with his past experience, his opportunities, his temperamental and acquired weaknesses and abilities. Not man in general but a particular man suffering from some particular disability aims to live healthily, and consequently health cannot mean for him exactly what it means for any other mortal.[17]

When one recognizes the importance of always focusing on the needs of individualized situations and applies this mode of approach to the field of moral questions, there is a similar shift in emphasis. "Morals is not a catalogue of acts nor a set of rules to be applied like drugstore prescriptions or cook-book recipes. The need in morals is for specific methods of inquiry and of contrivance: Methods of inquiry to locate difficulties and evils; methods of contrivance to form plans to be used as working hypotheses in dealing with them."[18]

Dewey himself refuses, therefore, to set up and recommend some fixed set of moral values or rules, since this would go contrary to the main thrust of his position. Moral decisions have to be made for each case as it arises. The recommendations or evaluations of how to act cannot be predetermined or set out in advance without knowing all the concrete details —the particular sources of conflict, the particular needs, the competition among which specific 'apparent goods' are operating in a given situation. Any intelligent moral decision would have to be reached through the use and application of the method of experimental intelligence in that particular situation.

Rejection of traditional distinction between 'higher' and 'lower' values

Dewey's approach to the sphere of moral values differs from the traditional ones not only in its call for the use of experimental intelligence in deciding on what is right or good. It also rejects the characteristic division made in traditional schemes or scales of value between '*higher*' and '*lower*' values, as well as between activities or institutions that serve merely as means to certain ends and self-justifying ends. This division is frequently connected with the difference in the kinds of values realized in types of life led by certain classes of individuals in society, as contrasted with the values realized in the lives of other groups of individuals.

Dewey opposes the traditional view of most moral philosophies that there is some one ultimate good in life at which all men should aim. For example, Aristotle called the supreme good 'happiness' and identified part of this good with the life of the contemplative intellectual 'knower'. Spinoza called the supreme good 'the intellectual love of God'. For the orthodox religious believer the supreme good is personal salvation; this is variously interpreted as a matter of living according to God's dictates, emulating God's love, or achieving 'union' with God. Dewey denies there is *one supreme* good, since he rejects a hierarchical conception of moral values.

Every case where moral action is required becomes of equal moral importance and urgency with every other. If the need and deficiencies of a specific situation indicate improvement of health as the end and good, then for that situation health is the ultimate and supreme good. It is no means to something else. It is a final and intrinsic value. The same thing is true of improvement of economic status, of making a living, of attending to business and family demands —all of the things which under the sanction of fixed ends have been rendered of secondary and merely instrumental value, and so relatively base and unimportant. Anything that in a given situation is an end and good at all is of equal worth, rank and dignity with every other good of any other situation, and deserves the same intelligent attention.[19]

For Dewey there is no one universal scale of values—a standard moral measuring rod, as it were—that can be applied to different people's lives to see how much moral value they exhibit or realize. There is no such single common scale of values that should govern everybody's life. People's lives differ. Individuals have different interests, needs, capacities, opportunities. No one mode of life is *the* best mode of life for a *human being as such*. There is no such entity as a human being as such. There is not something called Man; there are only individual human beings, with their individual differences, as well as their varyingly common or shared interests, problems, and needs. Moral evaluation and deliberation should concern themselves with maximizing the goods possible to different individuals. Regimentation is to be condemned and avoided.

The view that there is some one supreme value of life, with all other goods subordinated to it, is correlated with social and political philosophies that draw distinctions of rank among different classes in society. We saw a typical example of this in Plato's philosophy, where the producers serving 'merely' economic functions were the lowest class, the auxiliaries the next higher class, and the philosopher-kings or ruling class the highest. Analogous social distinctions are found in the traditional caste system of India or the class stratifications of feudal society. All such aristocratic, monarchical, hierarchical social and political philosophies are the targets of Dewey's attack. Dewey's own democratic and egalitarian political philosophy connects with his thesis in the field of moral philosophy that there is no fixed hierarchical scheme or scale of values culminating in some one supreme moral value.

The belief in fixed values has bred a division of ends into intrinsic and instrumental, of those that are really worth while in themselves and those that are of importance only as means to intrinsic goods. . . . Historically, it has been the source and justification of a hard and fast difference between ideal goods on one side and material goods on the other. At present those who would be liberal conceive intrinsic goods as esthetic in nature rather than as exclusively religious or as intellectually contemplative. But the effect is the same. So-called intrinsic goods, whether religious or esthetic, are divorced from those interests of daily life which because of their constancy and urgency form the preoccupation of the great mass. Aristotle used this distinction to declare that slaves and the working class though they are necessary for the state—the commonweal—are not constituents of it. That which is regarded as merely *instrumental must approach drudgery; it cannot command either intellectual, artistic or moral attention and respect. Anything becomes* unworthy *whenever it is thought of as intrinsically lacking worth. So men of "ideal" interests have chosen for the most part the way of neglect and escape. The urgency and pressure of "lower" ends have been covered up by polite conventions. Or, they have been relegated to a baser class of mortals in order that the few might be free to attend to the goods that are really or intrinsically worth while. This withdrawal, in the name of higher ends, has left, for mankind at large and especially for energetic "practical" people the lower activities in complete command. . . .*

No one can possibly estimate how much of the obnoxious materialism and brutality of our economic life is due to the fact that economic ends have been regarded as merely instrumental. When they are recognized to be as intrinsic and final in their place as any others, then it will be seen that they are capable of idealization, and that if life is to be worth while, they must acquire ideal and intrinsic value.[20]

The emphasis on growth   One way of summing up the main thrust of Dewey's moral philosophy is to say that there is no one substantive type of activity as the goal toward which all people's lives should move; rather, everyone should seek to *grow* and enrich his or her experience according to his or her propensities and interests. What growth would mean for one individual, however, will not necessarily coincide with what it would mean for another. What this might be, for any particular individual, is not to be found out by reading Dewey's or anybody else's books. There is no manual or code to consult. The goal of ethics should be not to lay down some predetermined plan or catechism but rather to stress the importance for each individual to use, repeatedly and continually, the method of experimental intelligence to maximize his or her own opportunities and abilities.

The conception which looks for the end of action within the circumstances of the actual situation will not have the same measure of judgment for all cases. When one factor of the situation is a person of trained mind and large resources, more will be expected than with a person of backward mind and uncultured experience. The absurdity of applying the same standard of moral judgment to savage peoples that is used with civilized will be apparent. No individual or group will be judged by whether they come up to or fall short of some fixed result, but by the direction in which they are moving. The bad man is the man who no matter how good he has been is beginning to deteriorate, to grow less good. The good man is the man who no matter how morally unworthy he has been is moving to become better. . . .

The process of growth, of improvement and progress, rather than the static outcome and result, becomes the significant thing. Not health as an end fixed once and for all, but the needed improvement in health—a continual process—is the end and good. The end is no longer a terminus or limit to be reached. It is the active process of transforming the existent situation. Not perfection as a final goal, but the ever-enduring process of perfecting, maturing, refining is the aim in living. Honesty, industry, temperance, justice, like health, wealth and learning, are not goods to be possessed as they would be if they expressed fixed ends to be attained. They are directions of change in the quality of experience. Growth itself is the only moral "end".[21]

With the foregoing central core of Dewey's conception of moral philosophy as a starting point, one could proceed in various directions within the total range of his thought to see how he applies and amplifies these themes. There are two such areas of application—educational and political philosophy—to which Dewey devoted so much of his attention and has had so much influence that brief mention must be made at least of the direction of his ideas.

The notion of *growth*, the key idea in Dewey's approach to moral philosophy, affords a clear link to his views on education. For "the educative process is all one with the moral process, since the latter is a continuous passage of experience from worse to better." The key concept in education, for Dewey, is also *growth*. This is to be understood not in a purely biological sense but rather as having to do with the continual and unending *enrichment of experience*. Dewey challenges those traditional views of education according to which education is essentially a matter of *schooling*, and is thought of as a *preparation* for 'real' life. In that approach, education is taken to consist of acquiring certain skills or information, completing certain courses, fulfilling specified requirements, and getting degrees and certifications of one sort or another. And the traditional justification for doing all of this (even though the reasons for the details may not be known by the one subjected to the schooling) is that it is a necessary and preliminary condition for what comes later. Childhood is a preparation for adulthood; school is a preparation for life in the 'real world'; acquisition of skills, information, habits, gives one the necessary means for eventually becoming independent of others.

Dewey rejects the basic orientation of this concept of education. For him, education is not synonymous with schooling. Education is something that ought to be a lifelong process. And that doesn't necessarily mean going to school for the rest of one's life and taking more and more courses, acquiring more and more degrees. Education is not a matter of accumulating credits or degrees. Education should be thought of literally as a matter of 'leading out' from a less rich, less informed, less skilled stage to one that is more informed, more skilled, and more enriched, in whatever directions of interest and need an individual freely chooses.

If at whatever period we choose to take a person, he is still in process of growth, then education is not, save as a by-product, a preparation for something coming later. Getting from the present the degree and kind of growth there is in it is education. This is a constant function, independent of age. The best thing that can be said about any special process of education, like that of the formal school period, is that it renders its subject capable of further education: more sensitive to conditions of growth and more able to take advantage of them. Acquisition of skill, possession of knowledge, attainment of culture are not ends: they are marks of growth and means to its continuing.[22]

Another characteristic principle of many traditional philosophies of education that Dewey attacked is the distinction made by these older theories between *effort* and *interest*. According to these theories, the important thing in educating the student is to give him what the teacher knows he needs, whether or not the student recognizes the need for it. The student must absorb a certain amount of packaged material, and show (through examinations, recitations, performances) that he has acquired the necessary skill, information, or whatever. What is called for on the student's part is *effort* in learning. Whether he has any genuine *interest* or self-motivated concern to find out more, or to improve his performance because he *wants to* and because he sees it as necessary in order to make progress toward goals that he himself has set, is completely beside the point. The teacher (like the doctor) knows what is good for you, and whether you like it or not it is up to you to learn the prescribed materials.

Dewey set himself in his philosophy of education to oppose this rigid contrast between interest and effort. Of course, Dewey doesn't deny the importance of effort, discipline, orderly sequence of acquisitions of skills, information, and so on. Recall the story of the man who was asked whether he could play the violin and who replied "I don't know, I haven't tried!" Dewey's plea is for the *union*, wherever possible, the copresence of interest *and* effort. Where the student or anyone participating in a genuine educative activity, at whatever age, has genuinely felt interests and needs that motivate him to satisfy them, the effort expended in acquiring the necessary means toward the achievement of those ends will not be a matter of drudgery or of an unwilling, forced compliance with an externally imposed discipline. It will, rather, be expended willingly and cooperatively on the part of the individual himself. Take, for example, someone who takes a course in pottery or photography because he wants to perfect his skills in these arts. He doesn't have to be prodded. He searches out the best available sources of help: teachers, books, magazines, visits to museums, exhibits, studios of other artists, conversations with those who might offer help—in short, all those things that can serve as aids or means to achieving the goals set by the individual. Desire doesn't evaporate in mere wishful dreaming, nor is effort coerced by an external authority. There are, instead, continuity and mutual reinforcement of effort and interest. This sort of thing, with all the appropriate accommodations and necessary qualifications that take into account the age of the individual or the nature of the subject matter, would apply, on Deweyan principles, to all levels and dimensions of education. If all of the foregoing seems by now commonplace, this very triteness is in no small measure due to the influence that Dewey's philosophy of education has had.

Even this bare hint of Dewey's educational philosophy is enough to show how radically different his approach is, for example, from that of Plato. For Plato, elementary education is primarily a matter of indoctrination and training, whereas higher education for the select few requires the exercise of an infallible faculty of reason. There is a sharp discontinuity between those eligible for elementary education and those equipped to become rulers. Dewey's whole approach to education is in complete disagreement with such a class-oriented division, as well as with the view that education is a matter either of training along predetermined lines or else of an elitist rational apprehension of fixed truths. Dewey would charge there is no recognition in Plato's philosophy of the concept of *growth*.

In a broad use of the term 'education', as we have seen, the educative process is synonymous with that of growth and so is coextensive with the whole domain of moral experience, itself generously and widely conceived as encompassing all kinds of values to be realized in human life. Taken in this broad sense, all social and cultural institutions—schools, government, business, religion, science, and art—are to be judged from a moral (educative, growth-contributing) perspective. How they function to promote or inhibit the growth of individuals affected by these institutions determines their moral value.

It is with this general point as a background that Dewey's contributions to political philosophy have to be understood. Dewey wrote extensively on the theory of political democracy, the character of totalitarianism, the varied changes in conception of liberalism and individualism, and the nature of legal institutions, as well as on a great number of particular issues and events of social import during his long life.

Political democracy

The concept of political democracy has crucial links with two principal themes in Dewey's thought: the use of the method of experimental intelligence and the concept of growth in experience. "Democracy has many meanings," Dewey asserts, "but if it has a moral meaning, it is found in resolving that the supreme test of all political institutions and industrial arrangements shall be the contribution they make to the all-around growth of every member of society."[23] Dewey vigorously opposes any form of elitist social philosophy, from Plato onward, that favors some individuals or class of individuals over others. Dewey is a *moral egalitarian*. He is committed to the view that a sound system of government should not let the judgment of what is good or right for all members of society rest in the hands of the few. Since the purpose of government is to make possible the full development of all members of society, only the judgment of those affected by the laws and policies of a government should be allowed to judge their effectiveness. Political democracy is the best institutionalized mechanism for the use of the method of experimental intelligence, when this is applied to settling public issues and problems. It leaves to those affected by the plan (law, policy) the decision of how well it works. The original *proposals* for laws and policies, even the *administration* of those enacted, may be left to *experts*, but the evaluation of their effectiveness is not to be left to the experts or to the administrators alone.

Dewey's claims in behalf of political democracy are not a matter of defending this or that specific political mechanism (for example, whether elections of a President should be held every four years or at some other interval, or what constitutes the proper number of representatives in a legislature, and so on). Instead, Dewey is primarily concerned to analyze and defend the root democratic concept of what it means to speak of the *freely given consent of the governed.* Nor is Dewey concerned to argue for this or that substantive law or policy, for example, for some tax law or tariff policy. It is essential to his view that there need be no fixed and permanent set of policies and laws. Even where the method of full and free discussion has resulted in the passing of a law that experience shows to have worked well, there is no guarantee that it will continue to do so. His primary concern, then, is not to argue for this or that law and substantive pattern of managing public affairs. It is, instead, with the *method* used to arrive at and support any proposal for such management. Mistakes, shortcomings, abuses, and failures abound in a democratic system. Dewey is as fully aware of this as anyone. It is his root conviction nevertheless that, in the long run, political democracy is the best and safest way of providing the material conditions for the growth of all members and segments of a society.

Concluding remarks

Dewey's thought sums up an era in the development of a naturalistic, humanistic, and pragmatic philosophy.* It is to some extent a measure of his influence that what at one stage seemed strange and even shocking should have come to appear 'obvious' to large numbers of people and to have become part of their everyday thought and practice.

Still, as we survey the current philosophic scene, we must admit that, far from continuing to discuss the themes Dewey took as his own or using his own favorite conceptual distinctions, many philosophers who now command the forefront of attention have, to a large extent, accomplished

---

* The writings of other American philosophers whose work was roughly contemporary with that of Dewey and who shared in the formulation of a naturalistic philosophy (although not agreeing in all details with Dewey's version) include George Santayana, *The Life of Reason*; Morris R. Cohen, *Reason and Nature*; F. J. E. Woodbridge, *An Essay on Nature*. A convenient collection of essays representative of the philosophy of naturalism of this period is to be found in Y. H. Krikorian (editor), *Naturalism and the Human Spirit.* For a discussion of the development of pragmatism in its various phases, see H. S. Thayer, *Meaning and Action: A Critical History of Pragmatism.*

a shift in perspective and in interests from those of Dewey and his followers. It is rare that a philosophy is refuted, if indeed the concept of refutation makes any sense at all in connection with a total philosophy. Rather, another process seems to be at work in the development of major replacements of philosophies, as in other intellectual areas. It is what I have called a 'shift in perspective and interests'. A new constellation of concerns and themes comes to occupy the attention of large numbers of thinkers. And even those issues or insights that are retained from an older way of thinking are now restructured and reexpressed in a new language, a new way of looking at things. This realignment of perspectives and interests is what has taken place in the field of philosophy since the days when Dewey's thought came into its own full expression. We find ourselves at the present time in a period of change and transition.

No single factor or cause brought about this change. It is hardly necessary to remind ourselves that our world, especially since the days of World War II, has seen profound upheavals in all dimensions of culture. The problems that people face are of enormous complexity and challenge. Whether human intelligence will in fact be adequate to their solution is a matter about which many persons have come to develop either strong doubts or a cautious reserve. They have adopted an attitude of something less than the general optimism and fundamental confidence that Dewey exhibited.

For our present purposes, there are two examples, two directions in which we can see the workings of such a shift in basic perspective and attitudes as reflected in the field of philosophy itself.

One has to do with the growth of 'analytic philosophy' and especially of an interest in examining the resources and varied uses of *language*. Those attracted to this mode of 'doing' philosophy are in general disenchanted with, and wary of, any program of constructing large and comprehensive schemes of thought. Instead, they would focus on problems of limited scope and undertake to deal with these one at a time. In performing their analyses, they pay much attention to the very language used in setting up the problem, as well as in the variety of linguistic tools that might be used to make the necessary distinctions and in finding possible solutions to the problem under investigation. As a clear and important example of this emphasis on linguistic analysis in the approach to philosophy, I shall consider (in Chapter 13) the views of Ludwig Wittgenstein, who has exerted an enormous influence in contemporary philosophy. In the course of examining some of his leading theses, I shall also have occasion to point out how his approach to language affords still another way of critically responding to a philosophy such as Plato's. For Wittgenstein's analysis of language offers a powerful tool for showing the difficulties in accepting Plato's Theory of Forms.

The other shift of perspective in recent philosophy derives from an altogether different kind of criticism of older ways of thought from that offered by analytic philosophers. This second group of writers (for all their internal differences from one another) would tend to look elsewhere than simply to a reliance exclusively on 'reason' or piecemeal linguistic and conceptual analysis in developing a philosophic viewpoint. If I may use for the moment an older religious term, these thinkers are motivated by the desire for personal 'salvation'. They are primarily concerned to develop a total attitude to life and to the world in which we live. They would look to philosophy to save us from being duped or enmeshed in the world. They would offer us a type of insight, a level or dimension of awareness that lies 'beyond reason' (but not in the sense of being anti-rational or favoring irrationality). What they would call attention to is a means of accomplishing a certain elevation of spirit, a way of achieving a tranquility of mind. But this result and the way it is to be reached, let me hasten to add, are not to be found by reverting to the traditional practices and ways of thought of theistic religion in the West. The kind of spirituality or transcendence of reason here being expressed has a different base and orientation from that associated with traditional theism.

We shall examine in Chapter 14 two major examples of this second broad pattern of thought. The first is associated with the tradition of Zen Buddhism. The second belongs to the thought of the German philosopher Martin Heidegger.

V
Some Recent Developments

Die Welt ist alles was der Fall ist.

Die Welt ist die Gesamtheit der Tatsachen, nicht der Dinge

~~Was der Fall ist, die Tatsache, ist das Bestehen von Sachverhalten~~

Die Tatsachen begreifen wir in Bildern

Das logische Bild der Tatsachen ist der Gedanke

Der sinnliche Ausdruck des Gedankens ist das Satzzeichen

Das Satzzeichen mit der Art und Weise seiner Abbildung ist der Satz

Der Gedanke ist der sinnvolle Satz

Der Satz stellt das Bestehen und nicht Bestehen der Sachverhalte dar

2 Der Sinn des Satzes ist seine Übereinstimmung, und nicht Übereinstimmung, mit den Möglichkeiten des Bestehens und nicht Bestehens der Sachverhalte

3 Die Wahrheitsmöglichkeiten der Elementarsätze bedeuten die Möglichkeiten des Bestehens und nicht Bestehens der Sachverhalte

4 Der Satz ist der Ausdruck der Übereinstimmung und nicht Übereinstimmung mit den Wahrheitsmöglichkeiten der Elementarsätze

5 Der Satz ist eine Wahrheitsfunktion der Elementarsätze

6 Die Allgemeine Form der Wahrheitsfunktion ist:

$$[\bar{p}, \bar{\xi}, N(\bar{\xi})]$$

chapter 13

Linguistic Analysis

Wittgenstein

Ludwig Wittgenstein (1889–1951) is one of the most important philosophers of the twentieth century. Although no single label is adequate to describe his philosophy, his contributions to the movement known as 'linguistic' or 'analytic' philosophy best serve to indicate where his most original contributions lay and where his influence on other thinkers can be most readily recognized. One major focus of Wittgenstein's philosophy is the nature of language. He was concerned to analyze the logical structure of language, its limits and uses (what it can and cannot do), and the varieties of uses for language. Two of his major works are *Tractatus Logico-Philosophicus* (completed in 1918) and *Philosophical Investigations* (1953, published after his death). Despite some elements in common between his earlier and later writings, there is a marked and important basic discontinuity. Indeed Wittgenstein's later philosophy had as one of its main targets his own earlier philosophy. In examining Wittgenstein's philosophy I shall select for more detailed analysis some leading themes in his later writings—particularly what he has to say about the nature of names, 'language games', and 'family resemblances'. We shall then see how, in one direction of the application of these ideas, Wittgenstein is led to criticize a philosophy such as Plato's in its appeal to the notion of the independent reality of abstract entities.

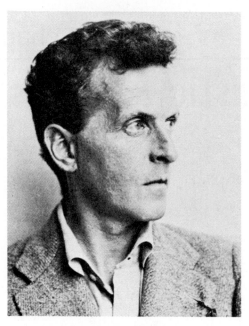

Ludwig Wittgenstein

Biographical sketch   Ludwig Wittgenstein was born in Vienna in 1889 and died in Cambridge, England, in 1951. His grandfather was a Jew who converted to Protestant Christianity. His father was a wealthy industrialist, a prominent leader of the iron and steel industry of Austria. Wittgenstein's mother was Catholic, and he himself was baptized in the Catholic Church and given a Roman Catholic burial. Ludwig was the youngest of eight children, a member of a family rich in intellectual and artistic talent. Music played an important role in the Wittgenstein home.*

Until the age of fourteen, Wittgenstein was educated at home. He later attended schools in Austria and Germany. Wittgenstein had great gifts for designing, constructing, and even repairing machinery, and he chose at first to study engineering. In 1908 Wittgenstein went to the University of Manchester in England, where he spent three years in the study of aircraft mechanics. There he developed a special interest in the design of jet reaction engines and propellers. Since this work required highly technical mathematics, Wittgenstein found himself getting more and more interested in the sphere of pure mathematics itself—in its basic concepts and methods, in short in the 'foundations' or philosophy of that discipline. For

---

* The composer Johannes Brahms was a friend of the family. One of Ludwig's brothers (Paul) was an internationally famous pianist. Ludwig himself played the clarinet and had a great talent for whistling: he could whistle, from memory, entire concertos.

this purpose he made a close study of Bertrand Russell's work *The Principles of Mathematics*, which had appeared in 1903. He was deeply impressed by that work. Russell's thought, in this area, owed much to the pioneering investigations of the great German logician Gottlob Frege (1848–1925). (Later, Russell was to collaborate with another celebrated logician, mathematician, and philosopher, Alfred North Whitehead. Their joint work, *Principia Mathematica*, was destined to become a major classic in the field of modern symbolic logic, the logic that challenged and replaced the older Aristotelian logic that had been taught in the schools for centuries.) The problems with which Frege and Russell were preoccupied, of giving a precise and carefully formulated analysis of the underlying logical patterns of our thought and language, aroused an enormous interest on Wittgenstein's part. Wittgenstein decided to give up engineering, and, on Frege's advice, went to study with Russell at Cambridge in 1911.* While at Cambridge, Wittgenstein also became the friend of the philosopher G. E. Moore and the economist John Maynard Keynes. In addition to his work on logic during this period, Wittgenstein conducted some experiments in the psychological laboratory on the nature of musical rhythms. After spending five terms at Cambridge, Wittgenstein went to live in Norway, where he built himself a hut, lived in isolation, and worked there until the outbreak of World War I in 1914.

Wittgenstein volunteered to serve in the Austrian Army, became an officer, and was repeatedly decorated for bravery. He was captured by the Italians in 1918. He spent part of his captivity as a prisoner of war at a camp in southern Italy. And it was here that he completed the manuscript of his first major work, later to receive the title *Tractatus Logico-Philosophicus*. (It was Wittgenstein's custom to write his philosophic thoughts in a series of notebooks. And all his major works were composed by making

---

* Russell, in his *Autobiography*, describes his early encounters with Wittgenstein: "He was perhaps the most perfect example I have ever known of genius as traditionally conceived, passionate, profound, intense, and dominating. He had a kind of purity which I have never known equalled except by G. E. Moore. . . . He used to come to see me every evening at midnight, and pace up and down my room like a wild beast for three hours in agitated silence. Once I said to him: 'Are you thinking about logic or about your sins?' 'Both', he replied, and continued his pacing. I did not like to suggest that it was time for bed, as it seemed probable both to him and me that on leaving me he would commit suicide. At the end of his first term at Trinity, he came to me and said: 'Do you think I am an absolute idiot?' I said: 'Why do you want to know?' He replied: 'Because if I am I shall become an aeronaut, but if I am not I shall become a philosopher'. I said to him: 'My dear fellow, I don't know whether you are an absolute idiot or not, but if you will write me an essay during the vacation upon any philosophical topic that interests you, I will read it and tell you'. He did so, and brought it to me at the beginning of the next term. As soon as I read the first sentence, I became persuaded that he was a man of genius, and assured him that he should on no account become an aeronaut" (Bertrand Russell, *Autobiography*, Vol. II, 99).

arrangements of these 'notes'. During the entire time he was in the Army, Wittgenstein kept such a notebook.) Wittgenstein showed a copy of the manuscript of his work to Russell, who finally succeeded in getting it translated into English and published. Russell himself wrote an introduction to the work. (However, Wittgenstein felt that Russell failed to understand what he was really after.) This short work (it is only twenty thousand words long) is written in a highly compressed form as a series of numbered statements. Wittgenstein, at the time, thought it contained 'the solution to all philosophic problems'. It has indeed become one of the major philosophic classics of the twentieth century. Although short, it is difficult to comprehend, and like other great works of thought has spawned a great and constantly growing literature of commentary and interpretation.

The *Tractatus* deals with the general problem of the relation of language and the world. Two famous sentences of that work (one from the beginning, the other from the end) are "The world is all that is the case" and "Whereof one cannot speak, thereof one must be silent." In this book, Wittgenstein was primarily concerned to work out the underlying logical structure of 'what can be said', the conditions that make for meaningfulness in the propositions we use to represent the states of affairs in the world. Wittgenstein was concerned to draw the limits between what makes for sense and nonsense in our use of language. (At the same time, it must be recognized that Wittgenstein himself, unlike many other linguistic or analytic philosophers, had a strong affinity for, and awareness of, those aspects of our experience that cannot be expressed in language at all, and that he sometimes called 'the mystical'.) In any case, in the *Tractatus* he is concerned to set out the character of what *can* be expressed—and expressed clearly—when we do use language to state facts. And all of this lies on 'this side' of the limits of language.

A key idea of that work is frequently referred to as 'the picture theory of meaning'. If we think of language as made up of a series of propositions, the principal question is how to describe the kind of relation such propositions have to the world of fact. One influential suggestion or model for answering this question came to Wittgenstein one day in 1914 upon reading about a lawsuit involving an automobile accident. During the trial, miniatures of the automobiles, persons, and houses involved were displayed in the courtroom. The miniature figures referred to the actual objects and persons involved. The pattern in which these miniature figures were arranged was intended to correspond to the circumstances of the accident as it had actually occurred. One was a picture of the other. Wittgenstein's insight was that one may think of propositions (words in language, arranged in a certain way) as also offering a picture of reality. The task of logical analysis is to trim away all that is irrelevant in obtaining the bare bones of the 'logical picture' present in every meaningful proposition that undertakes to state some item of 'what is the case'. When true, the form or structure of a properly analyzed proposition corresponds to, or pictures, the fact or state of affairs in the world. (I shall return, later, to a fuller account of this way of thinking, and to some of the criticisms that Wittgenstein himself eventually came to make of this whole approach.)

Since he believed that in the *Tractatus* he had 'solved all philosophical problems', Wittgenstein, for some years, gave up active research in philosophy. In 1912 Wittgenstein's father (Karl Wittgenstein) died. Ludwig came into a large inheritance. However, one of the first things that he did upon his return from military service was to give away all his money, some of it in the form of anonymous benefactions to well-known writers and poets. Wittgenstein himself, all his adult years, led a life of extreme frugality and simplicity.

At the end of World War I, Wittgenstein attended a teacher's training school and during the years 1920–1926 served as a village schoolmaster in lower Austria. After resigning his post, Wittgenstein became for a short time a gardener's assistant in a monastery near Vienna. For a period of two years, Wittgenstein designed and supervised (in all its details) the construction of a mansion in Vienna for one of his sisters. The style of architecture of this house is extremely severe in its modern lines and free from all decoration. Its spare and straight lines reveal an austere logical simplicity reminiscent of the logically tight structure to be found in the *Tractatus*.

Toward the end of the 1920s, Wittgenstein's interest in philosophy was rekindled and he returned to Cambridge in 1929. Here he was awarded his doctorate degree and became a fellow of Trinity College. In 1939 Wittgenstein became a professor of philosophy at Cambridge University, occupying the chair previously held by G. E. Moore. Wittgenstein's seminars were held in his sparsely furnished rooms at Trinity College. He sat in his deck chair, dressed somewhat unconventionally, and, without using any notes, engaged in long, intricate discussions with a select group of students. According to the reminiscences of some of these students, Wittgenstein in these discussions showed an enormous intensity, seriousness, and purity of devotion as he grappled with how to respond to various queries and how to give expression to his own thoughts. Two sets of student notes, taken down during this period, came to be known as the *Blue Book* and the *Brown Book* (and were published subsequently under these titles). They represent preliminary studies for his major work *Philosophical Investigations*, published posthumously and, like the *Tractatus*, an outstanding classic of contemporary philosophy. The later writings of Wittgenstein contain the working out of a quite different approach to the philosophy of language from that to be found in the *Tractatus*. In addition to his central work in the philosophy of language, Wittgenstein in these later works wrote extensively on the philosophy of mathematics and the philosophy of mind.

From 1929 until his death Wittgenstein lived in England. He became a British citizen, although he was not especially fond of English ways of life. From time to time he left the academic atmosphere of Cambridge (which, too, he tended to dislike) to live for brief periods in other countries, for example, Norway, Ireland, and the United States. Wittgenstein's personality was of a tense, forceful, and troubled sort. He made severe demands on his close friends and yet had an extremely devoted band of followers. He once said "Although I cannot *give* affection, I have a great *need* for it."

Just before Wittgenstein took up his duties in 1939 as professor of philosophy at Cambridge University, World War II broke out. Wittgenstein at first served as a porter in a London hospital and later worked in a medical laboratory in Newcastle. By 1949 his health had begun to rapidly deteriorate, and it was found that he was suffering from cancer. He nevertheless continued to work at philosophy until the very end. He recorded some of his most technical thoughts (on the topic of 'certainty') up to two days before his death. He died on April 29, 1951, at the home of his doctor.

The Picture Theory of Meaning

The theory of language in the Tractatus

The view of language with which Wittgenstein operated in his earlier work, the *Tractatus*, concentrated on the way in which language may be used to give a picture of the world. Language is there thought of as a series of propositions that undertake to state facts. And propositions would be said to be true when they correctly state, picture, or correspond to what the facts are and to be false when they fail to do so. On such an approach, the basic unit of language is a proposition. A proposition is a combination of words that asserts something. It is taken to consist essentially of *names*. The meaning of these names consists in their having reference to various *objects*. The way in which the names are connected with one another in the proposition, if the whole proposition is true, will correspond to, or picture, the way in which the objects are connected with one another in the world. A *rough model* of this way of thinking is illustrated in the sentence "The cat is on the mat." The expression 'the cat' refers to a certain object; so does the expression 'the mat'; and the words 'is on' may also be thought to refer to a certain specific spatial relation between the previously named objects. If the cat, the mat, and the specific spatial relation between them are to be found in the world in the way this proposition asserts, then the proposition correctly pictures the actual state of affairs. It is then true; otherwise, it is false. To summarize: This approach to language thinks of propositions as made up of names; of the world as made up of objects to which names refer; of meaning as consisting of the objects referred to by names; of the essential function of propositions as a matter of giving a description of the facts.

The individual words in language name objects—sentences are combinations of such names. . . . Every word has a meaning. This meaning is correlated with the word. It is the object for which the word stands.[1]

This theory of language is known as 'the picture theory of meaning'. It is this conception and approach to language that Wittgenstein himself sets out to challenge and replace in his later writings.

Language Games

In the *Philosophical Investigations*, Wittgenstein offers a whole new way of thinking about the nature of human language. It also offers a new way to 'do' philosophy. Let me first put this new perspective on language negatively. Wittgenstein came to realize that to think of language as made up fundamentally of names and of meaning as having to do with the objects referred to by names is to fail to do justice to the enormous flexibility and variety of uses of language. He came to realize that his earlier approach offered too confining a framework within which to fit all the uses of language. In thinking of propositions as combinations of names whose essential function is to picture facts, he was overlooking that to use language to *describe* states of affairs is only one among a great variety of uses of language, and not by any means its sole or even principal use. There are, of course, names in language, and we do often use language to state facts. But to think of names as the only building blocks of language and sentences as merely ways to picture facts is simply the wrong way of trying to understand what language is.

The varied uses of language

There is a famous phrase (or slogan) that sums up, in a positive way, his new orientation to language. It says: "Don't look for the meaning, look for the use!" The expression 'meaning' is to be understood here in the way in which this is understood in his *earlier* thought: names have meaning, and their meaning consists in the objects they designate. Wittgenstein rejects this conception of *meaning*. The constructions and uses of language, as well as the purposes and life situations in which they are embedded and which they serve, are enormously rich and complex. He asks us to look at all these *varied uses* of language.

Language games   Instead of taking the proposition as a combination of names, as the basic item to be analyzed, and as having a fixed logical structure, he stresses what he calls a *'language game'*. To understand this, let us think of a typical life situation. A particular language game will bring out the distinctive use of language in that situation. A language game is a simplified model, a clear instance of some characteristic use of language. In one respect, a language game may be thought of as a tool for analysis. It helps us gain a deeper understanding of language as we find it. In another way of thinking of the matter, we may say that language, as a total human phenomenon, is made up of a very great number of individual language games. These are interwoven with one another in an intricate network of interrelationships.

To say that the use of language may be compared to a game is, of course, not intended to convey any suggestion of amusement, recreation, or sport. The terminology is intended to bring out, by way of analogy with what we ordinarily call games (e.g., chess, baseball, bridge), that the words used in language are combined according to certain 'rules of the game'. Some are strictly laid down, as in mathematics. In other cases there may not be any strict or explicit rules. These rules constitute the 'grammar' of the language. The words or other linguistic units employed in the several language games may be compared to the pieces in a chess game. Both have a 'role' in the game. To understand the use of a word is like understanding the use of a chess piece—say, the king, pawn, or bishop. We must understand what can be done with it, the way it functions.

One use of language games is to make explicit and teach the rules that govern the use of a word. To serve this need, a language game does not involve the actual *application* of the word. Its primary role is to make us acquainted with the *grammar* of an expression. It is comparable, for example, to learning the rules of chess by having the various pieces pointed out in sample moves on the board. To learn the rules—what the chess pieces can do—is to learn the 'grammar' of the chess pieces. It is not yet to play an *actual game* of chess. It is, however, preparatory to, a condition for, playing a game. After one has learned the rules, one can actually play a game. One faces an opponent, and moves the pieces *in accordance* with the rules. The moves, as now made in an actual game, are the result of decisions as to how to put into effect a certain strategy, in order to capture the opponent's pieces and win the game. The playing of a game is more than learning the rules through simple illustrative moves. The case is similar to learning a language and then 'playing' an actual game—i.e., applying the rules in an actual life situation. One must first learn how to use a term. This is a condition for using the grammatical rule in situations where the language is applicable.

As previously remarked, Wittgenstein thought it simply too narrow and constricting to think of all languages as consisting of names, or of all sentences as engaged in giving descriptions. There are many words that don't name anything, even though they have genuine and well-established *uses*. For example, the word 'Hello', used as a greeting, doesn't *name* anything. Wittgenstein replies to someone who might say "We name things and then we can talk about them, can refer to them in talk." He says:

As if what we did next were given with the mere act of naming. As if there were only one thing called "talking about a thing". Whereas in fact we do the most various things with our sentences. Think of exclamations alone, with their completely different functions.

> *Water!*
> *Away!*
> *Ow!*
> *Help!*
> *Fine!*
> *No'!*

Are you still inclined to call these words "names of objects?"[2]

Not only are not all expressions in language names for objects, it is also more obviously the case that not all uses of language are for purposes of giving a description.

But how many kinds of sentence are there? Say assertion, question, and command?—There are countless *kinds: countless different kinds of use of what we call "symbols," "words," "sentences." And this multiplicity is not something fixed, given once for all; but new types of language, new language-games, as we may say, come into existence, and others become obsolete and get forgotten. (We can get a rough picture of this from the changes in mathematics.)*

Here the term "language-game" is meant to bring into prominence the fact that the speaking of language is part of an activity, or of a form of life.

Review the multiplicity of language-games in the following examples, and in others:

> *Giving orders, and obeying them—*
> *Describing the appearance of an object,*
>   *or giving its measurements—*
> *Constructing an object from a description*
>   *(a drawing)—*
> *Reporting an event—*
> *Speculating about an event—*
> *Forming and testing a hypothesis—*

Presenting the results of an experiment
  in tables and diagrams—
Making up a story; and reading it—
Play-acting—
Singing catches—
Guessing riddles—
Making a joke; telling it—
Solving a problem in practical arithmetic—
Translating from one language into another—
Asking, thanking, cursing, greeting, praying.[3]

Any one of these multiple uses of language may itself have many different forms. For example,

Think how many different kinds of things are called "description": description of a body's position by means of its co-ordinates; description of a facial expression; description of a sensation of touch; of a mood.[4]

To determine which of the many uses of language is being employed, what language game is being played, one has to examine the language used in the context of the social situation or activity in which it is embedded, and for which a particular combination of words serves a particular role. Its 'meaning' cannot be read off from the words or the sentence as it stands, or independently of seeing it in its context. Take the sentence "Mary, I love you." One cannot give a 'logical' analysis of its 'real' meaning without considering the possible situations in which the same sentence, the same combinations of words, is used. It does not have a single underlying meaning. For example, that sentence might be used by someone who is actually in love with a girl named 'Mary'. He is about to 'pop' the question, and says to her, "Mary, I love you." In using that sentence he is conveying to her how he actually feels about her. On the other hand, that very same sentence may be used as an example to illustrate a point in English grammar for foreigners learning the English language. The teacher may write this same sentence on the board, and make various remarks about the grammar of the words in the sentence. However, the teacher is not using the sentence, as in the previously mentioned situation, to tell any particular person that he loves her. The teacher is simply using the sentence as part of a lesson in English grammar. Or suppose, in a class in elementary French, a student translates the sentence "Marie, je t'aime", as "Mary, I love you." In this context, the use of the sentence "Mary, I love you" is different from both of the foregoing uses. The sentence is here being used to give a translation into English of a sentence in French. Or, again, suppose a play were being put on, and one of the lines a character has to read and act out is the sentence "Mary, I love you." The same words are being used as in all of the foregoing situations, but their use, in portraying a character in a play, is unlike any of the others. Thus it would simply be wrong to think of the sentence "Mary, I love you" as essentially a combination of names each of which refers to some object, where the sentence as a whole pictures some fact, and where the description is either true or false. For some situations, there are not even any actual objects or persons to which the terms refer. This is the case in making a grammatical point or in translating. In some cases, 'Mary' may in fact be the name of a person who is being addressed, as in the case of the young man who is actually asking the real girl named 'Mary' to marry him. In other cases 'Mary' is not the name of a real person but only of a character in a play.

Take another simple case: If somebody asks "How are you?" when he meets you on the street, normally he does not intend to literally inquire about your health, or to wait for a detailed answer. On the other hand, if your doctor uses the same words and asks "How are you?" when you visit him as a patient in his office, he clearly is not simply greeting you or using these words as a matter of social convention.

Wittgenstein's main point in his use of the concept of language game is that we bear in mind the multiple uses of language. We need to see any particular use of language in its relation to an actual life situation, and not confuse different possible uses. We should not automatically apply what holds in one context to another where it does not apply. We must be prepared to note similarities and differences among various uses of the same words. We must avoid the simple-minded reduction of all these varied uses to one supposedly fundamental use.

In addition to thinking of languages on the model of *games*, he compares linguistic expressions to *tools*:

Think of the tools in a tool box: there is a hammer, pliers, a saw, a screw-driver, a rule, a glue-pot, glue, nails and screws.—The functions of words are as diverse as the functions of these objects. (And in both cases there are similarities.)

Of course, what confuses us is the uniform appearance of words when we hear them spoken or meet them in script and print. For their application is not presented to us so clearly. Especially not, when we are doing philosophy!

It is like looking into the cabin of a locomotive. We see handles all looking more or less alike. (Naturally, since they are all supposed to be handled.) But one is the handle of a crank which can be moved continuously (it regulates the opening of a valve); another is the handle of a switch, which has only two effective positions, it is either off or on; a third is the handle of a brake-lever, the harder one pulls on it, the harder it brakes; a fourth, the handle of a pump: it has an effect only so long as it is moved to and fro.

When we say: "Every word in language signifies something" we have so far said nothing whatever; unless we have explained what distinction we wish to make.[5]

According to Wittgenstein, a prime cause of philosophical confusion and puzzlement is the failure to have a clear understanding of the nature of language and the grammatical rules that govern the use of various expressions. Even the most celebrated thinkers are frequently trapped into wrong turns of thought and are held captive by certain analogies. They are taken in by the 'surface grammar' of utterances rather than probing their 'depth grammar'. For Wittgenstein, the task of philosophy is to untangle the various intellectual knots, "to show the fly out of the fly-bottle."

Philosophical grammar   The sense in which Wittgenstein uses the term 'grammar' has relatively little to do with ordinary syntactical distinctions or classifications of the parts of speech. Indeed, in some cases, to give a grammatical analysis of an expression, in Wittgenstein's sense of 'grammar', might even come into conflict with what would be called its 'grammar' in the ordinary use of this term. Thus according to ordinary rules of English grammar, if one says "I have a toothache" and "He has a toothache" the use of the verb 'to have' has the same meaning in both cases. However, as Wittgenstein argues, the sense of 'have' (its 'depth grammar', as distinguished from its 'surface grammar') is different in both cases. Indeed, one can say that there is no such thing, strictly speaking, as a *verification* of the proposition "I have a toothache." The reason, according to Wittgenstein, why verification has no sense in connection with the latter proposition is that the question "How do you know that you have a toothache?" is nonsensical.[6] Thus the statement "I don't know whether I have a toothache" is absurd, whereas it makes perfectly good sense to say of another person, "I don't know whether he has a toothache." Because of these differences, one cannot regard "*He has* a toothache" and "*I have* a toothache" as equally good examples of the use of the verb 'have' in a sentence of the general form "*X has* a toothache." The grammar (in the Wittgensteinian sense) of 'have' operates according to different depth-grammatical rules when used in first person singular present tense, in connection with a pain, from what the rule is for 'have' as used in connection with a pain ascribed to another person. On the other hand, in the sentences "*I have* an automobile" and "*He has* an automobile" the word 'have' means 'to own' or 'to have access to the use of', and in these meanings the word 'have' is used in the *same* sense, whether in first person or third person singular.[7]

To make discriminations of the preceding kind—to explore the similarities or differences in the use of ordinary words like 'have' in various language games—is the sort of thing that calls for extremely patient and subtle analysis. It illustrates one of the things meant by the phrase 'linguistic analysis' to describe a central interest of Wittgenstein's philosophy.

Wittgenstein's stress on the varied uses of language (on the different types of language games that make up language as a whole or that illustrate, in their simplified forms, the distinctive uses of language in different situations) discourages any attempt to set up some one language game as ideal, by which other uses of language are to be judged and evaluated. Instead, the important thing is to see how, for example, scientific language when used to describe and explain natural phenomena is similar to and different from language used by mathematicians; how these in turn differ from the language of jurists, historians, literary critics, and other specialists. Or, again, it is important to study carefully the typical uses of language in poetry, novels, religion, for ceremonial purposes, to utter commands, to give advice, to express feelings, and so on. With such a spectrum of language uses as the field for study, one notes overlappings and dissimilarities. The task of philosophy in all of this is not to reform language or to set up some ideal language. It 'leaves everything as it is'. Its task is essentially descriptive of the various 'logics' or 'grammars' of these different language games. Nor is this type of study to be undertaken in a wholesale way. It cannot be done by taking large chunks of types of discourse and examining them. To be done properly, one must examine individual cases, one by one. Wittgenstein strives to overcome the distaste of philosophers toward working with particular examples. For him it is only through the patient, laborious, and detailed examination of numerous individual cases that one begins to see their multiple interconnections, their similarities and dissimilarities, and, as a result of all this, to learn how to avoid familiar mistakes and confusions. None of this can be accomplished simply by learning certain general principles. One has to gain proficiency in the detailed practice of this *linguistic technique*. And this is a very difficult, specialized, and sophisticated sort of activity.

No one ideal language

Dispensing with Abstract Entities

Much of Wittgenstein's work consisted in considering many different examples of characteristic fallacies that are to be found in an uncritical use of language. His accomplishments in this direction were in exposing the errors to which many philosophers are prone, thereby dissolving various chronic puzzlements and making explicit the confusions upon which they rest.

We shall now examine the application of some of Wittgenstein's insights in judging a central feature of a Platonistic type of world view. As we have seen earlier in this book, Plato claimed there are certain abstract objects or entities (Forms, Ideas, universals) that constitute the meanings

Plato revisited

of general terms, are apprehended by reason, have precise definable essential properties, belong to an independent timeless domain of reality, and as such are distinct from the world of sensible, material particulars. You will recall Plato's arguments for this view. He writes, for example:

Whenever a number of individuals have a common name, we assume them to have a corresponding Idea or Form. . . . Let us take any common instance: there are beds and tables in the world—plenty of them . . . but there are only two Ideas or Forms of them—one the Idea of a bed, the other of a table.[8]

To each of these sets of many things, we postulate a single Form or real essence, as we call it. . . . Further, the many things, we say, can be seen, but are not objects of rational thought; whereas the Forms are objects of thought, but invisible.[9]

The mind, by a power of her own, contemplates the universals in all things.[10]

Nothing makes a thing beautiful but the presence and participation of Beauty. . . . By Beauty all beautiful things become beautiful.[11]

Wittgenstein's critique of Plato

There are two features, in particular, of Plato's views about Forms (or, in general, any 'Platonistic' conception of abstract entities) that Wittgenstein's analysis singles out for attack. One has to do with the assumption that abstract nouns or general words are to be treated as being species of names that designate some object as their 'meaning'. Thus it might be thought that in the sentence "Rectangularity is a geometric property" the term 'rectangularity' refers to a *special kind of object*—an *abstract entity*. This assumption underlies what can be called the '*Reference Fallacy*'.[12]

The other underlying assumption of Plato's theory is that the use of a general word requires that there be some precise and fixed set of properties that make up the essential meaning of the general term. This essential meaning is to be captured and stated in a definition of the general word that, in turn, designates the Form under investigation. This assumption commits what, in Wittgenstein's view, may be called the '*Essence Fallacy*'. Wittgenstein's stress on the notion of 'family resemblances' is intended to break the grip of the Essence Fallacy. "I cannot characterize my standpoint better," Wittgenstein says, at one point, "than by saying that it is opposed to that which Socrates represents in the Platonic dialogues. For if asked what knowledge is I would list examples of knowledge, and add the words 'and the like'. No common element is to be found in them all."[13]

The idea that in order to get clear about the meaning of a general term one had to find the common element in all its applications, has shackled philosophical investigation; for it has not only led to no result, but also made the philoso-

pher dismiss as irrelevant the concrete cases, which alone could have helped him to understand the usage of the general term. When Socrates asks the question, "what is knowledge?" he does not even regard it as a preliminary answer to enumerate cases of knowledge.[14]

Taking these cues from Wittgenstein, one may say that the *combination* of the Reference Fallacy and the Essence Fallacy lies behind Plato's postulation of the reality of Forms. If Wittgenstein's claims can be sustained, they go a long way to undermining the Theory of Forms, and perhaps altogether dissolving the various controversies down the ages that have surrounded it. We shall turn now to a fuller statement, first, of the Reference Fallacy and, second, of the doctrine of 'family resemblances' as a basis for exposing the Essence Fallacy.

The form of philosophical bewilderment and error at the basis of the Reference Fallacy arises when "we try to find a substance for a substantive."[15] For example, we assume that wherever we use an abstract noun (a substantive) there must be some kind of object or entity (substance) that the noun designates. We fall into the trap of "looking at words as though they all were proper names."[16] "Here the word, there the meaning." We treat the general word or abstract noun and its meaning as if we had "the money and the cow you can buy with it."[17] However, money can buy not just *things* (like cows) but also various *services* (like a haircut or admission to a football game): it can be thought of in terms of the various *uses* to which it can be put. So, too, one should look at words not necessarily as always referring to objects (the way proper names do when they refer to individual material objects or persons) but in terms of their varied *uses*.

Just as an ordinary proper name for a person (e.g., 'Socrates') or a physical object (e.g., 'the Moon') is introduced and comes to be learned in conjunction with the entity, so, it is thought by those who commit the Reference Fallacy, *all* words must name some object of some type or other. The tendency is to assimilate all other uses to the naming use and to establish their meanings by looking for various 'objects' to serve as the meanings of these various terms. Wittgenstein criticizes this whole tendency as philosohpically misleading and the source of much confusion. A person asking the question "What is the meaning of _____?" invites an answer in the form of pointing to, describing, or in some way identifying the 'object' with which the word to be learned is to be connected, even if the 'object' is not a particular physical object or an individual person. One thus asks "What is Time?" or "What is Mind?" or "What is the Circle?" or "What is Thought?" or "What is Memory?" or "What is Life?" and so on. In all of these cases the underlying assumption is that the answer is to be found by identifying some type of object to serve as the meaning

Reference Fallacy

of the word. One uses the 'name-object' model (just as 'Fido' is the name of the dog Fido) as supposedly adequate to understand the varied uses of all these expressions. And this, Wittgenstein says, is where all the trouble begins. Disputes arise among those who offer their own 'candidates' in responding to the original question. Yet the whole enterprise, including all the ensuing debates and controversies, is idle. It shows that language "has gone on holiday." This results from the failure of philosophers to stop and critically question the reliance on the 'name-object' model as adequate for all purposes. One assumes that just as the proper name 'Fido' designates the particular dog Fido, so, in general, the meaning of a *general* word must designate some entity or object as its meaning.

Nor are we helped by those who want to distinguish different *kinds* of *objects*—say, *abstract* ones, or *mathematical* ones, as distinguished from *concrete* ones. For in trying to assimilate all of these under the single classification of 'object', one misses the important differences in the way in which language functions. We need to distinguish the use of *general words* (as predicates or abstract nouns), *mathematical rules*, and *proper names*. Those who fail to make the necessary distinctions in the type of language game being played are like those who say that since "A railway train, a railway station, and a railway car are different kinds of objects," therefore "a railway train, a railway accident, and a railway law are different kinds of objects."[18] Although a train, a station, and a car *are* objects, it would be a misuse of the term 'object' to say that an *accident* (which is an *event*) or a *law* (or *rule*) is an *object* in the way a *train* is. The technique of appealing to language games would clarify how we use 'event'-words in distinction from 'rule'-expressions, and both of these from the way we use proper names to refer to individual objects.

Essence Fallacy

A second type of fallacy that Wittgenstein's approach would guard us against is the Essence Fallacy. This is found where it is assumed that whenever any general words or abstract nouns are employed there must be some set of fixed and essential properties that constitute the meaning of the word. This meaning would be set out in a definition and would show the precise boundaries of the meaning of the term to be defined. This is the conception of definition that underlies the typical search for the meaning of a term in Plato's dialogues.

'Family resemblances'

To counteract the expectation that such an 'essence' can be found, Wittgenstein introduces his doctrine of 'family resemblances'. When the point of this doctrine is fully recognized, it would weaken what he calls the 'craving for generality' and discourage the assumption that all general words *must* have precise definitions.

This craving for generality is the resultant of a number of tendencies connected with particular philosophical confusions. There is—

(*a*) *The tendency to look for something in common to all the entities which we commonly subsume under a general term.*—We are inclined to think that there must be something in common to all games, say, and that this common property is the justification for applying the general term "game" to the various games; whereas games form a family the members of which have family likenesses. Some of them have the same nose, others the same eyebrows and others again the same way of walking; and these likenesses overlap. The idea of a general concept being a common property of its particular instances connects up with other primitive, too simple, ideas of the structure of language. It is comparable to the idea that properties are ingredients of the things which have the properties; e.g., that beauty is an ingredient of all beautiful things as alcohol is of beer and wine, and that we therefore could have pure beauty, unadulterated by anything that is beautiful.

(*b*) *There is a tendency rooted in our usual forms of expression, to think that the man who has learnt to understand a general term, say, the term "leaf," has thereby come to possess a kind of general picture of a leaf, as opposed to pictures of particular leaves. He was shown different leaves when he learnt the meaning of the word "leaf"; and showing him the particular leaves was only a means to the end of producing 'in him' an idea which we imagine to be some kind of general image. We say that he sees what is in common to all these leaves; and this is true if we mean that he can on being asked tell us certain features or properties which they have in common. But we are inclined to think that the general idea of a leaf is something like a visual image, but one which contains what is common to all leaves. (Galtonian composite photograph.) This again is connected with the idea that the meaning of a word is an image, or a thing correlated to the word. (This roughly means, we are looking at words as though they all were proper names, and we then confuse the bearer of a name with the meaning of the name.)*[19]

In the following passage, Wittgenstein elaborates the notion of family resemblance by taking the general term 'game' and showing that there is no single essence or set of essential properties that is common to everything we call 'games'.

Consider for example the proceedings that we call "games." I mean board-games, card-games, ball-games, Olympic games, and so on. What is common to them all?—Don't say: "There must be something common, or they would not be called 'games' "—but look and see whether there is anything common to all.—For if you look at them you will not see something that is common to all, but similarities, relationships, and a whole series of them at that. To repeat: don't think, but look!—Look for example at board-games, with their multifarious relationships. Now pass to card-games; here you find many correspondences with the first group, but many common features drop out, and others appear. When we pass next to ball-games, much that is common is retained, but much is lost.—Are they all 'amusing'? Compare chess with noughts and crosses. Or is there always winning and losing, or competition between players? Think of patience. In ball games there is winning and losing; but when a child throws his ball at the wall and catches it again, this feature has disappeared. Look at the parts played by skill and luck; and at the difference between skill in chess and skill in tennis. Think now of games like ring-a-ring-a-roses; here is the element of amusement, but how many other characteristic features have disappeared! And we can go through the many, many other groups of games in the same way; we can see how similarities crop up and disappear.

And the result of this examination is: we see a complicated network of similarities over-lapping and criss-crossing: sometimes overall similarities, sometimes similarities of detail.

I can think of no better expression to characterize these similarities than "family resemblances"; for the various resemblances between members of a family: build, features, colour of eyes, gait, temperament, etc. etc. overlap and criss-cross in the same way.—And I shall say 'games' form a family.[20]

Fallacies underlying Plato's Theory of Forms

Let us now apply the foregoing accounts of the Reference Fallacy and the Essence Fallacy to an examination of Plato's Theory of Forms.

(1) Part of Plato's error was to commit the Reference Fallacy. The fact that we use general words or abstract nouns, for example, in the sentences "Socrates is *wise*" and "*Wisdom* is a virtue" does not require that there be an 'object' that is being *referred* to by the terms 'wise' and 'wisdom'. It is important, rather, Wittgenstein would say, to examine, for example, the *use* of the general word 'wise' in the sentence in which it occurs and in the context in which that sentence as a whole is being used. When one uses the word 'wise' in the sentence "Socrates is wise" the predicate is not referring to anything by itself; it is being used to *describe* Socrates. As a general word, it can be used to describe not only Socrates but other individuals as well. The only *object* involved is the individual— in this case, Socrates. We note some particular feature connected with Socrates' character and thought to which we apply the word 'wise'. The general predicate word 'wise' is used to say something about Socrates; it is used to describe Socrates. The word 'wise' does not itself *refer* to some abstract entity or timeless object—Wisdom.* Thus instead of making, as Plato would, an *ontological* remark about some *abstract entity*, we clarify the *linguistic use* of the general word 'wise' or the abstract noun 'wisdom'.

* Nor does the term 'wisdom' as an 'abstract noun' or noun-substantive have reference to an abstract entity in analogy with that of a proper name in its reference to a 'concrete' individual. For the term 'wisdom' can be regarded as a nominalization of the *predicate* or predicable term 'wise'. The predicate term 'wise', as previously pointed out, serves to *describe* individuals. It itself does not refer to an entity. Similarly, the term 'wisdom' would be analyzed as derived from or as encompassing the various predicational (descriptive) uses of the adjective or adverbial form of 'wise'.

We need not invoke some special and mysterious domain of Forms. Individual men, the particular sentences they utter or write, and the words they use are all genuine entities. But we need not posit, in addition, some separate domain of abstract entities to which general words refer.*

(2) The other part of Plato's error, in positing a domain of abstract entities, derives from his assumption that such entities must be open to definitions that state a final set of essential properties. Wittgenstein's analysis shows that it is not necessary that there be a fixed set of common or 'essential' characteristics in using a general word. We use, fruitfully, many general words (e.g., 'red', 'language', 'healthy', 'game', 'good', 'wise', 'number', 'tool', 'meaning', 'leaf', 'alive', 'true', 'hard', 'clear') without requiring a *common* set of features that hold for *all* uses of the term. Nor is it necessary that every general term be definable by specifying *precise boundaries* that would apply in its 'correct' use. The absence of precise boundaries does not require, as a consequence, that the term would *lack* sense or use. Depending on the context, sometimes a term that may be considered vague for certain purposes may be exact enough for others. Consider an analogy. Suppose, in playing a game with children, the teacher says to Johnnie "You stand *here* in this corner!" The word 'here', in this context, may have a sufficiently clear or exact use if Johnnie stands *roughly* within a certain zone indicated by the teacher. However, if one is being given an X-ray by a radiologist, her saying to the patient, "Stand here!" has a far more precise zone of limitation in her use of the word 'here' than in the former example. Similarly with other words. For certain purposes, to say "This wall is painted *white*" may be correct enough, whereas to a very finicky interior decorator it is not enough to use the term 'white' in describing the color of the wall or in giving instructions to the painter. It must be a particular *shade* of white. Some more precise use of the term 'white' is required. Similarly, suppose a teacher were to say to the children in a kindergarten class "Let's all sit around in a circle, and I will tell you a story." And suppose some one child sits a bit farther out

* In considering the applications of a Wittgensteinian approach to language as a basis for criticizing a Platonic theory of the reality of abstract entities, we have focused on the use of certain general words and abstract nouns in ordinary language. However, it will be remembered that Plato himself, in arguing for his Theory of Forms, believed that the notion of Forms yielded a satisfactory metaphysical basis for making sense of the achievements of mathematical knowledge. For Plato (as well as for later Platonists) mathematics can be looked upon as a science that can make certain *discoveries* concerning the eternally fixed character and relationships among certain types of abstract entities. Wittgenstein, in his own philosophy of mathematics as set out in his *Remarks on the Foundations of Mathematics*, was opposed to such Platonism. This topic, however, is a highly technical one and cannot be pursued here.[21] For views opposed to Wittgenstein's own and upholding a 'realist' or 'Platonist conception of mathematics', see the literature referred to in footnote 21.

from the others. Does that mean that the group of children is not really 'sitting in a circle'? Is the geometer's 'exact' definition of the circle the only one that captures the true essence of the term 'circle'? No! There are the various *uses* of the term 'circle'. For Plato there is only one real circle—the Form Circle. Its essence is stated correctly by the geometer's definition. Instead, Wittgenstein would say to look at the various uses of the term 'circle' in the different life situations in which this word is used. No one is necessarily ideal or perfect, nor is there one meaning that corresponds to the eternal essence of Circle. The varied uses of the word 'circle' (or 'circular' or 'circularity') form a family. The same would apply to any other general term, whether used as a predicate or an abstract noun. There are obviously important differences of precision or exactness in the use of general words. However, it is not necessary to assume that there is a unique, ideal meaning.

We are unable clearly to circumscribe the concepts we use; not because we don't know their real definition, but because there is no real 'definition' to them. To suppose that there must *be would be like supposing that whenever children play with a ball they play a game according to strict rules.*

Take another example: Socrates' question "What is knowledge?" Here the case is even clearer, as the discussion begins with the pupil giving an example of an exact definition, and then analogous to this a definition of the word "knowledge" is asked for. As the problem is put, it seems that there is something wrong with the ordinary use of the word "knowledge". It appears we don't know what it means, and that therefore, perhaps, we have no right to use it. We should reply: "There is no one exact usage of the word 'knowledge'; but we can make up several such usages, which will more or less agree with the ways the word is actually used." . . .

Many words in this sense then don't have a strict meaning. But this is not a defect. To think it is would be like saying that the light of my reading lamp is no real light at all because it has no sharp boundary.

Philosophers very often talk about investigating, analyzing, the meaning of words. But let's not forget that a word hasn't got a meaning given to it, as it were, by a power independent of us, so that there could be a kind of scientific investigation into what the word really means. A word has the meaning someone has given to it.[22]

Concluding remarks

The principal route to philosophy that Wittgenstein followed was a critique of language: of what language can and cannot do, its uses and misuses. At the time he wrote the *Tractatus*, Wittgenstein's approach to this broad theme consisted in trying to understand the relation between language and the world. What are the basic elements of the world? What constitutes a matter of fact? How can language give an accurate picture of 'what is the case'? What, moreover, *cannot* be expressed in factual language and so lies beyond its limits? In carrying through this project, Wittgenstein sketched an ontology (a theory of the world) as much as he worked out the logical structure of a language adequate to describe the basic features of the world as the 'totality of facts'.

In his later writings, with their fresh approach to language, Wittgenstein stressed different themes from those we find in the *Tractatus*. He dropped an interest in working out an ontology and in showing the relation between a logically purified language and the structure of the world. His interests shifted primarily to language itself in its manifold uses. He concentrated his attention on exposing the various fallacies, snares, and puzzlements into which people fall when they don't see their way clear in the use of words. His major contributions here consisted in many detailed analyses of particular concepts, including 'understanding', 'imagining', 'intending', 'following a rule', 'remembering', 'seeing colors', 'being certain', as well as many others. In addition to devoting a good deal of his attention to the analysis of concepts of a broadly psychological bearing, Wittgenstein wrote extensively on certain basic concepts having to do with the foundations or philosophy of mathematics as well as on certain concepts in the field of esthetic and religious experience.*

The field of linguistic and analytic philosophy owes much to the impetus of Wittgenstein's thought. Although some philosophers have stayed fairly close to Wittgenstein's own manner of handling problems, others have moved considerably beyond his approach. For example, the growth of the science of linguistics in recent decades has brought with it an enriched treatment of the central problems of the nature of 'meaning', the notion of 'grammar', and the problems of semantics. Much valuable work is being done in this general area of investigation. However, the details of these investigations and the new philosophical problems associated with them are of a technical nature and lie beyond the scope of the present book.[23]

---

* The works to be consulted in connection with mathematics are Wittgenstein, *Remarks on the Foundations of Mathematics*, and Cora Diamond (editor), *Wittgenstein's Lectures on the Foundations of Mathematics*. For his views on esthetics and religious experience, see Wittgenstein, *Lectures and Conversations on Aesthetics, Psychology and Religious Belief* (edited by Cyril Barrett).

chapter 14

Nonconceptual

Awareness

and Serenity

In studying the naturalistic philosophies of Spinoza and Dewey, we found that, despite important differences, they shared a common emphasis on the central importance of applying reason in all spheres of human thought and action. They would agree that science, as the most sophisticated and refined form of the use of human intelligence, is the most reliable method for understanding the world about us and for explaining natural (including human) phenomena. Reason is committed to the belief that the world is intelligible and that it can be increasingly understood with the progress of inquiry. Furthermore, when brought to bear upon the practical problems that human beings face and the decisions about how to act (whether on a personal or social level), reason is the most reliable human resource. It promises (without guaranteeing) the best chances of success. Our lives become more and more adjusted, secure, peaceful, harmonious, pleasurable, and satisfactory to the extent that the method of intelligence gains effective control. It is therefore in reason or intelligence that people should place their greatest confidence, and to whose use and application they should bend all their energies. Of course, we all know that mankind is far from realizing this ideal; that, in fact, recent history includes examples of the most extreme forms of irrational human behavior ever recorded. And it is a commonplace, too, that vast numbers of individuals, on a personal level, lead lives of quiet desperation. But those who have confidence in the possibility of improving matters, of correcting abuses, and of gaining increasing control over the course of human affairs, thereby enabling people more and more to achieve a decent and rewarding life, are not daunted by these facts. The all-too-familiar facts about the prevalence and extent of irrationality in human life only point up all the more vividly, they would say, the desperate need for extending and implementing the use of the method of reason.

In recent thought, as in that of previous epochs, various reservations have come to be expressed about taking reason as the only or principal guide to life. Those who express such reservations would point to the positive value of certain levels or modes of human experience that lie beyond the province of conceptual analysis and the practical uses of intelligence altogether, and yet that should also be given their due weight in an adequate philosophy of life. There are different ways in which this broad theme can be (and has been) developed.

First, there are the ideas associated with the older types of religious thought developed over the centuries in India (Hinduism and Buddhism), in China (Taoism), and in Japan (Zen Buddhism). In their manifold ways, these traditions have always stressed certain kinds of 'insights' or 'modes of awareness' not normally found in the dominant religious traditions of the West. They have brought to the fore an emphasis on the achievement of a type of *enlightenment* that does not derive from accepting certain dogmas, i.e., in adopting a certain *faith*. In recent decades these ancient ways of 'Eastern' thought have begun to command a considerable amount of attention in 'the West'. Their impact would need to be reckoned with in any survey of recent thought.

Second, much of the literature that goes by the name of 'existentialism' can be considered as also falling within the broad stream of contemporary thought that looks 'beyond reason' for its main concerns. The writings of the nineteenth-century thinkers Sören Kierkegaard (1813–1855) and Friedrich Nietzsche (1844–1900) belong here. So do those of the more recent writers Jean Paul Sartre, Karl Jaspers, Albert Camus, and Martin Heidegger, among others. In one way or another, many existentialists give prominence to those aspects of human life that involve the 'element of the absurd'. Man finds himself 'thrown into' a world in which "God is dead" (Nietzsche), and nothing in the world or his own human experience can be found to possess or be transformable into a rational and meaningful scheme.

In what follows, we shall briefly consider examples of each of these two major strands of contemporary thought. First, we shall examine the notion of '*satori*' (enlightenment) in the teachings of Zen Buddhism. Second, we shall examine the place that the central concept of 'Being' occupies in the philosophy of Martin Heidegger, and the importance it has for him.

Zen and Satori

Gotama the Buddha (*c.* 563–483 B.C.) is the founder of one of the world's great religions. As a way of life and system of thought, Buddhism, like other major religions, is an extremely rich and complex matter. It is no part of our present purpose here to explore either the major overall aspects of its history or its doctrinal complexity. We shall, instead, single out for consideration one strand—that which goes by the name of 'Zen Buddhism'—and, in this connection, focus simply on one feature that bears on our present theme.

In A.D. 527, Bodhidharma carried the message of Buddhism from India to China, where it underwent many significant changes and adapted itself to the distinctive features of Chinese culture. What goes by the name of 'Zen Buddhism' arose from the teachings of Bodhidharma as these were transmitted and modified by a series of influential disciples. In the thirteenth century this strand of Buddhist thought was brought to Japan, where it underwent still further modifications. Over a period of many centuries it exerted a manifold powerful influence on many aspects of Japanese culture—in painting, poetry, calligraphy, the art of swordsmanship, the tea ceremony, and other areas. The spread of Zen to the United States is a relatively recent phenomenon. The person who virtually single-handedly familiarized the West with its teachings is Daisetz Teitaro

Daisetz Suzuki

Suzuki (1870–1966), professor of Buddhist philosophy at Otani University, Kyoto. He was the author of many books and articles, most of which have been translated into English. In the following account we shall lean upon Suzuki's interpretation of Zen, although it should be emphasized that there are many internal differences of approach within Zen, and not all who would consider themselves practitioners of Zen (let alone of Buddhism, in general) would necessarily share Suzuki's orientation.

In his account of Zen as a fundamental attitude and way of life, Suzuki stresses the central role of *satori* or enlightenment.

Satori

The essence of Zen Buddhism consists in acquiring a new viewpoint of looking at life and things generally. By this I mean that if we want to get into the inmost life of Zen, we must forgo all our ordinary habits of thinking which control our everyday life, we must try to see if there is any other way of judging things, or rather if our ordinary way is always sufficient to give us the ultimate satisfaction of our spiritual needs. If we feel dissatisfied somehow with this life, if there is something in our ordinary way of living that deprives us of freedom in its most sanctified sense, we must endeavour to find a way somewhere which gives us a sense of finality and contentment. Zen proposes to do this for us and assures us of the acquirement of a new point of view in which life assumes a fresher, deeper, and more satisfying aspect. This acquirement, however, is really and naturally the greatest mental cataclysm one can go through with in life. It is no easy task, it is a kind of fiery baptism, and one has to go through the storm, the earthquake, the overthrowing of the mountains, and the breaking in pieces of the rocks.

This acquiring of a new point of view in our dealings with life and the world is popularly called by Japanese Zen students 'satori' (Wu in Chinese). It is really another name for Enlightenment (annuttara-samyak-sambodhi), which is the word used by the Buddha and his Indian followers ever since his realization under the Bodhi-tree by the River Nairañjanā. There are several other phrases in Chinese designating this spiritual experience, each of which has a special connotation, showing tentatively how this phenomenon is interpreted. At all events there is no Zen without satori, which is indeed the Alpha and Omega of Zen Buddhism. Zen devoid of satori is like a sun without its light and heat. Zen may lose all its literature, all its monasteries, and all its paraphernalia; but as long as there is satori in it it will survive to eternity. I want to emphasize this most fundamental fact concerning the very life of Zen; for there are some even among the students of Zen themselves who are blind to this central fact and are apt to think when Zen has been explained away logically or psychologically, or as one of the Buddhist philosophies which can be summed up by using highly technical and conceptual Buddhist phrases, Zen is exhausted, and there remains nothing in it that makes it what it is. But my contention is, the life of Zen begins with the opening of satori (kai wu in Chinese).

Satori may be defined as an intuitive looking into the nature of things in contradistinction to the analytical or logical understanding of it. Practically, it means the unfolding of a new world hitherto unperceived in the confusion of a dualistically trained mind. Or we may say that with satori our entire surroundings are viewed from quite an unexpected angle of perception. Whatever this is, the world for those who have gained a satori is no more the old world as it used to be; even with all its flowing streams and burning fires, it is never the same one again. Logically stated, all its opposites and contradictions are united and harmonized into a consistent organic whole. This is a mystery and a miracle, but according to the Zen masters such is being performed every day. Satori can thus be had only through our once personally experiencing it.

Its semblance or analogy in a more or less feeble and fragmentary way is gained when a difficult mathematical problem is solved, or when a great discovery is made, or when a sudden means of escape is realized in the midst of most desperate complications; in short, when one exclaims "Eureka! Eureka!" But this refers only to the intellectual aspect of satori, which is therefore necessarily partial and incomplete and does not touch the very foundations of life considered one indivisible whole. Satori as the Zen experience must be concerned with the entirety of life. For what Zen proposes to do is the revolution, and the revaluation as well, of oneself as a spiritual unity. The solving of a mathematical problem ends with the solution, it does not affect one's whole life. So with all other particular questions, practical or scientific, they do not enter the basic life-tone of the individual concerned. But the opening of satori is the remaking of life itself. When it is genuine—for there are many simulacra of it—its effects on one's moral and spiritual life are revolutionary, and they are so enhancing, purifying, as well as exacting. When a master was asked what constituted Buddhahood, he answered, "The bottom of a pail is broken through."

From this we can see what a complete revolution is produced by this spiritual experience. The birth of a new man is really cataclysmic.[1]

There are various practices and techniques of Zen. These include *zazen* or sitting meditation, and the use of *koans*, i.e., logically insoluble riddles such as the well-known question "What is the sound of one hand clapping?" These are all directed to making the individual achieve a state of awareness that is altogether different from what characterizes the use of our normal perceptual powers or the use of ordinary processes of thinking, conceptual analysis, or problem-solving. To have this special mode of Zen-awareness does not mean that one has withdrawn from the world, that one completely rejects or excludes the use of the senses or the intellect, that one ceases to carry on one's daily affairs or to pursue one's ordinary activities. Rather, in doing all these things, it is the attitude and the *way* in which these are carried on that marks the one who has achieved *satori* (enlightenment).

Satori is not a morbid state of mind, a fit subject for abnormal psychology. If anything it is a perfectly normal state of mind. When I speak of a mental upheaval, one may be led to consider Zen something to be shunned by ordinary people. This is a mistaken view of Zen, unfortunately often held by prejudiced critics. As Nansen (Nan-ch'üan) declared, it is your 'everyday thought'. When later a monk asked a master what was meant by 'everyday thought', he said,

"Drinking tea, eating rice,
  I pass my time as it comes;
  Looking down at the stream, looking up at the mountains,
  How serene and relaxed I feel indeed!"

It all depends upon the adjustment of the hinge whether the door opens in or out. Even in the twinkling of an eye, the whole affair is changed, and you have Zen, and you are as perfect and normal as ever. More than that, you have in the meantime acquired something altogether new. All your mental activities are now working to a different key, which is more satisfying, more peaceful, and fuller of joy than anything you ever had. The tone of your life is altered. There is something rejuvenating in it. The spring flowers look prettier, and the mountain stream runs cooler and more transparent. The subjective revolution that brings out this state of things cannot be called abnormal. When life becomes more enjoyable and its expanse is as broad as the universe itself, there must be something in satori quite healthy and worth one's striving after its attainment.[2]

In order to appreciate what brings about this radical change, it is necessary, to begin with, to draw a distinction between two types of consciousness or 'knowledge'. For the realization of *satori* is associated with, or arises from, one of these types of consciousness or knowledge. It is one that is either completely ignored or underdeveloped by the vast majority of mankind, who rely instead on the other, more familiar type. The kind of knowledge whose cultivation leads to *satori* is called *prajna*, whereas the ordinary kind of knowledge is called *vijnana*.

Two types of consciousness or 'knowledge': prajna and vijnana

In Buddhism generally two forms of knowledge are distinguished; the one is prajna and the other is vijnana. Prajna is all-knowledge (sarvajna), or transcendental knowledge, i.e. knowledge undifferentiated. Vijnana is our relative knowledge in which subject and object are distinguishable, including both knowledge of concrete particular things and that of the abstract and universal. Prajna underlies all Vijnana, but Vijnana is not conscious of Prajna and always thinks its is sufficient in itself and with itself, having no need for Prajna. But it is not from Vijnana, relative knowledge, that we get spiritual satisfaction. However much of Vijnana we may accumulate, we can never find our abode of rest in it, for we somehow feel something missing in the inmost part of our being, which science and philosophy can never appease. . . . [S]piritual yearnings are never completely satisfied unless this Prajna or unconscious knowledge is awakened, whereby the whole field of consciousness is exposed, inside and outside, to our full view. Reality has now nothing to hide from us.

The Zen master's life-efforts are concentrated in awakening this Prajna, un-conscious consciousness, knowledge of non-distinction, which, like a vision of will-o'-the-wisp, unobtrusively, tantalizingly, and constantly shoots through the

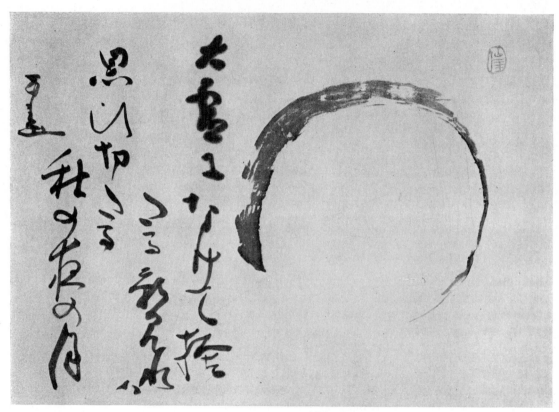

The Moon

When I see (Reality's) shadow
Thrown into the emptiness of space,
How boldly defined
The moon
Of the autumnal night!

"When the ego is thrown out into the vacuity of nothingness, or better, when the ego is identified with the absolute Emptiness (śūnyatā), how free, how unimpededly expanded one feels! The autumnal moon symbolizes the state of mind one then realizes. It is 'the moon of suchness' that Buddhist poets talk so much about, and Sengai tried to picture it for us."

DAISETZ SUZUKI, *Sengai: The Zen Master*

mind. You try to catch it, to examine it on your palm, to name it definitely, so that you can refer to it as a definitely determined individual object. But this is impossible because it is not an object of dualistically-disposed intellectual treatment.[3]

The reliance on the mode of awareness called *prajna* in Zen does not mean an abandonment or disparagement of our ordinary use of the intellect and the senses. However, by being totally immersed in these, one remains ignorant of their limitations. One is caught in what Suzuki calls the opposition of subject and object or a dualistic way of thought. And insofar as one remains entirely within this level of experience, one is 'in bondage' and prevented from achieving the kind of liberation that a cultivation of *prajna* offers. This latter mode of 'knowledge' is nondualistic, does not focus on any particular object or sets of objects, does not undertake to solve any problems, is not concerned with achieving any purposes or goals, and is nondiscriminative. It directs its attention to an aspect of reality *beyond* the limits of either the intellect or the senses. It deals with what is variously called 'the undifferentiated', 'is-ness', 'suchness', the 'Unattainable', or 'emptiness'.

Zen never despises intellection as such, but it wants intellection to know its place and not to go beyond the sphere it properly belongs to. . . . Inasmuch as we are living in the world of sense-intellect, and so constituted as to ask questions at every situation we come to meet, there is nothing wrong on our part in resorting to our intelligence and trying to find a solution intellectually. What Zen objects to is when we take the intellect for the sole agency to give us some sort of solution to any question we may raise. It is in the nature of the intellect to probe into the mysteries of life. But it will be a grave mistake to trust it absolutely or to think that it will give us satisfaction in every way when the questions are concerned with our being itself.

Such questions are raised in fact not by the intellect in its own right, but they come out of a very much deeper source than mere curiosity. They rise from the depths of consciousness, which are beyond the reach of the intellect. For the latter belongs to the periphery of our being. . . .

It is the intellect that asks the questions, seeking reason for everything, but there is one thing we have to take in its is-ness without asking any question about its being-so. And the strange fact is that when we have the thing itself we do not have to ask anything about it.[4]

The achievement of *satori* needs to be distinguished, as a type of spiritual experience, both from that which is meant by 'spirituality' in the context of familiar theistic religion and from what is meant by the attainment of 'Nirvana' in Buddhist thought itself.

Religion talks of faith, teaching that God somehow takes care of us, all the intellectual difficulties notwithstanding. Let the antithesis of being and non-being remain as it is; for what is beyond our intellectual comprehension may best be left in the hands of God. The faith that somehow or other things are all well with God, in whom we have our being, delivers us from doubts and worries.

The Zen way of deliverance, however, is not that of religion; to be free from doubts and worries, Zen appeals to a certain inner experience and not to a blind acceptance of dogmas. Zen expects us to experience within ourselves that the suchness of things—the antithesis of being and non-being—is beyond the ken of intellectual painting or dialectical delineation, and that no amount of words can succeed in describing, that is, reasoning out, the what and why of life and the world. This may sound negative and may not be of positive use to our spiritual life. But the real trouble with us whenever we try to talk about things beyond intellection is that we always make our start from intellection itself, although this may be natural and inevitable; therefore, when Zen-experience and other such things are talked about they sound empty as if they had no positive value. But Zen proposes that we effect a complete volte-face and take our stand first on Zen-experience itself and then observe things—the world of being and non-being—from the point of view of the experience itself. This is what may be designated as an absolute standpoint. The usual order of things is hereby reversed; what was positive becomes negative and what was negative becomes positive. 'Emptiness' is reality and 'reality' is emptiness. Flowers are no longer red, and the willow leaves are no longer green. We are no longer a plaything of karma, of 'cause and effect', of birth and death; values of the changing world are no longer permanent ones; what we consider good or bad from the worldly point of view is neither good nor bad, for it has only a relative value. Logically, too, the antithesis of being and non-being holds good only for our relative knowledge, for our discursive understanding. After the Zen-experience, an entirely new order of things takes place, a complete change of front is effected, and the result is that a relative world of changes and multiplicities is contemplated sub specie aeternitatis. *This in a way may be considered the meaning of "No paintings, no delineations can do justice to it."*[5]

Furthermore, Zen is also different from those strands in Buddhist thought which stress the attainment of Nirvana in the sense of 'self-annihilation'. Self-annihilation in this context does not mean, of course, suicide. It means, rather, escaping from the domain of 'samsara'—the entanglement in the pursuit of ordinary goals and desires, being engrossed in the gratifications of the senses, and devoted to 'craving' and its satisfaction. Nirvana means 'extinction', a 'snuffing out of the flame'. Nirvana is realized when craving is ended. Ordinary life is looked upon as being a kind of burning, a ceaseless rushing around trying to satisfy this or that desire or need. One is constantly on the go. For anyone enmeshed in life in this form, life is suffering. Such suffering results from 'ignorance', from a failure to realize that liberation and peace can only come, not from re-doubling one's efforts in the pursuit of these ordinary goals, but from abandoning them. Nirvana is not an escape to another world, but a way of living in this world, in which the strivings of our animal and social self are reduced to a minimum or, as far as possible, eliminated altogether. Nirvana is a stilling or calming of the ruffled waters of life. Insofar as it stresses *satori*, Zen is to be distinguished from this conception of Nirvana. It does not seek to escape from life, or to repress and deny the various drives and needs of the self. One who has *satori* continues to do what everyone else does. He pursues his normal activities but with a difference. The presence of *satori* prevents any total absorption or entanglement in life, to the point where these become a source of suffering and frustration.

The term Zen etymologically comes from Dhyana and scholars are apt to take Zen to mean practising Dhyana as it was practised by the Indians, that is, being absorbed in the Absolute, which is tantamount to entering into Nirvana, the cessation of all activities. But as Zen is actually and historically understood it is far from being such a practice in self-annihilation; it is the understanding of things not only from the aspect of manyness but from the aspect of absolute oneness; it is to take hold of the one as embodying itself in the multitudeness of things, and not as standing aloof from them.

Even when Zen is absorbed in Dhyana, or Shamatha, or in meditation, it never loses sight of a world of sense and intellect. Zen is not only thought but non-thought; it discriminates and at the same time holds in itself that which transcends discrimination. It acts, but acts in such a way as not to have any purpose. Zen's life is not teleologically defined; it is like the sun's rising in the East and setting in the West; it is like the plants flowering in spring and bearing fruits in autumn. It is we humans who take all these phenomena of Nature as having some definite design in relation to human destiny and welfare, but this homocentric interpretation of the world always ends in tragedy, if not in an utter confusion of thought.

Zen's world is at once purposeless and purposeful; it is purposeful as long as we conceive it in terms of space and time and causation, but it is utterly purposeless when it takes us to a world where there is neither thinker nor that which is thought, nor what is known as a thought. Some may say that there is no such world as far as human understanding is concerned, but Zen would say that there is such a world, that we are actually living in it and do not know it. In point of fact, Zen is not to be refuted by arguments; when it says things are so, the affirmation is final, and the only thing you can do is either to accept or reject it. This is in the very nature of Zen, that is, of Prajna.[6]

Summary

In the preceding passage, Suzuki remarks that "Zen is not to be refuted by arguments." In this he is undoubtedly correct. For *satori*, as the end result of Zen training, is not a kind of 'insight' or attitude toward life that emerges as the end product of a process of argument or reasoning. It does not come as the conclusion of a chain of inferences. A person reading about Zen, therefore, cannot pick some argument apart to judge its validity or soundness, and thereby establish whether to accept its conclusion on rational grounds. The only way one might possibly come to judge whether what Suzuki or some other Zen master is talking about makes any sense is by actually undergoing a certain kind of experience—by being brought to the state of mind to which the Zen master alludes. There are various techniques to be used in achieving this result, but the process of rational analysis and argument is not among them. You either have (or can acquire) this state of mind or you don't. And if you do, you can 'confirm' what he is talking about. If not, all you are left with is his (or someone else's) encouragement, praise, or suggestions of things to *do* to (possibly) reach this end result. However, you cannot reach this result by following a course of reasoning in which the conclusion is *understood*, in the ordinary conceptual way, as following from the premises of the argument. *Satori* involves a *leap* onto another level of experience from the conceptual one.

Heidegger and the Quest for Being

In turning next to the thought of Martin Heidegger, we shall be dealing with a thinker whose whole background and training have been primarily in the traditions of Western philosophical thought. Yet he, too, as we shall see, comes to certain results that, although reached by an altogether different path from that of Zen Buddhism, converge on the latter. For Heidegger, in his treatment of the theme of 'Being', makes the point over and over again that one's apprehension of Being lies beyond the powers of ordinary conceptual thought. Yet, paradoxically, he has himself written many philosophical works to establish this very point. Heidegger uses philosophy not only to come to his conception of Being but also to criticize other philosophers who have failed to pay any attention to this theme, as well as to show that, ultimately, one must fall back on a non-logical 'disclosure' of Being.

Martin Heidegger (1889–1976) is one of the most influential German philosophers of the twentieth century. He is frequently identified as a leading figure in the movement known as 'existentialism'. However, he himself repudiated that label. The author of many books, he is best known for his early major work *Being and Time* (1927). Heidegger had a brief and, for many people, troubling association with the Nazis when, under their auspices, he served as a rector of one of the German universities (1933–1934). Although not himself primarily a political person, there are on record some of his remarks that show him to have been swept up by the political fervor of the time. These must forever remain a blot on his name. Another negative thing about him is that unfortunately much of his writing is couched in obscure language and in terminology that he either invents, or, if taken from ordinary usage, gives highly idiosyncratic meanings to. Reading him, therefore, not only in the original German but also in English translation, demands considerable patience and determination. These facts about him have put off many potential readers, as well as caused him to be totally condemned and rejected by virtually all 'analytic' philosophers. Thus unless one is genuinely concerned to get to the bottom of what he is after, one can be easily alienated or discouraged.

Nevertheless, among those who have made the effort there are many who feel that these negative considerations should not deter one from coming to take seriously what he is anxious to communicate. For once the central theme of his writings is understood, what he brings to our attention, it is claimed, is of the deepest significance and originality.

There is at bottom only one theme on which all of Heidegger's thought circled throughout his long and prolific career. It is 'Being'. But what this simple and familiar word means and why it has the importance it does for him are not easy matters to make clear. Here is at once the major prob-

The centrality of the question of Being

Martin Heidegger

lem in coming to grips with his thought and the most difficult and elusive of philosophic topics.

In some autobiographical remarks, Heidegger tells us how he came to be engrossed in this theme early in his career:

My academic studies began in the winter of 1909–10 in theology at the University of Freiburg. But the chief work for the study in theology still left enough time for philosophy which belonged to the curriculum anyhow. Thus both volumes of Husserl's Logical Investigations *lay on my desk in the theological seminary ever since my first semester there. . . . I had learned from many references in philosophical periodicals that Husserl's thought was determined by Franz Brentano. Ever since 1907, Brentano's dissertation "On the manifold meaning of being since Aristotle" (1862) had been the chief help and guide of my first awkward attempts to penetrate into philosophy. The following question concerned me in a quite vague manner: If being is predicated in manifold meanings, then what is its leading fundamental meaning? What does Being mean?*[7]

Many years later, in the opening paragraphs of *Being and Time*, Heidegger takes as his point of departure a quotation from Plato's dialogue *The Sophist* (244a), which reads as follows: "For manifestly you have long been aware of what you mean when you use the expression '*being*'. We, however, who used to think we understood it, have now become perplexed." And Heidegger himself continues:

Do we in our time have an answer to the question of what we really mean by the word 'being'? Not at all. So it is fitting that we should raise anew the question of the meaning of Being. But are we nowadays even perplexed at our inability to understand the expression 'Being'? Not at all. So first of all we must reawaken an understanding for the meaning of this question.[8]

Heidegger's own work throughout his life was devoted to 'reawakening an understanding of the meaning of this question'. Put negatively, his charge against the entire history of Western philosophy is that, except for a brief glimpse of Being at the earliest beginnings of that history in the work of some of the Presocratics, there has been a 'forgetting' and ignoring of the question of Being. Even what goes by the name of 'metaphysics' or 'ontology' in philosophy has, in his judgment, failed to emphasize or to do justice to this theme. In making this wholesale charge of total neglect by philosophers (let alone others), Heidegger does not ignore, of course, the many differences among the various epochs of Western philosophy or the internal differences among different movements, schools, or individual thinkers. He thinks that, despite these differences, they all share in a common disregard for what, for him, is the central theme that any sound philosophy should dwell on—the nature of Being. He conceives his task to 'reawaken' men to the centrality of this topic.

Being not an entity

Heidegger adopts many routes by which to bring to our attention and 'clarify' the 'concept' of Being. The words 'clarify' and 'concept' are in scare-quotes in the preceding sentence because he does not undertake to give us a clarification in the ordinary sense of a definition or a specification of essential traits. This is impossible with respect to Being. We should not expect to obtain a clarification of *it*, as we would normally look for such clarification in connection with concepts that apply to this or that entity (for example, 'sonata', 'chromosome', 'neurosis', and so on). *For Being is not an entity*. Nor does the term 'concept' apply to it either, in any strict sense. For by 'concept' we ordinarily mean some general term that describes many different examples or instances to which it may be applied. However, Being is so wholly unique that it cannot be treated after the manner of concepts in the ordinary sense. Nevertheless, Heidegger's whole labor as a philosopher is in some way to 'clarify' the 'concept' of Being. And he does this by exploring many different routes, one or another of which might perhaps succeed in 'lighting it up' for us.

"Why is there something rather than nothing?"

One route Heidegger follows toward this end is to examine the question originally formulated by Leibniz: "Why is there something rather than nothing?" In his book *An Introduction to Metaphysics*, Heidegger characterizes this as "the most far-reaching, deepest, and most fundamental of all questions." Of course, the question can itself be understood in many different ways. One familiar, traditional way is that seized upon in the tradition of theism. In that tradition the question is interpreted to mean: "Why does the world exist at all?" The question expresses an underlying need to give a reason to explain *why* the world exists. Theists, who share such a need, answer the question so understood by claiming that God is the Supreme Being who brought the world and all that it contains into existence. Heidegger rejects both the interpretation of the question along these lines and this type of answer to it. Nevertheless, he takes the same expressions used in Leibniz's formulation of the question and reinterprets them in accordance with the requirements and distinctions of his own philosophy. For example, as we shall see later, he gives the term 'nothing' an altogether different meaning from what it ordinarily possess.

Being and beings

However, in order to understand the new slant Heidegger gives to the question, we have to begin by taking note of what, for him, is a crucial philosophic distinction. In German, he expresses this as the distinction between *Sein* and *seiendes*. In English this can be translated as the difference between *Being* and *beings*. (Instead of 'beings', some translators use the term 'essents' or 'what-is-es'.)

According to Heidegger, virtually all philosophy, ever since the days of Plato and Aristotle, has been dominated in one form or another by a preoccupation with *beings* (*seiendes*). Not just all traditional philosophy, but all science and everyday language and thought are similarly preoccupied with 'beings'. They too deal with things, substances, objects, events, entities, 'what-is-es', or 'essents' of one sort or another. Even theology conceives of God as *a* unique and special being, an entity, despite the fact that God is beyond the world and thereby different from all other beings. And in all of this preoccupation with beings, Being (*Sein*) is wholly overlooked. Heidegger conceives his mission to be one of reawakening human beings to the awareness of Being: to call them away from a total preoccupation with beings (*seiendes*).

Dasein

Among the various beings in the world, man alone (the human being) has the capacity to become aware of Being. Insofar as the human being has the privilege, capacity, and opportunity to become aware of Being, Heidegger calls him *Dasein*. '*Da*' literally means 'there', and '*Sein*' means 'Being'. The 'there' in which the human being is 'located' is not to be taken literally, however, in any spatial or geographical sense. If you were to say "I am here, in New York," you would not be responding as a *Dasein*, as a human being to Being. You would be locating yourself geographically as a being situated in spatial relations with other beings—just as if someone were to ask where his hat is, and the answer were to be given "Here, on this shelf, next to that scarf." Heidegger does not mean by '*Dasein*' that kind of 'being there'. He means: 'being *open* to Being'. *Dasein* 'makes a clearing' in Being. It serves as 'the voice of Being'. It is the means by which Being itself is disclosed to itself in man. All these expressions ('being open', 'voice', 'disclosed') are used by Heidegger as metaphors. He tries by means of such metaphors to suggest the kind of experience he wishes to call attention to. However, the means by which *Dasein* comes to 'know' Being does not involve ordinary processes of logic, calculation, or inferential thought. It is not the outcome of a process of deliberation, analysis, or reasoning. A special type of 'thought' is needed. It is a type of thought that Heidegger calls 'meditative' or 'contemplative'. The ordinary thinking of the practical man or of the scientist deals with things, objects, projects, problems, processes—in short, with 'beings'. In describing ordinary 'logical' or 'calculative' thinking, Heidegger says:

Its peculiarity consists in the fact that whenever we plan, research, and organize, we always reckon with conditions that are given. We take them into account with the calculated intention of their serving specific purposes. Thus we can count on definite results. This calculation is the mark of all thinking that plans and investigates. Such thinking remains calculation even if it neither works with numbers nor uses an adding machine or computer. Calculative thinking computes. It computes ever new, ever more promising and at the same time more economical possibilities. Calculative thinking races from one prospect to the next. Calculative thinking never stops, never collects itself. Calculative thinking is not meditative thinking, not thinking which contemplates the meaning which reigns in everything that is.[9]

In calculative thinking, the standards of logic and the rules of responsible and careful thinking (inquiry) have relevance and applicability. But logic and intelligence have no appropriate use when it comes to knowing Being: they are not the kind of 'thinking' that dwells on Being.

No matter where and however deeply science investigates what-is it will never find Being. All it encounters, always, is what-is, because its explanatory purpose makes it insist at the outset on what-is. But Being is not an existing quality of what-is, nor, unlike what-is, can Being be conceived and established objectively.[10]

The kind of truth that science and ordinary common sense are concerned with is *propositional truth*. A proposition is true when it states correctly what the facts are—how particular matters (beings) stand in the world. By contrast, the kind of 'truth' *Dasein* is after, in its concern with Being, Heidegger designates by the Greek term *'aletheia'*. This type of truth is not to be equated with the property of *being true* that belongs to some proposition or statement. The Truth of Being is not mediated by propositions. It does not involve saying something about this or that being or group of beings. *Aletheia* is something, rather, that comes through a direct or immediate *'disclosure'*. It's like coming out of a dark and tangled mass of buildings and winding streets, and suddenly seeing in full light the expanse of the ocean before you. There it is! You see it. It's right before your eyes, directly and immediately. It is 'lit up' for you. It is this kind of direct 'seeing' that Heidegger finds in *Dasein's* knowing the Truth of (not *about*) Being.

But in all of this it is important to realize that Being is not *a* being, a collection of beings, or even the totality of beings that make up the world. Being is not a thing or class of things at all. It is Nothing! It is No-thing. In this sense, Being is wholly other than, or different from, any thing or being.

'Aletheia'

This, the purely "Other" than everything that "is," is that-which-is-not (das Nicht-Seiende). Yet this "Nothing" functions as Being. It would be premature to stop thinking at this point and adopt the facile explanation that Nothing is merely the nugatory, equating it with the non-existent (das Wesenlose). Instead of giving way to such precipitate and empty ingenuity and abandoning

Nothing in all its mysterious multiplicity of meanings, we should rather equip ourselves and make ready for one thing only: to experience in Nothing the vastness of that which gives every being the warrant to be. That is Being itself.[11]

The equivalence between Being and this special meaning of 'Nothing' has to be understood in the special way Heidegger intends: No-thing. In its ordinary meaning, 'nothing' means the absence, disappearance, or ceasing to exist of something or other. "There is nothing on the table" means there are no objects on the table—they have been removed, are not to be found there now, or are absent. This meaning of 'nothing' is to be understood in the context of things, objects, occurrences, events (beings). The absence, removal, disappearance, or cessation of some thing is the sense of the 'nothing' here involved. When, too, in traditional theology, God creates the world 'out of nothing' (*ex nihilo*), the nothing is the absence or nonexistence of the world as the totality of things (beings). God, as the Supreme Being (the entity whose being is independent of the world), brings the world into existence. This theological meaning of 'Nothing' is *not* the meaning of 'nothing' that Heidegger has in mind when he equates Being with Nothing.

When, therefore, Heidegger deals with the question "Why is there something, rather than nothing?" he does not undertake to answer it in the manner of the theist, because for Heidegger the term 'nothing' does not have the meaning it has for the theist. For Heidegger, the question needs to be reinterpreted to read "Why has there always been this tremendous emphasis on 'something'—i.e., on things, beings, entities? Why, instead, should men not also have been aware of *Being* (i.e., No-thing)?" His answer to *this* question is primarily a historical one. The whole history of *Western* culture, as reflected in its philosophy, science, approach to practical affairs, and (more and more in recent times) technology, has been dominated by a concern with beings. Men have not been open to Being (*Sein*). Heidegger sees the spiritual destiny of the West as the need to become aware, instead, of Being. It is this mission of bringing about a spiritual awakening to Being to which all of his efforts as a philosopher have been directed.

Zen and Heidegger: some general comments

Even our brief glimpse of Zen Buddhism and Heidegger will undoubtedly have suggested to the reader a certain parallel, if not identity, between their central teachings. The achievement of *satori* rests on the use of *prajna*, an unsayable awareness of what the Buddhist calls 'suchness' or 'Emptiness', whereas all we can point to, describe, or even deal with by means of ordinary 'relative' knowledge (*vijnana*) are particular objects, situations, and experiences. Similarly, for Heidegger, all our everyday contacts with the world, whether in practical affairs, science, art, or conventional philosophy, are with beings of one sort or another. Here we use what he calls 'logical' or 'calculative' thinking. But unless we are open to Being —whose nature or essence is beyond logic, analysis, and calculative thinking—and use instead what he calls 'meditative' thinking we shall miss what is most crucial to *Dasein.*

It has been reported that a friend of Heidegger's one day found him reading one of Suzuki's books and that Heidegger remarked "This is what I have been trying to say in all my writings." Obviously Heidegger's intellectual roots were not primarily those of Buddhism, and the remark, if taken literally, would be a somewhat exaggerated expression of admiration on his part. Nevertheless, in these matters there is an often-noticed convergence of thinkers who may come from rather different starting points, use different vocabularies, and possess different cultural roots, yet find, when they encounter one another, a shared insight and emphasis. They understand one another, and readily make the appropriate translations and necessary accommodations in terminology. In illustration of this phenomenon, one could add to the names of Heidegger or Suzuki the names, for example, of the presocratic Greek philosopher Parmenides, the medieval German mystic Meister Eckhart, and the ancient Chinese poet Lao-Tzu.

There obviously is not just one way of arriving at this common meeting ground. Yet some routes may be more congenial and inviting than others for particular persons. The way of the Zen practitioner, in his refusal to engage in sustained philosophical talk and conceptual analysis, on the ground that they are (supposedly) hindrances to the goal sought, will clearly not be very attractive to one who prefers to follow a strictly philosophical or conceptual approach as far as it will take him. As for the Heideggerian path, some will come away with the feeling that, for all of Heidegger's repeated stress on the importance of distinguishing Being and beings, he has paid more attention to telling us about the shortcomings of always concentrating on beings than to making the notion of Being any clearer. There remains, in short, a basic unclarity in Heidegger's account of Being, even after one has made allowances for the fact that there may be some fundamental concepts that cannot be further analyzed.

Existence and Serenity

In this concluding section, the present author will offer some brief suggestions of his own as to what it might mean to have a certain type of 'nonconceptual' awareness that is of importance both to our view of reality and to our philosophy of life. This analysis will be carried out, first, by making a crucial distinction between the concept of 'the Universe' and a special use of the term 'Existence'. It will then be pointed out what it would mean to say that our awareness of Existence is 'nonconceptual'. Finally, we shall consider the value this type of awareness may have in making possible the cultivation of the quality of serenity in a person's life.

Our first task is to draw a fundamental distinction between the concept of 'the Universe' and one use of the term 'Existence'.

What are we to understand by the term 'the Universe'? One way of answering this question is to say the following: *The Universe is the unique, absolute, all-inclusive, spatiotemporal, individual whole to which everything belongs that can be given a spatial and/or temporal location.* Let us now examine this formula and see the reasons for putting the matter this way.

The Universe is unique since there is at least one Universe and at most one in existence. There are not *many* Universes in the way there are many persons, stars, mountains, atoms, flowers, and so on. There is only one Universe. To speak of many Universes is a misuse of terminology. At one time astronomers used the expression 'island universes'. What they were referring to are nowadays called 'galaxies'. There *are* many galaxies. However, these many galaxies are all parts of the (one) Universe. Cosmologists now believe that the Universe is made up of galaxies and clusters of galaxies as their basic astronomical units. If it should ever turn out, in the course of further research, that what astronomers now call 'the Universe', namely the totality of the *galaxies*, is itself part of some still more inclusive system, then the term 'the Universe' would be used to designate this more inclusive system. By definition, the Universe cannot be part of some still more inclusive whole. However, at any given stage of scientific research, what is taken to constitute the composition and extent of the Universe may be modified by further empirical research. Men will never in fact know with any certainty that they have identified or comprehended the absolute, unique whole that is the Universe. The term 'the Universe' should nevertheless be reserved for the unique, individual, spatiotemporal whole that includes everything that can be given a spatiotemporal location.

The Universe is an *absolute whole*. To say it is an absolute whole means that it is not part of some more inclusive whole. There are many wholes that are *relative* wholes, in the sense that although they are composed of parts, as wholes they are in turn also parts, in some way, of some more inclusive whole. Thus a person's heart is a relative whole whose parts are its valves, blood vessels, chambers, muscles, and so on. Yet the heart is part of a circulatory system, which in turn is part of the entire body. Further, the body is not itself an absolute whole. It too belongs, for example, as a *spatial* part of some more inclusive system of physical bodies. Or the person, as a relative whole, is a member of a wider social group, or of the human species as a whole, and so on. Similarly, the planet Earth is

The Universe

(a) Unique

(b) Absolute whole

a relative whole consisting of many parts. Yet as a relative whole it belongs to the more inclusive whole of the solar system. And that whole, in turn, belongs to the system of stars known as the galaxy. None of these is an absolute whole. However, the Universe is an absolute whole, for although all other entities in space and time belong to it, it itself is not part of some still more inclusive whole.

The Universe is an *individual*. All particular persons, atoms, grains of sand, stars, animals, plants, galaxies, and so on belong to it. They make up the individual whole that is the Universe. On a cosmological scale of magnitude, astronomers have a *sample* or segment of the Universe open for inspection and observational exploration by means of their instruments. The domain of this sample is sometimes referred to as 'the observable universe'. This expression has reference to the population of galaxies within range of the available instruments of the astronomers. This population, however, does not exhaust all that is presumed to lie *beyond* the range of the astronomers' present instruments. Thus 'the observable universe' does *not* refer to the Universe as a whole. It refers only to some portion of the Universe that is open to observation. Indeed, it would be best not to use the expression 'the observable *universe*', since it refers to only a *segment* of the Universe proper. On an astronomical scale, astronomers do not have now (and perhaps never will) the Universe as an entire individual under observation. Nevertheless, the science of cosmology consists in trying to figure out the structure of the Universe as a whole. Cosmologists do this by taking clues from what is found in the observable sample within range of observation and extrapolating from this sample. For the interpretation of these observational data, they also make use of the theories of physics. The 'picture' that cosmologists draw for this purpose (usually in highly technical, mathematical-physical language) of what the Universe as an individual whole is like, is known as *a model of the Universe*. The science of cosmology consists in constructing and testing various models of the Universe in accordance with the best available empirical evidence, and on the basis of the best available physical theories. Scientific cosmologists have made enormous strides, in recent decades, in the subtlety of the models of the Universe they construct. Although some models have been discarded, and others seem more promising and better confirmed, there is, as yet, no single model of the Universe as a whole that the entire community of scientific cosmologists has accepted.

To say that the Universe is an *all-inclusive spatio-temporal whole* means two things. First, it is the most *extensive* domain, in spatial and temporal terms. Nothing is *larger* in spatial terms than the Universe. And nothing extends in temporal duration over a *longer* period of time than does the Universe. Second, it is the most *inclusive* whole in the sense that nothing which has space-time existence is left out or excluded from the Universe.

(c) Individual

(d) All-inclusive

Whatever exists in a spatial and/or temporal way belongs to it, whatever its size, duration, complexity, position in an evolutionary scheme of development, or value to human beings. Thus the Universe includes not only the galaxies as the basic astronomical units; it also includes everything else situated within this vast domain, however small, trivial, or 'insignificant' it may be. For example, snowflakes, gnats, and electrons belong to the Universe just as much as do the galaxies.

However, although the Universe is the all-inclusive whole of whatever exists, this does not mean that one can give a *complete list,* at any time, of all the varied contents of the Universe. Men are constantly enlarging their knowledge of the kinds of things to be found in the Universe. For example, physicists and astronomers have recently discovered quasars, neutrinos, and the possibility of black holes, just as, on another level of research, biologists may constantly discover new species of living organisms. And who knows what wholly strange entities may exist in far off corners of the Universe, of which men now have no inkling at all? Furthermore, it is not simply a question of the limitation of men's observational or instrumental resources that keeps us from making a complete list. It may be that there is something we may call 'chance' or 'creativity' in the Universe. This is another way of saying that new and unpredictable entities will be brought into existence in the Universe, in an open-ended future, of which no one can possibly have any adequate foreknowledge!

In saying that the Universe is an all-inclusive whole, all that is meant is that if and when anything does come into existence, it belongs as a part to the Universe. The Universe will include it along with everything else as part of itself. The term 'all-inclusive' has a negative role. It points to the fact that *nothing is to be excluded* from the contents of the Universe, if it can be located in a spatiotemporal way. But it does not mean that anyone is able to give a complete list of the contents of the Universe.

Existence
The term 'existence' (like the terms 'exist' and 'existent') has been used in a great variety of senses. Instead of examining at this point all these different uses, we shall focus our attention on one of these. We shall mark it by using the capitalized expression 'Existence'. This use of the term has to do with trying to make sense of the statement "The Universe exists."

Most persons would agree that this is certainly a true statement, if anything is. Granted it may sound a bit odd to come right out and say "The Universe exists"! (And where else, except in the context of a philosophical discussion, would you expect anyone to find the occasion to make such a statement?) Nevertheless, once you overcome a possible sense of strangeness in making explicit this wholly obvious statement, the question may be raised: Why bother? What is to be gained? Indeed, aside from saying in slightly different terminology what is also perfectly obvious to most people—namely that the Universe is real—what is the philosophical point of considering this statement at all?

One of the end results of our discussion will be to try to show that it is by no means philosophically trivial to make this statement explicit, if it leads us to distinguish the use of the terms 'the Universe' and 'Existence'. For to say "The Universe exists" is to direct our attention to the special importance of the term 'exists' as employed in this proposition in connection with the Universe. We are calling attention to this importance by converting the verb 'exists' into a noun and capitalizing it: Existence. Another way, therefore, in which we could have reexpressed the statement "The Universe exists" is by saying "Existence belongs to, or holds true of, the Universe." But what does *this* mean?

One way of summing up the conclusion to which we shall be led is that whereas it makes sense to say we can gain increasing information or knowledge about the Universe, the same cannot be said of Existence. Moreover, unlike our previous analysis of the term 'the Universe', we cannot give an analysis of the term 'Existence'. The latter term is so fundamental that it cannot be broken down or taken apart at all. And for this reason we should find it useful to say that although we can be *aware* of Existence, we cannot *comprehend* it.

As a first step in helping to establish these results, let us consider what is meant by speaking of the mental act of *bracketing*. For one way of getting at the meaning of 'Existence' is to 'bracket the Universe'. By 'bracketing' is meant the adoption of a mental attitude or approach whereby one disregards, suspends, or excludes from one's attention or standpoint some aspect or features normally present in an experience, in order to bring into prominence and give one's sole attention to what remains.

Bracketing

Some simple illustrations of this sort of thing are as follows. Suppose a situation arose in which a surgeon's father needed a very difficult and dangerous operation, and that the only surgeon readily available to perform the operation was his own son. In such a situation, the son, having all the normal love and concern of a son for his father, would need, as far as possible, when performing the operation to put out of his mind any anxieties or feelings of love toward his father as patient. He would need to bracket these. He would need to adopt the same 'impersonal', professional relationship to his father as patient as he would normally adopt toward any stranger. To fail to bracket his emotions in this situation might perhaps interfere with the successful performance of the operation. As another illustration of bracketing, let me recall the case earlier used in connection with the discussion of Attributes in Spinoza's philosophy. I there used the example of the printer who, as a printer, dwells entirely on the physical aspects of the words in a manuscript and brackets all considerations of literary style, truth, and so on connected with the text before him. Many other examples of a similar sort will occur to the reader.

I now want to suggest that one can become aware of Existence by performing the mental act of 'bracketing the Universe'. To bracket the Universe in order to become aware of Existence requires that one focus exclusively on the sheer fact *that* the Universe exists and not on *what* the Universe is. Wittgenstein once expressed this by saying: "It is not *how* things are in the world that is mystical, but *that* it exists."[12] In becoming aware of Existence, everything else 'drops out of sight'. All the qualitative, intellectual, practical, or value-oriented experiences we normally have in our everyday life are submerged or suspended from our attention, in order to let the sheer undifferentiated fact of Existence occupy the center of our attention.

To perform this act of bracketing the Universe in order to let Existence occupy the foreground of attention calls for an unusual act of mental reorientation. The everyday attention of most people is directed toward the details of this or that experience, activity, or project. As parts of the Universe, we are ourselves normally occupied in interacting with other parts. And even the scientific cosmologist, who seeks to comprehend the space-time structure of the Universe as a whole, has an overall structure of parts at the center of his field of interest. To become aware of Existence as such calls for suspending (and only for the purpose of this exercise) these normal types of interests. One has to temporarily 'forget about' everyday preoccupations—earning a living, eating meals, running a household, participating in social activities, satisfying biological needs, engaging in research, helping other people, learning various skills, acquiring information of one sort or another, and so on. These are not being abandoned or rejected. Indeed, they could not be, so long as we are alive. They are only being bracketed so that one might attend to the sheer fact of Existence. Moreover, after one has gained some proficiency in doing this, it is no longer a matter of 'pausing' to become aware of Existence while all our normal activities in which we are engrossed are 'suspended' or 'bracketed'. Rather, it becomes a matter of both kinds of experiences being present *simultaneously*. The awareness of Existence then comes to accompany and permeate all our normal activities.

The contrast between the Universe and Existence

As here being used, the terms 'the Universe' and 'Existence' refer to different aspects of one and the same ultimate reality. The Universe is complex, in terms of both its structure and its contents. The Universe has various properties or qualities. It is describable and its phenomena are explainable. It is open to rational inquiry. With the growth of science it becomes increasingly intelligible. What we come to know about the Universe, either as a comprehensive whole or with respect to its many parts, can be formulated in statements whose truth can be evaluated by appropriate criteria of evidence. The knowledge thus gained about the Universe can be communicated from one human being to another.

By contrast, Existence *as such* is simple and undifferentiated, not complex. It has no parts, contents, qualities, internal structure, or properties of any kind. Existence cannot be identified observationally; one can't *point to* it in the way one can to some object or occurrence. It is so unique that one cannot compare it with anything else. It cannot be described or satisfactorily explained. It cannot be rendered intelligible, because it is beyond intelligibility. There is no possible progress in coming to know (in the sense of to understand) more and more about Existence. There is no increasing depth or wider extent of Existence to be probed, or hidden aspects brought to light. There are no fresh discoveries to be made about Existence. One can only be ultimately silent in the presence of Existence. The silence, however, is a pregnant silence, filled with a unique and overwhelming sense of awe.

Whereas the Universe is an object for inquiry and *knowledge*, Existence as such is something of which one can only, at best, be *aware*. The awareness, when had, is not a special or secret kind of knowledge that is difficult to communicate. It is primarily an experience that is had or undergone rather than communicated. The awareness of Existence engages a special level or type of human response that, as far as is known, only human beings are capable of. Even so, very few human beings manifest or develop this awareness. Our survival as human beings or the mere efficiency of our lives depends, to a large extent, on the exercise of intelligence. However, the awareness of Existence is not necessary to survival or efficient living. And yet the awareness of Existence possesses a spiritual quality that, when joined or added to intelligence, introduces a special dimension to our experience.

Having reached this point, the reader will undoubtedly ask: "Even if we assume that somehow one may be brought to the level where that person has the special type of experience called 'an awareness of Existence', of what possible value is it to the person who has it? Does it contribute in any way to the quality of life to have such an awareness?"

Of what value is the awareness of Existence?

By way of conclusion and summary of our discussion, I shall offer one type of reply to this question: that the awareness of Existence brings with it a distinctive quality of serenity in life—the deeper the awareness, the greater the serenity. Perhaps very few people ever reach this goal to a very high degree. Let us try nevertheless to get a glimpse of what this quality amounts to in such degrees as it may be present.

The quality of serenity in life

To prevent misunderstandings, let me first distinguish the benefit I am pointing to from other kinds. Some of these more familiar types are obviously at far remove from it, whereas others, although much closer in character, are not to be confused or identified with it. Thus, to begin with the most obvious cases, the benefit to be derived from an intensified awareness of Existence is not comparable to the sort of benefit that consists in having a remedy to specific weaknesses of performance, bodily ills, or psychological anxieties. For any of these (different as these are from one another), effective aids and remedies may be readily available. Thus the value of having an awareness of Existence is not like taking aspirin to relieve a headache, getting lessons from a golf pro to improve one's game, going away on a vacation in order to relax, taking tranquilizers or going to a psychotherapist to learn to cope with particular anxieties and stresses of daily living. All such remedies, when effective, are directed to specific problems or situations. Their applicability and the need for them, if present at all, will vary from one person to another. They serve to correct particular deficiencies or weaknesses, some of which may be transitory, others of variable seriousness and complexity, and still others not applicable for everyone. None of these features characterizes or arises from the situation that calls for the kind of value or benefit an intensified awareness of Existence may bring. For this value awaits realization by *any* human being, regardless of his or her special interests, needs, problems, or weaknesses. It does not come to remedy some particular deficiency. It responds, rather to the common and inescapable human situation of *all* men. When effective, it permeates a person's life in all his dealings, activities, and experiences. It is not limited, therefore, in its scope and relevance. It is not transitory or variable. It has to do with the total attitude and quality of a person's life, with respect to everything he or she does. It is a 'silent partner', an 'unexpressed accompaniment' to any activity or experience in which one is engaged. Once acquired, and depending on the degree to which it is had, it qualifies and suffuses all of a person's activities.

Various modes of achieving 'spiritual health'

What we are talking about, therefore, has a certain analogy with other major prescriptions for achieving an overall quality of 'spiritual health' in life. It is a diagnosis and response to the human situation, as such, in which all beings find themselves regardless of their individual propensities, careers, opportunities, and abilities. What the special quality of the awareness of Existence brings to life needs to be compared and contrasted with these other major conceptions of how to achieve 'spiritual health'. For purposes of such comparison and contrast, I shall select two examples, both of which we studied in earlier portions of this book. These are the viewpoints of theism and of Spinoza. Each, in its own way, offers and promises a way to achieve a type of 'salvation', 'blessedness', or 'peace of mind'. Each in its own way, therefore, when genuinely realized in an individual life, makes possible its own form of *serenity*. For the traditional religious believer, the serenity is born of *faith* in God's power, wisdom, infinite goodness, justice, and love. To one beset by life's evils, there is an abiding *hope* grounded in such *faith*. The believer is enabled to carry the burdens and challenges of life in a distinctive manner. It sets him unmistakably apart from the nonbeliever.

On the other hand, for Spinoza the blessedness to be sought for does not derive from faith in the goodness of a personal God and a confident hope in the triumph of justice—a triumph to be realized if not in this world then in the next. For Spinoza, blessedness is to be found in the practice of what he calls the 'intellectual love of God'. The world, Spinoza believes, is a thoroughly intelligible and causally determined structure. It possesses an order—although not a designful or teleological one—of which all events, human as well as nonhuman, are illustrations and parts. That order can be laid bare by the growing competency of science. It is open to discovery by a dispassionate understanding equipped with adequate ideas. The 'faith' called for is not one in the goodness of Nature, since Nature has none; Nature (God) is amoral. The requisite faith is that of the scientist in the power of reason to make explicit the intelligibility of the world as a logical and physical order. "The order and connection of things is the same as the order and connection of ideas." The wise man will recognize this causally and logically determined character of the world and accommodate himself to it. His peace of mind, his blessedness, and his serenity come from an understanding of the *necessity* of things—not a necessity deriving from the willful decrees of an all-powerful, supreme, and transcendent governor, but from the logical and physical necessity of a causal network within the world itself. The wise man will do what he can to live according to his own power of reason within the framework of this necessary order. His serenity comes from *understanding* the impersonal order of events and from resigning and accommodating himself to it. For Spinoza, then, blessedness is a by-product of the intellectual understanding, not, as with the theist, of faith. And, instead of the theist's *hope* in the ultimate triumph of God's infinite goodness and mercy, Spinoza's wise man would fall back on a quiet *acceptance of and resignation* to the structure of the world as he finds it.

Here then we have two familiar, influential, and tremendously powerful recipes for achieving serenity. One is the serenity born of religious faith, the other the serenity born of scientific understanding. The question now to be faced is how the serenity born of an intensified awareness of Existence is in any way different from either of these routes to spiritual health. In what does it consist? And what, if anything, recommends it in preference to either of the foregoing methods?

To begin with, the obvious point of contrast with the theist's recipe for serenity is that an intensified awareness of Existence is wholly unlike a faith in God and his goodness. Existence, unlike God, is not a Supreme Being, the source of the Universe and of man. Existence is not an entity, not even a supreme entity or being of any sort. Existence is not a Creative

The awareness of Existence contrasted with the faith of the theist

Mind or Power or Person. It has no will or purpose of any kind. It does not possess any type or degree of goodness, love, mercy, or justice, since it has no quality or capacity of *any* kind. Thus it makes no sense to *have faith* in Existence, or to place any *hope* in the ultimate 'triumph' or 'dominance' of Existence. For Existence has no superior degree of reality as compared to the Universe or anything contained in the Universe. Existence is not the 'ground' of the Universe, nor is the Universe the 'ground' of Existence. They are on a par, since they are different sides or aspects of one and the same ultimate reality. The human *awareness* of Existence, accordingly, is not a matter of faith or hope. Existence doesn't evoke love, because it has no love to give. Since neither the Universe nor man is derived from Existence, it makes no sense to seek 'union' or 'reunion' with Existence, in the way the theist and religious mystic seek union or reunion with God. We are not the creatures of Existence. We can, at best, therefore become aware of Existence. If we don't have such awareness, Existence doesn't care, because it can't 'care'. Existence doesn't call for worship or prayerful obedience. These are irrelevant and inappropriate as responses to Existence. We can be 'open' to Existence, but Existence doesn't look for or expect that we be 'open' to it. It neither suffers disappointment nor finds satisfaction when it is made the object of human awareness.

The awareness of Existence contrasted with a Spinozistic 'intellectual love of God'

Spinoza's prescription for blessedness stresses an intellectual comprehension and accommodation to the intelligible structure of Nature. What he emphasizes is of the highest importance and value. It is a necessary component of any naturalistic philosophy of life. However, in the light of the terminology earlier developed, we could say that what Spinoza is focusing on is *the intelligibility of the Universe*. His own philosophy does not distinguish, however, the ultimacy and parallel ontological status of Existence as such. Hence Spinoza's intellectual love of God leaves no room and makes no provision for the intensified awareness of Existence as such. Whereas the Universe does have an intelligible structure and is a complex of parts whose interrelationships with one another are capable of being described and understood, this cannot be said of Existence. For Existence is not intelligible. Nor is it unintelligible. It is not a complex of parts and is not possessed of any qualities. Hence it cannot be understood or inquired into. One cannot have an *intellectual* grasp of it, either in part or synoptically, in the way one might have such an intellectual grasp of the Universe as a whole or of any of its diverse parts. One can be aware of Existence, but one cannot understand it. So not only would the awareness of Existence be different from the religious person's *faith* in God. It would also be different from the Spinozist's *understanding* and accommodation to the necessary *intelligible structure* of *Nature*. Existence is neither God (in the traditional sense) nor the Universe. If anything, then, the awareness of Existence needs to be added to the intellectual comprehension of the Universe. The serenity and blessedness an awareness of Existence make possible are of a different order and quality from either the faith of the religionist or the understanding of the scientist. The 'intellectual love of God' is only one half of the story, not the whole of it. The type of 'spirituality' or serenity I am pointing to lies beyond Spinoza's remedy. It needs to be *added* to it, *not substituted* for it.

How, then, does serenity arise from an intensified awareness of Existence, and what are its distinctive characteristics?

The distinctive characteristics of serenity deriving from an awareness of Existence

Every human being is a part of the Universe. The vast majority of human beings throughout their lives devote all their attention to their interaction with other parts of the Universe, usually those in their own immediate environment. Some individuals, on occasion, 'lift up their eyes' and in some fashion or other (through the agencies of myth, religion, philosophy, or science) also frame some view about the Universe as a whole. To become aware of Existence, on the other hand, in the sense I have given this term, requires special philosophical discrimination. The route I have pointed toward that discrimination is not the only way of becoming aware of Existence. Yet whether the way I have suggested or some other be preferred, it is likely that very few individual persons ever reach or manage to sustain in any significant degree a constant, intensified awareness of Existence.

When one manages, in some degree, to become aware of Existence, it does not mean that one has ceased to be a part of the Universe. To become aware of Existence does not require (as in certain systems of Indian thought) that we regard the Universe or any of its parts as belonging to a realm of Maya, or illusion. It does not counsel us to withdraw from or minimize our contacts with 'the world'. To develop an awareness of Existence involves no such drastic and unwarranted response. To have an awareness of Existence adds another dimension to our experience. It does not call for abandoning, minimizing, condemning, reducing, or disparaging in any way other familiar modes of experience and interaction with the world about us, e.g., practical, social, esthetic, intellectual, or whatever. Everything remains as it was. The awareness of Existence comes to supplement and suffuse all these more familiar modes of experience; it does not come to supplant them.

Having an awareness of Existence is not to be confused with the sort of thing that happens when we engage in a new and different *activity*. It is not, for example, like taking up tennis, if one had never before played tennis, or learning calculus, traveling to a place one has never visited, becoming involved for the first time in an active way in politics, in business, in gardening, or getting married, raising children, and so on. Becoming aware of Existence is not another and new activity to be compared to 'taking up' any of these. For in doing any of these, we, as parts of the

Universe, still remain 'within' it and continue to interact with other parts of the Universe. We have simply enriched, modified, or shifted our interests within that all-encompassing framework. However, becoming aware of Existence is not to still remain 'within the Universe' in any of these ways. It is rather to add to our ways of experience of whatever we do, insofar as we belong to the Universe, by virtue of the fact that we now are also aware of Existence. A human being who becomes aware of Existence continues inextricably to be a part of the Universe. He is now, however, open to *both*. He is at the point where, through his own experience, they intersect and meet.

We, in being part of the Universe, are *caring* creatures. We have needs, desires, drives, interests, hopes, ambitions, satisfactions, and frustrations. Each of us engages in various projects, makes plans, has dreams. We are biological and social creatures, not just clumps of unconscious chemical or physical matter. Being endowed with minds, however, we can also enjoy a special type of awareness of Existence. Although for the vast majority of individuals *only* the Universe, in some way, concerns or involves them, to one who has become aware of Existence, this new dimension of reality has entered into his or her total experience. But it would be a mistake to expect to find such a person *doing* different things as a result of this addition. The only difference is to be found in one's *way* of doing whatever one would normally do. Recall the famous saying of the Zen master: "Before the Zen enlightenment, mountains are mountains and water is water; when one gains an initiatory experience, this is denied, but when one gets into the ultimate understanding, everything is asserted again; mountains are mountains and water is water." To become aware of Existence does not mean that mountains have ceased to be mountains, or water, water. Everything remains as it was, but with a difference. One 'sees' things differently. One sees them no longer *only* as parts of the Universe. Nor can one point to anything about them that cannot be seen by someone else. Where, then, is the difference, and what does it mean to say, as I did earlier, that it consists in the *way* one experiences 'mountains and water', or whatever it is one does or interacts with?

To try to answer this question, let me first make use of a simple analogy with the experience of visiting a Japanese house where, in a room completely empty (by Western standards), one finds at the end of the room tastefully displayed on the wall a single painting (or a single vase of beautifully arranged flowers). The effect is unmistakable. One focuses on the painting (or the flowers). One's appreciation and enjoyment of it is enhanced precisely because it is found in a setting of emptiness. The emptiness is not another object to study. It has no color or structure. But insofar as one is aware of this surrounding emptiness, one dwells all the more attentively and lovingly on the painting (or the flowers).

Existence is not itself another 'part of the Universe' or the Universe itself. It is the 'emptiness' 'surrounding' the Universe. Being without form, structure, quality, meaning, purpose, or intelligibility, it lends—for that very reason—all the more emphasis to what we can find, accomplish, or do insofar as we are parts of the Universe. All meaning, purpose, and intelligibility are to be found *in* the Universe. But all of this, even when found, made, or introduced (whether briefly, haltingly, progressively, personally, or collectively) is set within a total framework of ultimate reality that includes the sheer and unmeaning fact of Existence. The Universe and men's lives, for all their meaningfulness and creative accomplishments, are set within the surrounding 'sea' of 'meaningless' and 'unintelligible' Existence. And the awareness of *this* fact is what comes to permeate and suffuse all one's experiences, whether happy or unhappy, momentous or trivial, filled with goodness and joy or with horror, pain, and evil. The awareness of Existence qualifies any and all of these experiences. The awareness of Existence is a 'silent partner' and 'unexpressed accompaniment', which makes possible the kind of serenity available to a human being without benefit of either religion or science. By means of it one learns to 'care and not to care' at the same time.

Epilogue

chapter 15

Concluding Remarks

on the

Ways of Philosophy

In drawing the present book to a close, it is appropriate to pause, briefly, to take a backward as well as forward glance at the study of philosophy. We have had an introductory glimpse of some of the 'ways' of philosophy. What can be said of the road so far traversed? What lies ahead?

In their first formal contacts with the study of philosophy, most persons come away with a mixed bag of reactions. The study may have been helpful in acquiring a certain amount of historical and terminological information. Also, no doubt, here and there some ideas will have become clarified, or some of one's prior beliefs and commitments may have become strengthened and deepened. On the other hand, some of one's former views may also have come in for a good deal of challenging criticism. And perhaps this has been sufficiently searching and disturbing to result in dislodging those beliefs, yet without yielding anything satisfactory enough to take their place. To find oneself in this situation is an uncomfortable matter, and sooner or later the individual will need to settle on some replacement (however tentative this may be). Or perhaps the study of philosophy has succeeded, through this process of criticism, in proposing some view that seems more attractive than the old, and so the new comes to replace the old.

What I have just described as typical of the varied experiences in a person's first contacts with the study of philosophy is, however—let it be recognized at once—characteristic in some degree of the study of philosophy at any stage, and no matter how far one has pursued it! The serious study of philosophy, as one continues to engage in it, normally raises at least as many questions as it helps to clarify and settle. One is continually haunted by a sense of incompleteness. This is especially all too clearly the case in early stages of the study of philosophy. One has a pressing sense then of questions raised but left unanswered, of important questions not even raised (much less answered), of broad unfocused goals to be approached. If all this is true, in some degree, of the reader, then this introduction to philosophy has been successful. For, from the days of Socrates onward, philosophy has been a process and activity of search, of raising questions, of critically exploring alternative options. Whatever difficulties there may be (as we saw at the very outset) in characterizing philosophy as the pursuit of *wisdom*, and whatever else philosophy is, it is at least a *pursuit*. Of course, one may succeed, through persistent search, in clearing up and systematizing a number of one's beliefs in some particular area. However, there is never a final stage reached, even for one who 'does' philosophy professionally or spends full time at it. Still, this fact of always-receding horizons to match every advance will not discourage anyone who has once come to see the genuine value and benefits of philosophy. Philosophy, like any other worthwhile pursuit, is an unending quest, although like life itself it can be brought to an end. The fact that there may be an arbitrary cutoff point in someone's pursuit of philosophy does not in any way diminish or impugn the value of the quest itself.

What about the 'ways of philosophy' we have explored in this book? We have concentrated our attention on three major world views and philosophies of life (Plato's philosophy, theism, and naturalism). We have also had some very brief glimpses into two types of movements in recent philosophy. Our examination of these topics has been neither thorough nor free from the possible distortions of a selective presentation. To get a firm grasp of even these same philosophies would obviously call for a more complete investigation.

Much, too, has been omitted or bypassed altogether in our survey. There are many themes and issues in philosophy we have not even touched on or have done so only tangentially and briefly. For example, there are some major figures (let alone others) in the history of philosophy whose work would call for careful study in any attempt to enrich one's knowledge of the subject: for example, Aristotle (384–322 B.C.), Thomas Hobbes (1588–1679), John Locke (1632–1704), Gottfried Leibniz (1646–1716), George Berkeley (1685–1753), David Hume (1711–1776), Immanuel Kant (1724–1804), G. W. F. Hegel (1770–1831), to go no further.

There are, too, many important questions of a philosophic character (some no doubt recognized by the reader) to which we have not even begun to do justice in our own discussions. These questions would be explored in the various branches or specialized parts of philosophy which go by such names as 'ethics', 'ontology', 'logic', 'philosophy of science', 'philosophy of history', 'political (and social) philosophy', 'philosophy of law (jurisprudence)', 'philosophy of art (esthetics)', 'philosophy of education', 'philosophy of religion', 'philosophy of language', 'philosophy of mind (philosophical psychology)', 'epistemology (theory of knowledge)', and so on.

Finally, the whole rich and complex field of contemporary (i.e., twentieth-century) philosophy, with its many movements, leading figures, and cross-currents, would need to be carefully studied by any serious student. Among such movements and figures, the following may be mentioned: In the general area of 'philosophical logic', 'philosophy of language', and 'analytic philosophy' are the works of Gottlob Frege, Bertrand Russell, Ludwig Wittgenstein, G. E. Moore, John Austin, Gilbert Ryle, Peter Strawson, W. V. O. Quine, Saul Kripke, Michael Dummett, Noam Chomsky. Representative of the philosophy that goes by the name 'logical positivism' are the writings of Moritz Schlick, Rudolf Carnap, Hans Reichenbach. Under the headings of 'phenomenology' and 'existentialism' are the writings of Edmund Husserl, Maurice Merleau-Ponty, Martin Heidegger, Jean Paul Sartre, Karl Jaspers. In addition, there is the interesting and important (yet not easily classifiable) work of such philosophers as Henri Bergson, George Santayana, A. N. Whitehead.

A notable feature of contemporary philosophy (of which we ourselves have had a very small sampling) is the extent to which great diversity and sometimes sharp conflict and even mutually expressed contempt for one's rivals are displayed in the works of its various practitioners. Confronted by this phenomenon, one is tempted to raise the following questions: How are these newer developments related to older patterns of thought—among them, for example, the kinds we have ourselves examined in this book? Are these newer philosophies, each in its own way, enlargements of or embroideries on some fundamental pattern of thought whose basic themes and orientations had been worked out in previous epochs? Or are they, rather, genuinely novel departures whose full development and outcome yet remain to be seen? Can the many sharp cleavages that run through contemporary philosophy find effective modes of reconciliation or synthesis that themselves are not mere eclectic hodgepodges? Questions such as these not only would need to be refined and made more specific, but also, if answerable at all, would obviously call for far more extensive study than our own preliminary ventures into philosophy would allow. I mention them by way of suggesting that in broadening his or her knowledge of philosophy the student will gain the satisfaction that such deepening knowledge brings and will also, by carrying on the *activity* of philosophy, possibly come to help in answering some of these questions.

Notes _____

CHAPTER 2
(*The Examined Life*)
1. Plato, *Phaedo*, 116–18 (transl. Jowett).
2. *Theaetetus*, 150 c–d (transl. Cornford).
3. *Apology*, 21 (transl. Jowett).
4. Ibid., 22.
5. Ibid., 29–30.
6. Ibid., 31.
7. A critique of the Socratic conception of definition will be taken up later in this book (Chapter 13) in connection with Wittgenstein's philosophy.
8. *Euthyphro*, 5–6 (transl. Jowett).

CHAPTER 3
(*Eternal Forms and Temporal Flux*)
1. *Letter* 7, 341 b–d (transl. W. K. C. Guthrie).
2. *Republic*, VI, 510 (transl. Cornford).
3. *Phaedo*, 74–5.
4. *Republic*, I, 336.

5. Ibid., I, 338–41.
6. Ibid., X, 596.
7. Ibid., VI, 506.
8. *Theaetetus*, 185.
9. *Parmenides*, 147 d–e.
10. *Hippias Major*, 287 c–d.
11. A critique of Plato's Theory of Forms will be found in Chapter 13.

CHAPTER 4
(*The Ideal Society*)
1. *Republic*, II, 358–62.
2. Ibid., II, 368.
3. Ibid., II, 370.
4. Ibid., II, 372–3.
5. *Phaedo*, 66 c.
6. *Republic*, IV, 423 c–d.
7. Ibid., V, 457–66.
8. Ibid., IV, 420–1.
9. Ibid., IX, 580 e.
10. Ibid., V, 473.
11. Ibid., VII, 514–21.
12. Ibid., V, 455 e.

CHAPTER 5
(*The Religious Heritage of the West*)
1. George Santayana, *Reason in Religion*, 92–7.

CHAPTER 6
(*The Ontological Argument*)
1. See the references under Theism (B. Ontological Argument) in "Suggestions for Further Reading," p. 365.
2. Anselm, *Proslogion*, Ch. II.
3. E.g., *Proslogion*, XIV, XVIII; *Monologion*, XV.
4. Descartes, *Meditations*, V.

CHAPTER 7
(*The Cosmological Argument*)
1. Aquinas, *Summa Theologica*, 1a, 2, 3.
2. Ibid.
3. Cf. *Summa Theologica*, 1a, q. 46, 2.
4. Hume, *Dialogues on Natural Religion*, Part IX.

CHAPTER 8
(*The Right to Believe*)
1. Kierkegaard, *Philosophical Fragments*, Ch. III.
2. James, "The Sentiment of Rationality," in *Essays on Faith and Morals* (Longmans, Green, New York, 1947), 92–3.
3. Letter to F. H. Bradley, June 16, 1904.
4. "The Will to Believe," in *Essays on Faith and Morals*, 32–3.
5. "The Sentiment of Rationality," 90.
6. Ibid., 96–7.
7. "The Will to Believe," 35–6.
8. Ibid., 55.
9. Ibid., 34–5.
10. Ibid., 56–7.
11. W. K. Clifford, "The Ethics of Belief," in *Lectures and Essays* (Macmillan, London, 1886), 343, 344, 346.
12. "The Will to Believe," 42.
13. Ibid., 59.
14. Ibid., 36–7.
15. Ibid., 57–8.
16. Ibid., 57.
17. Ibid., 60–1.
18. "The Sentiment of Rationality," 109.
19. He does discuss this matter, however, in his *Varieties of Religious Experience*.

CHAPTER 9
(*I-Thou*)
1. *Eclipse of God* (Harper Torchbooks, New York, 1957), 30–1.
2. *I and Thou* (transl. Walter Kaufmann) (Scribners, New York, 1970), 129.
3. *Origin and Meaning of Hasidism*, 94.
4. *Between Man and Man* (Macmillan Publishing Co., Inc., New York, paperback edition, 1975), 13–4.
5. James, "The Will to Believe," 58.
6. *Between Man and Man*, 209–24.
7. *At the Turning*, 44.
8. D. J. Moore, *Martin Buber*, 235–6.
9. *Eclipse of God*, 128.
10. *I and Thou*, 114–5.
11. *I and Thou*, 85.
12. *Eclipse of God*, 129.
13. *Daniel* (1913), 148 f.
14. *I and Thou*, 57–9.
15. *Between Man and Man*, 22–3.
16. Ibid., 35.
17. Ibid., 3–4.
18. Ibid., 19.
19. Ibid., 36–7.
20. *I and Thou*, 62.
21. Ibid., 67.

22. Ibid., 68.
23. "Replies to My Critics," in *The Philosophy of Martin Buber* (Paul A. Schilpp and Maurice Friedman, eds.), 694.
24. *I and Thou*, 158–9.
25. Ibid., 160–1.
26. *I and Thou*, 127.
27. "Replies to My Critics," 690.
28. *Eclipse of God*, 126.
29. *I and Thou*, 181.
30. Ibid., 181–2.
31. "Replies to My Critics," 690.
32. *Eclipse of God*, 60.
33. Ibid., 14.
34. Ibid., 60.
35. *At the Turning*, 57.
36. *On Judaism*, 212.
37. *Between Man and Man*, Afterword, 221.
38. "Replies to My Critics," 690.
39. *Between Man and Man*, 58.
40. "Replies to My Critics," 712.
41. *I and Thou*, 123.

CHAPTER 10
(*Science and the Modern World*)
1. Anatole France, *The Garden of Epicurus* (Dodd Mead, New York).
2. A. Berry, *A Short History of Astronomy* (London, 1898), 159.
3. Descartes, *Discourse on Method* (transl. Haldane and Ross: Part I, 86–7.
4. Loc. cit.
5. *Rules for the Direction of the Mind* (in Haldane and Ross), 13.
6. Cf. J. Wheeler, *Geometrodynamics* (Academic Press, New York, 1962), and J. C. Graves, *The Conceptual Foundations of Contemporary Relativity Theory* (MIT Press, Cambridge, Mass., 1971).

7. *Works of Descartes* (C. Adam and P. Tannery, eds.), Vol. VIII, 65.
8. *Discourse on Method*, Part II.
9. Ibid.
10. *Rules for the Direction of the Mind*, II.
11. Ibid., III.
12. Ibid.
13. Ibid.
14. *Principles of Philosophy*, Author's Letter.
15. *Discourse on Method*, Part IV.
16. Ibid.
17. *Meditations*, I.
18. Ibid.
19. *Discourse*, Part IV.
20. *Meditations*, II.
21. Ibid.
22. *Discourse*, Part IV.
23. Ibid.
24. Ibid.
25. *Reply to Objections* II, Proposition IV.
26. *Meditations*, VI.
27. *Passions of the Soul*, Article XXXV.
28. Letter to R. P. Arnauld, in *Works* (Adam and Tannery, eds.), V, 222.
29. Gilbert Ryle, *The Concept of Mind* (London, 1949), 11–5.
30. Cf. Jerome A. Shaffer, *Philosophy of Mind* (New York, 1968).

CHAPTER 11
(*Nature and Man's Well-Being*)
1. *Improvement of the Understanding* (transl. R. H. M. Elwes).
2. Ibid.
3. Ibid.
4. Ibid.
5. Ibid.
6. *Ethics*, Part I, Definition III (transl. W. H. White).
7. Op. cit., Part I, Axioms I, II.

8. Op. cit., I, Def. IV.
9. Ibid., Def. VI.
10. Op. cit., Part II, Proposition VII.
11. Ibid.
12. *Ethics*, Part I, Appendix.
13. Ibid.
14. I, Prop. XV, Scholium.
15. I, Prop. XVII, Schol.
16. IV, Prop. XLV, Schol.
17. III, Prop. II, Schol.
18. IV, Prop. VII.
19. V, Prop. XLII, Schol.

CHAPTER 12
(*Pragmatic Humanism*)
1. Quoted, G. Dykhuizen, *The Life and Mind of John Dewey*, 204.
2. *The Influence of Darwin on Philosophy*, 1–2.
3. Ibid.
4. "From Absolutism to Experimentalism," in *Contemporary American Philosophies* (G. P. Adams and W. P. Montague, eds.).
5. *Quest for Certainty*, 255–6.
6. *Logic: The Theory of Inquiry*, 104–5.
7. Ibid., 108–9.
8. Ibid., 108.
9. *How We Think*, rev. ed.
10. "The Logic of Judgments of Practice," *Journal of Philosophy*, XII (1916), 505 f.
11. Loc. cit.
12. Loc. cit.
13. *Quest for Certainty*, 260.
14. J. Dewey and J. H. Tufts, *Ethics*, Part I, Sec. 3.
15. *Reconstruction in Philosophy* (Henry Holt, New York, 1920), 163 f.
16. Op. cit., 165.
17. Op. cit., 166–7.
18. Loc. cit., 169 f.
19. Op. cit, 175–6.
20. Op. cit., 170 f.
21. Op. cit., 176 f.

22. Op. cit., 184 f.
23. Op. cit., 186.

CHAPTER 13
(*Linguistic Analysis*)
1. *Philosophical Investigations*, 1. (Numbers, here, refer to sections.)
2. Ibid., 27.
3. Ibid., 23.
4. Ibid., 24.
5. Ibid., 11, 12, 13.
6. Cf. G. E. Moore, "Wittgenstein's Lectures, 1930–1933," in *Philosophical Papers*, 307.
7. Cf. loc. cit., 303.
8. Plato, *Republic*, 596.
9. Ibid., 506.
10. Plato, *Theaetetus*, 185.
11. Plato, *Phaedo*, 100.
12. Cf. Garth Hallett, *A Companion to Wittgenstein's Philosophical Investigations*, 28, 30 ff.
13. Wittgenstein, manuscript, 302, 14; quoted, Hallett, op. cit., 33.
14. *Blue Book*, 19–20.
15. Ibid., 1.
16. Ibid., 18.
17. *Philosophical Investigations*, 120.
18. *Blue Book*, 64.
19. Ibid., 17–8.
20. *Philosophical Investigations*, 66, 67.
21. The interested reader may consult the following works: Mark Steiner, *Mathematical Knowledge* (Cornell University Press, 1975); Paul Benacerraf and Hilary Putnam (eds.), *Philosophy of Mathematics* (Prentice-Hall, 1964); S. Körner, *The Philosophy of Mathematics* (Hutchinson University Library, 1960); Michael Dummett, *Elements of Intuitionism* (Clarendon Press, Oxford, 1977).
22. *Blue Book*, 25, 27–28.

23. Cf. Jerry A. Fodor and Jerrold J. Katz (eds.), *The Structure of Language* (Prentice-Hall, 1964); Richard Rorty (ed.), *The Linguistic Turn* (University of Chicago Press, 1967); Leonard Linsky (ed.), *Semantics and the Philosophy of Language* (University of Illinois Press, 1952); Gareth Evans and John McDowell (eds.), *Truth and Meaning: Essays in Semantics* (Clarendon Press, Oxford, 1976); Midwest Studies in Philosophy, Vol. II, *Studies in the Philosophy of Language*, 1977; G. H. R. Parkinson (ed.), *The Theory of Meaning* (Oxford University Press, 1968); Donald Davidson and Gilbert Harman (eds.), *Semantics of Natural Language* (Reidel Publishing Co., 1972).

CHAPTER 14
(*Nonconceptual Awareness and Serenity*)
1. D. T. Suzuki, *Essays in Zen Buddhism*, first series (Grove Press, New York, 1961), 229–31.
2. Ibid., 264–5.
3. D. T. Suzuki, *Living by Zen* (Samuel Weiser, New York, 1972), 80–1.
4. D. T. Suzuki, "Self and the Unattainable," in *What Is Zen?* (Perennial Library, Harper & Row, New York, 1972), 53, 58–9.
5. D. T. Suzuki, *Studies in Zen* (Delta Books, New York, 1955), 72–3.
6. *Living by Zen*, 150–1.
7. M. Heidegger, "My Way to Phenomenology," in *On Time and Being* (Harper & Row, New York, 1972), 74.
8. M. Heidegger, *Being and Time* (transl. J. Macquarrie and E. Robinson) (SCM Press, London, 1962), 1.
9. M. Heidegger, *Discourse on Thinking* (Harper Torchbooks, New York, 1969), 46.
10. M. Heidegger, "What Is Metaphysics?" in *Existence and Being* (Werner Brock, ed.) (Vision Press, London, 1949), 384.
11. Ibid., 384.
12. Wittgenstein, *Tractatus*, 6.44.

Suggestions for Further Reading

General

The Encyclopedia of Philosophy (Paul Edwards, ed. in chief) (Macmillan Publishing Co., Inc., New York, 1967).

Socrates

GUTHRIE, W. K. C., *A History of Greek Philosophy*, Vol. III: *The Fifth-Century Enlightenment* (Cambridge University Press, Cambridge, 1969).

TAYLOR, A. E., *Socrates* (London, 1932; reprinted, Anchor Books, Doubleday, New York, 1953).

VERSENYI, L., *Socratic Humanism* (Yale University Press, New Haven, 1963).

VLASTOS, G. (ed.), *The Philosophy of Socrates: A Collection of Critical Essays* (Anchor Books, Doubleday, New York, 1971).

Plato

BAMBROUGH, J. R. (ed.), *Plato, Popper and Politics: Some Contributions to a Modern Controversy* (Cambridge and New York, 1967).

CORNFORD, F. M., *Before and After Socrates* (Cambridge University Press, Cambridge, 1932; reprinted).

CROMBIE, I. M., *An Examination of Plato's Doctrines*, 2 vols. (London and New York, 1963).

CROSS, R. C., and WOOZLEY, A. D., *Plato's Republic: A Philosophical Commentary* (London and New York, 1964).

CROSSMAN, R. H. S., *Plato Today* (New York and London, 1937).

FIELD, G. C., *The Philosophy of Plato* (Oxford University Press, London, Home University Library, 1949; 2nd ed., 1969).

FITE, W., *The Platonic Legend* (New York, 1934).

GUTHRIE, W. K. C., *A History of Greek Philosophy*, Vol. IV: *Plato, the Man and His Dialogues: Earlier Period* (Cambridge University Press, London and New York, 1975).

LEVINSON, R. B., *In Defense of Plato* (Cambridge, Mass., 1953).

NETTLESHIP, R. L., *Lectures on the Republic of Plato* (London, 1897; reprinted, 1963).

POPPER, K. R., *The Open Society and Its Enemies*, Vol. I: *The Spell of Plato*, 5th ed. (London, 1966).

RANDALL, J. H., JR., *Plato, Dramatist of the Life of Reason* (New York, 1970).

RYLE, G., *Plato's Progress* (Cambridge University Press, Cambridge, 1966).

SESONSKE, A. (ed.), *Plato's Republic: Interpretation and Criticism* (Belmont, Calif., 1966).

SHOREY, P., *What Plato Said* (Chicago, 1933).

TAYLOR, A. E., *Plato, the Man and His Works* (London, 1926; reprinted, 1960).

VLASTOS, G. (ed.), *Plato: A Collection of Critical Essays*, 2 vols. (Anchor Books, Doubleday, New York, 1971).

WOODBRIDGE, F. J. E., *The Son of Apollo: Themes of Plato* (Boston and New York, 1929).

Theism

A. General Works

FLEW, A., *God and Philosophy* (Hutchinson, London, 1966).

FLEW, A., and MACINTYRE, A. (eds)., *New Essays in Philosophical Theology* SCM Press, London, 1955).

GILSON, E., *God and Philosophy* (Yale, New Haven, 1941, 1959).

HEPBURN, R. W., *Christianity and Paradox* (Watts, London, 1958).

HICK, J., *Faith and Knowledge* (Cornell University Press, Ithaca, 1957).

HICK, J. (ed.), *The Existence of God* (Collier, New York, 1963).

HICK, J. (ed.), *Faith and the Philosophers* (St. Martin's, New York, 1964).

KAUFMANN, W., *Critique of Religion and Philosophy* (Harper, New York, 1958).

MACQUARRIE, J., *God-Talk* (SCM Press, London, 1967).

MARTIN, C. B., *Religious Belief* (Cornell, Ithaca, 1959).

MASCALL, E. L., *He Who Is: A Study in Traditional Theism* (Longmans, London, New York, 1943).

MATSON, W. J., *The Existence of God* (Cornell, Ithaca, 1965).

MUNITZ, M. K., *The Mystery of Existence* (New York, 1965; reprinted, New York University Press, 1974).

OTTO, R., *The Idea of the Holy* (Oxford, 1925; Penguin, 1959).

PHILLIPS, D. (ed.), *Religion and Understanding* (Blackwell, Oxford, 1967).

PLANTINGA, A., *God and Other Minds* (Cornell, Ithaca, 1967).

ROYAL INSTITUTE OF PHILOSOPHY LECTURES, *Talk of God*, Vol. 2 1967/68 (Macmillan, New York and London, 1969).

Smith, J. E., *Reason and God: Encounters of Philosophy with Religion* (Yale, New Haven, 1961).

B. Ontological Argument

Barnes, J., *The Ontological Argument* (Macmillan, London, 1972).

Hartshorne, C., *The Logic of Perfection* (La Salle, Ill., 1962).

Hartshorne, C., *Man's Vision of God* (Harper, New York, 1941).

Hick, J., and McGill, A. C. (eds.), *The Many-Faced Argument* (New York, 1966).

Plantinga, A. (ed.), *Ontological Argument from St. Anselm to Contemporary Philosophers* (Anchor Books, Doubleday, New York, 1965).

C. Cosmological Argument

Burrill, D. R. (ed.), *The Cosmological Arguments* (Anchor Books, Doubleday, New York, 1967).

Kenny, A., *The Five Ways: St. Thomas Aquinas's Proofs of God's Existence* (Routledge, London, 1969).

Rowe, W. L., *The Cosmological Argument* (Princeton, 1975).

D. James

Perry, R. B. (ed.), *The Thought and Character of William James* (briefer version) (Harper Torchbooks, New York, 1964).

Thayer, H. S., *Meaning and Action: A Critical History of Pragmatism* (Bobbs-Merrill, Indianapolis, 1968).

E. Buber

Diamond, M., *Martin Buber: Jewish Existentialist* (Harper Torchbooks, New York, 1968).

Edwards, P., *Buber and Buberism: A Critical Evaluation* (Department of Philosophy, University of Kansas, 1971).

Friedman, M., *Martin Buber: The Life of Dialogue* (Chicago, 1976).

Schilpp, P. A., and Friedman, M. (eds.), *The Philosophy of Martin Buber* (Library of Living Philosophers, Open Court, La Salle, Ill., 1967).

Naturalism

A. Historical and General

Gillispie, C. C., *The Edge of Objectivity: An Essay in the History of Scientific Ideas* (Princeton, 1960).

Krikorian, Y. H. (ed.), *Naturalism and the Human Spirit* (Columbia University Press, New York, 1944).

Randall, J. H., Jr., *The Making of the Modern Mind: A Survey of the Intellectual Background of the Present Age* (New York, 1926, 1976).

B. Descartes

Kenny, A., *Descartes* (Random House, New York, 1968).

Ryle, G., *The Concept of Mind* (Hutchinson, London, New York, 1949).

Sesonske, A., and Fleming, N. (eds.), *Meta-Meditations: Studies in Descartes* (Belmont, Calif., 1965).

C. Spinoza

CURLEY, E. M., *Spinoza's Metaphysics* (Harvard University Press, Cambridge, Mass., 1969).

GRENE, M. (ed.), *Spinoza: A Collection of Critical Essays* (Anchor Books, Doubleday, New York, 1973).

HAMPSHIRE, S., *Spinoza* (Pelican Books, 1951; Barnes and Noble, New York, 1961).

KASHAP, S. P. (ed.), *Studies in Spinoza: Critical and Interpretive Essays* (University of California Press, Berkeley, 1972).

MANDELBAUM, M., and FREEMAN, E. (eds.), *Spinoza: Essays in Interpretation* (Open Court, La Salle, Ill., 1975).

WOLFSON, H. A., *The Philosophy of Spinoza*, 2 vols. (Harvard University Press, Cambridge, Mass., 1934; reprinted, Schocken, New York, 1969).

D. Dewey

BERNSTEIN, R. J., *John Dewey* (New York, 1966).

DYKHUIZEN, G., *The Life and Mind of John Dewey* (So. Illinois University Press, Carbondale, 1973).

GEIGER, G. R., *John Dewey in Perspective* (New York, 1958).

HOOK, S., *John Dewey: An Intellectual Portrait* (New York, 1939).

HOOK, S. (ed.), *John Dewey: Philosopher of Science and Freedom* (New York, 1953).

SCHILPP, P. A. (ed.), *The Philosophy of John Dewey* (Library of Living Philosophers, Vol. I, Northwestern University Press, Evanston, 1939).

Some Recent Developments

A. Wittgenstein

BARTLEY, W. W., III, *Wittgenstein* (Quartet Books, London, 1974).

FANN, K. T., *Wittgenstein's Conception of Philosophy* (Blackwell, Oxford, 1969).

FANN, K. T. (ed.), *Ludwig Wittgenstein: The Man and His Philosophy* (Delta Books, New York, 1967).

FINCH, H. L., *Wittgenstein: The Later Philosophy: An Exposition of the Philosophical Investigations* (Humanities Press, Atlantic Highlands, N.J., 1977).

HARTNACK, J., *Wittgenstein and Modern Philosophy* (Anchor Books, Doubleday, New York, 1965).

MALCOLM, N., *Ludwig Wittgenstein: A Memoir* (Oxford, 1958; rev. ed., 1966).

PEARS, D., *Ludwig Wittgenstein* (Viking, New York, 1970).

PITCHER, G. (ed.), *Wittgenstein: The Philosophical Investigations: A Collection of Critical Essays* (Anchor Books, Doubleday, New York, 1966).

SPECHT, E. K., *The Foundations of Wittgenstein's Later Philosophy* (Barnes and Noble, New York, 1969).

B. Zen

Kapleau, P., *The Three Pillars of Zen: Teaching, Practice, and Enlightenment* (Beacon Press, Boston, 1965).

Suzuki, D. T., *Essays in Zen Buddhism*, first series (Grove Press, New York,
1961).

Suzuki, D. T., *Living by Zen* (Samuel Weiser, New York, 1972).

Suzuki, D. T., *Studies in Zen* (Delta Books, New York, 1955).

Wienpahl, P., *Zen Diary* (Harper & Row, New York, 1970).

C. Heidegger

Barrett, W., *Irrational Man: A Study in Existential Philosophy* (Anchor
Books, Doubleday, New York, 1962).

Biemel, W., *Martin Heidegger* (Harcourt Brace Jovanovich, New York,
1976).

Mehta, J. L., *The Philosophy of Martin Heidegger* (Harper Torchbooks, New
York, 1971).

Schmitt, R., *Martin Heidegger on Being Human: An Introduction to Sein
und Zeit* (Random House, New York, 1969).

Versenyi, L., *Heidegger, Being, and Truth* (Yale University Press, New
Haven, 1965).

D. The Universe and Existence

Munitz, M. K., *Existence and Logic* (New York University Press, 1974).

Munitz, M. K., *The Mystery of Existence: An Essay in Philosophical Cosmology* (New York, 1965; reprinted, Delta Books, 1968; reprinted, New
York University Press, 1974).

Munitz, M. K., *Space, Time, and Creation: Philosophical Aspects of Scientific
Cosmology* (Free Press, Glencoe, Ill., 1957; reprinted, Collier Books, New
York, 1961).

Munitz, M. K. (ed.), *Theories of the Universe: From Babylonian Myth
to Modern Science* (Macmillan Publishing Co., Inc., New York, 1957).

Index